CW01664753

LADY BUTLER

LADY BUTLER

War Artist and Traveller

1846–1933

CATHERINE WYNNE

FOUR COURTS PRESS

Set in 11pt on 14.5pt AdobeGaramondPro by
Carrigboy Typesetting Services for
FOUR COURTS PRESS LTD
7 Malpas Street, Dublin 8, Ireland
www.fourcourtspress.ie
and in North America for
FOUR COURTS PRESS
c/o IPG, 814 N Franklin St, Chicago, IL 60622.

A catalogue record for this title is available from the British Library.

ISBN 978-1-84682-649-8

SPECIAL ACKNOWLEDGMENT

This publication has been made possible by financial assistance from the Ferens Education Trust at the University of Hull and the Marc Fitch Fund for Research and Publication (established by Marcus Felix Brudenell Fitch CBE DLitt HonFBA FSA in 1956).

MARC FITCH FUND

DAMUS UT DETUR

Printed in Spain
by Castuera, Navarra.

For Alexander and Lawrence

Contents

Illustrations

Acknowledgments

This book would not have been possible without Oliver Hawkins – I owe him a deep debt of gratitude for access to the materials at Greatham, the Sussex home of Alice and Wilfrid Meynell. Warmest thanks to Oliver and his family for their kind welcome and enthusiasm for the project. My second debt of gratitude must go to Lord Gormanston who provided me with materials from the Butler side and spoke to me about his family memories of Elizabeth. Rupert Butler was extraordinarily supportive in getting this project launched and I am grateful to him for his memories of his father, Patrick Butler. Ian Wray's extensive knowledge of the Thompson family and of their connections with Dickens brought the early chapters alive. I spent some wonderful days with Ian and Georgina in Malton, North Yorkshire.

Many generous scholars and specialists have helped me on my journey by reading chapters, providing advice on archives, supporting grant applications or advising on Butler paintings. I would like to warmly thank: Nicholas Allen, Colonel Simon Bate, Sir Christopher Frayling, Kirstie Hamilton, Keith Hanley, Ann Heilmann, Sophie Hetreed, Catherine Holt, Tess Hunter, Simon Johnson, Colonel Nigel Jones, Brandon Lindberg, Mark Llewellyn, Críostóir MacCárthaigh, Clara Morgan, Veronica O'Mara, Lieutenant Colonel Richard Osbourne, Lucy Peter, Alison Price-Moir, Tariq Sadiq, Kirsten Simister and Nigel Walsh.

I am deeply grateful to the Marc Fitch Fund for supporting this project and I would also like to warmly thank the Ferens Education Trust at the University of Hull.

I am fortunate to have staunch allies: Deirdre Flood, Bethan Jones, Edel McGloin and Sabine Vanacker. Thanks also to Sabrya Albalawi, Laila Alharthi, James Booth, David Beck, Christopher Catling, Lesley Coote, Kevin Corstorphine, Victoria Dawson, Peter Duckers, Sahar el Mougy, Jonathan Greenwood, Joanne Hardy, Jason Lawrence, Andrew Lycett, Jackie McAndrew, Sophie McConnell, David Omissi, Brigitte Resl, Valerie Sanders, Jane Thomas and Sara Williams.

Butler was the subject of a major exhibition in 1987 at National Army Museum. The extraordinary work for that exhibition and the comprehensive catalogue produced by Paul Usherwood and Jenny Spencer-Smith made my task much easier. Martin Ryan, the biographer of William Butler, was very generous in directing me to relevant archives.

I had wonderful visits to museums, art galleries and regimental museums and, in particular, I would like to thank Bury Art Gallery and Museum, Christie's,

National Museum of Ireland, Collins Barracks, Dublin, Downside Abbey, Ferens Art Gallery, Hull, Isle of Wight Heritage Centre, Leeds Art Gallery, Manchester Art Gallery, Museums Sheffield, National Library of Ireland, Shropshire Regimental Museum, Tate Britain.

I am grateful to the staff of the Royal Household of St James's Palace for allowing me to see *The Roll Call*. I experienced tremendous pleasure in following the footsteps of the great Pre-Raphaelite John Everett Millais, who walked the length of the painting with Elizabeth at the Royal Academy, questioning her on its detail. Lunch in an army mess (which will remain anonymous) was one of the highlights of my research as well as a visit to Chelsea Army Barracks to see *The Retreat from Mons*. Justin Rouse walked me through the gardens of The Dell in Bonchurch where Elizabeth sketched.

Thanks also to Richard O'Sullivan from the London Irish Rifles Museum for supplying *The London Irish at Loos* and to Library and Archives Canada for *Cede Nullis*. The Department of Folklore at University College Dublin deserves a special mention for their generosity, as does the Princess of Wales's Royal Regiment and Queen's Regiment Museum, Dover Castle.

Thanks to Leila Salem and staff at the University of Tunis for their invitation to delivery a keynote conference lecture on Butler in 2014 and to Janine Hatter, Helena Ifill and Jane Jordan for their invitation to deliver a keynote on Butler at their 2017 Victorian Popular Fiction Association conference at Senate House in London. I would also like to thank Emma Butcher for an invitation to speak at a research seminar on nineteenth-century war trauma at the King's Manor, University of York in 2017, and Scott Brewster for an invitation to speak on Butler at the University of Lincoln in 2016. Martin Fanning at Four Courts Press deserves a special note of thanks for his work, advice and patience. Martin Healy was scrupulous in his attention to detail for which I am very grateful.

Thanks to my brother David for keeping the home fires burning and my cousins Pat Winters and Gemma Winters for listening to my thoughts on Butler. Christiana Thompson, Elizabeth Butler's mother, figures prominently in this book. She is a tribute to mothers who are dedicated to their children's education. The work of my mother Rose never ceased and I am deeply grateful to her for this. My father has sadly passed away but would have delighted in this work.

I visited Elizabeth Butler's grave in Stamullen, Ireland, with my husband Keith and young son Lawrence in the autumn of 2014. Some pruning of branches had been done in the graveyard and a stray branch had fallen on her gravestone. My husband uncovered it. I promised Elizabeth that we would place flowers on her grave when I completed her biography. That journey can now be made, appropriately enough for a painter of war on the centenary of the end of the First World War. We will have another little one, Alexander, in tow.

May 2018

Prelude

My divine Lole was born at 13½ past two in the morning.
XXXXXXXXXX[1]

This is what Christiana Thompson recorded in her diary for 3 November 1846. Elizabeth Thompson was the 'divine Lole' and she would grow up to become Victorian Britain's greatest war artist. Better known today as Lady Butler, Elizabeth was born at the Villa Claremont in Lausanne, Switzerland, where her parents Thomas and Christiana had settled after they had completed their ten-month honeymoon in Italy. At Lausanne her parents joined their friend Charles Dickens, and in the weeks before Elizabeth's birth the couple socialized with Dickens and his wife and attended readings of the opening chapters of the writer's new novel. *Dombey and Son* was not, however, an encouraging story for an expectant Christiana in the final trimester of her first pregnancy. Early in the novel Mrs Dombey dies in childbirth after delivering a frail son, Paul. Dickens's poignant description of this must have been difficult for Thomas who had lost his first wife in 1834, when she was twenty-three, after the birth of their second child, Fanny. Christiana's diary entries make no direct reference to the impending delivery so the declaration of the birth comes rather as a surprise. Although this was a much-loved child, the ten xs are not recording a suffusion of affection for the new daughter but represent a break in the diary of two weeks, corresponding to the traditional period after birth when Victorian mothers were confined to rest. Christiana, however, was up before the end of the traditional month's confinement.

The real Elizabeth Thompson and the fictional Paul Dombey were birthed in Switzerland. But the entry into the world of the 'divine Lole', unlike that of her novelistic contemporary, was an auspicious one, and quite remarkable for a girl child born in the mid-nineteenth century. Indeed, Dickens connected Elizabeth's birth with Paul Dombey's by quoting his character Mrs Tox's observations shortly after Paul's entry into fiction in the congratulatory letter he sent to Thomas on the morning of the birth: 'hearty and cordial congratulations on the event. We are all delighted that it is, at last, well over. There is an uncertainty attendant on Angelic Strangers (as Mrs Tox says) which is a great relief to have so happily disposed of'.[2] The delicate Paul dies at the age of six, the robust Elizabeth lived a full life to the age of nearly eighty-seven. In *Dombey and Son* Dickens provides a portrait of a dysfunctional family in which a father disregards his daughter and although his son is the source of his pride, he is unable to love either of his children in a meaningful way. Indeed, the children are destroyed by their father's desire for power and his inability to see beyond the separate spheres that dominated middle-class English life in the mid-Victorian period and beyond.

By contrast, Elizabeth was born into a loving and supportive family. 'I made', she notes in the opening lines of her 1922 autobiography, 'a good start with the parents Providence gave me'. The Thompson family 'oscillated' between Italy and England. Elizabeth's bohemian life was shaped by travel, music, art and literature, and an early predisposition towards art was encouraged by her parents, who were wealthy enough to live comfortably abroad and periodically in England during Elizabeth's childhood and adolescence, and whose own artistic and scholarly activities drew them in their early married lives into Dickens's orbit of genius.

The Thompsons cultivated their daughters' talents – their second and last child, Alice, was born in Barnes, England, in 1847. 'My father', Elizabeth notes, 'devoted his leisure to my and my sister's education'.[3] The opening of Elizabeth's memoir highlights the influence of her father as a diligent educator, but Christiana, a self-confident and a talented musician, whose early career as a pianist had drawn her into the public sphere, was instrumental in the shaping of her painter-daughter's success. Novel-writing, which many comparable Victorian women excelled in, could operate comfortably from the private sphere of the home, but success in the art world, with its required exhibitions of paintings and pursuit of commissions, was a public affair. It also required more space – a room or studio of one's own.

Christiana had gained plaudits for her music in the early 1840s before marriage ended her career. Her daughter trained at the South Kensington Art School and in Florence. Elizabeth became a sudden sensation in the 1870s at the age of twenty-seven for her paintings of soldiers: in *The Roll Call* they are depicted war weary and exhausted; and in *Scotland for Ever* – one of her most famous paintings – she captures the moment of the charge of horses and men before eventual annihilation. A single woman in her twenties painting soldiers and the travails of war in the 1870s was extraordinary. Elizabeth shared some of her mother's exuberance and she was, her daughter Eileen recalls, 'zestful and happy in the gift that had shown itself early'.

As a child, Elizabeth sketched alongside her mother, who also had artistic leanings, on the Italian Riviera, at the Somerset coast, on the Isle of Wight, and in English hayfields and Italian vineyards. Eileen recalls: 'By example, as well as precept, [Christiana] taught Elizabeth what landscape painting in watercolour ought to be; and Elizabeth came to love this medium. Wherever her travel-filled later life brought her, my mother sketched' – just like Christiana before her.[4] Elizabeth's early specialism was horses, a training that proved useful in the battle canvases that made her reputation as an artist.

Both Thompsons cultivated their daughters' talents; Thomas, a scholarly gentleman and traveller of no fixed profession, was one of Dickens's amateur actors. Both daughters were instructed for professional lives, although their education was conducted, Elizabeth notes, along the 'principle of "little and often"' but they had 'no regular holidays: a day off occasionally, especially when travelling'. Both girls exhibited an extraordinary work ethic. They were, Elizabeth affirms, 'fanatically devoted to Charlotte Brontë, since our father had read us *Jane Eyre* (with omissions). Rather strong meat for babes!'[5] *Jane Eyre* is, of course, the exemplary Victorian novel of female triumph over adversity and the biographical relations between the Brontë sisters were surely a template for the Thompson siblings' successes and sisterly solidarity throughout their lives. But *Jane Eyre* had another aspect which may have ignited the sisters' interests – their father was from Jamaica. Thompson was born to a Creole mother and a planter father whose family had come from Lancashire – it is likely that he was illegitimate.

'How', Eileen asks, 'came it to happen that these two sisters ... should have both been so gifted as to vie with one another in celebrity, the one as an artist, the other as a writer?'[6] As painter and poet respectively, they excelled: Elizabeth became famous in 1874; Alice's career as an acclaimed poet and essayist flourished in the 1880s and 1890s. For the young sisters, travel enabled them to experience life outside mid-Victorian Britain, and the rich Italian colours and brightness cultivated an artistic predisposition in Elizabeth. Progress for women was gathering a slow, uneven and non-linear pace over the course of the nineteenth century. But contrary to beliefs held by Dombey, a character described in an essay by Alice as a 'finely wrought figure of pride', girls, it would seem, were everything, if they could not, in Victorian society, still be everything.[7] While Florence Dombey in *Dombey and Son* occupies the private sphere and proves her worth as a daughter in her steadfast devotion to her father, Elizabeth Thompson achieved public greatness in a way that Dickens could not envisage, or possibly even desire to, for his female characters.

On Saturday, 14 November 1846, in Lausanne, Christiana left her confinement and came into the drawing-room where she was greeted by violets sent by her elder sister Betsy. On 5 December, Christiana noted how 'the Angel babe was christened at home in the drawing room by Mr Cheesborough – she did not cry – sunshine & great revelling'. Christiana thus commenced her mode of describing her children – they are always 'angel babes' – constantly admired for their cleverness.[8]

Switzerland was merely the beginning of Elizabeth's travels. Her comment in her autobiography that the family 'travelled much' is an understatement.[9] The Thompsons' life was dominated by constant movement and change. After her marriage to an Irish Catholic officer on imperial postings, Elizabeth's opportunities for travel extended to Egypt, France and South Africa, and finally to retirement in Ireland in the politically and socially turbulent early decades of the twentieth century. To properly know Elizabeth Thompson Butler, we must appreciate her life in travel –

her travels as a child with her family, as an adult with her military husband, her historical travels to Waterloo and the Crimea in her art, her representation of contemporaneous imperial conflicts and colonial landscapes, and the battlefields of the First World War. While travel was very much a lived reality, as a female painting in the last three decades of the nineteenth century and the first three decades of the twentieth, the battlefield was out of bounds for her. The Crimean War, which took place when Elizabeth was a child, was the last war in which British women could accompany their men to the front. Elizabeth's battlescapes, then, are travelled to in her imagination and through rigorous research and interviews with serving and retired soldiers. She was the soldier's painter and veterans of old Crimean campaigns posed for her in her studio. Her championing by Queen Victoria, and her husband's high-ranking army postings, ensured that troop manoeuvres were conducted for her so she could study horses and men in motion.

This story of a partially deaf and socially shy female's triumph through talent and industry is quintessentially Victorian in its fortitude. Like Jane Eyre, Elizabeth led a restless life; fittingly, for an artist who spent her life in travel, it starts in Liverpool. Dickens appears at its beginning, but little did the writer know how Elizabeth's particular tale would unfold, when he arrived in the port city in 1844 and became infatuated with her mother.

CHAPTER ONE

Liverpool to Lausanne, 1844–6

Christiana Weller – Meeting with Dickens – Thomas Thompson – Courtship and honeymoon – Paris – Genoa – the de la Rues – Italian tour – Birth of Elizabeth – Lausanne

I put in a book
Once by hook or by crook,
The whole race, as I thought, of a feller,
Who happily pleased
The town's taste (much diseased),
And the name of this person was Weller.

I find to my cost,
That one Weller I lost,
Cruel destiny so to arrange it;
I love her dear name
Which has won me some fame
But great Heavens! how gladly I'd change it.

Charles Dickens for Christiana Weller[1]

Christiana Weller, eighteen years old, was a well-regarded concert pianist when she performed at Charles Dickens's lecture at Liverpool's Mechanics Institution on Monday, 26 February 1844. Educated by parents with cultural inclinations – her father ran Cheltenham's Literary Saloon in the 1820s and her mother operated a school for girls – Christiana became a pianist. After success in Liverpool and Manchester, in December 1842, her Irish debut was announced in the Dublin press. It noted that she was 'appearing under *the* Thalberg, and that alone should be sufficient to establish her as a first-rate'.[2] Sigismund Thalberg (1812–72) was one of the greatest piano virtuosos in Europe at this period, rivalled only by Franz Liszt. Handsome and tall, Christiana inspired admiring tributes in the early 1840s for both her talent and her figure. At Liverpool's Philharmonic Concert in March 1843, she was described as sitting down 'at the piano as one conscious of being its perfect master'. Indeed 'tutored by her accomplished mother, improved by her own taste and industry, and encouraged by Thalberg, with whom she lately played a grand duet in Dublin, she had felt competent to the task she had undertaken'.[3] As a performer she was described as 'brilliant, imaginative and energetic'.[4]

At the Mechanics Institution lecture in Liverpool on that February evening in 1844 '1200 gay, happy and intelligent beings thronged to listen to the voice of him whose writings – by their truthfulness in the delineation of character in the lights and shadows of life – had before touched their feeling'. In his lecture Dickens praised the work of the Mechanics Institution in the spread of knowledge, encouraged its recent endeavour to 'aid of the formation of a girls' school' and of admitting women to the Institution on the widest possible extent. As he explained to the ladies in the audience, 'any ray that falls upon you at your own firesides, from any book, or thought communicated within these walls, will raise you nearer to the angels in the eyes you care for most'.[5] This is a common Victorian theme – the education of girls in the service of home and family.

Dickens's address was succeeded by his introduction of the pianist, claiming that 'he had some difficulty and tenderness in announcing her name'. Christiana shared her surname with Dickens's comic manservant, Sam Weller, in *The Pickwick Papers*. While Christiana 'played a fantasia with all her accustomed delicacy, power, and beauty', Dickens, the *Preston Guardian* records, 'kept his eyes firmly fixed on her every movement' and in his final thanks pronounced that while his writings had been praised for their heart, he 'felt a loss of heart' with the warm reception he had received that evening and that the 'last remnant he had left of it went out of him into the piano on which Miss Weller had been playing'.[6] Dickens was enthralled by the pianist and proceeded in the coming days to attempt to exert his fascination over her – he was, after all, a practising mesmerist. But Christiana Weller was no Trilby to Dickens's Svengali. Moreover, she was chaperoned by her father.

Public performance, however, had its complications in terms of propriety. Victorian actresses were, for example, at the extreme end of female display and that profession was still regarded with moral disdain until the late nineteenth century. As a pianist, Christiana was under scrutiny for her looks as well as her playing. A reviewer of one of her later performances notes, 'For the information of those who look at the person as well as the artist, we may add that Miss Weller is tall, with an exceedingly handsome and intelligent face'.[7]

Dickens, a married father, penned the Pickwickian ditty to capture the 'Weller [he] had lost' and in his quasi-courtship he moves into the realm of fantasy as he attempts to mould her into one of his characters. In real-life, however, it was not Dickens who could change her name, and indeed, career, but the friend who accompanied him to Liverpool. Thomas James Thompson also was enamoured by Christiana. Thompson, Dickens told his wife by letter, had arrived at Radley's Hotel in Liverpool before him and was waiting for Dickens by his fireside.[8]

Thompson's story starts in Jamaica. He was the son of a planter and born on the Mario Bueno estate, parish of Trelawny. The family's income was derived from sugar plantations and property in the West Indies and Lancashire. On his father's death, his grandfather brought Thomas, his two siblings, Elizabeth and Amelia, and their mother, Mary Edwards, to England. Mary Edwards was Creole and possibly of mixed race. Her granddaughters certainly thought so. Elizabeth's sister, Alice, honoured the family's Creole ancestry in a poem to her own daughter Olivia born in 1890. Here she celebrates the 'ancestral lights' which 'Kindled anew' in her child's 'dark-bright eyes'. ('To O – Of Her Dark Eyes').

> Across what calm of tropic seas,
> 'Neath alien clusters of the nights,
> Looked, in the past, such eyes as these?
> Long-quenched, relumed, ancestral lights!
> …
> Hereditary eyes! But this
> Is single, singular, apart:—
> New-made thy love, new-made thy kiss,
> New-made thy errand to my heart.[9]

Thomas was educated at Trinity College Cambridge and had stood unsuccessfully for Parliament on two occasions. He had two children, Thomas Melville, born in 1833 and Matilda Frances (known as Fanny), after her mother, in 1834. Thomas Melville (Mel) experienced mental health difficulties and spent some of his life incarcerated in an asylum. The children did not know their mother who was buried on 28 July 1834 in Kensal Green cemetery in London after Fanny's birth. Thompson was widowed for almost ten years when he met Christiana in Liverpool. His sister, Elizabeth Smithson, took care of his young children and they lived in the early 1840s with her husband, Charles, and her unmarried sister, Amelia (Milly), at Easthorpe Hall in Malton, Yorkshire. Elizabeth and Milly were also members of the Dickens circle; Smithson was the partner of Dickens's lawyer, Thomas Mitton, and the novelist was godfather to the Smithsons' daughter, Mary.

Thomas was a member of the Liberal Reform Club and of the Travellers Club (the latter set up to accommodate gentleman who travelled or lived abroad and who had travelled over 500 miles from London).[10] Nine years after his death, Alice wrote a tribute to her father, 'A Remembrance'. This is his epitaph, published when both his daughters were well established in their respective professions. 'When memories of two or three persons now upon earth shall be rolled up and sealed with their records within them, there will be no remembrance left open except this of a man whose silence seems better worth interpreting than the speech of many another. Of himself he has left no vestiges'. He was, she recalls, 'reticent' and 'reserved'. 'Delicate' is a word she repeats: 'delicate, liberal, instructed, studious, docile, austere' and with a 'selflessness that made him languid'. He was not, she says, 'inarticulate, he was only silent' and '[l]oving literature, he never lifted a pen except to write a letter'.[11] This was the man who pursued the exuberant Christiana Weller. Inspired by Christiana's music and beauty, Thomas Thompson was anything but languid in his courtship.

On the day following the lecture at the Mechanics Institution, Dickens invited himself and his friend to the Weller family for lunch or, as Wilfrid Meynell – Alice's future husband – describes it in his collection of Dickens's letters to the family, *A Dickens Friendship* (1935), 'riding out to her home near Liverpool the next morning, he bore with him the wakeful verses in which he had linked the Weller of his own creation with the living bearer of the name'.[12] But when Dickens proceeded to Birmingham for his next lecture, Thompson stayed behind. Dickens expressed his feelings for Christiana to Thomas by letter on 28 February:

> I cannot joke about Miss Weller; for she is too good; and interest in her (spiritual young creature that she is, and destined to an early death, I fear) has become a sentiment with me. Good God what a madman I should seem, if the incredible feeling I have conceived for the girl could be made plain to anyone![13]

'Fragile young virgins', Kathryn Sutherland observes, 'aroused in Dickens a mixed response of reverence and prurience and morbid fantasies of early and stainless deathbed'. Christiana, however, proved 'thoughtlessly robust and attached to life'.[14] Dickens continued his fantasy courtship of Christiana from London, impulsively sending her father his personal volumes of Tennyson's poems given to him by the poet. When Thompson declared his interest in Christiana, Dickens was melodramatic in his return letter to him on 11 March: 'I felt the blood go from my face ... and my very lips turn white' not because 'it contained a word to astonish me, but because I never had imagined you remaining in Liverpool, or seriously admiring her'. Impetuosity, Dickens confirmed, was not in Thompson's character: 'I did not think it lay in your temper or habit to do so unless it had become a thing of pretty long custom'.[15] But when Thompson asked Dickens for advice on how to proceed, Dickens quickly assumed the role of facilitator, but rather than relinquish control of the plot, his directions to Thompson were mediated through Dickens's own feelings: 'If I had all your independent means ... I would not hesitate ... But would win her if I could'. Christiana was removed from the realm of ordinary women and became a figure of fantasy, as Dickens asserted: 'hours of hers are years in the lives of common women. That it is in such a face and such a spirit, as part of its high nature, to do at once what less etherial creatures must be long in doing'.[16]

The Wellers, however, had other plans for their daughter. Her father wanted her to continue as a musician. Interestingly, Dickens directed the path for the couple's future travels when, again acting by proxy, he instructed Thomas: 'I *would* point out [to Weller] … that the course to which he is devoting her, should not be called her life but Death; for its speedy end is certain. I saw an angel's message in her face that day that smote me to the heart … Repose, change, a mind at rest, a foreign climate would be, in a springtime like hers, the dawning of a new existence'.[17] In this letter, as Rosemarie Bodenheimer points out, Dickens begins to argue as if he were talking 'directly with T.E. Weller' and by 'fighting on behalf of one man against another for the possession of an 18-year-old girl, Dickens entered the quadrangle of the Thompson-Weller marriage negotiations'. He was 'quite out of control'.[18] After dwelling on the fantasy of Christiana's early death, Dickens romanticized about 'the quiet happiness we might enjoy abroad, all of us together, in some delicious nook, where we should make merry over all this … Such Italian Castles, bright in sunny days, and pale in moonlight nights, as I am building in the air!'[19] When an engagement was announced between Thomas and Christiana, Dickens rhapsodized on the 'noble prize' in a letter to Thomas on 29 March and inserted himself into the romance in the third person as Dick – a character in his own melodrama of a woman loved by two men:

> Shall we ever forget that night when she came up to THE Piano – that morning when Dick, the energetic Dick, devised the visit! Shall we ever cease to have a huge infinite delight in talking about the whole Romance from end to end – in dwelling upon it, exaggerating it; recalling it in every possible way, form, shape, and kaleidoscopic variety!
>
> Ask her to save the dress – the dress with the fur upon it. Let it be laid up in Lavender. Let it never grow old, fade, shrink, or undergo millinerial alteration, but be a household God, Immortally Young and Perpetually Green. *Wasn't* it Green? I think so.[20]

During this time, Thomas had pressing family problems as his brother-in-law, Charles Smithson, had died in Yorkshire, and he was forced to arrange matters for his sisters and for his children. Dickens told his wife that Elizabeth and Milly had £330 each a year, in addition to what Thomas paid them to take care of his children and this would have enabled them to live 'genteelly' anywhere.[21] Dickens wrote to Christiana from Malton Abbey on 8 April, where he attended Smithson's funeral, to intervene in what had now become rocky courtship. '[A]t this funeral I found [Thomas], to my great amazement, as chief mourner to his own hopes, and attending them to an early grave' because he had 'heard, in the very height of another distress, from Her; and She had told him that he had been a little premature'. Dickens exhorts her that he had 'Faith … in Her, and that whatever she worked out would be for Good'.[22]

Christiana's life was very much grounded in the practicalities of earning a living as a performer. The Wellers sought Dickens's help in this regard to establish her in

London and despite his reservations on her continuing career, Dickens offered to introduce her to individuals in the musical world who might assist her. The family moved to London to launch Christiana's career in the capital. One observer perceptively remarked that she demonstrated not only a 'most remarkable genius for the pianoforte' but she was 'moreover, an artist full of enthusiasm for the beautiful'.[23] Elizabeth inherited this aspect of her mother's personality. The beautiful, its pursuit and cultivation, defined Christiana and she sought it in nature, in her travels and artistic endeavours. Elizabeth recalls how as child in Italy her

> mother's piano sent bright melody out of the open windows of the drawing-room when she wasn't painting mountains, the sea, the flowers. She had the 'semi-grand' piano brought out into the balcony one full-moon night and played Beethoven's 'Moonlight Sonata' under those silver beams, while the sea, her audience, in its reflected glory, murmured its applause.[24]

Thomas finally succeeded in his efforts to marry Christiana. Christiana continued to perform intermittently to friends and on social occasions. But while a happy marriage had the benefit of financial security, Christiana's creativity was frustrated and she focused her ambitions on her daughters. By the time of her marriage, Christiana was the more famous member of the couple and the press records of the wedding drew attention to Christiana rather than Thomas. The marriage, as the *Standard* announced, took place on the 21 October in Barnes Parish Church, southwest London and Dickens was a witness.

> MISS CHRISTIANA WELLER. – This charming and accomplished young lady was married on Tuesday last at Barnes Church, to T.J. Thompson, Esq., of Gloucester-road, Hyde Park. A large party of ladies and gentlemen, including 'the inimitable Boz', graced the ceremony with their presence. The bride and bridegroom left town the same day for Tonbridge Wells, *en route* for Italy, where they intend to pass the winter.[25]

On the marriage certificate Thompson's recorded age was thirty-five and Christiana was twenty.

From Genoa to Lausanne

> Our last morning in England broke beautifully. The mists of the two or three preceding days were dispelled and left nothing more than silvery haze thro' which the now visible castle appeared to the greatest advantage.[26]

This honeymoon journey sets the scene for the family's unsettled lifestyle at home and in Italy for the next two decades. The Thompsons left Dover en route for

Boulogne on Saturday, 1 November. Such journeys in the 1840s were still largely conducted by horse-power and the expedition took several days, although the Thompsons took a break in Paris along the way. While a cold obliged Christiana to stay in her rooms, Tom 'walked out & brought me home tantalizing accounts of the grandeur & gaiety of the outer world'. He returned with Galignani's guidebook on Paris, a bulky compendium, from which he read to his wife. Tom reading to his family would become a feature of their domestic life. Christiana's impressions of Paris, when she was well enough to venture outside, were not favourable: 'What have the Parisians I should like to know to compare with the beautiful parks & sensory gardens of London' and the Parisian women were 'frumpish'. Meanwhile in Paris the cosmopolitan Tom with his 'anti-provincial tastes' was 'somewhat shocked' when Christiana declared that the Champs-Elysées reminded her of Cheltenham's promenade.[27] Paris, on this visit, failed to move Christiana – later, on their frequent journeys through the French capital to Italy it would become more interesting, particularly as a centre of the international art scene, while London would become increasingly associated with darkness and fog.

The Thompsons continued their onward journey south in early December through a 'wretched' and 'depopulated' French countryside until they reached the Côte-d'Or where 'a gleam of golden light fell upon the landscape as tho' to confirm the title but the scenery continued miserable … the evening star shone forth from a transformed blue sky & the moon began to shed her mysterious light upon the dark objects of the landscape – I adored it – Tom laughed at me'.[28] Eileen Gormanston describes her grandmother as 'exuberant' and that she 'indulge[d]' in the 'language of hyperbole' in her journal: 'the afternoon is "resplendent", the moonlight "blessed", the morning "magical", the children "the angels, the doves"'.[29] Another granddaughter, Viola Meynell, suggests that Christiana's 'brilliance was of feeling' and that her journal gives 'an idea of her influence over the children's early life'.[30] A keen sensitivity to landscape and colour, a heightened imagination and a language of the sublime emerge in the journal – traits that Elizabeth inherited and transformed into dramatic art. Scenes envisaged by Christiana as glorious by night pall in daylight:

> I looked over what appeared to me an immense plain. The mountain gloom draped it up in romantic ideas – the spot where I stood seemed the battlements of a castle & I pictured a far different scene beneath it to what proved to be the next morning, tho' it was then not bad for France. The moon shone beautifully. I proposed a walk but I spoke wildly – the roads were ankle deep in liquid mud.

A steamer from Chalon sur Saône brought the couple to Avignon. The entry into Lyons by water was 'extremely grand and imposing' and at the Hôtel de l'Europe Christiana's exuberance was further demonstrated in their suite which was 'more like a gallery in some public exhibition private rooms', its oaken floors enabling her to slide about. However, contrary to Christiana's enjoyment of the hotel, Tom had 'unconquerable ideas' that it 'was dirty to excess (the impressions of a previous visit)' which prevented him from eating his dinner. Christiana saw her world through pictures. When Tom fell asleep before the fire she observed that he produced a 'Rembrandt effect charming to behold'.

As Italy beckoned the scenery improved: 'Picture after picture all varying & vying with each other for novelty & beauty enchant the eye'. Christiana's embryonic fascination with Catholicism emerged when in Avignon (a former seat of the Papacy) in the Cathedral of Notre-Dame des Doms she saw 'the Virgin draped up in real clothes & wearing together with the infant Christ a wreath of artificial flowers & ribbons; relics of saints & other symbols were displayed on each side of her. The Gothic pictures were also new to me – one represented a woman being run over by a cart – the virgin appearing in a cloud at a little distance & by whose supposed agency the poor creature in jeopardy was rescued'.[31] Catholicism, in its southern Gothic aspects, fascinated and disturbed.

Visas and passports, an onerous undertaking for the Victorian traveller, had to be checked and while all of this was going on at the Custom House, Christiana 'waited in an agony in sight of the promised land, but once at liberty jumped out of the carriage & we danced & ran & sang into Italy'. Her exuberance on this occasion infected the normally reserved Tom. Nice, a 'charming place', belonged to northern Italy's Duchy of Savoy until 1860, and marked the entry into Italy: 'Above us was an Italian sky not blue but violet-colour fading with azure towards the horizon'.[32] By mid-December they were in Genoa where they stayed for two months.

The Thompsons' journey to Italy mirrored Dickens's trip of the previous year which had resulted in *Pictures from Italy*, published in September 1846, although Dickens took a steamer from Marseilles, in contrast to the Thompson's overland route. With numerous books on Italian tours and references to Italy in other genres, the country was, by the mid-1840s, a 'fully "scripted" environment'. Christiana was undoubtedly influenced by the vogue in recording her impressions of travel. For the Victorian tourist, 'travelling and reading were seen to complement each other, constituting a cyclic ritual in which readers both shaped their expectations and relived their past travels, through texts'.[33] Dickens's presence is felt in the journal as the Thompsons became akin to literary tourists, visiting the places where Dickens stayed. Directed by the author who was still, to some extent, orchestrating the couple's relationship, the Thompsons went to the Peschiere, the imposing mansion in which Dickens had rented rooms the previous year, with a view to renting an apartment there. However, Christiana was not entirely satisfied with it:

> This, I was much, tho' not perfectly pleased with:- the approach is exceedingly characteristic & well kept – its terraces, grottos, fountains, & statues are

unique – but near the house, the gardens look dilapidated & run to seed & the wild luxuriance of nature seemingly so neglected produces quite a melancholy effect upon the spirits. We exclaimed 'oh! If an English nobleman had this what a fairy land he would make it![34]

Dickens describes it in *Pictures from Italy*:

> The Villa Bagnarello: or Pink Jail, a far more impressive name for the mansion: is in one of the most splendid situations imaginable. The noble bay of Genoa, with the deep blue Mediterranean, lies stretched out near at hand … You walk into a seedy little garden, all wild and weedy, from which the vineyard opens; cross it, enter a square hall like a cellar, walk up a cracked marble staircase, and pass into a most enormous room with a vaulted roof and whitewashed walls.[35]

The Thompsons, again directed by Dickens, became friends with Emile and Augusta de la Rue – a Swiss banker and his English wife. During the previous year, Dickens, who had no medical training, had practised mesmerism on Augusta de la Rue, treating her for symptoms of neurasthenia. Like his fantasy courtship of Christiana in 1844, Dickens had involved himself again in 1845, albeit therapeutically, with another woman. Mesmerism, a controversial science, had been introduced to England in 1838 by Professor John Elliotson, one of the founders of London's University College Hospital and a friend of Dickens. Mesmeric treatment was problematic as it often betrayed, and certainly in the Dickens–de la Rue case, a 'mutual need in the operator-patient relationship'.[36]

Immediately after viewing the Peschiere the Thompsons called on Madame de la Rue and 'found her in an elegant apartment decorated quite in the Italian style, the ceilings divided into compartments & painted in fresco'.[37] Claire Tomalin describes the de la Rues as living in 'a pretty, high-windowed and comfortable apartment at the top of a Genose palazzo, up many stairs and across many landings lined with antique busts'.[38] A couple of mornings later, despite the inclement weather, Madame de la Rue accompanied them on a walk and Christiana noted how the 'narrow streets … will always be connected in my mind with Dickens who was our topic'.[39] The Thompsons were drawn into what Tomalin describes as the '*folie à trois*' between the writer and the de la Rues.[40] Unfortunately, Christiana did not entrust what was said about Dickens to her journal. Over the course of the coming weeks, the couples socialized together and the Thompsons were guests at the de la Rues' Christmas dinner and took excursions with them in the mountains. Emile took them to Dickens's first Italian residence, Villa Bagnarello:

> Drove out to Albaro & beyond to Nervi with Monsieur de la Rue … [He] took us to see the wretched dwelling at Albaro … It was indeed a green spot & approached by a lane so narrow that their carriage had to be measured

> before entering it. We rang several times at the dilapidated stable looking door of the court but the barking of a dog was our only response. Very near upon the wild sea shore stands the ruins of a church, the tower of which is the oldest in Genoa. It is exactly the spot for a poet.[41]

For the Thompsons and the de la Rues, Dickens was the usual subject of conversation at the gatherings in the de la Rue home. Christiana also underwent mesmeric experimentation on New Year's Day 1846: 'M de la Rue mesmerized me. – at least as far to prove I should be an excellent subject for experiments. Unfortunately the moment I went off they roused me up & the various influences acting at once produced something of an hysterical feeling … The Pope by the bye has forbidden the practise, & we must never speak of it openly here'. That mesmerism became part of the Thompsons' life is evident from the fact Tom also practised mesmerism on Christiana's sisters, Betsy and Anna. Betsy suffered from blinding headaches, and Anna regularly suffered with her mental health during her adult life and unhappy marriage to Fred Dickens.

Christiana and Tom departed Genoa on 9 February. Their honeymoon tour of Italian cities continued until they reach Rome on the 21 February:

> The gradual growing of the city upon the eye with the domes & towers & great objects, & lastly, as we rounded a projection commence the wonderful St Peter's itself rising like the sun & putting out the stars. Tom placed himself in a position of great jeopardy & inconvenience to enlighten me upon the scene standing on some projection outside the carriage & holding on by the apron & lamp I think – for I was with Harris [her maid] inside, in a state of pent up emotion quite painful to bear.[42]

Italy was synonymous with culture, and Rome was the pinnacle. By now, Christiana was in the first trimester of her pregnancy but showed few signs of slowing down. They crossed the Pontine marshes to Naples and then to Herculaneum and Pompeii and on the 1 May, the couple ascended Vesuvius. Salerno, Amalfi, Sorrento and Capri occupied the early days of May and Florence was arrived at towards the end of the month where the heat made Christiana tired.

By the end of June, the couple reached Venice. 'The country we passed thro' as far as Mestri, where we had determined to take a gondola, & so approach the island city by sea, was as characterless as the environs of Warrington. Birmingham or Manchester might have been our goal'. A trip to the Lido was 'divine' for 'the sun had not set when we started & the colour & light on the San Georgio – on the sea – on the horizon I don't know what language can describe – it was gold with a rosy bluish tinge'. They left Venice on the 24 July and visited Padua, Verona, Turin and Milan and then to Como and on 8 August they took the Simplon Pass to Switzerland travelling through 'clean & happy' Swiss villages. However, as Christiana recorded, 'the approach to Lausanne by the lakeside disappointed' her but she 'strove much to mask' her 'feelings'.[43]

At Lausanne, the Thompsons joined a circle which incorporated writers and social reformers. Lausanne's residents included William de Cerjat, the philanthropist William Haldimand and his sister, Jane Marcet-Haldimand, who had published a popular scientific work *Talks about Chemistry* and *Talks on Political Economy*. Elizabeth de Cerjat, William's sister, had with William Haldimand founded philanthropic institutions for the blind and for prisoners. Shortly after Elizabeth's birth Thompson and Dickens visited the Blind Institute.[44]

In Lausanne Christiana embraced motherhood with exuberance. On the 14 December, she recorded in her slim little diary (the honeymoon journal is broken off during the Lausanne period) a 'fine effect of snow on the mountains – the whole expanse of country now slightly covered – angelic Lole grows more exquisite & intelligent every day'.[45] Christiana's diaries, unlike the honeymoon journal, are short on description and filled with hurried phrases, 'they telegraph themselves onto the page as if they were recorded in the actual hurry of their happening'.[46] On 31 December the Thompsons received Dickens's fourth Christmas novel, *The Battle of Life*, which he dedicated to his English friends in Switzerland and Tom read it to Christiana in the evening. Meanwhile Elizabeth was 'glorious to behold – a velvet flower to touch bless her' and the proud new mother was annoyed when their friend, Mr Cerjat, who brought them the third number of *Dombey and Son*, published the previous December, took no interest in the infant: Elizabeth 'stared at him for a quarter of an hour which however failed to cheat a word from him on the blessed subject'. The third number of Dickens's novel (chapters 8–10) describing the development of Paul's character and education was, however, 'inimitable – first rate it is in fact "Boz".'

The Thompsons were not secluded in their Lausanne retreat. Christiana read about 'the frightful famine in Ireland' and on the 24 January, there was a 'fast on account of Ireland'. She recorded with disapproval how the vicar, Mr C, 'attributed the calamity of the poor Irish and Scotch to the national sins'. She further observed: 'It is well to have money in ones purse'.[47] Many years later the deprivation of the Irish peasant experience would find a remarkable champion in Elizabeth's painting *Evicted* (1890).

In these final months in Lausanne Christiana spent her time writing to Dickens's wife, Catherine, and to Augusta de la Rue, walking to Lausanne and revelling in her new baby. The family departed Lausanne for England on 6 May 1847. Elizabeth was six-months old and was accompanied by her Swiss maid, Amelie. Stopping in Paris on their way to London, the family visited the Exposition of Modern Pictures in the Louvre which, for Christiana, contained an 'immensity of trash' and a 'few exquisite things & many moderate ones – a large collection of the usual atrocious portraits more hideous and dowdy than I can describe ... All this is Tom's opinion also'. But one painting captivated her: 'a very peculiarly beautifully coloured glimpse of dancing Bacchanalians or idealized Neapolitans by one Muller – a gorgeous southern colour lost in the light of sunset as I have seen objects in Italy'. The light and colour of Italy beckoned as the family reached London on 11 May. 'LONDON AWFUL! Smoke unbelievable'.[48] The south of England would be their home for the next four years as the political unrest of the late 1840s spread across the Continent.

CHAPTER TWO

South of England to the Italian Riviera: the making of an artist, 1847–61

Birth of Alice – Fred and Anna Dickens – Trip to Italy – Italian Riviera – Fanny marries – Home life in Italy – Elizabeth's education – Rosa Bonheur – Albaro –Elizabeth's proficiency in art – Military matters – Garibaldi – Back in London

> Colour seemed flung down anyhow, anywhere; every sort of colour piled up in heaps pouring along in rivers – the periwinkles looked exactly as if they were being poured down each side of the steps – and flowers that grow only in borders in England, proud flowers keeping themselves to themselves over there, such as the great blue irises and the lavender, were being jostled by small, shining common things like dandelions and daisies and the white bells of the wild onion, and only seemed the better and the more exuberant for it.[1]

Elizabeth von Arnim's *Enchanted April*, published in the same year that Elizabeth produced her autobiography, is a story of how a group of women, strangers who meet through an advertisement, travel to Portofino, to escape their English lives and find emotional renewal in a rented castle in Italy. This Italian landscape opens up lives closed by the constraints of English society. Von Arnim uses the language of flowers as a metaphor for these women's existences. Flowers that keep to themselves in the borders of English gardens are 'jostled' in the Italian fields by a luxuriance of weeds to become more 'exuberant'. Such representations, however mythic or constructed, of the Italian countryside as liberating or awakening had a powerful hold over the Victorian and post-Victorian creative imagination and suggest a way of understanding how Elizabeth's formative years in the environs of Portofino in the 1850s prepared her for an artistic life. In the English cultural imagination at this time Italy was perceived as a place of spontaneity and creativity.[2] Liberal England, of which the Thompsons were products, deepened its engagement with Italy as the Italian landscape went through its own processes of recreation and unification. As children, Elizabeth and Alice were enthralled, as was most of Britain, by the allure of Giuseppe

Garibaldi. As 'highly exalted *Garibaldians*', Elizabeth describes how she and her sister saw 'the Liberator' in Genoa in early May 1860 and she quickly 'made a pen and ink memory sketch of him which my father told me to keep for future times'.[3]

However, in the summer of the Thompson family's return to England in July 1847, Tom was preoccupied with Dickens's theatricals. The amateur company which, in addition to Tom, comprised the dramatist John Poole and writer Douglas Jerrold, the illustrators and painters John Leech, Frank Stone and Augustus Egg, the critic George Henry Lewes and the journalists Dudley Costello and Mark Lemon (the founder of *Punch* magazine) performed Ben Jonson's *Every Man in His Humour* at Covent Garden, London, on 14 July, with Tom in the role of Wellbred, and on the following Monday produced *The Merry Wives of Windsor*, before travelling to Manchester. En route the pregnant Christiana shared a carriage with Dickens' illustrator George Cruikshank. *The Morning Post* declared Jonson's play a success in Manchester's Theatre Royal where it was performed before a 'crowded and fashionable house' and realized £300 net profits.[4] The touring party travelled on to Liverpool, Christiana's adolescent home. Here Tom gets a mention in the press with others who 'acquitted themselves admirably' in the interlude piece – John Poole's *Turning the Tables*.[5]

The Thompsons arrived back in Barnes, South London, on 10 August to find 'blessed Topy asleep & very well'. On 11 October Alice was born at '16 ½ past 7 in the morning'. While Elizabeth's pet name changed over the course of the next few years to Lole and then to Mimi, the name she used for the rest of her life with family and friends, the young Alice was called Babe in her early years and both girls were collectively referred to as 'babes' or 'angels'. On 5 May Christiana's attempt to have the 'babes christened' took her to Barnes Church but 'babes came too late & no sponsors'. Five days later they were christened, although Elizabeth had already been christened by Mr Cheesborough in Lausanne.

The one-and-a-half-year-old Elizabeth was already showing signs of a cosmopolitan upbringing: 'Glorious Topy says "How doo do" ... with a most fascinating foreign accent ... she is too exquisite'. The breathless pace of the Thompsons' lifestyle continued as they moved to Cheltenham in May 1848 where Christiana read *Jane Eyre*: 'the most wonderful written fascinating & charming novel I ever read'.

Elizabeth's first attempts at painting take place on 21 October 1848, although she showed few signs of talent beyond that of the average toddler: 'Little Mim has got box of paints which she amuses herself with for half an hour or more at a time – she made a little green dab in colour & said Voila arbe Mama! When I asked her what colour she would have for the arbe she said Vert Mama – for the sky bu (blue)'.[6] Over the course of the next year, under the influence of her Swiss nurse, Amelie, Elizabeth learned French. The family's existence seemed bucolic. The girls' young lives were shaped against the backdrop of art. Christiana painted on a daily basis and the children enjoyed long walks in the countryside around Cheltenham.

All, however, was not quite as comfortable with Christiana's relatives. On 30 December 1848, her sister Anna married Fred Dickens, much against Charles's wishes. It was through Dickens and Thomas that Fred met Anna in June 1844.[7] Dickens, however, registered a strong opposition to Fred's courtship of Anna from the start, arguing that Fred's earnings were a problem. Fred's income as clerk at the Treasury was not ample but it was sufficient, at £360 a year, to support a family.[8] Anna's youth was also a problem – she was only 14 when they first met. Dickens's main objection to the marriage was directed at the Weller family, describing them as 'feverish, restless, flighty, excitable, uncontrollable, wrong-headed ... The presence of this flutter and fever in anybody's house – but especially in a poor man's, with the world before him – is not the presence that would make it comfortable, rich, or happy'. Dickens admitted Anna's 'cleverness' but doubted whether she would ever grow into a 'reasonable woman'.[9] Fred was also in debt. The union was disastrous for both, but particularly for Anna who suffered from Fred's mistreatment and neglect.

The wedding took place in Prestbury, near Cheltenham. The guests 'waited a long time for the bridal party – at length they came up the aisle & great was the hushed excitement – dear little Anna in white silk with bunches of flowers & lace' while Fred was 'most gorgeous & looking very pale'. Despite Fred's paleness, the ill-fated marriage seemed to start promisingly with the support of the Wellers. The wedding breakfast 'looked like a repast suddenly called up by the enchantment for a fairy prince or a beauty lost in a wood who had suddenly espied a castle of shining gold'. Elizabeth and Alice were dressed in 'scarlet cashmere'.[10]

This auspicious start did not last. When the Thompsons went to London the following May for the Royal Academy exhibition, after a commotion at Anna's lodgings which seemed 'outwardly good but kept by drunken wretches', Anna had to be rescued from her bed by 'Pa Tom & Fred' and brought to her mother's house.[11] By June 1849, it was a relief for Christiana to return to Prestbury to her 'babes' – 'Oh what a joy to see them'. On a mid-summer afternoon Christiana was out 'in hayfield all afternoon with angels – read Ruskin's Modern Painters in the hay!' And then 'up the hill with babes on donkies'. Mimi 'sitting alone on side saddle'. Meanwhile, Elizabeth's ability to alternate between French and English continued as Christiana observed: 'I was admiring little babe [Alice] in a nude state one eve – when Mimi says of les petits bras – si belle – et puis la pointing to the lovely curve of her little back – et la pointing to her blessed little chest with evident appreciation of the beautiful – "mimi ansi belle n'est ce pas?"' On a visit to the Somerset coast Christiana took her children to watch the waves: 'Elizabeth amazed & leant over a rock to watch them for half an hour. A lovely picture'. During this period, Christiana constantly exposed her children to art as they experimented with painting on a daily basis. As she developed into adolescence Elizabeth's talents would far exceed her mother's, but she certainly inherited Christiana's determination to use every opportunity to sketch. Christiana's surviving paintings in oil and watercolour are landscape scenes and demonstrate only average ability. Christiana was, however, dedicated. One diary entry records how in October 1849 a bad cough prevented her from continuing her sketching and she lamented how her opportunity to paint faded 'thro' the window' as she was 'obliged to stay on the bed'.

The winter of 1849 brought the family back to London and at three years old, Elizabeth is described as a 'bonny bouncing intelligent wonderful creature with an expressibly glorious face!'[12] The London stay was punctuated with visits to St Leonards and Hastings. By February 1850, 'Little babes do arts now – nuages & des vagues – et des collines. Wild lines of various colours'. When, in April 1850, Elizabeth identified the flower of the wild strawberry, which was hardly distinguishable from the surrounding grass, her parents were 'amazed', delighting in what they saw as their child's precocity. This, Christiana affirmed, 'would be intelligent in a grown up botanist'.

On the return to London in late April 1850, Anna's health had deteriorated. Dickens, now reconciled to his brother's marriage, used mesmerism to treat her. Christiana observed: 'He did it completely' and was 'very cordial' but the strained relations between the families was now evident as Catherine Dickens was 'stiff'. Christiana criticized her brother-in-law, as Fred did 'nothing but loaf'.[13] Meanwhile Tom mesmerized Anna every evening in August 1850. He also practised mesmerism on Christiana's sister Betsy who, due to pregnancy, was suffering from what Christiana described as 'wheel headaches' and was obliged to confine herself to a darkened room – Alice would later suffer from similar migraines.

Life was better in the Thompson family and the babes back in Cheltenham practised their singing while Tom cultivated his languages in preparation for foreign travel. By February 1851 Christiana described how 'Angel Mimi has a glorious contralto voice & catches a tune now very readily'. A letter from Emile de la Rue in early January 1851 focused the Thompsons' attention on Italy as the family 'fully intend[ed] going to Genoa in September. Little babes very much charmed'.[14] These stays abroad were for financial as well as cultural reasons. It was cheaper to live on the Continent and the Thompsons, never good with money, were required to budget. As well as his second family, Tom also had to consider the interests of his son and first daughter. The 1851 census locates the family as living at 61 High Street Prestbury Green with 16-year-old Fanny (Matilda), the children's Swiss nurse and two servants. Anna Dickens was registered as a visitor at this time. In this final summer in the English countryside Christiana recorded how she went with her 'angels' to a 'sweet field – tried to do some hay art but men so vile & talking shocking language' that they were obliged to leave: 'angels playing about in exquisite long grass full of tall waving flowers – back thro' sweet cornfield'.[15] One of Christiana's oil paintings from this period captures the Thompsons' life as Christiana depicts the diminutive figures of her infants strolling through English summer fields.

The Italian Riviera

With 17-year-old Fanny in tow, the Thompsons set off to a new life in Italy in September 1851. Fred and Anna accompanied them to Paris for the first part of their journey. Unlike her honeymoon experience in the French capital six years before, Christiana was now more impressed with the city: 'who in their senses can compare London with this – everything tells – every bit of architecture' and Anna was 'charmed & astonished'. In a happy picture of family life, the babes enjoyed a 'morning flane' on Tom's shoulders with 'their legs dangling'.[16] Departing from Anna on the 7 November was difficult for Christiana. She missed her sister's company and intimacy.

In the autumn of 1851 an onerous winter journey lay ahead for the Thompsons and their little children as they made their way from Paris to Genoa. In Chalon Alice was taken ill. Christiana, Fanny and Mimi went to buy her a doll but the streets were filthy and muddy. Meanwhile Mimi, a 'sweet merry soul', amused herself watching boats from the hotel window 'for hours at a time'. Barely recovered Alice had to endure the boat to Lyons as the family continued their journey by water: 'My life', Christiana remarks, 'seems to be spent in struggling with tightly filled carpet bags & portmanteaus'.[17] Indeed, in one of Elizabeth's surviving notebooks there is a list of 'boxes, & what they principally contain' for an unspecified journey.[18] One item of clothing in the list dates the trip as sometime after 1860 as Elizabeth had packed a 'white Garibaldi', referring to either the blouse or jacket that became popular alongside its originator's apparel – a loose baggy red shirt.[19] Clearly, Elizabeth was wearing the jacket in honour of her hero. Usually red with gold military trimmings, although white versions also appeared, the Garibaldi jacket certainly helped to fix Elizabeth's interest in military uniforms.

On their first trip down the Rhône in 1851 the 'Poor babes [were] obliged to be down in a little stifling cabin on account of cold', as Christiana on deck 'recognized the old dear scenes' from her honeymoon trip 'but oh! how drear & different'. At Valence, Christiana and Mimi, blinded by steam, nearly tumbled into the river but their rooms, at least, were clean and large. They arrived in Marseilles on 15 November to 'bad smells along the shore' but saw the Mediterranean which 'delighted' the babes. Anxiety did not diminish on the 'wild' sea journey to Genoa and 'Poor Tom [was] very anxious about us particularly the babes' who seemed, contrary to the adults, to pass the journey quite well. Genoa then rose before them as a 'magnificent spectacle' and at the Hotel d'Italie their 'glorious room [was] perfectly <u>ideal</u> Italian'. However, Christiana 'Found my poor arts' (her paintings) 'quite ruined by the way I had packed them up which drove me quite wild'.

The family initially settled at Nervi and Tom and Fanny set about 'busy as bees unpacking great cases'. Here the Thompson life resumed its English ways as Christiana 'Sketched view in the morn & after dinner sat on rock & coloured it.

Divine sunset sweet babe's climbing up the rocks near me – guarded by Tom'. Painting was now the norm for Mimi. On the last day of 1851 the children painted outdoors: 'After dinner with angels to rocks & did my art & they bless them, made couchers de soleils near me in water colour. [Alice's] sun & reflection was like a great green cauliflower & stalks. Little Mimi at last moment very busy in getting down a long rose coloured cloud'.[20] Elizabeth enjoyed the robust pleasures of art-making in the open air. Her art was not confined to the nursery or drawing room, the traditional orbits of Victorian femininity. Taking possession of the landscape as a child equipped her to later compete in a male-dominated art world. The point is an important one in a Victorian culture that validated female physical and mental incapacity. Deborah Cherry points out that this 'delicacy of bodily and mental constitution was given as an argument against middle-class women's professional work, vocational training and higher education as well as outdoor pursuits such as landscape painting and sketching'.[21]

Elizabeth's early recollections of Italy are those of change and sunshine – at 'Ruta, on the saddle of Porto Fino, that promontory which has been called the "Queen of the Mediterranean" … we began our lessons, and, I may say, our worship of Italy'. The children led a Bohemian life as Elizabeth is keen to emphasize the vigour of their rather unfeminine 'escapades':

> Our dear Swiss nurse was often scandalized at our escapades, but our mother, bright and beautiful, loving music and landscape painting and practicing both with an amateur's enthusiasm, allowed us what she considered very salutary freedom after study. Still I don't think she would have liked some of our wild doings and our consorting with Genoese peasant children and Surrey ploughboys, had she known of them. But, careful as she was of our physical and spiritual health, she trusted us and thought us unique.[22]

Albaro, Ruta, Portofino, Genoa, Sori and Nervi trip out of the pages of Elizabeth's autobiography, as the family peregrinated over the Riviera, rarely settling in one place for very long. 'In all their wanderings it was to this Ligurian coast that they returned most constantly; and this more than another scene of that rootless childhood was home' for the girls.[23] In Genoa, the Thompsons were drawn into a social circle that contained the de la Rues, the English Consul Timothy Brown, his wife Stuarta and son Monty, banker Charles Gibbs and the English vicar Alfred Stretsell and his family. Fanny fell in love with an Italian army officer and engineer Carlo Brocchi, who would later become a follower of Garibaldi. Brocchi was 27 years old, 9 years older than Fanny. They married at the British Consulate at Genoa on 5 October 1852. The Thompson family now had roots in Italy which would draw Elizabeth and Alice back to the country for the rest of their lives, or as Elizabeth describes it, Fanny 'settled in Italy, becoming one of our attractions to the beloved Land'.[24] Alice and

Elizabeth's relationship with their half-sister remained strong until the end of their lives. They often visited her in Italy. Evidence of the nature of the relationship can be seen in a letter which Alice wrote to Fanny during the First World War, assuring her that her London flat in Granville Place had escaped a bombing and urged her half-sister to 'Keep well for the sake of those who hold you so precious'.[25]

Family matters and business interests at home drew Tom and Christiana separately to England and sometimes with their children over the course of the 1850s and letters exchanged between the couple provide an insight into Elizabeth's Italian childhood. In June 1853, Christiana returned home, possibly to see Anna. Tom wrote on 2 June: '[I] hope Anna is better – give my love to her and tell her I shall write'. He was anxious about Christiana's welfare on the journey: 'What I have suffered from the thoughts of what you must be suffering!'[26] Both Elizabeth and Alice wrote in large, joined script, but with imperfect punctuation. Elizabeth described how they were 'going to bathe in the sea to-morrow and every day. It is very smooth and the sun shines very hot and bright' and she promised to be 'very industrious' while her mother was away. 'I hope I shall be able to read very well when you come back'.[27] Alice wrote in a similar vein and Tom, in a note at the bottom of his children's missives, informed his wife that the 'composition having extended over several days somewhat feels stilted at the commencement' and that the weather precluded bathing. He envied Christiana her London visit as there must be 'glorious things in the Academy' and urged her to 'renew her acquaintance with C[harles] Kean' at the Princess's theatre.[28] As a teenager Christiana had been an ardent admirer of Kean, a leading actor of the period.

In a subsequent letter, Mimi tells her 'dear Lily of the Valley' that they walked to Recco to see Fanny's baby: 'a little tiny wee baby and she has black hairs and she has black eyes and I am an aunt' and 'I send you some drawings one I have made of Porto Fino from the balcony and the sun shines very bright the sea is very beautiful'.[29] Tom's postscript to Elizabeth's letter informed Christiana that the 'little ones are perfectly well and in high spirits & would write all day, but I confess it is generally necessary to bring their compositions to an untimely end for the superintendence after a certain time becomes rather wearying'. After having lost Fanny's mother in childbirth, Tom was no doubt relieved to be able to inform Christiana that Fanny was through the ordeal and 'going on very well – no drawbacks at present I believe – the baby also'.[30]

In an essay on their Italian cook, Agostino, published in the *Pall Mall Gazette* in 1898, Alice recalls the domestic circumstances of the family – 'an English family fond of Italy and capriciously inclined to spend now a winter and now a summer, as the Italian longing took them, at Genoa or somewhat to the eastward'. Indeed they 'seldom knew much beforehand of their own movements, but short as were their decisions Agostino knew, by some invisible way of communication, that they were coming; and his light figure with the dancer's step was always the first thing to meet them, whether on the platform of the station or among the brown porters and the screaming apple-women, the mules and whips and chaos of the port'. The two little girls 'throve on Agostino's exceedingly Italian cookery'.[31] Meanwhile they were 'proud of their intimacy in Genoese affairs' and saw 'far more of the servants' lives than their parents knew' and talked the 'strongest kind of Genoese even to each other in their games' and delighted in secretly consuming garlic bread in the kitchen, in exchange for which they attempted to teach one of the maids to read. The children revelled in the maids' singing and 'the dearest of many affectionate words was always "beautiful".' They grew up on the sounds of "Bello", "Bella" which were 'perpetually in the mouths of these Genoese'. Alice's childhood memory is of freedom and gaiety mingled with religious observance and duty.[32]

A caricatured insight into the family's Italian life is recorded by Dickens. When the writer visited Genoa in October 1853, he went to see the Thompsons who were then living at the Villa dei Franchi at Sori. The Thompsons rented the villa for what Elizabeth describes as 'two exquisite years'. It was a '*palazzo* of rose-coloured plaster and white stucco, with flights of stone steps through the vineyards right down to the sea'.[33] Into this idyllic setting, Dickens called and in a letter to his wife described how he found them living in a 'beautiful situation' in a 'ruinous' palace similar to the Villa Bagnarello which the Dickens's had rented at Albaro in 1844:

> Coming upon them unawares, I found Thompson with a pointed beard, smoking a great German pipe, in a pair of slippers – the two little girls, very pale and faint from the climate, in a singular untidy state – one (Heavens knows why) without stockings – and both with their short hair cropped in a manner never before beheld, and a little bright bow stuck on the top of it. Christiana said she had invented this head gear as a picturesque thing – adding that perhaps it was – and perhaps it wasn't. She was greatly flushed and agitated, but looked very well and seems to be much liked here. We had disturbed her at her painting in Oils; and I rather received an impression that what with that, and what with Music, the household affairs went a little to the wall. Thompson was teaching the two little girls the multiplication table, in a disordered billiard room.[34]

Meanwhile the 7-year-old Elizabeth's precocity as a painter is confirmed in an 1854 letter from Christiana's sister. Betsy praised 'precious Mimi's wonderful battle scene' which was sent to her in a letter: 'what may we expect of her some day.[35] Letters to Christiana, then on a visit to her family in England in July 1856, shed further light on the family's Italian retreat and Elizabeth's life in Stresa. Here Tom told Christiana on 6 July that the 'chicks' were 'rusticating charmingly'. Stresa was the 'pearl of this side of the lake in regard of situation. The cooking of the hotel was 'very pleasant' but more expensive than the family could afford. The children got up at 'five to bathe' each morning and Elizabeth sketched.[36]

Tom's reading matter at this time embraced popular science, art criticism and music. He instructed Christiana to buy him Combes' *System of Phrenology* and *Phrenology Applied to the Arts* – an unsurprising choice given his practice of the allied quasi-science of mesmerism. Phrenology examined the relationship between the skull and an individual's character and some mesmerists deployed phrenological ideas to manipulate the skull in their treatment practice. Founder of the Edinburgh Phrenological Society in 1820, Combes attracted a middle-class audience interested in science. Tom was drawn then to quasi-scientific areas that operated alongside but often challenged medical orthodoxy, as Victorian scientific knowledge underwent processes of development. Tom also requested the fourth volume of Ruskin's *Modern Painters* and Thomas Moore's *Irish Melodies*, which had been illustrated by one of his friends from the Dickens circle, the artist Daniel Maclise. But money concerns in the meantime forced Tom to opt only for Combes. Meanwhile Elizabeth and Alice continued their studies under the instruction of their father. 'Their great amusement now', he wrote to Christiana on the 19 July, 'is writing history – the history of their respective islands. [Elizabeth] illustrates hers with portraits of the sovereigns, not without vanity & character'. The girls' top knots which Dickens found so strange were 'dispensed with' and it 'will be for you to restore them. I shall not'.[37]

While correcting his daughters' spellings, which Elizabeth recalls caused him 'many an agonized twinge', Tom was also reading a life of the history painter Benjamin Haydon, whose diaries catalogue the frustrations and thwarted ambitions of the artist whose rise to fame was meteoric and his fall just as sudden.[38] Tom was so enthralled by Haydon that he urged Christiana to go to Deepdene near Dorking to see Haydon's work: 'I have been reading once more Haydon's life – it has not lost its fascination. It keeps me awake thro' most improper hours. As I put out my candle I see the day breaking over the snow sprinkled Alps that close and the head of the Lake that spreads out before me. Not a bad view I confess to look at through an open window as one lies in bed'.[39] Christiana duly went to Deepdene in Surrey, home of the collector Thomas Hope, and commented on Haydon's painting of Joseph and Mary on the road to Egypt: 'gt feeling of repose and solemnity'.[40]

But it was at the Royal Academy some days prior to her Deepdene visit in July that Christiana saw a much more important painting, the Pre-Raphaelite artist Holman Hunt's *The Scapegoat* (1854–6). Painted with meticulous attention to the landscape of the Holy Land where Hunt began his painting, it depicts a goat straying in an Old Testament desert with the animal in the foreground 'staggering with glazed eye'. The painting represented 'atonement' and the goat a sacrifice, but Christiana could not 'contain [herself] before this – for the inhumanity injustice imbecility blasphemy of the hideous idea'.[41] The Pre-Raphaelites, an artistic movement formed in 1848 by Hunt, Dante Gabriel Rossetti and John Everett Millais, were leading the way towards a greater naturalism in art and some of Elizabeth's work would be identified with Pre-Raphaelite strands, particularly her attention to landscape and the fields of battle.

The Thompson family's interest in contemporary art is underscored by Tom's further instructions to Christiana to 'Go well into pictures. Rosa Bonheur's *Horse Fair* is exhibiting at Leggatts Cornhill (or was) go & see it'.[42] The French animal painter Rosa Bonheur (1822–99) was the artist that Elizabeth was compared to in her early career. Her aunt Amelia Thompson concluded an 1860 letter giving her love to 'Rosa Bonheur's future rival and her pretty sister'.[43] *The Horse Fair* (1853) was Bonheur's most celebrated painting and to undertake it Bonheur cross-dressed to avoid drawing attention to her gender when she went to the Paris horse fair twice a week for a year-and-a-half. The painting was celebrated on the Continent and in Britain, where it impressed the viewers with the extraordinary movement and grandeur of the black and white horses. The large canvas occupied a whole side of the room at the exhibition of French paintings, Pall Mall. The style was celebrated by *The Critic* on 1 August 1885 as one of 'prodigious force and firm breadth of treatment' and a painting 'rich in life and action' that sends 'a perpetual current of vital activity through the spectator.[44] When the writer George Eliot saw Bonheur's painting she declared: 'What power! This is the way women should assert their rights'.[45]

With Christiana back from England, the Thompsons rented the Villa Bagnarello – Dickens's Pink Jail – at Albaro in November 1856. For Christiana it was a 'sweet & grand place' and her diary provides a sketch of the floor plan and occupancy of the rooms. Tom's room was 'splendid', Christiana's 'exquisite' and the babes' bedroom had their beds alongside each other, denoted by the first letters of their names.[46] More interesting is the fact that the babes' playroom was adjacent to the studio, as play and art intersected in their young lives.

As an adult Elizabeth recounted her memories of her Italian childhood with her sister:

> [H]ow many things I could say of her girlhood! Her goodness & courage; her grace in dancing & in the saddle; her devotion to her Father & her helpfulness to me who used to go to her in all my troubles & dilemmas. How she used to get me out of many a bad bit of spelling which our Father wd have scolded me for, most severely. (I was a bad speller up to my latter teens.) Though my junior she was intellectually my senior & tho' physically so much more fragile had a stronger nature.[47]

Alice was Elizabeth's early model and the description provides an insight into the painter's early themes – horses and soldiers:

> Very patient & obliging if wanted to serve little 'Mimi' as an imaginary horse harnessed to some imaginary vehicle, trotting to the stimulating crack of a whip with a string of twine. Later on as a charging soldier and later as a graceful maiden always handy as a model according to Mimi's mood. Very irksome some of those poses must have been. The charging soldier lapsing into

forgetful melancholy or the horse forgetting to prance – these things amazed the sister with the pencil.[48]

In the summer of 1857 the Thompson family were in London where they saw Bonheur's *Horse Fair* on 8 June. Mimi finally had an opportunity to see Bonheur's celebrated painting which Christiana described as a 'marvellous picture'. A move to the countryside saw Mimi practice sketching trees in Betchworth Park near Dorking. Christiana noted on 11 June how Mimi described how the 'gigantic trees' seemed to 'have arms'. However, much to Christiana's annoyance, on 16 June, a 'pompous artist found out poor Mimi and criticized her tree'. By August Mimi was proficient in watercolours. By the 24 September 'Little Mimi [was] doing wonders in drawing – in men their attitudes & expressions – also in watercolour landscape backgrounds'. The Thompsons did not live in the secluded world of art; they engaged with contemporary issues, which would form the basis for Elizabeth's interest in historical and political art. On 7 October, Christiana noted how they were having a 'Fast day' for the Indian Mutiny, describing the events in India as 'a judgement on the nation for its sins' but the 'punishment was made to fall on the head of creatures whose innocence no one can doubt – viz little children – leaving alone the women'. Christiana blamed 'an unwise government' which had 'brought about these evils'.[49] Elizabeth recalls: '[a]s time went on my drawing-books began to show some promise so that my father gave me great historical subjects for treatment, but warning me, in that amused way he had, that an artist must never get spoilt by celebrity, keeping in mind the fluctuations in popularity'.[50] He had remembered Haydon.

Wider family matters intervened again as Tom was obliged to act as a mediator in the separation of Anna and Fred. Anna's petition for a judicial separation was filed on the 30 October 1858. It reveals the sordid underbelly of this married life with details of separation, reconciliation and Fred's adultery – the latter charge Fred first denied and then contended that Anna condoned it. Fred was ordered by the court to pay alimony of £60 per annum, but gave up his job, alleging grounds of ill-health, which the court refused to accept on 2 February 1860.[51] Fred's subsequent flight resulted in jail where he filed for bankruptcy in order to avoid supporting Anna. Meanwhile in 1858 the breakdown of Charles Dickens's marriage became a source of gossip amongst the writer's Genoese friends with Stuarta Yeats Brown, the Consul's wife, informing Christiana, in a letter which she told Christiana to burn after reading, that she felt sorry for Catherine Dickens before commenting on Elizabeth's burgeoning career: 'Poor Mrs Dickens, her position is a very sad one. I can't conceive a sadder one. I hope Mimi goes on with her drawing'.[52] The Dickens' marriage and Mimi's artistic prowess were interchangeable items of news in this closely knit English community.

In September 1859, the Thompsons returned to Italy and were drawn back into the de la Rue's social circle, with Christiana, Fanny and the girls spending Christmas night with them: 'Magnificence at the De la Rues' [...] large assemblage. Everyone there of the colony & Italians besides'.[53] But Elizabeth's attention was turning firmly in the direction of military matters. By 1859 when the Thompsons returned to Genoa, Italy was poised for Garibaldi's campaign of Italian liberation. It was not his first and would not be his last, but the late 1850s possibly marked the zenith of Garibaldi's achievements. His story, his biographer Alfonso Scirocco remarks, 'reads like an adventure novel' and his 'ability to stand up to stronger adversaries earned him the aura of a hero' in a life that 'inspired a sense of awe and gave free rein to the imagination'.[54] Garibaldi's campaign coincided with Elizabeth's increasing attention to her art and the evidence of her 1860 sketchbook confirms that military subjects were at the forefront of the teenage artist's mind. From an early age she almost always painted men.

Garibaldi was a glamorous and deeply charismatic figure with an international exoticism. In 1815 after the fall of Napoleon who had invaded the country, Italy was again fragmented into various states with varying levels of autocratic government largely under the control of the Austrians. Genoa was part of the Kingdom of Sardinia which included the territories of Liguria, Nice, Savoy, Piedmont and Sardinia. As a young man, Garibaldi joined Mazzini's Young Italy movement and became involved in plans to start a revolution in Genoa in 1834. Nothing happened but Garibaldi was forced to flee Italy. Taking refuge in South America, initially to generate support for Young Italy amongst the Italian emigrant community there, he became involved in a nationalist movement in the province of Rio Grande do Sul in Brazil and later fought with Uruguayans against Argentina. Experiences in South America had caused him to discover his vocation: 'to engage in armed struggle to defend oppressed people' and his motto was 'War is the true life for a man'.[55] In 1848 with insurrections brewing in Palermo and the Sardinian King Charles Albert's incursion into the Austrian territory of Lombardy, Garibaldi returned to Italy where he attained command of the army of Milan's provisional government. In Sicily, he participated in a rebellion against the Bourbon monarchy and proceeded to Rome where he assisted the Roman Republic declared after the Pope fled the Papal States. The Welsh sculptor John Gibson, whose studio the Thompsons had visited on their honeymoon tour of Rome, describes Garibaldi 'seated on his white horse ... perfectly statuesque in his virile handsomeness'.[56] By September 1849 the short-lived constitutional regimes established by the revolution were over and only the new King of Sardinia, Victor Emmanuel, promised to maintain constitutional reforms. The first War of Independence was over.

When Garibaldi relaunched his campaign for Italian freedom in the 1850s he allied himself to Victor Emmanuel. In 1859, he became a general in the Sardinian army but resigned when he was prevented from invading the Papal States. In May 1860 Garibaldi was in Genoa where he launched his campaign in the Kingdom of the Two Sicilies, as the Italian State that comprised the island of Sicily and Southern

Italy was called, by invading Sicily. On 2 October, he defeated the Bourbon army at Volturno and handed Southern Italy and Sicily to Victor Emmanuel. In 1861, the Kingdom of Italy was proclaimed.

The Thompsons were following Garibaldi's activities with great excitement. The writer A.L. Gretton, who was living in Genoa, gave the Thompsons a copy of her *Vicissitudes of Italy* in which Gretton discourses on the history of Italian politics and anticipates the present moment of 1859 when the 'the great struggle against Austria' will decide whether the 'peninsula is to participate in the civilization, the discoveries, the improvements of the age'.[57] Such intensity of feeling was replicated by supporters of Garibaldi everywhere. Maura O'Connor points out that 'Garibaldi personified all that the romance of English narratives of an Italian nation promised because he managed, through the example of his manly and heroic military means, to instil a moral awakening in the Two Sicilies, thus helping create a nation on the Italian peninsula where none had existed before'.[58]

Mimi's developing talent as an artist coincided with the intense phase of the Italian liberation struggle. On 24 March 1860, Christiana observed in her journal: 'Mimi drawing wonderfully – has just made a scene – "catching wild horses on prairie" – <u>is</u> perfectly marvellous'.[59] The excitement of Italian politics was further entwined with the family as Brocchi became one of Garibaldi's followers. Garibaldi is first mentioned on the first page of Elizabeth's autobiography in connection with Brocchi who was killed at the Battle of the Volturno and references to Italian politics pepper the early chapters:

> One day as we were running along the road in our pinafores near the Zerbino palace, above Genoa, along came Victor Emmanuel in an open carriage looking very red and blotchy in the heat, with big, ungloved hands, one of which he raised to his hat in saluting us little imps who were shouting 'Long live the King of Italy!' We were only a little previous (!). The next year came Garibaldi enthusiasm.[60]

Elizabeth saw Garibaldi in Genoa before his famous campaign to liberate Sicily. On 30 April Christiana recorded how 'Mimi & Babe had seen Garibaldi – Mimi 3 times' and that he was 'sitting on a wall looking at sea' but was an 'unimportant looking man – rather short reddish beard & moustache'.[61] Garibaldi was, in fact, staying at a house behind the Brown's – the Villa Spinola – where he mobilized his famous army of the One Thousand 'young men and not so young men [who] flocked in and were keen to liberate their oppressed brothers from the tyrant'.[62] 'He was talking', Elizabeth confirms, 'to the gardener'.[63] On the evening of 5 May the Thompsons saw 3 or 4 boats of Garibaldi's men going off to join a brigg in the moonlight: 'oh why did we not go down to cheer them', Christiana lamented, this 'glorious little band some of them knowing nothing of war going to almost certain death or life imprisonment' on a 'wild but glorious enterprise to aid the poor Sicilians now struggling desperately to be free themselves from the hated Neopolitans'.[64] Garibaldi's men commandeered two steamships and at 'half past eight Garibaldi left Villa Spinola. He was wearing his red shirt, which from now on he would always wear'.[65] De la Rue, Christiana recalls, was in great 'wrath' about the loss of the steamships but Christiana merely laughed at him.[66]

By June that year Elizabeth was immersed in hero-worship shared by her father who had a bust of Garibaldi but desired a photograph of him as well. Elizabeth sent her mother, who was back in England, a drawing of Garibaldi as she had seen him. Her father wrote to Christiana on 15 June that Elizabeth's sketch 'might go into the *Illustrated News*'. He further noted that Elizabeth had become 'big & strong' but was critical of her looks: 'I hear her everywhere admired – beyond her deservings I think for I cannot think her beautiful'.[67] Elizabeth's sketchbook, she recalls in her autobiography, was filled with 'charges of Garibaldian cavalry on discomfited Neopolitan troops (the despised *Borbonici*), and the waving of tricolours by bellicose patriots'.[68] Mimi shared this excitement with most of Liberal England. Elizabeth Barrett Browning, a distant cousin of the Thompsons, writing from Florence in that same month, describes how 'We are all talking and dreaming of Garibaldi just now in great anxiety. Scarcely since the world was a world has there been such a feat of arms. All modern heroes grow pale before him'.[69] Garibaldi was also the subject of poetry and, in London, a melodrama, *Garibaldi*, written by the influential dramatist Tom Taylor, was staged at Astley's Theatre.[70]

On 28 July, Christiana records how Brocchi was 'in the confidence of Garibaldi' and kept Fanny informed by letter. On 6 August, he wrote to say that they were preparing to land on mainland Italy. Christiana describes Garibaldi's soldiers as 'wonderfully picturesque men – dramatic' and 'admirably artistic'. By 12 October tragedy was looming. Fanny wrote to tell her family of a report in several papers that Brocchi was killed at Volturno on 1 October. By 20 October the news was confirmed: 'an officer reported to Fanny's servant that he had been wounded in the arm & would not stay away from the battle – & was then killed by a canon shot'. Fanny was 'wretched' and Christiana and the girls went with her to get 'black things' on 25 October.[71] This was a timely reminder for Elizabeth of the sacrifices of war. A month later, there was another family death as Amelia Thompson wrote from the Isle of Wight to inform her brother that their sister Elizabeth was dying.

By April 1861 when the family was back in London, Elizabeth's continuing interest in military matters showed little signs of abating. Sketches of the newly formed citizen soldiers occupied her: 'I stuffed my sketch books with British volunteers in every conceivable uniform, each corps dressed after its own taste'. Her grandfather, Thomas Weller, joined the St George's Rifles and engaged in several practice fights. Her developing ambition prompted her to send a 'design for a uniform to the *Illustrated London News*, which was returned with thanks. I felt hurt'.[72]

The family visited the Royal Academy's summer exhibition on 22 May where there were 'some hideous things ... others very interesting and instructive'. Christiana was much moved by an abolitionist painting by Richard Ansdell. *The Hunted Slaves* (1861) depicts a runaway couple who are warding off attacks from a vicious hound. It was a topical painting, exhibited in the same year as the outbreak of the American Civil War. Christiana described the 'awful scene of poor escaped slave & his wife defending themselves against bloodhounds! Devilish Americans!' The painting caused her to feel ill and she had to be led to the ladies room. Later that day, they called on the Dickens's but 'all out'.[73] Elizabeth recalls in her autobiography how she noted the visit in her diary: 'Mamma and I paid calls, one on Dickens (*sic*) – out, thank goodness'.[74]

By the autumn of 1861, Tom was back in Italy nursing a seriously ill Fanny but was still sending instructions to his wife on his younger daughters' education: 'if they would rub up their declensions (Latin) when they have nothing else to do, it would be no loss to them. Any little application of this kind they will find gives a great zest to the general freedom of the day – the more so if voluntarily self-imposed as a duty'.[75] He also urged plenty of fresh air and exercise. Christiana joined Tom in Italy in October leaving the girls in the care of Tom's sister, Amelia.[76] By the autumn Fanny had recovered much to Elizabeth and Alice's relief. Meanwhile, the girls followed their lessons with their cousins Mary and Amelia – Elizabeth Smithson's daughters. Amelia (affectionately known as Lalla) would later marry the French artist, Theodore Roussel. On 6 November 1861, three days after her fifteenth birthday, Mimi wrote to her mother at Albaro: 'To think you have walked in the old villa again under the dear garden' and to her father: 'When are you going to return? Do not be long. I am looking forward to a winter in London with great impatience for being now 15 years of age I would like to begin drawing seriously and would so like to study at the Kensington Museum'.[77] The Italian years were at an end and the artist's formal career was about to begin.

CHAPTER THREE

Road to fame, 1862–73

Elizabeth's training in London – Isle of Wight – Northern Europe and Waterloo – South Kensington School of Art – Exhibiting and London artistic society – Florentine art training with Bellucci – The Magnificat *– A studio of her own – Franco-Prussian War –* Missing *– Catholicism and pilgrimage to Paray-le-Monial – A* Graphic *artist*

In an undated watercolour, Christiana captures a female artist, her back to the viewer, painting the luscious, rolling landscape that stretches out before her. Protected by an umbrella to ward off the rays of the sun and with a red shawl slung carelessly on one shoulder, the artist, her black hair caught in a bun, faces her easel and is completely enthralled by her art.[1] You do not see the unknown woman's face. This genteel image captures the artist's absorption in her work. Focusing on the landscape in front of her, she shuts out the rest of the world. The painting conveys a sense of a woman as an artist and is obviously modelled on Christiana's and Elizabeth's painting outdoors. Eileen Gormanston describes how Elizabeth was so involved in her painting that on one occasion her young model, who was required to 'lie in one position so long on the ground after sunset' for the young officer in *The Dawn of Waterloo* (1895), fell asleep and woke up with a cold. 'To me as a child (and doubtless also to my elder sister and brothers), it had been quite natural that mothers should paint six-foot canvasses for each year's Academy'.[2] Natural though it may have been for her young family to become accustomed to their mother's painting, just as Elizabeth was accustomed as a child to her mother's artistic endeavours, being a professional female artist in the Victorian period was a formidable undertaking – it was, as Germaine Greer observes, an 'obstacle race'.[3]

Of course, amateur art was very much part of an upper- and upper-middle class young woman's accomplishments in the nineteenth century. At the highest level of society, Queen Victoria was a painter, as well as an art patron, although she expressed some anxieties about artists themselves. Art, as a genteel occupation, was well represented in literature. In Jane Austen's *Emma* (1815) the wealthy Emma has specimens of her accomplishments in art – 'landscapes and flowers' (the proper themes for a woman's artistic activities) – on display in her family drawing-room.[4]

Her portfolio is filled with half-finished portraits as she lacks steady application. She need not apply herself to anything – she is, after all, an heiress. A realization, however, by the middle decades of the nineteenth century that some women would have to work for a living and be trained as art workers finally led to art schools opening for them. Helen Huntingdon, from Anne Brontë's *The Tenant of Wildfell Hall* (1848), is often seen by feminist art critics as an example of the proto-feminist female artist figure. Helen, an heiress, makes a bad marriage to a violent drunk. As a woman's property was the preserve of her husband after marriage for most of the nineteenth century, Helen loses her fortune when she flees the family home and is forced to use her accomplishment in art in order to support herself and her child. Even here, however, she requires a male figure, her brother, as mediator between her and the commercial art world. Another literary example of a working female artist is Dinah Mulock Craik's *Olive* (1850). Here Olive uses her artistic talents to pay off her late father's debts and support her blind mother. Olive is trained by a bombastic older male artist, Michael Vanburgh, who offers her marriage and an opportunity to study in Rome, which she declines. It is clear that her talent would be subservient to his. Indeed, Craik, who had a good knowledge of the art world, is certain that a woman would always be an inferior artist: 'no woman can be an artist – that is, a great artist' – her womanliness precludes it.[5] Craik's writings, Paula Gillett confirms, 'helped to strengthen the widely held belief that, while art practice could indeed be readily accommodated within the setting of feminine domesticity, the highest levels of artistic achievement were almost certainly – and appropriately – out of the reach of women'.[6] Both *The Tenant* and *Olive* show women artists competing in the commercial world, but love and marriage, which both characters attain by the end of their respective stories, are presented as ultimately more satisfying.

These literary representations of the nineteenth-century female artist reflect the wider social and political conditions of middle-class and upper middle-class women – conditions that did not offer much hope for an aspiring artist. There were always exceptions. Rolinda Sharples (1793–1838), whose best-known work is often drawn in conjunction with Austen's fiction for its portrayal of Regency life, was an accomplished portrait painter from a family of portrait painters. The family worked in Britain before emigrating to America, and then returning to Bristol.[7] In *The Artist and Her Mother* (1816) Sharples depicts herself seated at her easel, boldly looking at the viewer, while she works on her painting with brush and mahl-stick. Her widowed mother, also an artist, is looking appreciatively at her daughter's canvas in a studio filled with paintings. This painting celebrates the artist's relationship with her mother and conveys a forthright and unapologetic sense of Sharples's identity as an artist.[8] Similarly, Christiana was the figure who oversaw Elizabeth's art and her success at the Royal Academy.

In the mid-Victorian period, however, when Elizabeth was emerging as a teenage artist, Britain was dominated by the ideology of the separate spheres, which dictated that professional activities were the preserve of males, and women were required to beautify their homes. Amateur art could be accommodated within this ideology with examples of women's artistic output gracing, as fictional Emma's early example demonstrates, the drawing-room. Art, at this level as well, could be conducted from the drawing-room. Both Brontë's and Craik's artists use their drawing-rooms. In the Thompson household Christiana combined art with her family life, even if Dickens caustically observed on his 1853 visit to the family in Italy that domestic matters were largely ignored.

Femininity was also at stake. The proper art for women was landscape, still-life or 'figures', as the fictional Emma's are, and the proper medium was watercolour not oil. Still-life paintings were, Deborah Cherry notes, 'perceived as expressions of innate femininity'.[9] At the same time it was possible to use traditional genres to achieve success as Sharples, who worked in conventional genres, managed to turn a traditional female accomplishment into lucrative work and exhibited at the Royal Academy in the 1820s. However, Elizabeth's branch of art – history painting – was not deemed suitable for women. How could professional women artists balance the claims of domesticity and family with the all-engrossing activity of art? Patricia Zakreski notes how the *Art Journal*, which was generally sympathetic to female artists, sought to reassure its readers on the compatibility of art and domestic life.[10] Eileen Gormanston's recollections of her mother, however, revel in Elizabeth's disregard for domestic matters. Six-foot canvases were normal for the family and when Eileen 'hurtled down to the studio to announce a waiting meal' the fact that the 'air that surrounded [her] mother should smell deliciously of a mixture of lavender oil and paint' seemed entirely customary. Her image of her mother is of a figure both diminutive and powerful: 'whenever I get a whiff of lavender oil, the picture of my mother – rather small and slight, with delicate face but strong hands, standing at her easel in a long garberdine, a mahl-stick in one hand and palette and brushes in the other – is conjured up'.[11] Here the daughter projects an image in writing of the artist mother, just as Sharples's self-image incorporates her own mother as observer and admirer.

Successful female artists, like Sharples, tended to come from families of artists. Rosa Bonheur, for instance, was the daughter of an artist and Kate Greenaway, who later trained with Elizabeth at the South Kensington School, was the daughter of an engraver. Indeed, Meliora Vanburgh, the sister of the painter Michael Vanburgh in *Olive*, confirms to Olive that there had been women painters such as Angelica Kauffman and Elizabetta Sirani, but more numerous were the 'wives, or daughters, or sisters who helped [the Italian masters] a great deal'.[12] Cherry points out that art was often a family affair and that while women benefited from 'access to tuition, materials and work-space' as well as advice on the exhibitions, commissions and sales, which allowed them to make their way in the art world, nonetheless, in artist families sons and daughters were not treated the same way, did not receive the same education and ultimately 'occupied a lower status in the artistic hierarchy'.[13] Elizabeth was not subsumed by the claims of a male relative, and was fortunate, in many respects, not to have an artist father or brother. In her 1929 biography of her mother, Viola Meynell asserts that Tom 'taught the two little girls all that he would have taught them had they been sons'.[14] Vita Sackville-West, attuned to the gender constraints for Victorian women, commented in 1947 in a centenary edition of Alice's work, that both Thompson sisters were fortunate that their father, a 'man of culture, scholarship and extreme sensibility should have lavished upon their education all the trouble he would have accorded to a son'.[15] There was, of course, the son from his first marriage, but Mel is written out of published accounts – mental illness was something that the culture silenced. Indeed, the existence of this ill son may well have focused Tom's attention on his three daughters. His strong attachment to Fanny, Mel's sister, is expressed in a letter towards the end of his life: 'Believe me it can bring nothing happier to me than the day when I can see you again whenever it may please Providence to bring that about'.[16]

While Elizabeth's development into a professional artist placed her at odds in a culture that prescribed domestic existence for women of her class and generation, she was certainly a product of another strand of mid-Victorian thinking in her devotion to work. Her dedication to her art from a young age coheres with Samuel Smiles's observations on artists (Smiles, of course, focuses only on males) in *Self Help* (1859). Although the artistic 'gift comes by nature', Smiles notes, it is 'perfected by self-culture, which is of more avail than all the imparted education of the schools'. Smiles emphasizes 'long and continuous labour'. Focusing, of course, on male artists, he argues that they triumphed over adversity through 'sheer industry and hard work'.[17] Regardless of gender, application to art was necessary for all artists, but professional female artists had to encounter huge obstacles and inequalities in terms of training in their field.

Two female painters, Angelica Kauffman and Mary Moser, were founding members of the Royal Academy of Art in 1768, but no other woman succeeded them in this powerhouse of the art world, until Laura Knight in 1936. Elizabeth came close to becoming an Academician, but lost by two votes to Hubert von Herkomer in 1879. 'Power in the art world', as Debra Mancoff notes, 'rested in the hands of men'.[18] During Elizabeth's life as an artist, then, women were accorded secondary status in the Fine Art world. Other areas of the art world started to open up as attention in the early Victorian period started to focus on the development of art and design training. The Government School of Design was opened in 1837 with the intention of training male designers for employment in the manufacturing industry. By the mid-century vigorous campaigns for the better general education, including art education, of women gained momentum. In 1843, the Female School of Art and Design was established, largely for women who were required to earn their living for 'commercial application',[19] and was aimed at women from the middle classes.

There was a clear distinction made between Fine Art (the province of the Royal Academy) and Design (the province of the School of Design) both in terms of class and training. At the School of Design and the schools that emerged from it, students followed a prescriptive programme. 'All students', Christopher Frayling notes, 'would start with basic geometric shapes, then progress to copying a range of architectural details from books or dictionaries, then, if they were lucky, they would copy from objects in glass cases – plaster casts of famous sculptures, ceramic tiles, metalwork, bowls and so on'. But at the outset they were banned from drawing moving objects as 'this activity might encourage students to become artists' and art was the preserve of the Royal Academy.[20] In other words, the Royal Academy offered training as an artist; the School of Design trained its students to become artisans.[21] By 1838, a change was initiated when the human figure was taught, but it was specifically taught for the 'purposes of ornament' in order to avoid overlapping with the Royal Academy's area of control.[22] The School of Design had a second-class status in the eyes of many aspiring artists who often sought to use it as a stepping-stone to Royal Academy classes. Another development, however, occurred for women artists in 1857 when the Society for Female Artists was established.

In 1857, the Head School of Design moved to South Kensington and became popularly known as the South Kensington School. While women could study at the South Kensington School from 1857 they were regularly rejected from admittance into prestigious Royal Academy training. In 1860 Laura Herford applied under her initials and, as it was assumed that she was a male applicant, she was admitted. The artist Estella Canziani recalls how her mother Louisa Starr used a similar 'strategem' and signed her name L. Starr in order to gain entry in 1862. 'The sex of the artist was not suspected by the Academicians, and there was general amazement and consternation when the young aspirant appeared in feminine guise and claimed to be received as a student!'[23] One of the ongoing problems, however, facing women artists was their prevention from studying the nude figure from a live model as this was seen as too indecent for them. 'While a male artist was encouraged to look at bodies, a female artist learned that doing the same sullied her reputation'.[24]

It was within such a climate that the 'liberally educated' and well-travelled Elizabeth urged her father to return from Italy in 1861 so she could start her training at the South Kensington School. Significant difficulties lay in her way not only in terms of her gender but in the quality of training on offer. It was, by all accounts, lacklustre. The work was 'desultory and tedious, involving a slow and painful progression from making elaborately stippled copies of antique casts before moving on to the life drawing class, in a pale imitation of practice in academies geared to fine art'.[25] Elizabeth recalls this period of her training: 'the lessons in the elementary class at the S. Kensington School of Art are not worth mentioning. The masters gave me hateful scrolls and patterns to copy, and I relieved my feelings by ornamenting the margins of my drawing paper with angry scribbling of horses and soldiers in every variety of fury. That did not last long'. Sketching in the margins is an apt description of female artists of the period but in Elizabeth's case this 'fury' would burst from the margins of her drawing paper to the six-foot canvases at the Royal Academy. Success would take more than a decade. In the meantime, she left the South Kensington School and continued her private art lessons, recalling in her autobiography: 'Mr Standish gave me two hours drill in oil painting. How grand I felt! He gave me his own copies of Landseer's horses' heads and dogs as models. This wasn't very much, but it was a beginning!'[26]

Isle of Wight

Art historians have partially ascribed Elizabeth's success to her family's wealth but this is not a complete picture. While the Thompsons had money enough to enable a leisured lifestyle, financial matters were always a problem for them, forcing them to economize abroad or sell books and paintings at various points in the 1860s. What was more important for Elizabeth's success was her family's desire for her to succeed as an artist and they focused on securing her future through art lessons and travel to Italy. With both daughters on the verge of adulthood, the Thompsons had by the early 1860s to consider a more permanent home. Back in England they tried to cultivate through their friend the engraver Richard Lane the acquaintance of John Everett Millais. In March 1862 Elizabeth visited Millais's studio with Lane and her father: 'I wanted the company to see I was a bit of a judge of painting, ahem! In fact, a painter myself, and approaching, very near to the wet picture of *The Ransom* (I think), I began to scrutinize. Mr Lane took me gently, but firmly, by the shoulders and placed me in a distant chair'.[27] A month later, on 17 April, Christiana recorded in her diary: 'Mr Lane was to have come with Millais to see my arts! but Millais prevented by a model'. Mother and daughter painted side by side and Elizabeth produced a horse's head which she sketched from a 'horse close to her over gate near where' Christiana 'paint[ed] on other side'. For her mother's birthday that July Elizabeth presented Christiana with a 'white horse with romantic rider bearing a banner – in oils – horses face beautiful. I never saw the child about it'. At the Royal Academy exhibition, the family were 'enchanted' by Frederic Leighton's *Odalisque* and here Elizabeth was earnestly taking notes.

By the end of July, the family were in the Isle of Wight and rented a newly constructed villa in Bonchurch called the Dell. 'Economy', noted Christiana, was 'the order of the day' and the rent on the Dell was £400.[28] Nestled into the cliff on the outskirts of Ventnor in an area of lush vegetation known as the Undercliff, the Dell looked out over the English Channel and was just a short walk to a stony beach where the family bathed. The Dell was constructed as part of the boom in development in the area from the mid-century. Below it and over to its left was Winterbourne, where Dickens had holidayed and wrote parts of *David Copperfield* in

1849. Bonchurch's semi-tropical climate, its exclusivity and the area's reputation as a health resort attracted the middle and upper classes. The Queen had a residence on the north of the island at Osborne and Tennyson lived on the east coast. The scenery was spectacular and Victorian visitors 'never ceased to marvel at the way wild and wet mornings could give way to flawless blue skies and unseasonal warmth'.[29] Bonchurch, Christiana asserts in her usual exuberant manner, was a 'dream of loveliness – like Porto Fino somewhat quite as lovely' and the 'sea & sky like Italy'. In Bonchurch the family also resumed its Italian ways bathing on Bonchurch beach and extolling its 'Radiant resplendent Italian light & sea'.[30] Bonchurch appealed, in particular, to artists and in the period in which the Thompsons resided at Bonchurch, various artists painted the shore and coastal scenery, including the popular watercolourist of sentimental scenes, Myles Birket Foster. Meanwhile Elizabeth was concentrating on horses and a white horse was brought to the front door of the Dell so that she could paint it outdoors at the end of October – the 20-year-old horse was kept docile by oats fed to it by a boy.[31] Elizabeth describes how her mother made 'a little garden herself at the highest point of the grounds, with grass steps, bordered with tall white lilies, and called it the "Celestial Garden"'.[32]

Despite the benefits of scenery, the Bonchurch years were not quite idyllic. Health and financial problems affected the family in the early 1860s. By October 1862 Christiana was recording in her diary how Elizabeth was having trouble with her hearing, with a doctor diagnosing 'general debility & want of power & growing too fast'.[33] Eileen Gormanston confirms how this affected her mother

> The partial deafness from which my mother suffered since her girlhood gave to her face a certain sadness, and to her nerves an uncertain proneness to fatigue. But, hampering as it did her intercourse with the outer world, it must also have had much to do with the complete unworldliness of her outlook on life – probably, too, with her entire lack of small talk.[34]

Alice had other troubles as her teeth, which were a problem since childhood, required attention in London. The drain on the family finances at this period resulted in Tom selling a painting by Carl Haag, the celebrated nineteenth-century Orientalist painter. In an 1863 letter he sent Christiana a cheque for £15 to cover Alice's dental expenses and urged his wife to 'make the most of' it, lamenting that 'I am tired of the old story and crying "Wolf"!'[35]

Elizabeth entered into Ventnor's social activities with mixed enthusiasm. Bonchurch, she recalls, had a certain 'Oxford primness' although the family enjoyed the company of the educationalist and writer Elizabeth Sewell and her sister Ellen. The religious climate at Bonchurch had a tendency towards High Anglicanism and it was at this period that Christiana started to embrace Roman Catholicism and was admitted into the Catholic Church on 18 July 1864. Her daughters would later convert – Alice was the first of the sisters to convert in July 1868. At Bonchurch,

Tom, a member of Ventnor and Bonchurch Literary and Scientific Institution, renewed his amateur acting interests, while Christiana played Chopin and her own musical compositions. Elizabeth deplored how during her mother's playing at parties conversation 'raged' and 'this after the worship of her playing in Italy' until at last she commanded attention, 'it being whispered that silence was better suited to such music' and 'it became quite the thing to stop talking'. Elizabeth's observation here can be read as more than just a reflection on local manners but rather how in the broader context of the mid-Victorian period female performance was relegated to the status of genteel accomplishment, a mere social lubricant. Female artists had to work harder to command attention. This proto-feminist consciousness also emerges in Elizabeth's further comments on social gatherings: 'The Ventnor dances were thoroughly enjoyable, and the croquet parties and the rides with friends, and all the rest of it. Yes, it was a nice life, but the morning lessons never broke off'.[36] For his part Tom was often frustrated with his daughters, telling his wife: 'I asked Alice a simple question in arithmetic this morning & she couldn't answer – got confused and thrown off her balance. I dread anyone putting a question to those children – they are so easily obfuscated'.[37] His daughters' talents lay elsewhere. Elizabeth recalls: 'I now and then come upon funny juvenile sketch books where I find my Ventnor partners at these dances clashing with charges of Garibaldian cavalry'.[38]

A long and detailed letter in June 1865 to Alice, who was in London, reveals Elizabeth's life in Ventnor and her feats of 'horsewomanship' – Tom had taught his daughters to ride, fence and play billiards. At one of the dances Elizabeth was invited to a meet on the following morning: '[a]s my officer had expressed a wish that I should be at the meet I complied all the more readily'. Her friend, 'wicked Sophy', assured her that they would only go as far as Shanklin and she would 'come home like a good girl as soon as the field moved off to cover'. Elizabeth proclaimed to be shocked when Sophy pushed on with the hunt but felt obliged to accompany her. Outwardly conventional in her comments on her friend's forwardness in joining the hunt, Elizabeth channels her delight in this male fray into her description of her horse: 'My horse was swimming, I never saw one in such a state of perspiration, it ran down his legs in showers. We certainly had ridden tremendously hard ... The condition on which Papa had allowed me to go was that my horse should not be likely to be excited ... But the one I rode was a hunter'. Elizabeth extolled her superior horse: 'I was much better mounted than Sophy, indeed the gentleman with whom I talked at the meet rather liked the looks of him, & looked knowingly at his legs. I said I thought he would go over anything'. Elizabeth was 'enchanted' by the 'gay scene' and although the 'gentlemen were very cheeky with Sophy & threw off all constraint' Elizabeth was keen to assert that they behaved properly with her. Her horse 'would not stand still' and he 'jumped about in a most delightful manner'. However, an 'officious man came wo-o-o-ing up & caught hold of my horse to my intense disgust, & instead of thanking him I peered at him in a way which I repent now'. Pressed ahead by Sophy who called her a 'horrid creature' if she left her, Elizabeth's horse was 'enjoying himself immensely' while her hair 'flopped' up and down 'disgracefully'. The pleasures of the hunt override these moments of unconventionality as Elizabeth delighted in her horse clearing a bank: 'I had gone over like a bird … we tore up to the Downs & seemed to be swimming thro' the heather, the horses now & then jumping over the bushes'. Finally, they returned, although she 'had great trouble in making Sophy come'. In Elizabeth's account Sophy is represented as the conventional flirt, forcing her friend to accompany her, but this only serves to accentuate Elizabeth's own pleasures of 'horsewomanship', her delight in entering into and holding her own in a male environment and her interest in horses.[39] Even here the military artist, forging a career in a male-dominated world, is being shaped.

These 'festive Ventnor doings were all very well', Elizabeth recalls in her *Autobiography*. However, 'it became more and more borne in upon me that, if I intended to be a "great artist" (oh! seductive words), my young teens were the right time for study'. While her father got her books on 'anatomy, architecture, costume, arms and armour, Ruskin's inspiring writings, and everything he thought the most appropriate for training', she wanted 'regular training in some academy'. Her father warned her of the difficulties: '"You will be entering into a tremendous ruck of painters, though, my child"' – to which she answered: '"I will single myself out of it".'[40]

The family were pushing their eldest daughter in the art world. Elizabeth wrote to Alice who was in London with her mother about her 'arts' as she had not known that 'dear little Mamma was going in person to Evans', the co-owner of *Punch Magazine*. Elizabeth instructed Alice: 'If she sees him I should like her particularly to say that I don't mind about the terms, so long as I can get an opening. That I am particularly fond of horses (that is with ever eye to "Punch") in fact all Mamma knows I want said'. She cautioned Alice: 'I don't think anything need be said about my age, or my not having even learnt &c &c. That wouldn't impress them to look with an eye of favour on the drawings I sent you'. She was also hard at work at new drawings – '3 horsey ones, depicting the adventures of a young lady who "only just went to see the hounds meet". I can also send a poetical one'.[41]

On 6 February 1865, Tom gave up his lease of the Dell and decided to take his daughters to northern Europe before Elizabeth would take up her art training in earnest. In Bruges, 'one of the few towns one loves with a personal love', Elizabeth made the most of every hour. In Cologne, she observed how the German officers differed from the Belgian ones: 'Big whiskered fellows with waists enough to make the Belgians faint'. They travelled down the Rhine to Coblenz and then to Bingen where 'market women and *pelotons* of soldiers with glittering helmets and bayonets make excellent foreground groups'. Cologne was 'ever to remain bright by the remembrance of its cathedral and that museum containing pictures which have so inspired my mind'.[42] The most important visit was to the site of Waterloo on the

3 November, Elizabeth's birthday. The 'awful field' of Waterloo captures the essence of her later battle art – the sacrifice and pathos of war:

> The day was most enjoyable, but what an inexpressibly sad feeling was mixed with my pleasure; what thoughts came crowding into my mind on that awful field, smiling in the sunshine, and how, even now, my whole mind is overshadowed with sadness as I think of those slaughtered legions, dead half a century ago, lying in heaps of mouldering bones under that undulating plain.

On their way to the battlefield, an old man called Sergeant-Major Mundy of the 7th Hussars, a veteran of the campaign, stopped their carriage and offered them a tour: 'we got into the old road, that road which the British trod on their way to Quatre Bras' and met an old woman of eighty-eight who had tended the wounded after the battle: 'There she was, she who at thirty-eight had beheld those men just half a century ago! It was overpowering to my young mind'.[43] The Thompsons visited the 'mouldy relics' of war in the museum before being walked through the battlefield by their veteran guide: 'What a story was that he was telling us, with the scenes of that story before our eyes! I, all in eagerness to learn from the lips of one who took part in the fight, the story of that great victory of my country, was always throughout that long day by the side of the old hussar, and drank in the stirring narrative with avidity'. She describes the tour through the battlefield as a 'walk through ghosts with agonized faces and distorted bodies, crying noiselessly'.[44] Elizabeth's account narrated over fifty years after her visit to Waterloo identifies the strands that define her battle art: episodes of war related as stories and empathy with the suffering of individuals. Reaching the site of one of the most intense scenes of battle Elizabeth transposes the language of the First World War onto Waterloo as she describes the 'concentrated horror' and the 'sickening terror of war'.[45] European battles – Garibaldi's contemporaneous campaigns and then the sight of Waterloo relived through an old soldier's memories – were shaping the war artist of the future.

Art Training

The year 1866 heralded renewed attention to her formal art study. An interview with Richard Burchett, Headmaster of the South Kensington School of Art, resulted in her being accepted into the Life School after preliminary work in the Antique. Burchett's *On the Central Art Training School* (1858) recommended training women in drawing for their domestic improvement: 'It will be found to confer advantages upon all; habits of order and precision will be acquired, and the girl who has been taught drawing in her school will have one element in her character towards forming a good housekeeper'.[46] Elizabeth brought him her portfolio and a scene of soldiers working on the new fort at Dover Castle, completed on the family's homeward route from their continental tour. Rejected by the *Illustrated London News* the sketch found favour with Burchett who 'strongly advised' her to become an artist. Study began in earnest on 2 January and comprised five hours a day: 'I felt very raw indeed, never having drawn from a cast before'.[47] By mid-January Burchett was praising her work, observing, however, that her early art education had been neglected: 'I console myself with the thought that I have not wasted my time so utterly, for all the travel I have had all my life has put crowds of ideas into my head, and now I am learning to bring those ideas to good account'.[48] By mid-February, Elizabeth was still in the Antique Class to the dismay of Richard Lane, 'my friend in the truest sense of the word', who informed her that Burchett had spoken highly of her drawing to him.[49] On 19 March, she finally entered the Life Class, describing her promotion in an effusive manner similar to her mother's personality. This was a '*golden* Monday', a 'joyous morn' where the model was a 'small man, perfectly clean shaven with a most picturesque face; quite a study' and as nervous as the trainee artist. Praise was followed by prizes when Elizabeth won best prize at the Sketching Club competition for her illustrations of Thackeray's *The Newcomes*. She ran back to Fulham to deliver the happy news to her parents and grandparents, the Wellers. She joined a class in Bolsover Street to study the undraped female model and worked there on alternate days, a journey that necessitated long rides on the omnibus. But even this time was not wasted: 'I always managed to post myself at the omnibus door, so as to study the horses in motion in the crowded streets from that coign of vantage'. She favoured movement in her early military sketches, remarking that 'a deep well of melancholy existed in my nature, and caused me to draw from its depths some very sad subjects'. She continues: 'How strange it seems that I should have been so impregnated, if I may use the word, with the warrior spirit in art, seeing that we had no soldiers in either my father's or mother's family'.[50]

In 1867, she exhibited *Horses in Sunshine* at the women artists' exhibition and this was followed by *Bavarian Artillery Going into Action* at the Dudley Gallery. She was delighted when her father told her that *The Times* critic, Tom Taylor, had seen her painting on the gallery walls during the press view.[51] Ruskin came to visit the family the following year on a 'Memorable Monday' in March. He told her that she had not 'studied enough from nature' in the drawings she showed him but was 'most pleased' with her artillery watercolour, *The Crest of the Hill*, and he 'knelt down before where it hung low down and held a candle before it the better to see it, and exclaimed "Wonderful!" two or three times, and said it had "immense power".' The painting had been rejected by the Dudley Gallery but was exhibited the following year at the Society of Female Artists. Ruskin also discussed Alice's poetry and Christiana's art, while Tom felt 'like the circus man, standing in the middle with the long whip, touching us up as we were trotted out before the great man'.[52]

It was not all hard work; she was making friends in art school and attending parties. A detailed letter to Christiana about one of these gatherings reveals the networks of the Victorian art world. In May 1868, Elizabeth wrote about a party at the home of the sculptors Thomas and Mary Thornycroft in Wilton Place, Knightsbridge. The Queen was their patron and Mary Thornycroft, the more famous member of the couple, made busts of the Royal family and inspired Princess Louise to become a sculptor. Thomas, though less successful than his wife, produced equestrian statues for civic adornment, most notably *Queen Boadicea* on Westminster Bridge. Four of the couple's children were either sculptors or painters; their daughter Alyce having exhibited her first sculpture, *Ophelia at the Brook*, at the Royal Academy in 1864. There were six studios to accommodate the Thornycrofts at Wilton Place.[53]

Such an environment was conducive to an aspiring artist. Mary Thornycroft encouraged Elizabeth's art and introduced her to other artists at her home. On a visit to the Thornycroft house she brought the 'self same packet of drawings [she] took before (for in her note Mrs T. most particularly begged [her] to bring them to show Mad. Jerichan & others)'.[54] Elizabeth Jerichan, born in Poland, lived in Denmark and, like Mary Thornycroft, was highly regarded in royal circles. The Thornycroft party was a large one but Elizabeth was confident that her silk dress 'did exactly, not being at all below the mark'. She was pleased by Jerichan's interest in her: 'Madame Jerichan is such a nice lady. She wanted to make my acquaintance, having, when she came to see the Schools a few weeks ago remarked on my study of the acrobat model which I was working at, and pronounced it the best in the room'. Elizabeth was also introduced to the painter Simeon Solomon who was there with his sister. Her 'old friend and instructor (?!) Cave Thomas was there, & kept harping upon the "British Bonheur" all the evening'. 'I flatly told him', noted Elizabeth, 'that I had no intention of becoming an animal painter'. Thomas, who specialized in historical and Biblical subjects was a fringe member of the Pre-Raphaelites. Despite having to assert herself with Thomas, Elizabeth was delighted by the compliments on her art:

> All the men were more or less artistic, & I never received so many compliments about my art at once as last night. I had five or six of them buzzing around me all the time there was no music. A certain art critic in particular went on so about the poetry & subtle expression of my figures, shown most particularly in my Launcelot & Guinevere. The Launcelot singing was a great favourite. The gentlemen were delighted with the horses, & complimented me especially on the way I made my men sit them. Mad. Jerichan was charmed with the two dejected bloats riding on their stoats. The sentiment & composition. She objected, however, to Guinevere's horse as too modern & suggestive of Rotten Row & they all advised me not to give him a white face in the picture, but just a star on the forehead. They were quite right.[55]

One of the young, celebrated painters was Louisa Starr. Starr was just a year younger than Elizabeth and had also spent time in Italy. By 1868, Starr had already made a name for herself; she won the first Royal Academy medal (a silver) ever awarded to a female painter in 1865 and won a gold medal in 1867. 'Starr was heralded in the mid-1860s as the "coming woman"' but she lost status with art critics in the 1870s when she turned to portraiture and perhaps, Pamela Gerrish Nunn observes, 'they could not forget or forgive the unprecedented trouncing of male ambition and smugness dealt out by her much-publicized success as an R. A. student'.[56] So when Elizabeth told her mother in the letter about the party at which she was compared to Starr, she was delighted: 'The art critic, Robertson (an excitable Scotchman more like a foreigner) was in a great state, & talked to me no end. He told me a great deal about Louisa Starr, what a wonderful girl she was; "but," he said "She hadn't half the invention & imagination that you have".' However, Robertson warned her against the detrimental effects of marriage: 'His great fear is that I shd marry & spoil everything'. Despite this Elizabeth was delighted that Jerichan had observed her 'remarkably fine head (!)'. She further noted: 'I had four gentlemen attending to me at supper, Robertson, Major Thornycroft (with whom I talked on military matters) the eldest Master Thornycroft, & C. Thomas. They were always clashing & I couldn't patronize them all'. More importantly, 'I am going to make Louisa Starr's acquaintance immediately for Miss Clarke, a fellow student of mine who has known her ever since she was 9 years old, is going to take me to her house, someday after school, if not on Monday, as soon after as possible'.

Elizabeth's letter also reveals a forthright personality. As the class's appointed 'spokeswoman' she had to 'implore, threaten & argue with the model'. The model 'does not keep her eyes open more than half a minute at a time. My bullying has no effect upon her. It rubs up my Italian, tho', nicely. All the complaints of the riled students have to pass thru' me, so that I lead rather a life'. There is no sympathy here for the model which is revealing of Elizabeth's class position.

Her technique was improving: 'I feel I am getting quite a facility of handling at last, & work so much quicker & more surely, putting one decided touch where before I shd have messed & modified no end'. Jerichan's interest in her resulted in an invitation to her studio: 'I am to go to Mad. Jerichan's studio whenever I like. They tell me she is engaged on a great cartoon with horses in it, so that I am anxious to see it'.[57] In another letter to her mother she describes a model: 'We had our own model at the schools today, a splendid old man, ever so tall & majestic, supposed to represent Crammer walking to the Tower. He wears a black velvet cap of curious shape, a long black gown & a muslin ruff, & a book clasped in his hands. I have drawn him in, in Miss Channon's own word, "beautifully", which is a great comfort. He is a splendid study of white beard and wrinkles'.[58]

Her intense focus on her art at this point also dictated her relationship with her family:

> About my sketch – I shall certainly not require more than a day for doing what I want to do at Littleh. viz to get Alice for the female figures. The male figures

> I can manage splendidly here and have indeed got them sketched in partly. Now I don't want to spend money unnecessarily, & if you think that as I have got on so far alone I may do the whole without going down, then I no doubt shall manage to get the women somehow or other without little Alice. After all it seems out of proportion to go to Littleh. on account of this sketch, but of course my nice Mamma & dear my Loze if you wd like me to come down, down I come, only don't let Papa think it is indispensable that I shd do so, for it is not at all.[59]

Frustrated by her parents' constant changes of location, she told her mother that she 'must not run about hither & thither, & take snatches of study instead of keeping on regularly' and that visits to her parents would necessitate having available horses to paint so that 'no precious precious time wd be lost'.[60] This year also saw her exhibit three works – an oil portrait of Alice at the Dudley Gallery and two other paintings at the Society of Female Artists, priced at eight and twelve guineas respectively.[61]

At the same time, Elizabeth was having fun in London socializing with her art school friends. By the end of May, a boat trip on the Thames to Hampton Court with the Thornycroft family delighted her. At Kingston station the young Thornycrofts suggested a race: 'I ran in my great waterproof, so came in 3rd'. Opportunities for study were not missed; when a Kingston eight (rowers) passed their steamer Elizabeth watched their arms and was 'particularly delighted with their triceps'.[62]

More serious was her competitiveness with Kate Greenaway; she was, she informs her mother,

> 'second best' this time, which was more than I expected, Miss Greenway [sic] is champion once more, & no wonder she bumped me seeing how hurriedly my little thing was done, & how much larger & more finished & interesting hers was. It was Lorenzo examining the mask of the laughing faun ... Mr Denby seemed to know that I was the author of no. 2, & told me he found it very good, as he held it out at arms length with Miss Greenways' [sic], but that he gave Miss G.'s the preference on account of the greater interest & variety of the subject.

But Elizabeth was not entirely outdone as she confidently told her mother that the other girls in the class 'were enchanted with what they called the "Leightonish" character of my sketch, particularly the youth in the white jacket. Those girls are thoro'ly artistic & always bestow their praise rightly'.[63] Nonetheless, both artists shared a studio for a time and Elizabeth commented in a biography published in 1905 after Greenaway's death: 'We were very good friends, she and I, in spite of our rivalry in the sketching club'. The two artists were such hard workers that they had the custodian lock them in after the other students had gone home so they could continue their work.[64] Greenaway's subject matter 'governed the fashions of the nursery' and her drawings 'were a sort of mould of form for babies and little girls'.[65] The two artists then could not have been more different with Greenaway's diminutive and feminine figures forming a sharp contrast to Elizabeth's war-ravaged men.

Elizabeth felt that her training in the South Kensington Art School was not entirely satisfactory. Alice observes in an 1883 essay: '[Elizabeth] never considered, however, that her course of study at South Kensington had done for her what it ought to have done in the time which she spent there, or that the system in force was personal or careful enough to develop individual power'. For that, she needed to go to Italy.

Continental Travels

In July 1868, the Thompsons headed to Florence. Alice notes: 'it was between two long courses of study there that she enjoyed the summer in Florence and the winter in Rome to which she thought she owed almost all the solid success of after years'.[66] The first stop was the 'old palazzo at Albaro and the old friends' but Elizabeth's work 'never relaxed' and she set up a 'little studio and went in for life-size heads'.[67] The journey was also taken to improve Alice's health, the reticent sister who had started to quietly write poems and the 'beginnings of whose career had been as hidden' as her sister's were 'conspicuous'.[68] Leaving Genoa in April the following year, the Thompsons opted to travel by carriage to Spezia. In a little place called Bogliasco, Elizabeth spotted 'handsome youths with bare legs and arms [who] were playing at a game of ball which called forth fine action. I did not know at first whether to look well at them all or sketch them down one by one, but did both, and I hope to make a regular drawing of the group from the sketch I took from memory'. The last part of the journey to Florence was taken by train:

> I am still so dazzled by the splendour of Genoa that my eyes cannot, as it were, comprehend the brown, grey and white tones of this quiet little city. I must *Florentine* myself as fast as I can ... Oh! may this city of the arts see me begin (and finish) my first regular picture.

The family settled in a villa on the road to Fiesole near the heart of the city and Elizabeth immersed herself in art. In the gallery that links the Uffizi to the Pitti Palace she particularly revelled in the 'sketches, studies, and the first thoughts of most of the great masters'. For her these early sketches were important to her own artistic development: 'One delights almost more in these than in many of the finished pictures. They bring one much more in contact, as it were, with the great dead, and make one familiar with their methods of work'.[69] Elizabeth was moved by the atmosphere and identified with its dead painters:

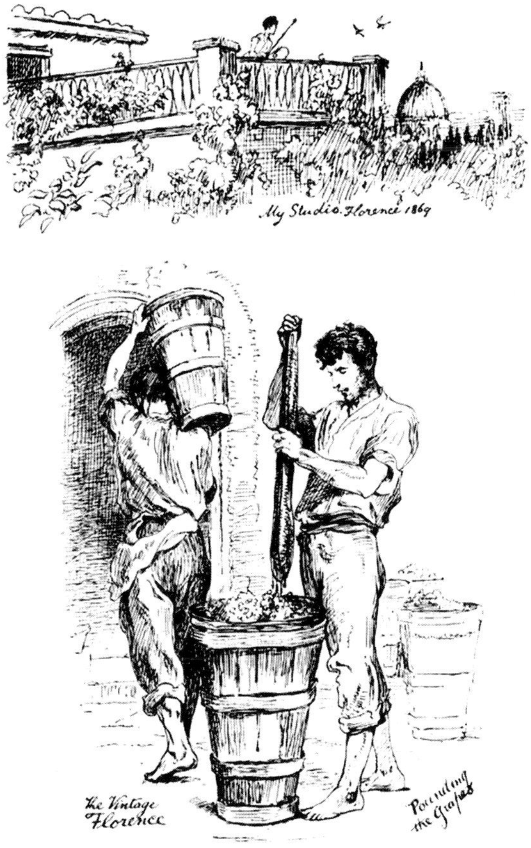

1 'In Florence during my studies' from Elizabeth Butler, *Autobiography*.

> I have never, before I came here where so many of them have lived, realized the old masters as our comrades; I have never been so near them and felt them to be mortals exactly like ourselves. This city and its environs are so little changed, the greater part of them not at all, since those grand old Michael Angelesque days that one feels brought quite close to the old painters, seeing what they saw and walking on the very same old pavement as they walked, passing the houses where they lived, and so forth.[70]

Florence was not just about seeing, but about learning. Elizabeth took lessons from Giuseppe Bellucci, 'the most eminent historical painter of his time in Italy'.[71] She got up before the rest of the family, breakfasted alone and walked with a maid to his studio (Figure 1). She describes how 'on alternate days to those spent in his studio [she] copied in careful pencil some of the exquisite figures in Andrea del Sarto's frescoes in the cloisters of the SS. Annunziata'.[72] Alice recalls how the 'sacristans of the old church – the most popular church in Florence – knew and welcomed the young English girl, who sat for hours so intently at her work in the cloister, unheeding the coming and going of the long procession of congregations passing through the gates'.[73] She worked in Bellucci's studio through the heat of the summer, taking time off only when the weather became too unbearable, and by October she had completed her studies:

> He drilled me in drawing more severely than I could have been drilled in England. For that purpose he had kept me a good deal to painting in monochrome, so as to have my attention absorbed by the drawing and modelling and *chiaroscuro* of an object without the distraction of colour. He also said to me I could now walk alone (*può camminare da sè*).[74]

The Thompsons then departed for Rome where the religious atmosphere prompted Elizabeth to put aside her military subjects.[75] Following Bellucci's instruction to 'walk alone', she ascended the Trinità dei Monti (Spanish Steps) to find her 'first model' from the 'costumed loafers' who 'used to sun themselves on the steps at that time':

> I had a half-frightened, half-delighted thrill when choosing my first *Ciociaro*. It was the judgement of Paris transposed. Three of them in peaked hats and goat-skins, stood grinning and posing before the English *signorina* while the Papal Zouave sentry and the whole lot of male and female models looked on and listened. When I gave the apple to Antonio on account of his good brown face and red waistcoat, and engaged him for the morrow, I felt I had started.[76]

As a female artist, she faced obstacles:

> What trouble mamma and I had had in trying to find a studio. A young lady working by herself! A thing unknown – no one would let me a studio, so we ended with the makeshift … in our apartment. 'That comes of being a woman at the starting,' exclaimed mamma.[77]

Their apartment was at 'No. 56 Via Babuino' and Elizabeth recalls how on one occasion she watched her model saunter up and down outside of the apartment for half an hour, wasting Elizabeth's time and pay:

> I had engaged him for eight o'clock for an eight-hour day (*giornata finita*), and there he was, strolling away franc's worth of sitting on purpose. 'But, Signorina, one cannot always arrive to the very instant', was the villain's excuse on coming in. I said nothing of what I had seen out of the window. Dear old Francesco, he was much prized for his laugh, which he could keep up for twenty minutes at a time.[78]

At her mother's request, she commenced *The Magnificat*, Mary's visit to Elizabeth, with Christiana as the model for Mary. On days off Tom and Elizabeth examined the paintings in the Vatican and the Villa Borghese and she recorded pages of notes. In

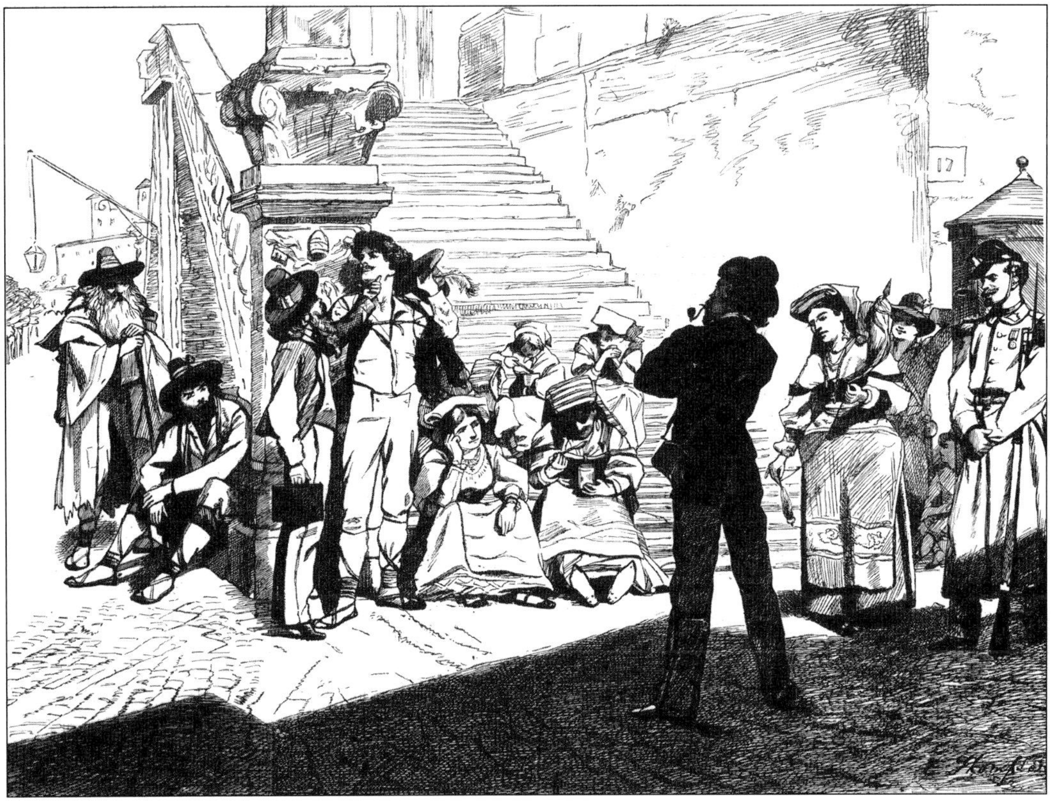

2 'Sketches in Rome – Artists Choosing a Model' from *The Graphic*, 9 August 1873.

the evenings, when they were not entertaining, Tom read Roman history to them but Christiana's 'brightness' soon attracted visitors including Mr Severn, 'in whose arms Keats died'.

In early 1870 Elizabeth entered *The Magnificat* into the Pope's international exhibition. Severn, promising to do all he could to help her, went to see if he could make the exhibition organizers hang her picture well. Elizabeth, however, was less satisfied with the painting than Christiana who wanted it placed where the Pope could see it. As a female, the artist was barred admittance to the venue until the opening day and Tom and Severn had to take responsibility for the picture. The judge 'said to Severn he had expected the signorina's picture to be rubbish (*porcheria*). I suppose because it was a woman's work. He retracted and said he would like to see me'. In the end, the painting received an honourable mention.

An 'old *ciociara*' whom she hired from the Spanish Steps was the model for her *Magnificat*'s Elizabeth.[79] She describes how on one occasion she chose a man with a 'finely cut profile and black hair'; three years later *The Graphic* magazine published her sketch of choosing models at the steps recalling this moment.[80] The sketch contains two male artists – one tilting the chin of a tall, black-haired young man while another artist observes the pair from a few yards distance. This second artist, his back to the viewer, and with a pipe in his mouth, commands a scene which includes groups of women and men huddled on the steps and overseen by a sentry (Figure 2).

At this point in Elizabeth's artistic career, travel and religious interests vied with military scenes. When the family returned to England in the summer of 1870, Elizabeth resumed for a short period her studies at the South Kensington School and then took a studio in one of the 142 custom-built studios at 76 Fulham Road called The Avenue. For Elizabeth and others such studios represented not only a 'properly appointed workplace' but an 'inspirational tool and material proof of the professional approach'. These studio spaces came with a waiting room, costume room and other 'necessary conveniences'.[81] Her 'regular exhibition career' dates, Alice records, from 1870.[82] In the 1871 census the 24-year-old Elizabeth's profession is recorded as artist-painter and the Thompsons were living at 8 Sunmer Terrace, Brompton.

However, *The Magnificat* was not accepted for the Royal Academy's summer exhibition in 1871 and was returned with a 'ragged hole in the carefully painted evening sky large enough to give a glimpse of the sky of London through the canvas'.[83] Another attempt at a semi-religious scene, the Papal zouaves saluting two bishops in Rome, was rejected in 1872. The religious material was clearly not the right course. Success followed at the Dudley Gallery, located in the famous Egyptian Hall in Piccadilly, when Elizabeth resumed her travel-inspired war art.

'Standing at Ease' – Bersaglieri Recruits, Genoa was a critical success at the Dudley Gallery's winter exhibition: 'An exceedingly clever drawing in all ways is signed with a name new to us – Miss Elizabeth Thompson', observes the *Pall Mall Gazette* on 13 February 1872. '[N]othing can be more lifelike, more *spirituel*, than the touch which gives each soldier boy his separate Italian temper of swaggering jauntiness, attentive smartness, sentimental regret, laughing self-compassion in his new situation, yawning sulkiness or sluggish indifference'.[84] Personalizing the individual soldier's experience is what would later define Elizabeth as an artist. Meanwhile *The Examiner* can hardly believe that such a 'racy, humorous picture, full of character and fun, relieved by a few touches of pathos, and painted with force and decision' was the 'work of a lady'.[85] Another review of 30 March observes how the painting 'hits off with truth and hardly-concealed fun the miseries of these conscripts. The soldierly set-up of the sergeant, who has evidently put them "through their facings" with a zeal they hardly appreciate, and his evident coolness of mind and body, are in forcible relief to their varied attitudes, all expressive of *ennui* in the hardier, and utter fatigue in the weaker of the batch'.[86]

Another work entered later that year garnered the praise of Tom Taylor:

> A figure (282) of a Chasseur 'en vedette' by Miss Elizabeth Thompson, deserved a better place than it has obtained at the top of the room. Man and horse are admirably drawn, and full of expression and truthful effect. This lady deserved better treatment if only as the painter of the particularly clever squad

of Bersaglieri on drill, one of the most remarkable drawings for character ever exhibited at the Dudley.[87]

The Pall Mall Gazette of 5 March 1873 describes her work as 'clever' with one of her paintings representing 'an English officer and men lolling or chatting at ease on horseback while their horses drink from a water-trough'; the other painting was of 'a squad of young Italian drummers standing in Genoese sunshine' and while these paintings had not 'gone beyond her exceedingly skilful debut, with the cavalry under fire of last year', the review confirmed that she showed 'the same kind of singular facility in catching, with the slightest shadow of caricature, the gestures and expressions of groups of soldiers'.[88] *The Examiner* praised *Autumn Manoeuvres, 1872* and *Drilling the Drummers – Genoa* as 'two clever military sketches'.[89] Such military scenes drew the attention of a man who would change her life; Charles Galloway, a Manchester industrialist, purchased her soldiers watering horses and commissioned a military painting in oil. It would turn out to be *The Roll Call.*

Meanwhile events in the early 1870s focused Elizabeth's attention on France; the first of these was the Franco-Prussian War and the second involved a pilgrimage. 'It was', Elizabeth recalls in her autobiography, 'the Franco-Prussian War and a return to the Isle of Wight that sent me back on the military road with ever diminishing digressions'.[90] Elizabeth's first minor success at the Royal Academy was *Missing* (1873) which 'commemorated one of those side-incidents of a campaign in which she believed that art might find a truer and more human interest than in the masses and generalities of battle', as Alice describes her sister's artistic vision. 'Two French officers, old and young, both wounded and with one wounded horse between them, have lost their way after a disastrous defeat; their names will appear in the sad roll as missing, and the manner of their death will never be known'.[91] Neither figure in the picture is looking at the viewer. Tom was the model for the seated officer who is glancing sideways into the distance, while the walking figure, grasping his mounted companion's arm looks disconsolately at the ground. The weary horse dragging his leg reflects the men's distress. Here Elizabeth, no doubt recalling the advice of Madame Jerichan and other artists at the Thornycroft party in 1868, painted the horse's head in brown with a white star on his forehead. With this painting Elizabeth had found her artistic voice. Disappointingly, it was hung too high up at the Royal Academy or, in technical terms it had 'skyed', but nevertheless, it had given her a foothold. With *Missing* and her later battle canvases Elizabeth was importing to Britain the French traditions of Detaille and Meissonier, who individualized the experience of war. From 1872 with Tom's help she started to study British soldiers at army manoeuvres in Southampton and in 1873 an opportunity to study the Cameron Highlanders presented itself when the unit was stationed near Ventnor. These 'splendid troops, so essentially pictorial' would become some of her favourite subjects.[92]

France beckoned in August 1873 for commercial and religious reasons. Both Thompson girls had followed their mother into the Roman Catholic Church and Elizabeth and Alice embarked on their first pilgrimage to Paray-le-Monial, the site of St Margaret Mary Alcoque's visions of the Sacred Heart in 1673–5. Elizabeth was commissioned by *The Graphic* to produce sketches. Conversion to Catholicism had gained momentum in Britain with high-profile converts like John Henry Newman. It was, however, treated with suspicion with Catholics often accused of being unpatriotic and frequently attacked.[93]

The trip to Paray-le-Monial was a new adventure for Elizabeth and one that the sisters took without their parents. The trip underlines how Elizabeth used the resources of travel for her profession. In her career as an essayist, Alice would do the same. The diary entries for the days before the pilgrimage provide an insight into Elizabeth's working practices at this time. On 25 August, she wrote in her diary: 'A very little art my artillery, being dreadfully hindered from working'.[94] By 30 August, Elizabeth was getting anxious about the impending trip:

> Alice and I, the intending pilgrims to Paray have been in dismal incertitude these last days on account of the dreadful weather wh. has made us all but give up going by the route fixed upon by the organizers of the Pilgrimage – we by Dieppe. We thought of going on our own hook by Boulogne for the sake of the far shorter passage as I am such a terrible sufferer from sea sickness, but today after days of hurricane the weather became utterly still & warm & this caused us to take the very necessary, but irrevocable step of making up our minds as to the route we should take – that route being via Dieppe. So we telegraphed to Cook for our tickets, there being no time to write, for we must leave here for Portsmouth on Monday. Let us hope there will be no hitch. Affairs seem to be rather in a muddle with the committee, no wonder, for it has been a tremendous undertaking for them to assemble & organize this heterogeneous multitude which flocks from all parts of the United Kingdom. As matters stand with us tonight we two are to go to Portsmouth on Monday & there start with Cook's tickets en route for Paray, joining the body of Pilgrims at Newhaven as they arrive on Tuesday morning from London by their special train. The Graphic wants me to send rough sketches done on the journey before Friday, so as to come out in the paper the week following, & to do a large, more elaborate drawing for the week after that. I wonder if I shall really cover our expenses by these sketches. Too busy today to do anything but a few dots to Tent Pegging for much has had to be got in order for the journey.[95]

Elizabeth and Alice left Ventnor for Portmouth accompanied by their father with Elizabeth in charge of their tickets and money and her 'all important sketchbook in which to dash down flying sketches on our way to Paray, for the *Graphic*'. At Newhaven, she sketched a steamboat for future illustrations, 'feeling some of it would prove useful as figuring in some scene on the morrow & [she] was right'. On the next morning, they waited in anticipation for the 'special' from Victoria which was bringing other pilgrims: 'We knew F. Bagshawe wd probably be in it, but besides him we did not expect to see one friend, & yet they all seemed to be warm old friends who were coming, so strong is the feeling of sympathy in the great family of the Catholic Church'. They embarked on the *Marseilles* although not everyone was happy to see the pilgrims depart. Elizabeth noted how a preacher pointed his umbrella at them and called them a 'disgrace' to their country but the 'more he bawled the more [they] cheered' as there was 'never anything so ridiculous'. The passage across was rough but

> our spirits [were] too high to be seriously dashed by the severest seasickness. I never forgot that besides a pilgrim I was also the Graphic artist & tho' as far as I could from my berth in the ladies' cabin, joined the mass we heard being celebrated on deck in spirits, as the latter I regretted not being able to see what must have been a thrilling subject for a sketch. I was later on persuaded to make the sketch from description … I have sent it with the others to the *Graphic*.

On arrival at Dieppe Elizabeth 'got up in time to join in the last half' of the hymn and 'then to take a rough outline of the scene whilst the front people were swarming off the boat'. Exhausted by the time they reached their hotel in the Rue de Rivoli in Paris, Elizabeth still had to think of her sketchbook: 'scarcely knowing where I was & unable to fix my attention … feeling more inclined to lie down on the floor & go to sleep, I had to sketch as hard as I could at one of the things I had to send off from Paray by Thursday. It was the "Mass at Sea", & if it comes out like any thing on the habitable globe, what with one thing & another, it will be more than I expected'. On reaching Paray, the sisters joined the crowds: '[W]ith all our hearts we struck up one of the many hymns we sang' through the 'unknown streets towards a mysterious, unknown church up in the sky & with a belt of lamps twinkling round its tower, & its great bells clamorously pealing out a heart-stirring welcome to us'. Later they found their lodgings for the night and on the following morning Alice, up before her sister, attended an early service. Elizabeth recalls the later 8 o'clock service in the Chapel of the Apparition:

> I found the wonderful little chapel densely crowded, chiefly, of course, with English, & a bishop was just finishing Mass, whilst at the side chapels, half hidden by the gorgeous folds of many banners supported against the walls at the openings of these chapels, priests were celebrating the Holy Sacrifice at

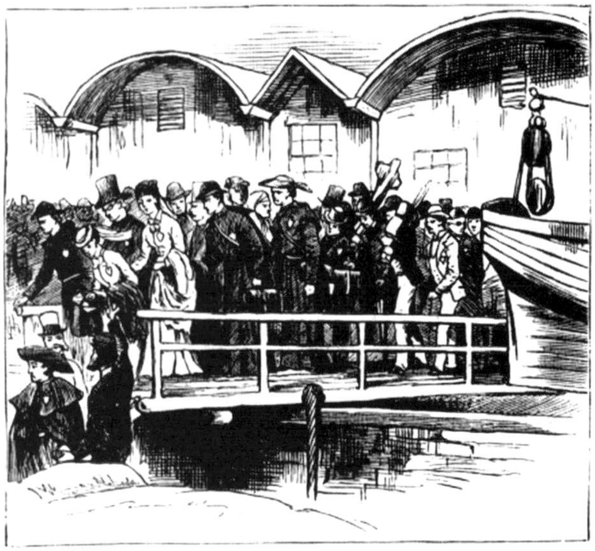

1. EMBARKATION AT NEWHAVEN

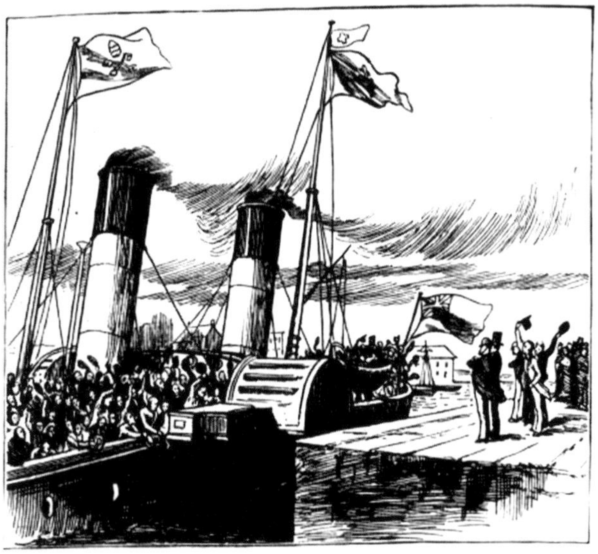

2. WE LEAVE WITH THREE TIMES THREE

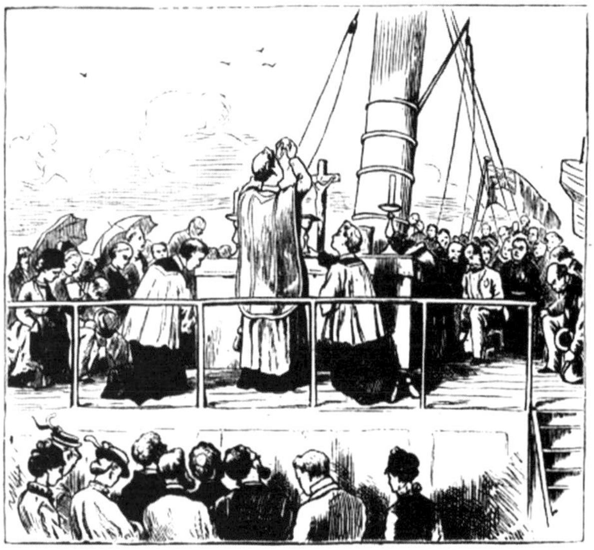

3. MASS ON BOARD THE STEAMER

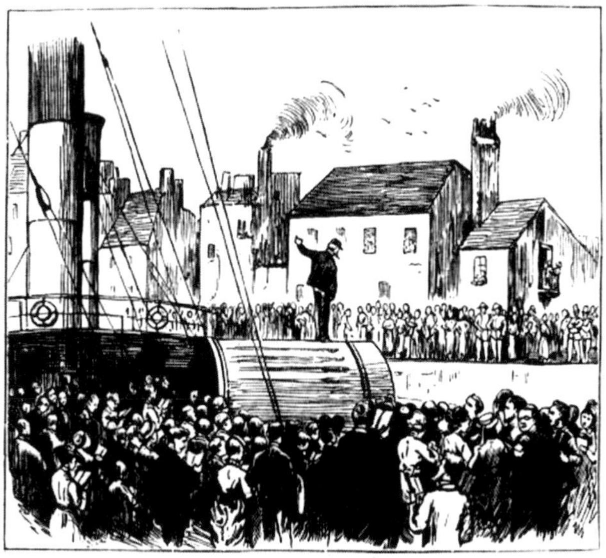

4. SINGING THE "MAGNIFICAT" AT DIEPPE

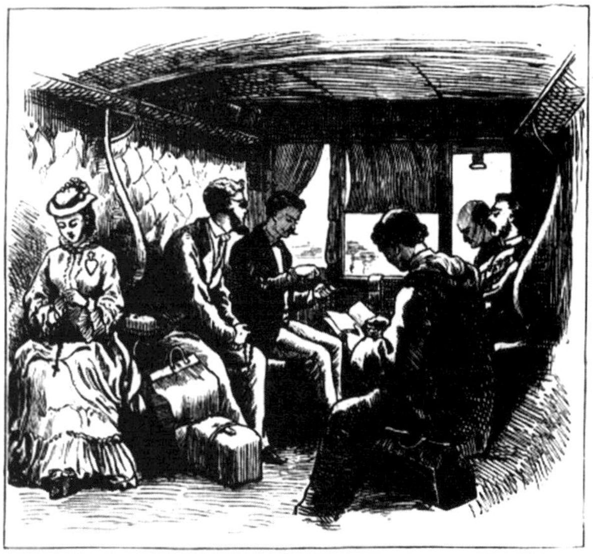

5. THE SERVICE OF THE ROSARY

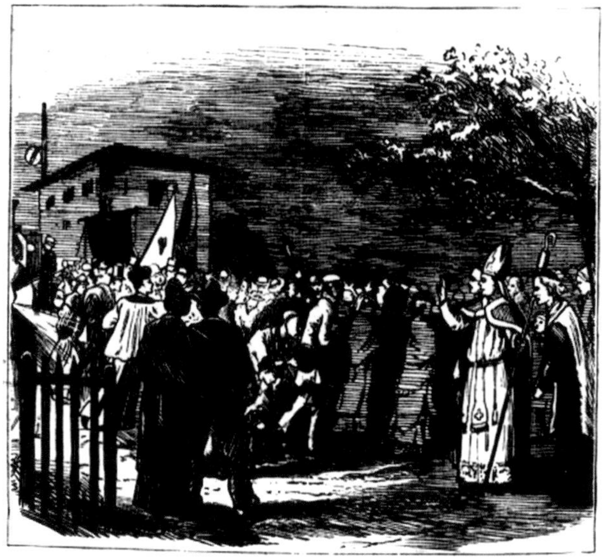

6. ARRIVAL AT PARAY

different stages I could not tell now what the walls of this interior were made of, & indeed I doubt whether I could see them so completely covered were they with these banners brought by proceeding pilgrimages & left their [sic] as offerings.

Later they attended the parish church: '[T]he dear church wh. had peeled out its welcome to us the night before ... The scene was of the gayest description, the ever moving crowd, brightens here & there with a veil in cotton & black or purple cassock, the picturesque surroundings – notably the magnificent Romanesque church itself ... Need I dwell on the spiritual beauty of the picture?'

Special permission was granted to the English pilgrims to visit the garden of the apparition in the convent grounds: 'And so we reached the gates of the convent Garden & entered that Enclosure WH. so few (literally) outsiders [had entered] especially members of the male sex ... We could not linger at this point, & had not time allowed us to stay & fix our minds on the awful sanctity of that spot, but we received leaves from the trees, which the priest picked for us, as mementos of the place'. Elizabeth, however, had to get her sketches posted to *The Graphic*. 'I had a touch or 2 to put to one of the sketches which I had counted on doing at the post office. Finding it all dark inside I expressed my disappointment & the woman thereupon showed us into a little room in their back premises where she gave us a dim Lamp [and] by his lights I touched up the sketches' before popping them in the box. That night she was 'far too full of pleasant & absorbing recollections to go to sleep till very late. Alice slept 3 minutes, for the fleas were most lively & even kept me from sleeping long at a time'. In the early hours of the following morning, the girls had to rise in darkness and, accompanied part of the way by the owner of their *pension*, made their way to the 4.30 a.m. train. The return journey was more relaxed as a 'wild young Irishman afforded us great amusement'. At the breakfasting station, Elizabeth had only time to grab two bits of sugar before the train announced the recommencement of its journey but the young Irishman came back 'all aglow with triumph' with a plate of veal. However, the 'poor fellow had forgotten it was Friday & when I told him he sank into his seat after tossing the tempting filet in the net wh. holds the hats &c'. One incident conveys Elizabeth's sense of humour when at the next 'victualling station', Elizabeth, 'struggling thro' the masses of surging humanity to try & get at the coffee cans at the top of the room', spied one of the clerical bigwigs actually '"galumphing" off with a whole chicken!', and decided to intervene:

3 'Sketches of the Pilgrimage to Paray-le-Monial' from *The Graphic*, 20 September 1873.

'It's Friday!' I exclaimed, with a faint hope half expressing itself not exactly in my heart – ahem! 'Oh!' was the welcome reply over my head, & at the Pilgrims generally 'the whole train's dispensed!' I heard no more, I turned, I fled, careened over the down line, over the up line, I flew along the train, amusing myself by shooting the telling intelligence into a compartment here

> & there, assuring the doubtful, cheering the incredulous until I reached our carriage. I came with empty hands indeed, but virtually with filet of veal that lay amongst the waterproofs & umbrellas in the netting, for I brought the permission to devour that same. Out came our penknifes, my tiny one disappearing into the meat as; aided by a cook, it endeavoured to cut off a slice, the motive power of both implements being the eager hands of the wild Irishman.[96]

Elizabeth's six sketches appeared in *The Graphic* on 20 September (Figure 3). Long trained in painting outdoors with her mother and taking possession of the landscape in front of her, Elizabeth had proved herself as a pictorial correspondent. The artist, however, was only identified as 'a pilgrim'. By May the following year she would be the celebrated painter of *The Roll Call* and as Viola Meynell observes: 'It is pleasant to think of her father and mother looking on. None of their journeys can have shown them anything more spectacular than Elizabeth's career now'.[97]

CHAPTER FOUR

The war path: from *The Roll Call* to *Inkerman*, 1874–7

Fame with The Roll Call – *The Royal Academy* – *Queen Victoria and the painting* – *Reviews and celebrity* – *Other exhibitions* – Quatre Bras – *Help from the army* – *The 'Black Hole'* – *Reviews* – *Visits Florence* – *Alice's* Preludes – Balaclava *and its reception* – *Alice and Wilfrid Meynell* – *Italy again* – The Return from Inkerman

On 7 May 1874, Christiana wrote in great excitement from Ventnor to tell Fanny of Elizabeth's outstanding success at the Royal Academy. *Calling the Roll after an Engagement, Crimea* had not only been accepted for the summer exhibition at Burlington House, but had been feverishly celebrated by the academicians and the public. 'A cause for rejoicing' had 'burst' upon the family with 'dear Mimi's wonderful & marvellous triumphs'. Christiana informed Fanny: 'The first intimation we had of the success was in a letter to Mimi from Herbert RA some 3 weeks ago telling her that when the picture was brought before them for judgement they took off their hats and cheered it'. Elizabeth, working in London, had brought the news home to her parents:

> This wondrous news Mimi brought down to us last Sat. fortnight. She came home for a fortnight as soon as she had sent the picture 'in'. Then she went up for 'Varnishing day' – all alone of course – saw her picture placed on the line & had a series of trumps from all the R. As. On the following Friday she went by invitation to the Private View – when such a series of bewildering trumps awaited her as cannot be told. From the Archbishop of Canterbury down thro' Dukes Duchesses Lords & Ladies – all crowded to be introduced & to beg for the picture – wild prices of 1000 guineas 1500 etc or nameless sums – for some said – name whatever sum you like for it – were offered. Then the Prince of Wales wished to have it & I grieve to say the gentleman of Manchester whose commission it is – & who has got it for £120 – refused extravagant sums for it in the room and finally flatly refused to give it up to HRH.

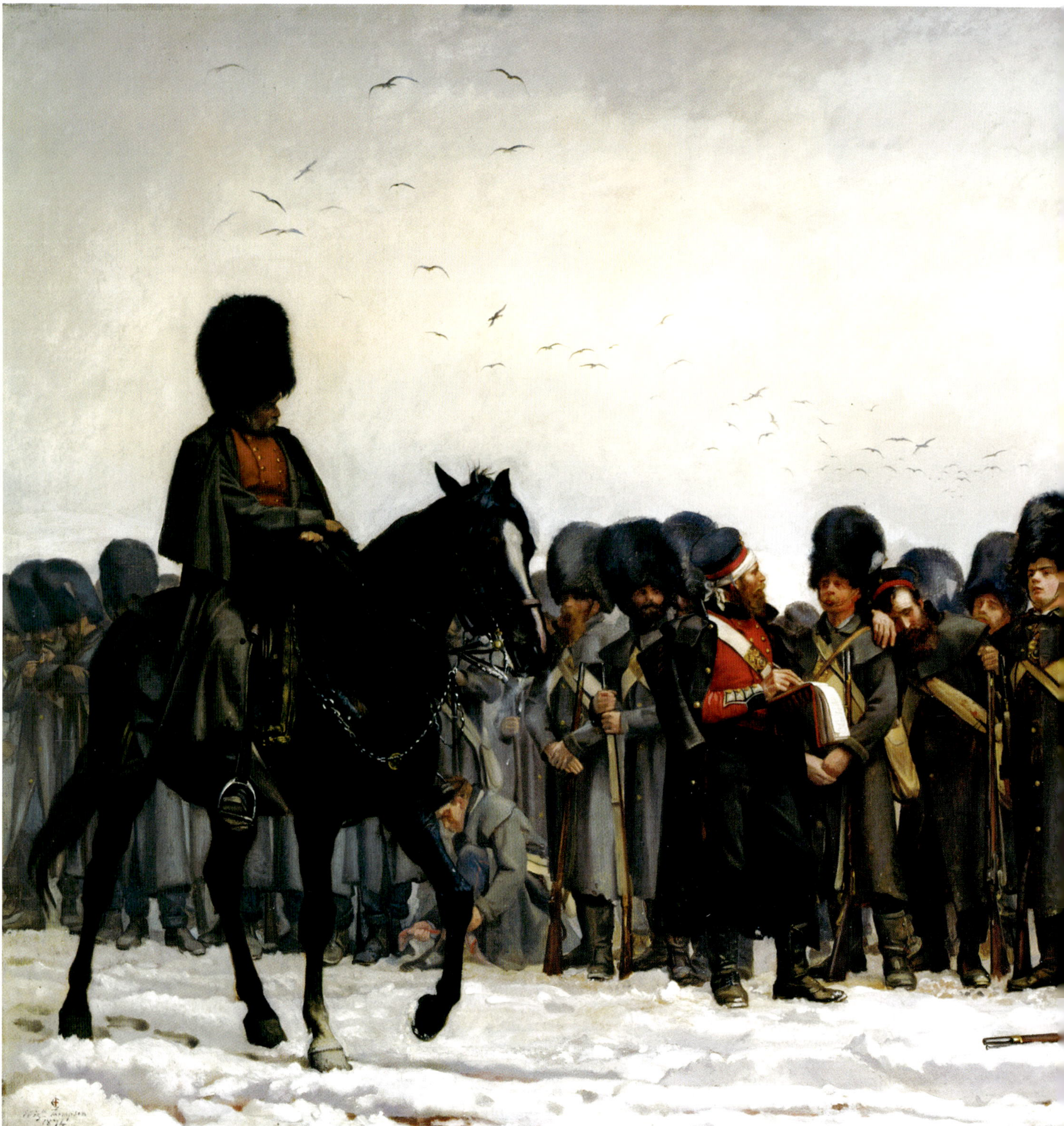

4 *Calling the Roll after an Engagement, Crimea (The Roll Call)*, 1874.
Oil on canvas, 91 x 182.9cm. Royal Collection. Bridgeman Art Library.

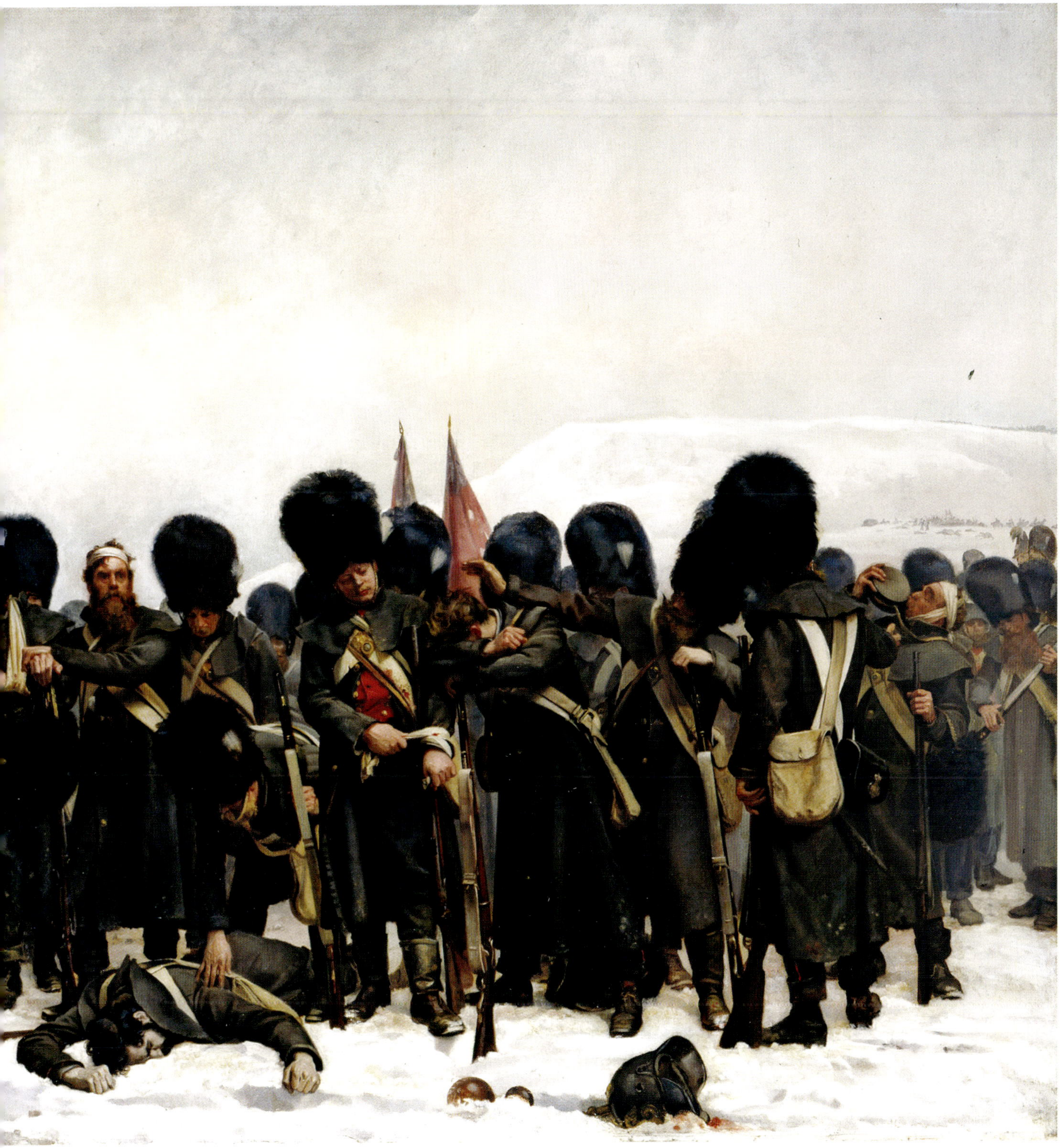

Ventnor is wild with excitement as you may imagine & I am knocked up with it – congratulations &c from all quarters.

A telegram just arrived from 'The Roll Call by command – for several hours at Buckingham Palace. A communication is expected from her Majesty' (so it must have been taken down from the walls of the RA – & sent in.) I will write more in a few days. I send today's Telegraph. Your Papa went to London yesterday to take Mimi to the grand ball at the Goldsmith's Hall – & we go up tomorrow for a fortnight.

The pace at which her daughter became suddenly famous is palpable in Christiana's account to Fanny. There is no exaggeration in the letter – crowds did gather before *The Roll Call* at the Royal Academy or, as Christiana puts it: 'A tremendous crowd always before the picture & people fighting to get a glimpse of it'.[1] To avoid potential damage to the painting, a policeman was posted beside it to deter the over exuberant viewers. Elizabeth was the toast of the Royal Academy's banquet. And then the painting disappeared temporarily from the Royal Academy so the Queen could see it and finally get to have it from 'the gentleman of Manchester', Charles Galloway, who had originally commissioned it.

The Roll Call was several months in the making (Figure 4). Elizabeth recruited her old teacher Burchett to help her find suitable models for her painting and he sent her 'nearly all ex-soldiers'. The sergeant who calls the roll in the painting was a Crimean veteran. They modelled for five hours a day, although towards the end Elizabeth had them work for six. Meanwhile, a family friend, Dr Pollard, rooted about in Chelsea's pawnshops and after one particular pawnbroker, Mr Abraham, had tramped the city to find her 'more accoutrements, helmets, coatees haversacks, etc' Elizabeth sallied back home with him, sharing his umbrella while discussing the pawnbroking trade. This was not a conventional undertaking for a woman of her time and class but then Elizabeth's choice of subjects for her paintings – soldiers and war – was not conventional either. Equipped with models and uniforms Elizabeth started the painting on 13 December 1873:

> Having made a little water-colour sketch previously, very carefully, of every attitude to the figures, I had none of those alterations to make in the course of my work which waste so much time. Each figure was drawn in first without the great coat, my models posing in a tight 'shell jacket' so as to get the figure well drawn first. How easily then could the thick, less shapely great coat be painted on the well-secured foundation. No matter how its heavy folds, the cross-belts, haversacks, water-bottles, and everything else broke the lines, they were there, safe and sound, underneath.[2]

On 29 and 30 March Elizabeth had her first 'Studio Sunday', a conventional occasion where artists opened their studios to the public. Galloway's agent, who had been anxious about the painting, came and was delighted. He duly sent Elizabeth a cheque for £126 (approximately £7,888 today) but she retained the copyright, which after the picture's fame she sold to Dickinson & Co., engravers, for £1,200 (approximately £75,130).[3]

Events gathered pace over the next few weeks. By mid-April Pollard informed her that the Academicians were in a 'commotion about it' and that the history painter Alfred Elmore wanted to meet her. Prior to the painting's acceptance, she had asked her friend Father Bagshawe to write on her behalf to the Academy about it. The history painter John Rogers Herbert replied:

> I may tell you with what pleasure I greeted the picture and the painter of it when it came before us for judgement. It was simply this: I was so struck by the excellent work in it that I proposed we should lift our hats and give it and you, though, as I thought, unknown to me, a round of huzzahs, which was generally done. You now know my feeling with regard to your work, and may be sure that I shall do everything as one of the hangars that it shall be *perfectly seen* on our walls.[4]

After taking the note round to Fr Bagshawe Elizabeth went home to Ventnor to tell her parents, as Christiana informed Fanny in her letter, before going back again to London for Varnishing Day on 28 April. The RA's longstanding custom allowed artists to make final adjustments to their paintings before applying the finishing varnish. On Varnishing Day artists would jostle with each to reach their paintings on the overcrowded Academy walls to make their changes. In an 1877 illustration for *Punch*, 'Varnishing Day at the Royal Academy', the artist George du Maurier depicts artists putting the last-minute touch to their paintings (Figure 5). Interestingly, three of the nine are women, celebrating, perhaps, after Elizabeth's fame in 1874, women's artistic claims.[5] Elizabeth, with her palette brushes and paintboxes, ascended the staircase alone as 'hurrying men' equipped like herself scurried past her. As she entered Room 2 she saw her 'dark battalion' '*on the line* with a knot of artists before it'.[6] In other words, her painting had been hung at eye-level – the most desired position. Herbert had kept his promise. Then she received an ovation. She was quickly surrounded by leading artists – Millais, Val Prinsep and Philip H. Calderdon – who questioned her on her training and examined her soldiers in detail. Arthur Severn, her friend from Rome, cleaned the picture for her in case she ruined her velveteen dress. Du Maurier told her that *Punch*'s editor, Tom Taylor, admired the painting. 'To be an object of such interest', she recalls, was 'delightful' and, as Taylor told her, she had 'burst into fame'.[7] A few months later *Punch* celebrated her in a cartoon by Linley Sambourne. An elegantly caricatured Elizabeth presides like an angel looking down over the key figures and events of the first eight months of the year as a cherub beside her holds up *The Roll Call* and blasts on a trumpet.[8]

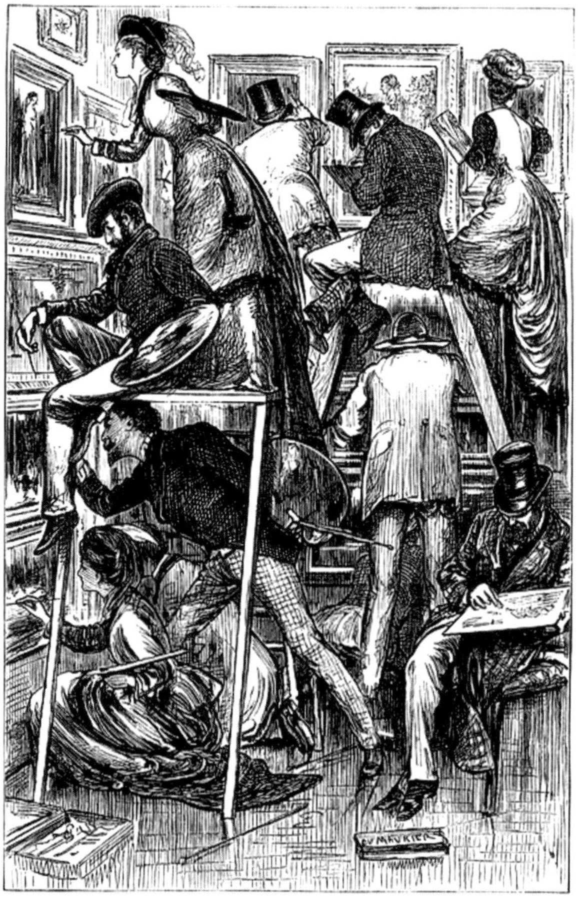

5 George du Maurier, 'Varnishing Day at the Royal Academy' from *Punch*, 19 June 1877.

What was this painting that burst her into fame and why did a Crimean War painting become so celebrated twenty years after the start of that war? The Crimean War was a conflict of the past for the enthralled artists and spectators at the Royal Academy in the spring of 1874, but it was also, in many ways, a war that occupied the present politically and culturally. It was the first media war and the extensive coverage of the conflict by William Howard Russell of *The Times* brought the war into people's lives in ways in which war had never done before. It was also a photographic war as the relatively new invention of the camera was deployed on the battlefield. It was also a disastrous war. Bureaucratic bungling and poor military leadership caused the unnecessary suffering of ill-equipped soldiers and starving horses in the harsh conditions of two Crimean winters. This moved the British public, well-informed by Russell's dispatches from the front, to anger and dismay. It was a war of poetry as Tennyson's populist 'The Charge of the Light Brigade' (1854) commemorated the heroism of ordinary soldiers sent to their annihilation by the confused orders of their superior officers. It was also the 'last of the "old-fashioned" wars, the last before science came to the aid of the military, the last before full dress was finally deemed unsuitable for active service, the last where smooth-bore artillery thundered and cannon-balls bounded through ranks of disciplined men, leaving a bloody path'.[9]

Elizabeth's painting was produced in a period when the Franco-Prussian War was initiating army changes at home. The Liberal administration under Gladstone was re-organizing the army. Under the Cardwell reforms, undertaken by the Secretary of State for War, Edward Cardwell, officers' commissions could no longer be bought; the aristocratic grip on the army was loosened and promotion would be based in future on merit not money. The 1870s were a period when, as Elizabeth's future husband William Butler was to note, 'everybody had something to do with military matters'. The old system of 'foul corruption' was replaced by selection which though 'theoretically pure' was also subject to 'political jobbery'. The change was motivated, according to William, by 'the spectacle of a neighbouring nation, struck suddenly to the ground by a mighty empire' and this 'caused the panic-stricken British people to overhaul and to reconstruct'.[10]

A multi-volume history of the Crimean War was also being published in this period and Elizabeth read Alexander Kinglake to research her paintings. Kinglake had not finished publishing his history of the war when Elizabeth exhibited her painting; his eighth and final volume appeared in 1887. Joan Hichberger notes that Kinglake's history subscribed to the view that 'the aristocrats who commanded the army had failed their country and that only the heroism of the ordinary soldiers had won the war'.[11] In 1874 Kinglake was writing the fifth volume of his history of the war focusing on Inkerman. He had accompanied Lord Raglan, the Commander of British forces, to the Crimea and was given Raglan's papers to write his version of the war. Raglan, who was an incompetent strategist, did not survive the conflict; he died from cholera on 28 June 1855.

The Crimean War was also a woman's war – its most famous female representative was Florence Nightingale, a wealthy Derbyshire woman, who brought her band of nurses to the remote peninsula to tend the sick and wounded soldiers and launched nursing as a professional career for women. The Jamaican Mary Seacole also set up a medical unit. Overall British losses in the Crimea amounted to 22,000, most of them from cholera and typhus. French casualties amounted to 95,000 with over 75,000 lost to illness and the Turkish estimate was 45,000.[12]

The Roll Call did not capture the aftermath of any particular Crimean battle but rather served as an archetypal representation of the conflict. However, a contemporary, Reverend Kilvert, who saw the painting at the Royal Academy on 25 June 1874, recorded in his diary that the scene represented the aftermath of the battle of Inkerman, which took place on the 5 November. Inkerman, however, was fought in rain and mist and not in the snow that in Elizabeth's painting so eloquently captures the general harsh conditions of the Crimea. Significantly, Kilvert's account confirms the volume of spectators and that the painting particularly attracted female viewers: 'There was a great press of people, 100 or more, round Miss Thompson's

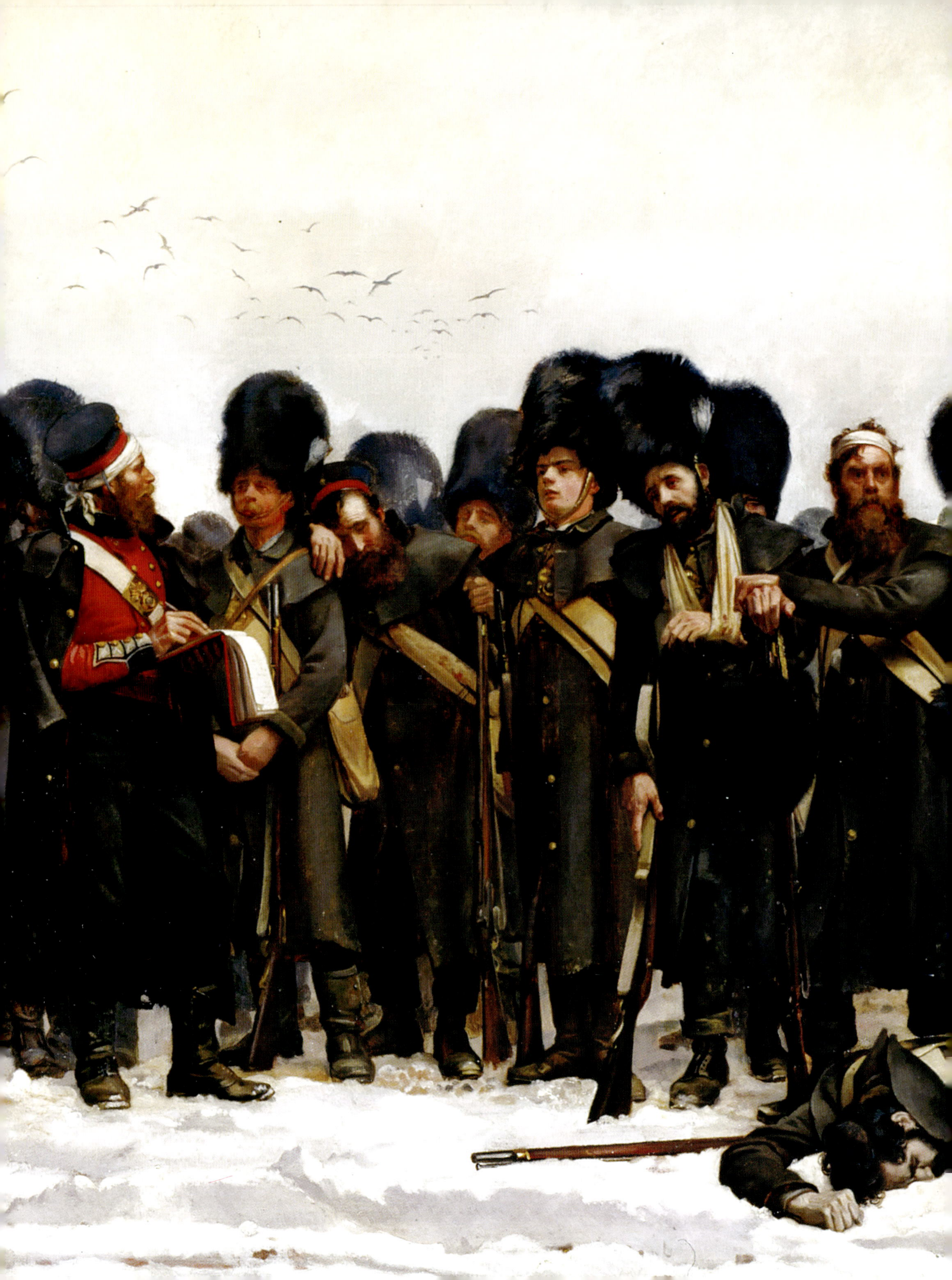

famous picture *Calling the Roll after the battle of Inkerman*. A policeman stands on duty all day by this picture from 10 o'clock till 6 in the evening saying, "Move on ladies. Ladies, please move on".'[13] Frederic Leighton, who was exhibiting *Moorish Garden*, wrote to the RA to ask if a rail could be put up along the whole end of Gallery 2 in order to protect his painting from the crowds coming to see *The Roll Call*; his request, however, was refused.[14]

In *The Roll Call* a line of wounded and war-weary Grenadier Guards gather to answer their names as a red-bearded sergeant, positioned off centre to the left, and the most robust figure in the group, records the names of the survivors in his roll. The whiteness of the page emulates the snow on the ground and the snow covered mountain in the background. The model for the sergeant was a veteran of the conflict who had provided Elizabeth with advice during the painting's composition. The hardier soldiers stand to attention leaning on their rifles, others lean on their companions' shoulders. At the painting's left, a mounted officer, slouching in his saddle, examines the survivors. One of the soldiers has recently collapsed at the front of the line, his rifle lying on the ground adjacent to his outstretched body and his grey clenched hands and the grey pallor of his face partially buried in the snow indicates that he has just died. His nearest companion in the line bends over him with his hand touching the prostrate figure's shoulder. Beside him another guard focuses his attention on rearranging the bloodied bandage on his wrist. The figure adjacent to him hides his face in his arms, propped on the barrel of his gun while his companion to the right of the viewer stretches his outstretched palm towards the man's head – not quite touching it. Another figure, with his back to the viewer, is seemingly reaching back into the line towards a guard with a bandaged head who is drinking from his water butt as if to implore a drink. Figures in the painting parallel each other. The bandaged head of the bearded sergeant calling the roll, is mirrored by a bare-headed, red-bearded soldier with a bandaged head, positioned slightly to the right. His hands are crossed on his gun (Figure 6). Remarkable for being the only bare-headed figure in the line, the man gazes out into the distance beyond the canvas's frame. Indeed, an earlier version of this figure has survived as a separate painting (Figure 7). The central figure, a young man, stands to attention, as the sergeant looks directly at him as he calls his name. In the painting's foreground to the viewer's right, a Russian helmet is strewn on the ground with the blood from its inside soaking into the snow (see Figure 8 for sketches of men).

6 Detail from *Calling the Roll after an Engagement, Crimea (The Roll Call).*

The war started when Russian imperial expansion into the declining Ottoman Empire resulted in Britain and France supporting Turkey. The Crimean campaign was defined by its slowness and by the suffering of soldiers and horses, ravaged by hunger and cholera, and criticisms of commanding officers, who were either inept or too old. British intervention was at first popular at home when the public learned how the Russians in an unprovoked attack entered Turkish waters and destroyed almost the entire Turkish navy at Sinope. The British and French mobilized their

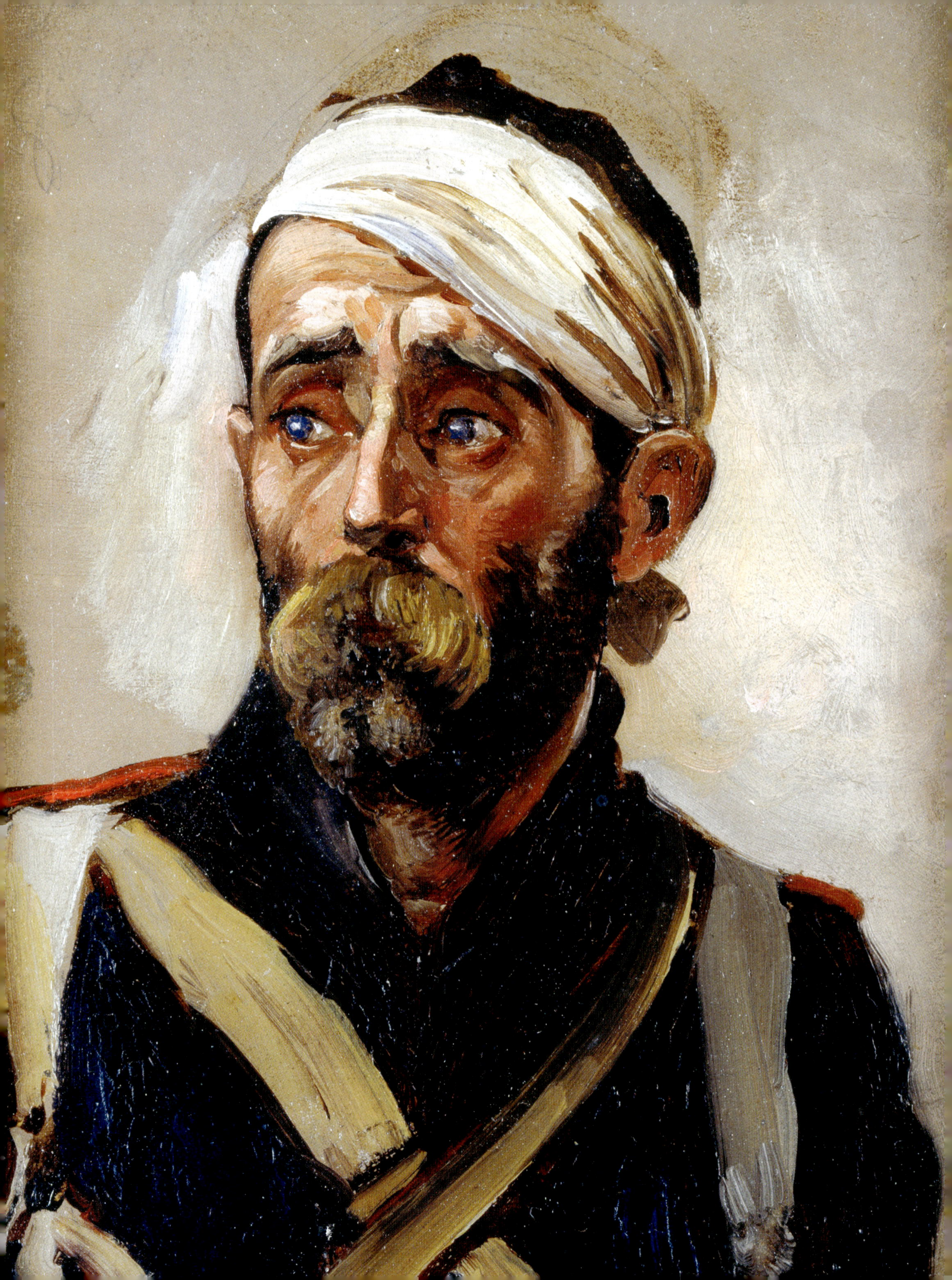

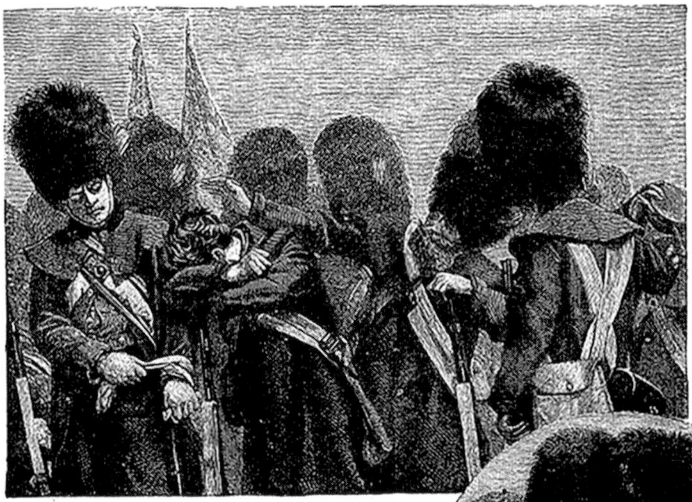

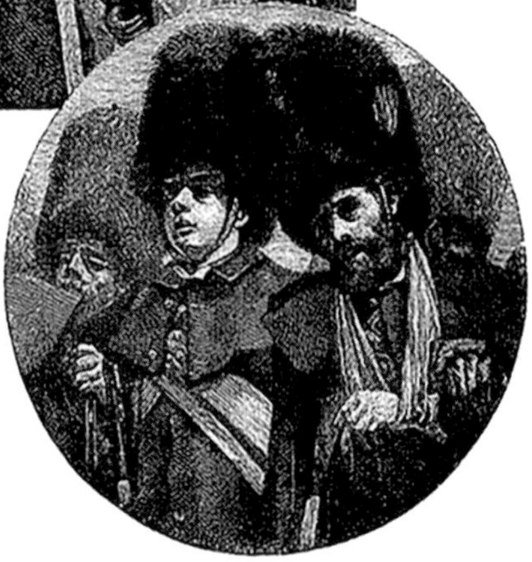

7 *(opposite) Study of a Wounded Guardsman*, 1874. Oil on a panel, 22 x 13.4cm. National Army Museum. Bridgeman Art Library.

8 Sketches from *The Roll Call* in 'Elizabeth Butler' by Alice Meynell, *St Nicholas Magazine*, 1 January 1883.

respective navy forces in the Black Sea and the army under Raglan's command was deployed to the region in February 1854, landing first at Varna from where the troops then attacked the Russian Black Sea port of Sebastopol. The campaign's first major success was at the Battle of Alma on the 20 September 1854 where the allied forces defeated the Russians. This was the only battle that Kinglake witnessed before returning from the Crimea. The Russians retreated to Russia's second-most important port of Sebastopol. Raglan was criticized for not immediately following up the victory by pursuing the Russians, thus allowing the enemy to shore up its defences, enabling it to withstand allied bombardment. The allies took up positions at Balaclava which became their supply route for the assault on Sebastopol but on 25 October the Russians launched a counter-attack on Balaclava. The most famous encounter in the entire war took place when, at 11 a.m., confused orders caused the Light Brigade of the British Cavalry Division (over 600 men) to charge a battery of Russian guns a mile beyond them in the valley. As they charged for approximately six minutes they came under attack by enemy fire on both flanks. Terry Brighton notes:

> Men and horses fell dead or mutilated at every stride. The carnage was horrific, yet still the survivors spurred their mounts on. To those watching from high

> ground to the rear as what remained of the Light Brigade disappeared into the smoke of the Russian guns, it seemed that these magnificent cavalrymen had charged into hell itself.[15]

The charge had been the result of bungled orders. Raglan had not intended that the Light Brigade should charge at the Russian guns. His order, written by General Richard Airey, was conveyed by an aide de camp, Captain Nolan, to Lord Lucan, Commander of the Cavalry Division, who in turn gave his order to Lord Cardigan, the Commander of the Light Brigade. When Cardigan asked Nolan what guns he was supposed to charge the aide de camp seemingly pointed in the direction of the Russian guns but after Cardigan issued the orders to his soldiers, Nolan pursued them. Whether Nolan was attempting to turn them back, knowing too late that they had turned in the wrong direction, will never be known as Nolan was killed in the charge.

Eye-witness testimony was provided by Fanny Durberley:

> I only know that I saw Captain Nolan galloping; that presently the Light Brigade, leaving their position, advanced themselves, although in the face of the whole Russian force, and under a fire that seemed pouring from all sides, as though every bush was a musket, every stone in the hillside a gun. Faster and faster they rode. How we watched them![16]

The Charge of the Light Brigade acquired mythic status with the British public celebrating the heroism of ordinary soldiers who were led into danger and death by the bungling of their officers. 'By consolidating in her paintings a realistic treatment of war with a sympathetic portrayal of the soldiers', Elizabeth represented, as Matthew Lalumia notes, 'Liberal England's answer to the preceding generation's vision of military affairs. She was the product of a reformist age in which the public understood the cost of armed adventurism'.[17] Elizabeth's paintings of the Crimean War, *The Roll Call*, and later *Balaclava* and *Inkerman* seized the public mood. Their appeal transcended social classes.

The Prince of Wales attended the private view at the Royal Academy on 30 April. When he saw *The Roll Call* he wanted it but Galloway, who installed himself near the painting, 'refused to give it up'. The furore added to the picture's fame but Elizabeth, surrounded by London society, claimed to remain unaffected by the attention. 'Do you remember', Elizabeth wrote to her father on 1 May, 'joking with me, when I was a child, about the exaggerations of popularity? How strange it felt to-day to be realizing, in actual experience, what you warned me of, in fun, when looking at my drawings'. She was introduced to Raglan's daughters 'who were pleased with the interest I took in their father' and 'Old Kinglake was also introduced, and we had a comparatively long talk in that huge assembly where you are perpetually

interrupted in your conversation by fresh arrivals of friends or new introductions'.[18] She told her father that 'Sir Richard Airey, the man who wrote the fatally misconstrued order on his holster and handed it to Nolan on the 25th October, 1854, was very cordial, and showed that he took a keen interest in the picture'.[19] Tom, as Christiana informed Fanny in her letter, was summoned from Ventnor to take her to a ball at Goldsmith's Hall.

In the meantime, the Prince of Wales praised the painting at the Academy's annual banquet on 3 May creating a frenzy of excitement. He commented that the Academy's walls contained 'pictures of the greatest artists this country can produce' and then after listing all male artists including Millais, Frederic Leighton, W.G. Watts, he drew their attention to the work of a woman:

> I hope these gentlemen who have come to the Royal Academy on this occasion have not forgotten to look at the picture in the next room which I think deserves attention. It is numbered 142 in the Catalogue, and is entitled – *Calling the Roll after an Engagement in the Crimea*. This picture, painted by a young lady, who I am given to understand is not yet 23, is deserving of the highest admiration, and I am sure she has before her a great future as an artist.[20]

Then Queen Victoria had the picture taken from the Royal Academy on 6 May to 'gaze at' at Buckingham Palace. Finally, the Queen won over both the Manchester industrialist and the Prince of Wales and had the painting. Press accounts recorded the Queen's wish to purchase the painting from Galloway: 'The admiration her Majesty has expressed for *The Roll Call* is necessarily highly gratifying to Miss Thompson, and must be no less pleasing to Mr Galloway, who has been indirectly the means of attracting attention to the artist's merit'.[21]

As the sensation of the exhibition Elizabeth became a figure of fantasy. One contemporary reviewer imagined the artist:

> The walls still ring with the echoes of the cheers with which the Council greeted this lady's work when it came before them, and, as my ears tingle with all that I have heard about it, I begin to build up, after my habit, a *tableau vivant* of the artist herself. I see her, strong, muscular, tall, broad-shouldered, short-haired, and comely-visaged, wearing a semi-masculine military costume of the vivandière stamp, and, for the purposes of her art, 'putting money in her purse, and following the wars'; for the soldier and his life have been her favourite themes ever since she began to exhibit.

While this, and her previously exhibited works, might, the writer notes, suggest a personal experience of war, Elizabeth's physicality rejects this idea:

> That young, delicate, clever-looking lady, over whose gentle head at the most five-and-twenty summers may have passed, cannot possibly be a campaigner; yet, in the midst of my mind's eye picture-painting, such a fragile being is pointed out to me as Miss Elizabeth Southerden Thompson.[22]

There is a strange mix here of Amazonian fantasy and 'fragile' femininity. Neither, of course, is accurate. Elizabeth was twenty-seven when she exhibited the painting but this desire to make her younger is an attempt to contain the artist and her unusual choice of subject matter. At the same time, the essay observes that Elizabeth 'is said to have marvellous memory, being able to remember not only personal descriptions of events which are related to her, but also every detail and variety of uniforms, down to stripes and buttons'.[23] A rumour circulated in the press that Elizabeth had nursed in the 'Franco-German war'.[24] Another argued that 'the picture is really the reproduction of a reminiscence of Miss Thompson's in the Crimea, where she served with Miss Nightingale'.[25]

Coverage of *The Roll Call* dominated the press. *The Times* noted that there was 'neither swagger nor sentimentalism' in the painting, but 'plain, manly, pathetic, heroic truth'. It describes the scene in detail:

> The sergeant is passing along the thinned ranks, roll-call in hand. Beside him rides the mounted field-officer, his charger, like himself, besmirched with the dirt and dust of a hard day's work, with a look in which the sternness of command struggles with the concern of a good soldier as he notes the ravage of battle in the ranks. Among the men all ages are represented, from the bronzed and battle-hardened veteran to the boy recruit. Some bind up wounds not severe enough to take them to the rear; one, who has miscalculated his strength, or whose death-wound has been concealed or overlooked, has fallen in his place, and lies, prone, dead in a swoon. A raw, young soldier is overcome by the shock of this sudden fall, and leans his face on his musket, all but fainting.[26]

The *Illustrated London News* noted that the 'subject is about the very last which we should expect from a female pencil; yet by force of imaginative sympathy the terrible havoc of war is realized with a vraisemblance that could only be expected from an eye-witness'. The psychological as well as the physical marks of war are observed here: '[O]ne poor fellow has fallen dead even at the muster; a comrade feels in vain for the beating of his heart; another wounded man sickens at the sight; one near him stares at vacancy, frenzied by a wound in the head; another binds up his bleeding hand'.[27] *The Graphic* celebrated its artist alongside its other artist, Luke Fildes, whose *Applicants for Admission to a Casual Ward* depicts a scene of 'metropolitan wretchedness' as London's poor queue outside a casual ward.[28] Both paintings, indeed, have aspects in

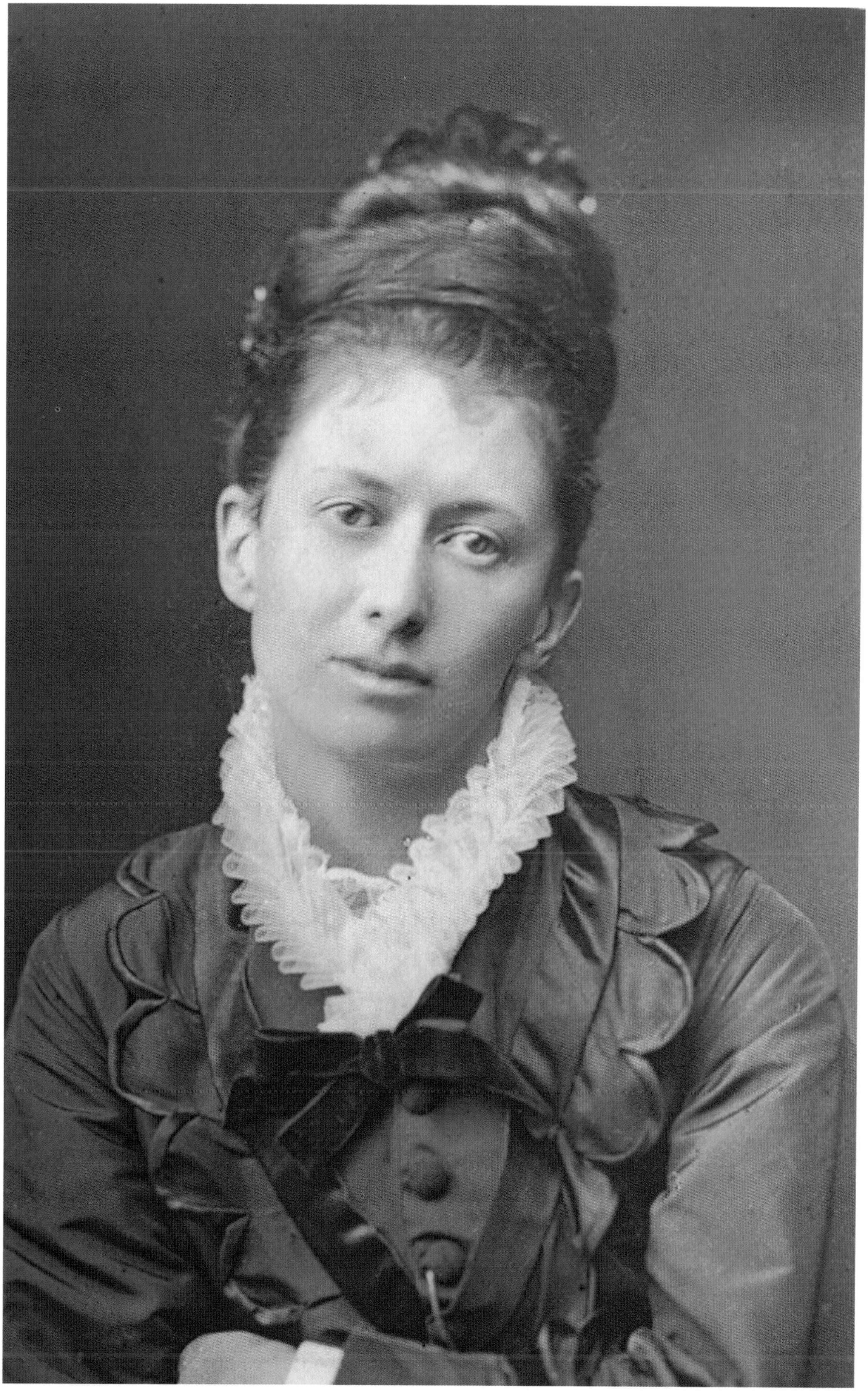

common; both represent a line of figures in various states of distress and both draw attention to the ordinary casualties of society and attempt to prick the social conscience of their viewers. With *The Roll Call* Elizabeth broke the 'norm' for battle paintings as Matthew Lalumia argues that the 'horizontal disposition of the figures, punctuated by narrative incidents along the entire length of the design' was innovative and replaced the traditional 'pyramidal format' of traditional battle paintings.[29] The democracy of its design generated its appeal.

Enthusiasm for the painting spread across Britain. As the painting made its way on a provincial tour, enthusiastic crowds clamoured to see it. Liverpool hosted it in September and in October the *Newcastle Courant* observed that 'upwards of 2,500 persons visited Mawson and Swan's Picture Gallery' on the 17th of that month.[30] In November the painting was in Birmingham's Masonic Hall. The *Birmingham Daily Post* informed its readers that the

> picture is a painful one, but there is no undue obtrusion of horrors, no morbid sentiment or sensational exaggeration. Everything necessary to the completeness of the story, from the trodden and blood-stained snow in the foreground to the carrion birds which are wheeling their flight overhead – from the spent cannon ball which lies half-buried in the snow to the battered helmet beside it – is carefully and truthfully depicted, but always in due subordination to the main idea, as expressed in the human elements of the composition.

The paper also mused on Elizabeth's rise to fame:

> Of the many recorded instances in which aspiring genius has shared Byron's oft-quoted experience by waking some morning to find itself famous, we know of none more remarkable than that of the gifted and fortunate young lady whose picture ... may be fairly described as the artistic event of the year ... since Frith's *Derby Day* we can recall no painting by an English artist, which has produced so deep a sensation or exercised so potent a fascination upon the great mass of the public.[31]

The *Lancaster Gazette* noted on 4 October that 'Miss Elizabeth Thompson, the painter of *The Roll Call*, has to pay the penalty that awaits success in any line. Her photograph is in all the shop windows'.[32] Photographs of celebrities were regularly exhibited in shop windows. This was the culture into which Elizabeth was launched. She recalls: 'Of course, the photographers began bothering. The idea of my portraits being published in the shop windows was very repugnant to me'. Finally, she consented and her grandfather, Thomas Weller, 'simply walked into the shop of the first people that had asked me, in Regent Street, and calmly made an appointment'.

She describes the result as a photograph of a 'rather harassed and coerced young woman'.[33] Two photographs of Elizabeth taken by the celebrity photographers Fradelle & Marshall show the artist's head and upper body. In one her head is slightly tilted away from the camera with her eyes looking into the distance. In the second the gaze is directed towards the viewer but the tilted head shows reticence (Figure 9). Neither depicts a happy subject. A Ward and Downey photograph shows the artist in a more comfortable pose. Seated on a chair her hands are clasped to the side of her body, her head is again turned to look into the distance. In all of these photographs, the nose is stronger and the lips are fuller than Elizabeth's 1868 self-portrait in oil (Figure 10). As Patrizia Di Bello notes of the Fradelle & Marshall photographs, there is nothing to suggest that the subject is an artist, although a 'stick poking from the bottom of the frame might be a paintbrush'.[34] The poet Edward Fitzgerald went to the Royal Academy in July 1874 and describes how he could not see Elizabeth's picture 'for a three deep file of worshippers before it' but the artist's photo left a 'favourable impression of her' as it 'really looks, in face and dress, like some of Sir Joshua [Reynold's] Women'.[35] Di Bello underlines the dilemma facing Elizabeth as a professional artist: 'Photographs could elevate any beautiful woman to the status of celebrity in the absence of any actual achievement. Conversely, for a handsome-looking woman, becoming a *carte* celebrity could threaten to erase actual achievement and reduce her to the status of "Professional Beauty", as people looking at her photographs would not ask themselves whether she is selling her work or herself'.[36]

9 Elizabeth Thompson [1874], b/w photo. Fradelle & Marshall. Watts Gallery, Compton, Surrey. Bridgeman Art Library.

Elizabeth was in demand. She had been introduced to Florence Nightingale's sister, Parthenope, at the Private View on 1 May and records how she asked if there was 'any possibility of my "most kindly" letting the picture' be taken to Nightingale's bedside.[37] Indeed, Nightingale maintained an interest in Elizabeth's career. In June 1879, she records how she was awaiting the engraving of Elizabeth's 'picture of the Charge of the Light Brigade' (*Balaclava*) so she could purchase it to send to the Balaclava Commemoration Society.[38] On 14 May Elizabeth recalls how she lunched with Lady Raglan, where she met Kinglake. '[W]e talked Crimea. I had read and re-read his much too prolix history, which I thought overburdened with detail but I had learnt much that was of utmost value'. General Hope Grant, who had made his military name in India during the 1857 Rebellion and who was also the brother of the President of the Royal Academy, Francis Grant, invited her to Aldershot the next day, where Elizabeth benefited from a 'sham fight' and had 'two charges of cavalry' put on specially for her but 'what with the dust storms half swallowing them up in dense dun-coloured sheets' and her eyes full of sand she could hardly see them, although she 'made the most of the situation' and 'got some good hints'.[39] She stood beside Grant's charger when the cavalry marched past the saluting base: 'I felt extraordinarily situated, standing there, half liking and half not liking the situation, with an enormous mounted staff of utterly unknown, gorgeous officers curvetting and jingling behind me and the general'. On 20 May Elizabeth was at Woolwich with Lady Elizabeth Herbert, the writer and friend of Florence Nightingale. The Czar of Russia, Alexander II, was here during his visit to Britain. 'The artillery manoeuvres were effective, and I sketched as much as I could'.[40] The press reported the visit and Elizabeth's presence at Woolwich alongside royalty: 'Miss Elizabeth Thompson, of *Roll Call* celebrity, sketched the scene from a carriage'.[41]

Elizabeth's painting provoked some controversy with regard to her horse's legs. When a letter to *The Times* criticized the legs, Elizabeth launched a robust defence on 12 May:

> Some well-meaning but mistaken individual has thought it his duty to write me an anonymous letter, pointing out what he considers an error in the position of the horse's legs in my picture of the *Roll Call.* He, in common with all people who have not observed the horse's walk for themselves, supposes that a horse moves his legs in the walk exactly in the same sequence as he does in the trot.

10 *Elizabeth Southerden (neé Thompson), Lady Butler,* 1869. Oil and pencil on card, 21.9 × 11.8cm. National Portrait Gallery.

This, she counters, is a 'vulgar error' and advised those interested in the matter to consult '"Stonehenge" in his admirable book on the horse'. Furthermore Elizabeth reveals her attention to French military art: 'In Meissonier's picture of the Retreat from Leipsic, entitled *1814*, the horses of Napoleon and his Staff afford a splendid illustration of the real, and not the conventional, rendering of this pace. In the trot, the near fore leg and the off hind leg are brought forward simultaneously, and *vice versa*; it is not so in the walk'.[42] She recalls that she had spent many hours moving alongside horses to see 'exactly how a horse puts his feet down in the walk! I told many people to go down on all fours themselves and walk, noting the sequence with their own hands and knees'.[43] When the controversy failed to abate Elizabeth declared in *The Times* on 16 May that she had 'no intention of carrying on a public controversy on the subject of horse action'.[44] An article in the *Daily News* came to the defence of artists: 'A little of this correction of details by experts may be tolerable and instructive to artists, if not to the public; but it might degenerate in the end into sending a milliner to pronounce on a Millais, and in accepting from a coastguard advice upon "seascapes"'.[45]

Meanwhile Elizabeth's sketches at Aldershot and Woolwich were developed and exhibited as pen and ink sketches at the Dudley Gallery's black and white exhibition in July entitled *'Halt!' A Reminiscence of Aldershot* and *Gallop: A Reminiscence of Woolwich. The Graphic* praised *'Halt!'* for demonstrating her 'mastery over the delineation of horses in rapid motion' and the 'wonderful amount of life and spirit about the officer who is giving the word of command and the bugler who is sounding the signal, and then when we look behind on the troop of Centaurs tearing along and raising clouds of dust we perceive that at the sound of these few brazen notes, they

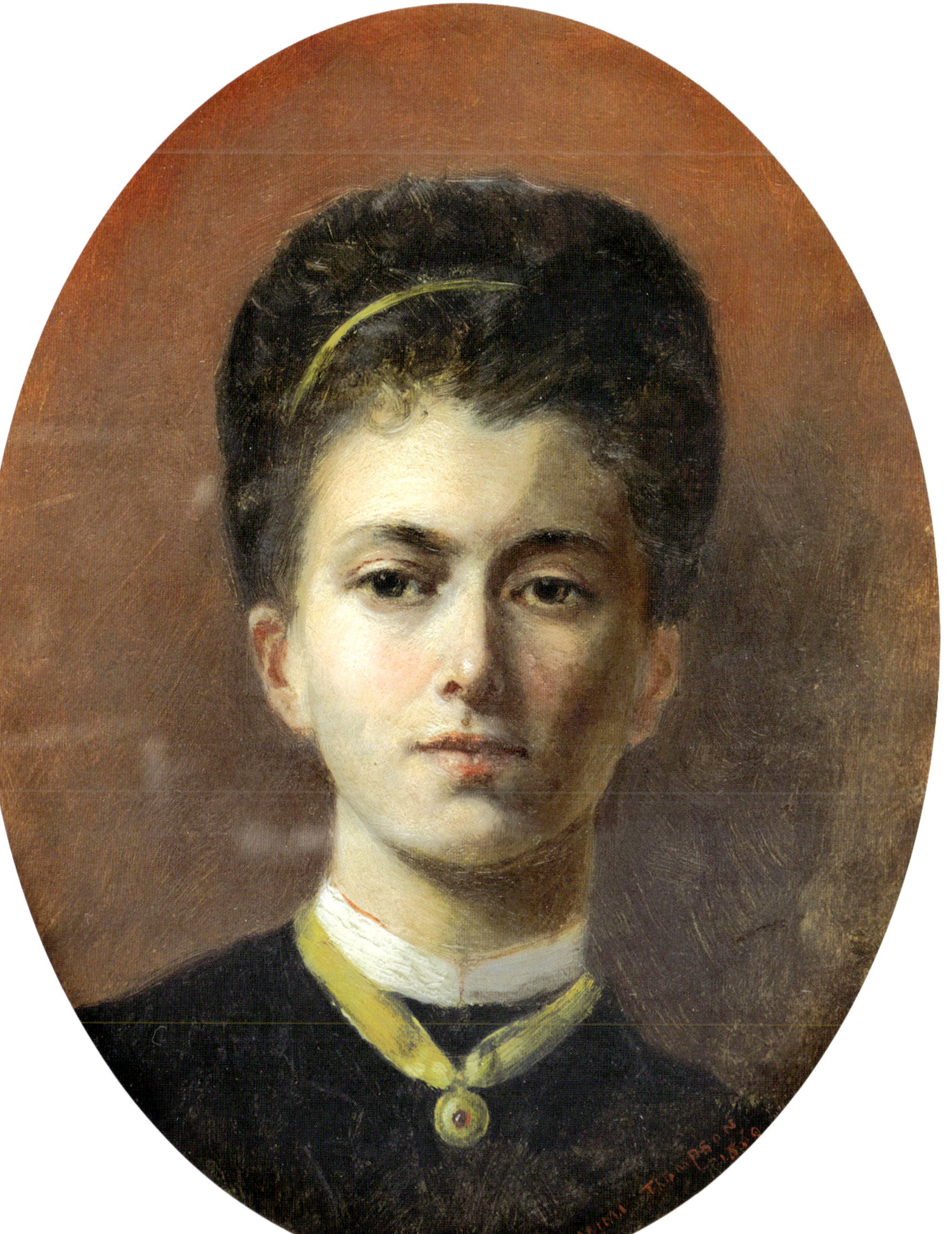

will presently be as motionless as statues'.[46] The *Illustrated London News* praised the 'power of drawing the horse in full action, together with a spirit and a vigour, that for a lady's work is most extraordinary' but there is a 'tendency to clever exaggeration which we do not find in the Academy picture'.[47] Later that year she exhibited *Choosing Models at Rome* at the same exhibition and *'Charge!' A Reminiscence of the Life Guards at Wimbledon* (a water-colour) was exhibited by the New Watercolour Society (to which she was elected membership) alongside *A 10th Bengal Lancer Tent-Pegging*. *The Graphic* alluded to this painting by Elizabeth when it described the game of tent-pegging in ancient Asia. A cavalry sport akin to polo, *The Graphic* describes how 'an ordinary tent-peg is driven firmly into the ground, and the aim of each competitor is to withdraw it at the point of his lance as he gallops past at full speed'. The exercise hones the skills of the cavalry soldier by 'furnishing the means of acquiring considerable physical skill' and 'an additional means of relieving the dreary monotony which too frequently forms one of the most discouraging features of British garrison life'.[48]

Quatre Bras

Despite the social whirl that surrounded her in the summer of 1874 Elizabeth was busy preparing her next Academy painting, *The 28th Regiment at Quatre Bras* (Figure 11). The painting was for Galloway but Elizabeth had no intention of selling this work as cheaply as *The Roll Call* – 'I could not paint it for that little £126 – so very puny now!' Galloway finally agreed to Elizabeth's price of £1,126 (broadly equivalent to £70,500 today).[49] As the negotiations with Galloway took some time, Elizabeth started work on another canvas, a French theme, *The Dawn of Sedan*. For the grey horses in the painting, Elizabeth made oil studies and the General Omnibus Company in London sent her 'all shades of grey *perchons* for this purpose'.[50] She also made 'life-size oil studies of the hands for *Quatre Bras*, where hands were to be very strong points, gripping "Brown Besses".' Although clearly a very able negotiator she observes that she had 'wise business heads to grapple with the business part of my work'.[51]

Elizabeth's support for the army was reciprocated by the army's attention to her work. For *Quatre Bras* she was taken to Chatham by a Colonel Browne 'where some 300 men of the Royal Engineers were awaiting us on the "lines"'. They were in 'full dress and knapsacks' as Elizabeth 'desired'. What Elizabeth required for this Waterloo painting was soldiers who could form 'the old-fashioned four-feet square', a defensive position.[52] It is extraordinary to consider Elizabeth's standing with the army. She could 'command' soldiers at a time when women of her class were consigned to the home. Her rise to this position with the army was also swift as this was, after all, only

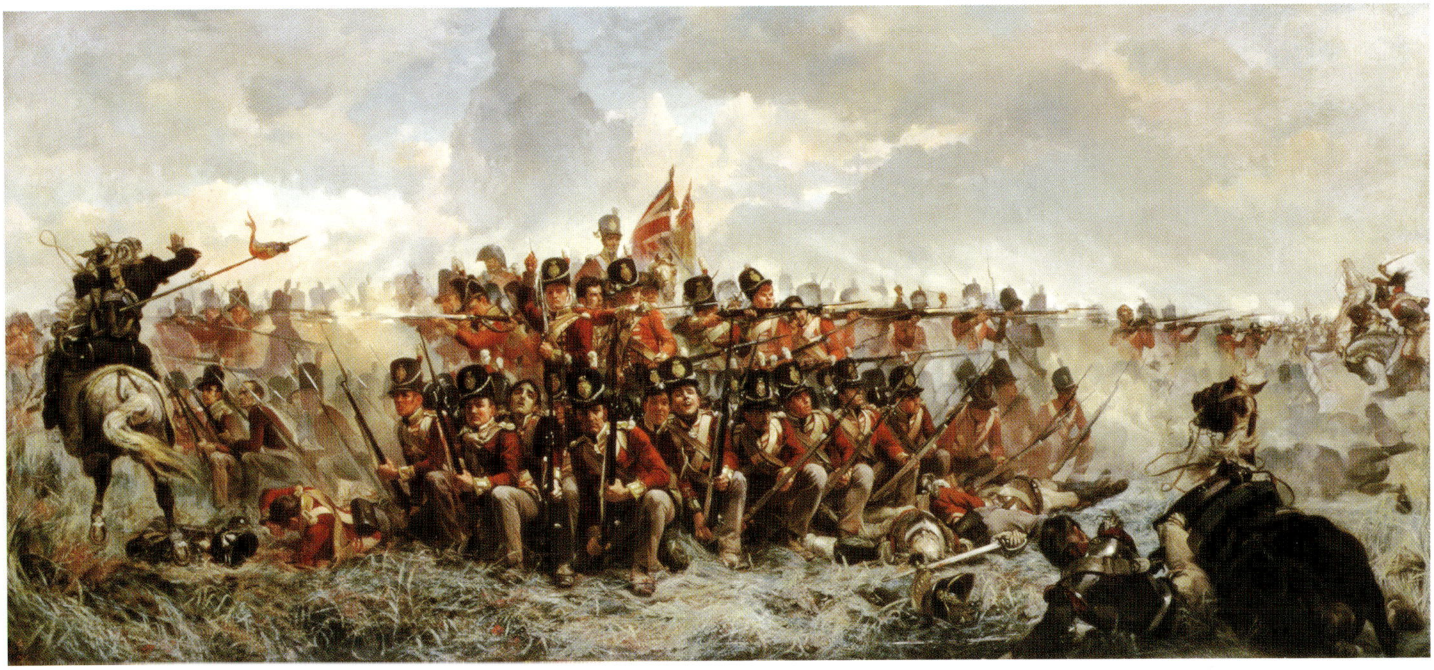

11 *The 28th Regiment at Quatre Bras*, 1875. Oil on canvas, 97.2 x 216.2cm. National Gallery of Victoria, Melbourne. Bridgeman Art Library.

her second war painting. For the purposes of her art, Elizabeth had the soldiers fire in 'sections' but the wind was so strong that the effect she was trying to achieve for her painting – 'masses of men seen through smoke' – could not be achieved. Afterwards the men were drawn into a line so she could choose ones without beards as models for her painting and the 'sergeant took down the name of each man as [she] pointed him out very unobtrusively'. After that she went to the guardroom where each of the men was brought in so Elizabeth could jot down their 'personal peculiarities'. Of the 300 paraded before her she eventually chose eight as models, although she had to dispense with three who were perceived as 'bad characters'.[53] The men were then quartered at Brompton near to Elizabeth's studio in The Avenue for her use. The army went to considerable lengths to accommodate her and she rewarded the army by presenting a modern vision of soldiers at war.

On 16 July Christiana and Elizabeth went to Henley-on-Thames to find a rye field for the painting. Eventually they found a piece that was uncut and purchased it from the farmer and then trampled it with the help of some local children. Finding that she had left her oil brushes behind in the chaise, 'Mamma went frantically to work with two slimy water-colour brushes to get down tints whilst I drew down forms in pencil'. Mother and daughter laughed that they were 'two regular "Pre-Raphaelite Brethren", to all appearances, bending over a patch of trampled rye'.

Her attention to detail is reflected in her discovery that she had missed a 'vital point'. She had her men in the 'front rank sitting on their heels in the kneeling position' contrary to the instructions in the drill-book.[54] Colonel Browne, on seeing it, shook his head and a sergeant-major was summoned from Chatham to advise: 'He showed me the exact position when at the "ready" to receive cavalry'. Elizabeth notes how she 'dread[ed] to think what blunders' she might have 'committed' and although '[n]o civilian would have detected them ... the military would have been down upon' her. She felt 'rather fettered' at having to observe such strict rules but confided in an artist colleague that 'she wished to show what an English square look[ed] like viewed quite close at the end of two hours' action, when about to receive a last charge'. As a woman, witnessing actual combat was denied her, but she invoked her imagination:

> I seem to have seen it – the hot, blackened faces, the set teeth or gasping mouths, the blood shot eyes and the mocking laughter, the stern, cool, calculating look here and there; the unimpressionable, dogged stare![55]

Instruction for the artist continued at Chatham where the sergeant-major showed her how to load the Brown Bess rifle (long since decommissioned). Meanwhile Galloway, who was promised this painting for having relinquished *The Roll Call* to the Queen, sold its copyright to the engravers Dickenson for £2,000 (approximately £125,218 today).[56] Galloway made a lot of money out of it. '[The engravers] must have faith', Elizabeth notes, 'in my doing it well'. Elizabeth also received at her studio a token of admiration from the Queen – 'a splendid bracelet set with pearls and a large emerald'.[57] At home in Ventnor for a holiday she studied Napier's six-volume *Peninsular War*. By September she was ready to tackle the canvas when the sergeant-major and Colonel Browne arrived. Browne had the Waterloo uniform made for her at the Government clothing factory. Elizabeth describes the event as a dress rehearsal, testimony to how much her paintings were theatrical, capturing a particular moment in a story. Her models included guardsmen, engineers and policemen. She required men without moustaches for which policemen were suitable but she found it hard to find a head 'suitable for the Waterloo time'. In November, she went to Sanger's Circus where two horses were put 'floundering on the ground, and rearing'.[58] These were the first of many horses that were 'put down' for her over the coming months so she could study them for the foreground horses of her painting.[59] In early December she had a short break in Paris with her father where she visited the studios of leading artists: Bonnat and Gerôme, Detaille and Henriette Browne. Meeting Gerôme she describes as 'an epoch' in her life.[60] When she returned her eye had been 'much sharpened, and very severe was that organ as it rested on my *Quatre Bras* for the first time since a fortnight ago'.[61] Because of the London fogs she had to start work at 9.30am and worked until late, taking pride in the fact that hers was the first morning fire to be lit in all The Avenue. On 23 March the sculptor Edgar Boehm advised her on how to complete her 'bounding horse'. She was visited by Galloway who, delighted with the painting, gave her £500 (about £32,000 today) on account and by the Duke of Cambridge who scrutinized her soldiers in the square.[62] By Studio Monday, when she opened to the public, Elizabeth's studio was thronged but the most interesting of the guests was Millais who focused on 'the drawing, character and expression'. His wife later told Elizabeth that Millais considered her 'an even stronger artist than Rosa Bonheur' although Elizabeth again distanced herself from a comparison with the French artist: 'I *may* be equal to Rosa Bonheur in power, but how widely apart lie our courses!'[63] When Millais died in August 1896 Elizabeth described him as the 'kind, enthusiastic friend' of her 'early days' and she recalled his 'hearty encouragement and praise'.[64]

On Varnishing Day, however, Elizabeth, to her great disappointment, discovered that her painting was displayed in the Lecture Room, which she describes as the 'Black Hole', where the light was poor as the room was never intended for pictures. She observed that Christiana would 'never forgive the R.A'.s for the Black Hole'.[65] Despite being in what was an unenviable location, the painting was crowded. Paul Usherwood considers that the location might have been a response from the notoriously conservative Academicians to Elizabeth's rise to fame. Although fêted the previous year and receiving commendations for her *Quatre Bras*, the Academicians might have feared that too much attention to a female artist might open the doors to other women.[66] Although an 'outsider' Elizabeth was invited to the private view, accompanied by her father. 'They make', she wrote in her diary, 'a pet of me at the

Academy'. There were, however, 'fewer great guns, and I was not torn to pieces to be introduced, here, there, and everywhere, most people being the same as last year and knowing me already'.[67] Another indicator of how the Academicians were distancing themselves from a female painter triumphing in their domain can be seen in Elizabeth's remarks that on opening day the painting had no policeman to protect it although it was so crowded with 'jammed people numbered in dozens' which rendered it 'invisible'. Viewers 'clashed in front of the canvas and, in struggling to wriggle out, lunged right against it'.[68]

Whereas *The Roll Call* captured the aftermath of conflict, *Quatre Bras* was a painting of action that captured an historical incident two days before the Battle of Waterloo when the 28th Regiment, outnumbered by the French, formed a defensive square outside Charleroi. The focus of the picture is on the square, as the men, similar to the figures in *The Roll Call*, exhibit varied emotions as they encounter the French light infantry. They look out towards the oncoming cavalry and towards the spectator. The square holds, although some in its ranks have fallen. In the front two ranks, the soldiers are on their heels in the military position with guns loaded and waiting for the command to fire – this was the position that Elizabeth initially struggled with before she was corrected by the drill book and sergeant-major. One dying soldier clutches his hand around his comrade's breast as his bloodied head collapses backward. His comrade faces forward with an implacable look, his gun propped and waiting for the command to fire. Another has fallen forward from this front line onto the rye on the painting's left. On the right, the bodies of two French soldiers are dead on the rye, with a British soldier dead between them. Various emotions appear on the faces of the men who vary from grim-faced hardened veterans to boys. The central figure in this front row is a mere boy, with an expression of laughter, or more likely hysteria, on his face, as he responds to a smiling youth behind him (Figure 12). The second row is in different stages of firing at the oncoming cavalry and the figures in the painting beyond and around them are shrouded in the smoke and dust of the battlefield. The third rank are in various stages of shooting and behind them are the officers with the colonel mounted on a charger. A bare-headed officer in an excited state points with his sword at some oncoming danger.

12 Detail from *The 28th Regiment at Quatre Bras.*

The horses, over which Elizabeth spent much time, appear in the picture's foreground. To the left a charging white horse carries a French soldier, with a spear out of his back and to the right of the painting, a horse has tumbled to the ground dismounting its rider. Through the mist on the right, another horse has tumbled to the ground while two other horses with their mounted riders are forced into the square – one with its head reared as its rider grasps its neck to prevent him from falling and the other with its head bowed against the onslaught of bullets. Elizabeth observed how in preparation for her picture the riding master of the Horse Guards had strapped a horse's foreleg in order to help her create the fallen horses in her

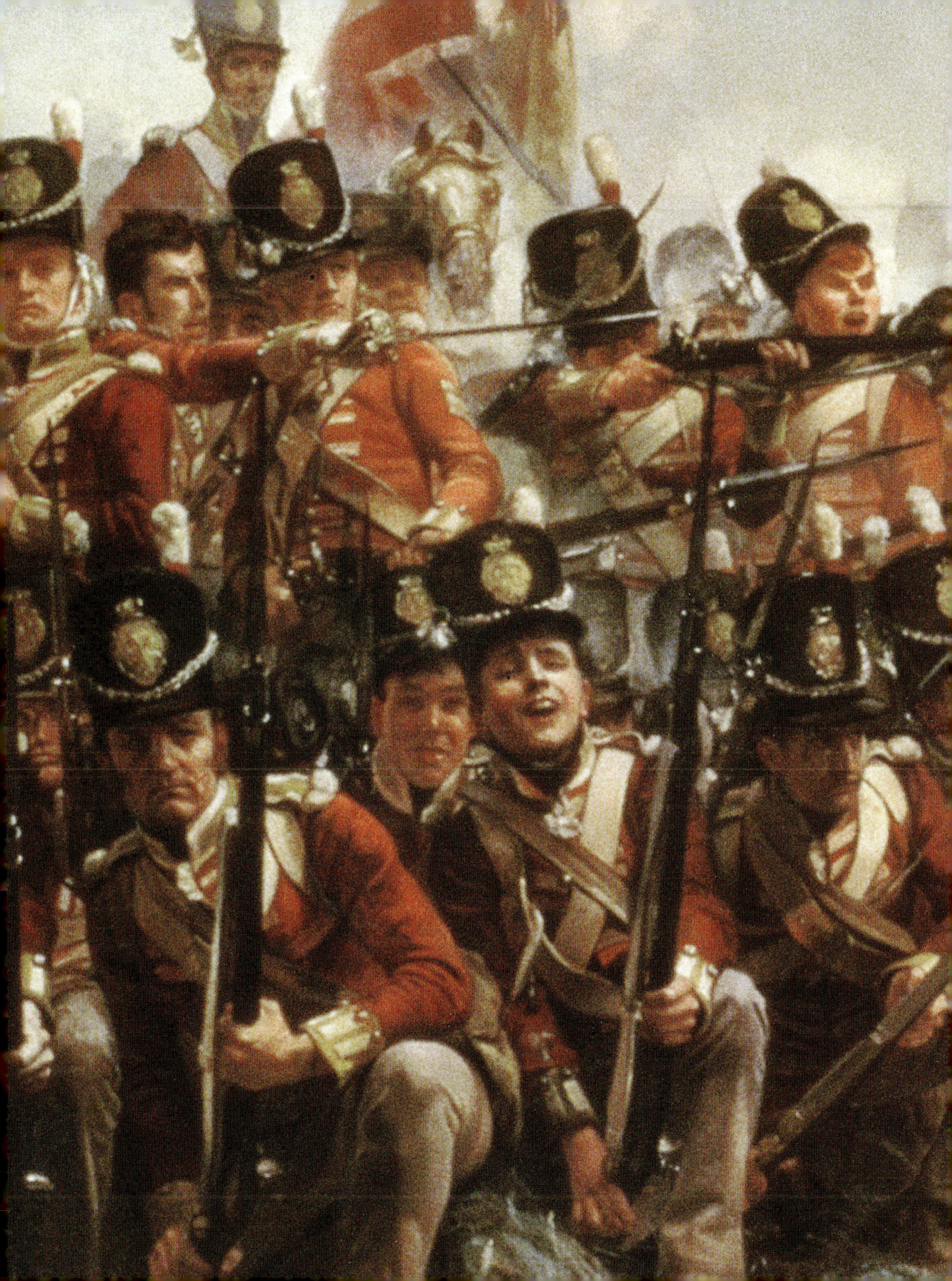

painting: 'What a commotion before he fell! How he plunged and snorted in clouds of dust till the final plunge' causing her to consider 'what it must be like for a horse wounded in battle'.[69] Like Elizabeth's previous Academy painting, the heroes, as Claire Bowen points out, 'are the troops' and 'the strategy is based on the painter's desire to record the dismembering nature of war and, in so doing, to encourage the spectator to re-member and to value its victim practitioners' – humans as well as horses.[70] Although the pathos of war is figured in the dying soldier, this painting, capturing the moment of combat, lacks *The Roll Call*'s attention to the traumatic effects of war and is less in tune with modern or, indeed, Victorian sensibilities. What Elizabeth is asserting here instead is her ability to depict actual military action – a point recognized by the *Birmingham Post* which points out the 'masculine force and freedom' of execution which was not 'observable in *The Roll Call*'.[71] Elizabeth was very clearly asserting her desire to compete in a man's world of art and in the traditionally male domain of military painting.

On 1 May *The Times* produced its notice of the Royal Academy exhibition and Elizabeth's painting received top billing. *The Times* declared that an opportune moment had arisen to 'strengthen the hands of those who plead for a liberal enlargement of the pale of Associateship' and that 'it will probably be about the second picture of an outsider, Miss Elizabeth Thompson, the painter of the unprecedentedly successful *Roll-Call* that most curiosity will be felt out of doors'. *Quatre Bras*, it notes, showed 'no falling off in power'. Elizabeth, it confirms, 'hit on a fashion of her own in thus recording the influences of what some have called the rage, some the joy, of battle upon individual character'. The review raised some objection to the colouring and that the uniforms and men's faces were too clean, but praised its 'uncommon qualities of power, determination, and originality of conception'. It was, however, deemed 'too remote to appeal to popular sympathy' like *The Roll Call*.[72] The painting's elaborate frame in gold gilt is inscribed with the campaigns and battles of the regiment embedded in myrtle leaves. An Egyptian sphinx underneath the word Egypt is featured in the middle of the frame. The ornate frame draws this particular moment of battle into the wider dimensions of war and demonstrates how the artist balances patriotism with sympathy for the plight of the individual in war and concern about war in general. Elizabeth maintained this balancing act throughout her career.

On 8 May *The Graphic* featured Elizabeth on its front cover (Figure 13). The artist posed in a manner similar to her own self-portrait. Positioned to the side, her head is tilted forward and she looks directly at the viewer. There is no doubt here as to her profession as her left hand holds a sketchbook and her right is in the process of sketching the background to a mounted dragoon. The magazine describes her as having worked 'very steadily and conscientiously in her vocation as an artist'.[73] By the end of the year, Elizabeth achieved praise from Ruskin. Although he had seen her earlier work at home, Ruskin proclaimed that he had approached '[*Quatre Bras*] with "iniquitous prejudice" as being the work of a woman'. Elizabeth observes: 'He had

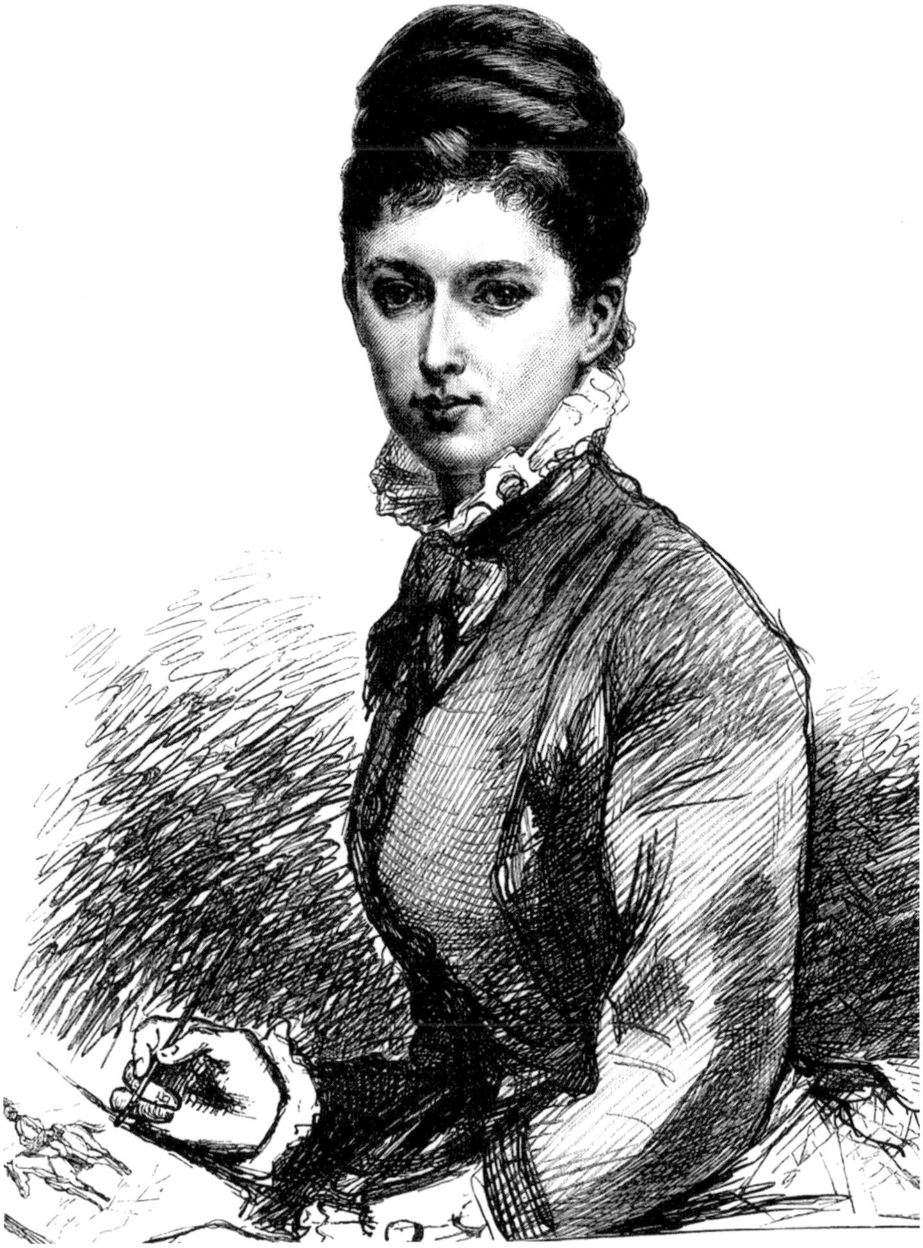

13 'Elizabeth Thompson' from *The Graphic*, 8 May 1874.

always held that no woman could paint, and he accounted for my work being what he found it as being that of an Amazon. I was very pleased to see myself in the character of an Amazon'.[74] Although, as Germaine Greer points out, Elizabeth was 'clearly influenced by the school of Meissonier', Ruskin compared her to the Pre-Raphaelites. The association was a mark of his 'appreciation of her technical skill'.[75]

In the summer of 1875 Elizabeth and Alice visited Florence and stayed with Janet Ross. Ross was the daughter of the Egyptian traveller, Lucie Duff Gordon, whose *Letters from Egypt*, where she had lived for several years in order to prolong her

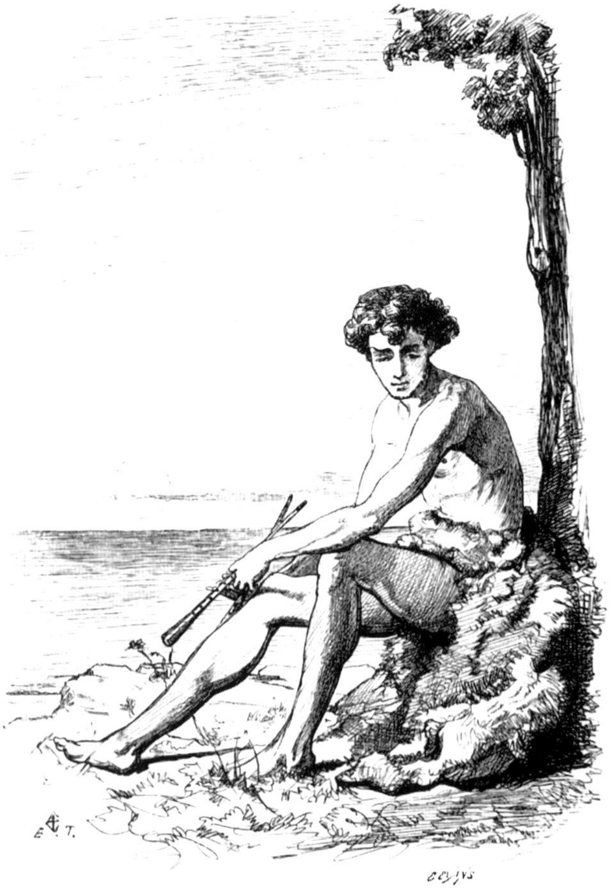

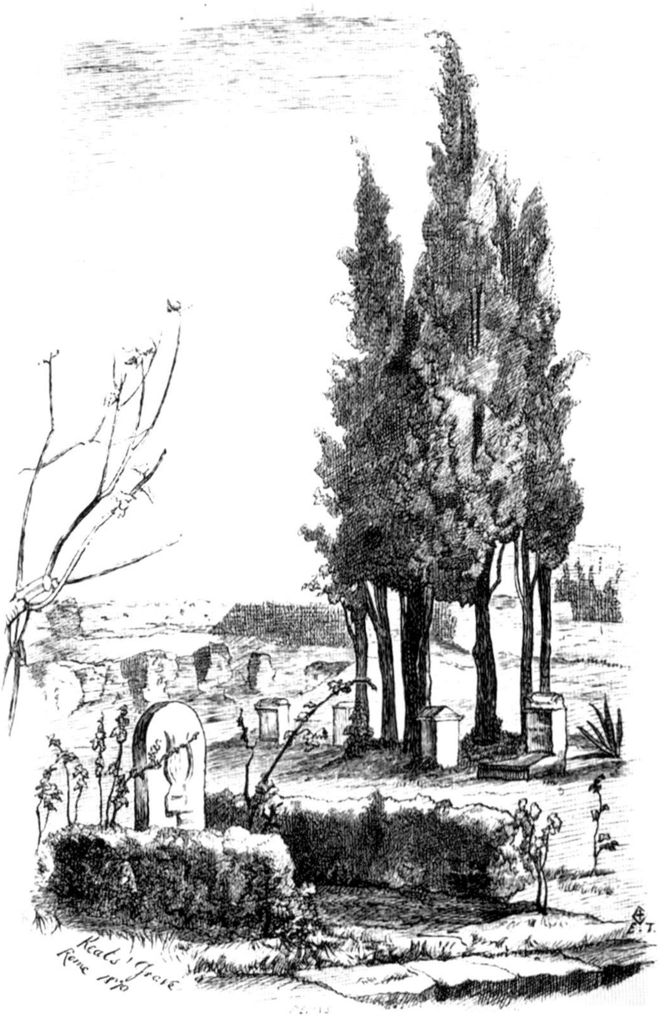

14 (*above left*) Frontispiece from *Preludes* by Alice Thompson (1875).

15 'Keats' Grave' from *Preludes* by Alice Thompson (1875).

life after contracting tuberculosis, made her famous in the 1860s. Ross maintained a literary and artistic salon in her villa Castagnolo outside Florence. Elizabeth describes how the 'fascination of the Castagnolo was intense'. The trip coincided with celebrations to mark the 400th anniversary of Michelangelo's birth. Elizabeth 'sketched hard every day in the garden, the vineyards, and the old courtyard where the most picturesque vintage incidents occurred, with the white oxen, the wine pressing, and the bare-legged merry *contadini*, all in an atmosphere scented with the fermented grapes'. These sketches in Italy were used to illustrate Alice's first volume of poetry, *Preludes*, which was published in 1875 (see Figures 14 and 15).

Duty, however, recalled her to England, via Genoa, where the sisters visited Fanny. By 19 October she had started *Balaclava*, the second, and most dramatic, of her Crimean paintings. She observes in her autobiography: 'My trip to Italy, and the glorious and happy and healthy life I have led there, and the utter change of scene and occupation, have done me priceless good, and at last I feel like going on at this picture *con amore*'.[76]

Balaclava

For this painting, whose full title was *Balaclava. On the Causeway Heights. After the Charge of the Light Brigade, October 25th 1854*, Elizabeth focused on survivors in the aftermath of the Charge of the Light Brigade – an emotive subject for a Victorian audience. The painting was not in time for the Academy and was exhibited instead by the Fine Art Society in Bond Street. She recalls at her private view on 20 April 1876 that it was 'disappointing' to her. 'In vain I call to mind all the things that judges of art have said about this being the best thing I have yet painted. Can one never be happy when the work is done?' Elizabeth was incorrect in her assessment of this painting. It was, and remains, a striking piece. The painting's impact on its contemporary audience is noted by Elizabeth: 'Virginia Gabriel, the composer, was

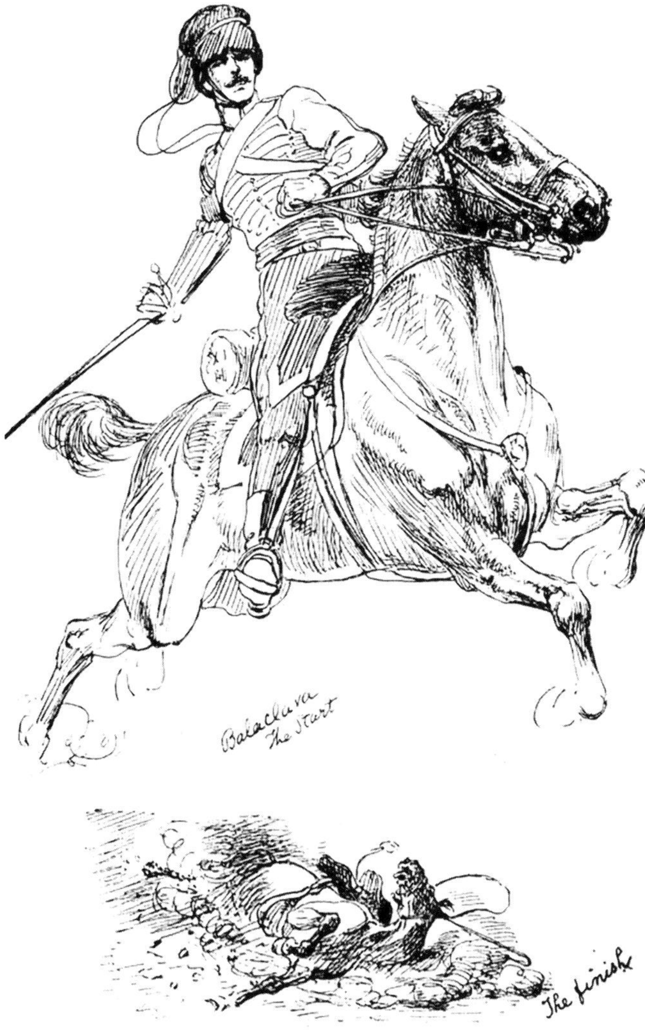

16 'Start' and 'Finish' of the Charge from Elizabeth Butler, *Autobiography*.

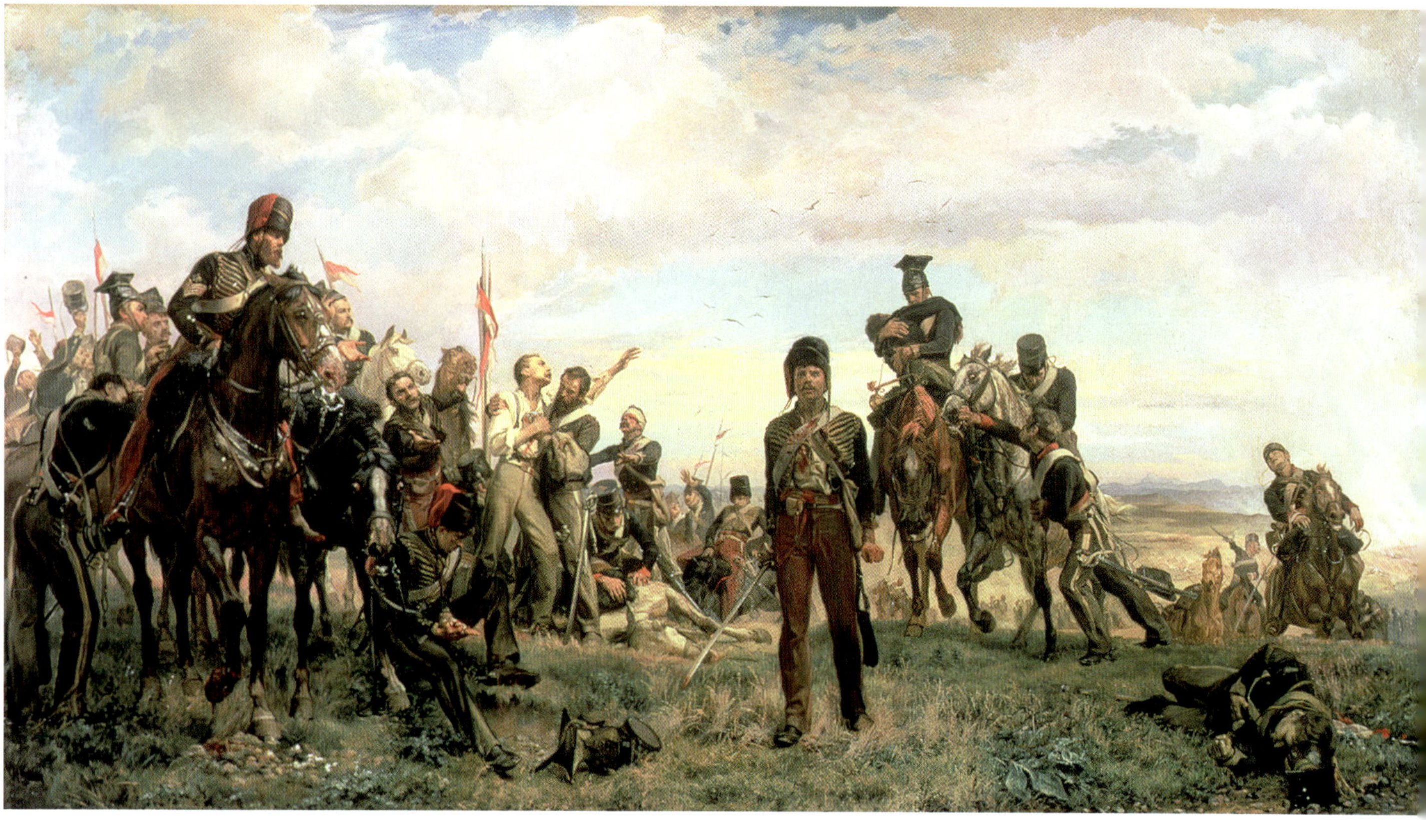

17 *Balaclava*, 1876. Oil on canvas, 103.4 x 187.5cm. Manchester Art Gallery. Bridgeman Art Library.

led out of the room by her husband in tears!'[77] Deeply affecting to the viewer, *Balaclava* has a melodramatic quality. A theatrical effect is created by the central figure of the composition, a survivor of the Charge, W. H. Pennington, who changed career from soldiery to acting after the Crimea. When he posed for the painting Pennington was manager of Sadler's Wells Theatre in London and was admired by Gladstone, particularly for his role as Hamlet. In the painting Pennington projects a sense of remoteness – he is a figure separated from his comrades both psychologically and physically.

The scene features the remnants of the Light Brigade as they gather on the Causeway Heights after their charge through the Valley of Death (see Figure 16 for the 'start' and 'finish' of the Charge). It is, as the *Nottinghamshire Guardian* notes, 'a strangely miscellaneous gathering, including troopers from all of the regiments on active service'. The review praises how Elizabeth adhered to accuracy in the detail of her uniforms: the Lancers of the Seventeenth are presented in their '"hour-glass" shakos, and with crimson and white pennons to their spears' while the 4th and 13th Light Dragoons have jackets of red and yellow facings respectively. The painting (Figure 17) is both a 'powerful and pathetic representation of the actualities of warfare' and 'a rigidly faithful transcript of an aspect of the British army', which was even by 1876 relegated to the past.[78]

The central and isolated figure of the group, modelled by Pennington, is a traumatized Hussar, grasping his bloodied sword in his right hand and his left hand clenched into a fist. Staring out with widened eyes into the distance, he looks beyond the spectator (Figure 18). The *Daily Telegraph* describes this figure as

> a dismounted trooper of the 11th Hussars, who, wounded, gory and dust-stained, has wandered out of the rout, and looks literally as though, like the man in the Book of Job, he has escaped 'with the skin of his teeth'. He is so dazed and bewildered, so utterly 'disorganized', as Americans might say, by the awful ordeal through which he has just passed, that he stalks onward in a kind of trance or coma, as one distraught, or one who has just been appalled by some hideous apparition, or as one walking in his sleep, clutching convulsively, yet, it would seem, unconsciously, his blood-stained battle-blade.

Pennington becomes Hamlet-like and his character gives 'not only technical but literary coherence to the composition' as his comrades seem to be 'expostulating with their "dis-organized" comrade, and striving to recall him to himself'.[79] The *Morning Post* perceives the hussar as 'demented'. Physically unwounded in the charge, his 'mind is gone'.[80] The mounted hussar expostulating with Pennington was modelled on Sergeant George Loy Smith, another survivor of the Charge. In his memoir Loy Smith records the events of the Charge:

As we moved off, the Russians opened fire from all their batteries. The round shot passed through us and the shells burst over amongst us, causing great havoc. The first man of my troop that was struck was Private Young, a cannon ball taking off his right arm. I, being close on his right rear, fancied I felt the wind from it as it passed me. I afterwards found I was bespattered with his flesh … We now came under terrific fire, for the [Russian] infantry … kept up a continual fuselage as we came opposite them, but the men hung well together, keeping their line and closing in as their comrades fell back wounded or killed. Many riderless horses were now galloping along with us, forcing their way into the ranks and keeping their places as well as though their masters had been on their backs.

On his return, Loy Smith describes his reactions after being greeted by the orderly room clerk:

I told him I had lost my horse and how fearfully the regiment had been cut up. He then said: 'What is this on your busby and jacket?' On picking it off, I found it to be small pieces of flesh that had flown over me when Private Young's arm was shot off.

I now sat down and the feelings that came over me are not easy to describe. I was moved to tears when I thought of the havoc I had witnessed, and that I had lost my beautiful horse. She was a light bay, nearly thoroughbred; I became her master three years before.[81]

18 Detail from *Balaclava.*

Below the mounted hussar (Loy Smith) is a traumatized young soldier seated on the ground concentrating on his wounded hand – the focus providing a psychological shield to the contemplation of greater horrors. To the viewer's left a black horse conveys fear in his eyes. Indeed, the horses' varied expressions – terror, exhaustion, astonishment – mirror the soldiers' experiences. The *Morning Post* review focused on the horses. One horse carrying an unconscious trooper has 'dilated nostrils' and his 'strange expression of eyes, and wild action bespeak his terror'. Another dragoon leads a 'fine grey charger, footsore and exhausted' to the crest – the horse, the review suggests, would not have reached safety but for the soldier who came to his assistance.[82]

In another grouping, a soldier stanches the wound on his comrade's chest. Grasping him into his shoulder he is intent on the immediate situation while the injured soldier reaches over his helper's body with his hand reaching towards another scene of pathos in which a young trumpeter is clasped like a baby in the arms of his mounted officer. The officer's large hands covering the boy's back convey the youth of this trumpeter and his bugle hangs off his back to rest on the chestnut horse. The horse with its downcast face seems to register the tragedy of this particular moment.

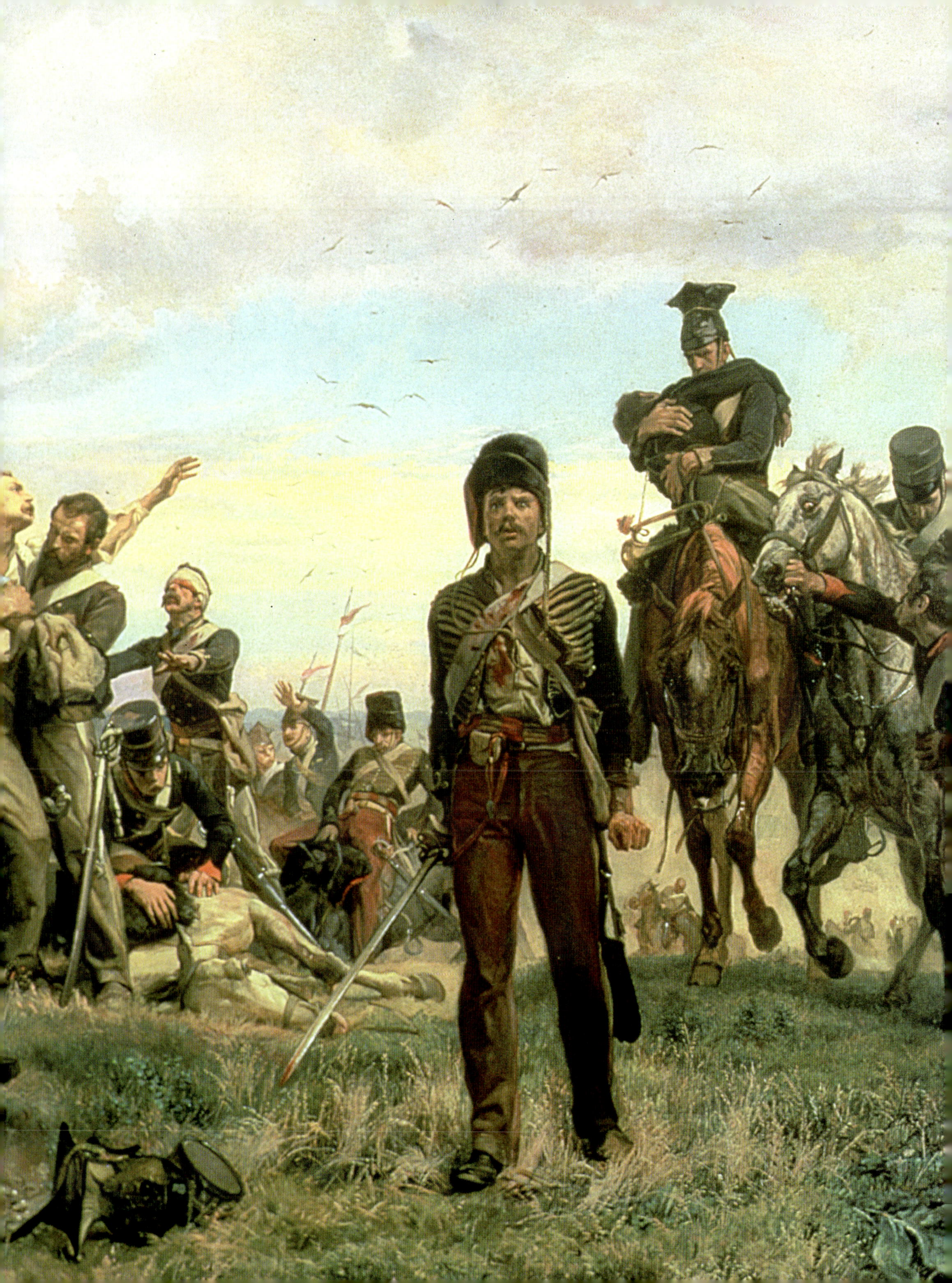

In the right facing the viewer is a lancer lying wounded on the ground with the grey pallor of death. In his dying moments, he has clutched at some grass which is held tightly in his fist. In the centre of the painting, to the background, a trooper with bandages over his eyes reaches out to find his way. Warfare in this painting is rendered 'wretched, squalid, deplorable' and we are behind the 'scenes of the theatre' which shows war as a 'bloodthirsty brawl', of 'mutilation, blood, ruin, agony and death'.[83] The *Morning Post* praised the painting as Elizabeth's 'best work' to date and described it as a 'poem in colours, not undeserving of equal rank with the Laureate's famous ode'.[84] Elizabeth recalls how an officer who had been through the charge had declared that he would never have come to see the painting if he had known 'how like the real thing it was'.[85] The *Sporting Gazette* agreed that it was Elizabeth's best work and describes Pennington, '[t]his graphic and ghastly single figure in the central group', as 'a worthy and marvellous centre of a great picture'. Furthermore, the 'expression of the sergeant calling out to his entranced and half-crazed comrade, that of the non-commissioned officer carrying the dead trumpeter, and that of the seated soldier to the right, who is half sulkily, half ruefully, looking at his shattered hand, are admirable; and in conception, in drawing, and in execution the central figure is absolutely perfect'.[86]

Meanwhile, during the summer season Christiana had 'at homes' on Wednesday afternoons in Kensington. Here Ruskin visited and seemed to agree with Christiana on 'many subjects' and Elizabeth recalls she remembered 'seeing him gently clapping his hands at many points she made'. W.P. Frith warned Elizabeth at one of these gatherings that she must send a painting to the Academy in order not to lose her chance of election as an Academician.[87] On 18 May she returned to her studio to begin work on *Inkerman*. However, she enjoyed the Lord Mayor's Banquet to the Representatives at the Mansion House on 10 June where she conversed with the painter Marcus Stone and discovered that when she 'tried it' she 'could talk pretty well'.[88] She danced with George du Maurier and John Tenniel of *Punch*. She recalls at one of these social occasions she created a *tableau vivant* of the scene in *Balaclava* of the 'dazed' hussar. Pennington irritated her by thwarting her directions. In the picture she had his busby pushed back but the actor had other ideas for when she looked away, he 'rammed it down at the becoming "smart" angle'. The episode provides an insight into Elizabeth's forthright character: 'The wretch pretended to obey, but, just before the curtain rose, rammed the busby down again, and utterly destroyed the meaning of that figure. We didn't want a representation of Mr So-and-So in the becoming uniform of a hussar, but my battered trooper'.[89] The painter and the actor were in conflict. Later that summer a visit to Tennyson failed to inspire Elizabeth who found the poet's behaviour odd as he attempted, without success on Elizabeth's part, to cultivate awe in his guests, making some 'commonplace remarks' about Elizabeth's paintings and criticizing her modern dress for being too tight.[90]

Life was changing for the family. Alice met her future husband, Wilfrid Meynell, after he was attracted to one of her sonnets. He became a frequent guest at the

Thompson's at homes. Although having the support of the Catholic clergy, Meynell had no money and Thomas initially opposed the union. 'The *only* difficulty seems to be a financial one', Alice wrote to Wilfrid. However, 'Mimi today suggested the very thing ... a magazine to which she could contribute – not continually but often enough to make her drawings its speciality. I think it would be a delightful employment for us both to edit and write for this magazine'.[91] There began the couple's life in journalism. They were married by the Bishop of Nottingham in the Church of the Servite Fathers in Fulham road on 16 April 1877 and moved into 11 Inkerman Terrace, next door to Alice's parents. The poet, Aubrey de Vere, although commending her choice of Wilfrid, warned her: 'Remember no other tie is to relax your first bond – your engagement to *Poetry*. Otherwise we Poets shall have to write Satires on Marriage'.[92] Journalism, however, intervened and poetry was put aside for over a decade.

The Return from Inkerman

For her next painting of the Crimean campaign, *The Return from Inkerman*, Elizabeth used the South Downs near Worthing for the foreground and visited Aldershot and interviewed veterans whose accounts varied considerably (Figure 19). Her main source was Russell's description of the battle in *The Times*. The war reporter published his book in 1855. Having fixed the composition of the painting in sepia on tinted paper, she returned to Italy at the end of August with Alice, spending time in Portofino with the Consul Monty Brown, before continuing on to Janet Ross in Florence. In May she had been elected a Foreign Member of the Academy of Florence. Among the pleasures of Italy, Elizabeth managed to sketch an oak bush to use in the foreground of *Inkerman* and some water-colour sketches as well as a sketch of Janet Ross in Turkish dress. What eventually forced her return to London was the 'stern necessity' of *Inkerman*.[93] Again she missed the deadline for the Royal Academy and *The Return from Inkerman* was exhibited at the Fine Art Society in Bond Street, who purchased the painting for 3,000 guineas (approximately £200,000 today) in a deal negotiated by Elizabeth's father. When the picture left the studio she danced with Christiana, their ritual on these occasions.[94]

Inkerman, Elizabeth concedes, may have been 'too sad' for some viewers. She took as inspiration Wellington's words that there is 'nothing sadder than a victory, except a defeat'.[95] The painting portrays the straggling remnants of regiments returning from victory at Inkerman. The battle, a victorious one against the odds for the allied British and French forces, was fought on a dark, wet and foggy day and the weather conditions make the painting more solemn. Russell describes the 'fog and vapours of drifting rain' which were 'thick' as morning dawned on 5 November. Russell describes the battle in these conditions as 'a series of dreadful deeds of daring, of sanguinary hand-to-hand fights, of despairing rallies, of desperate assaults'.[96]

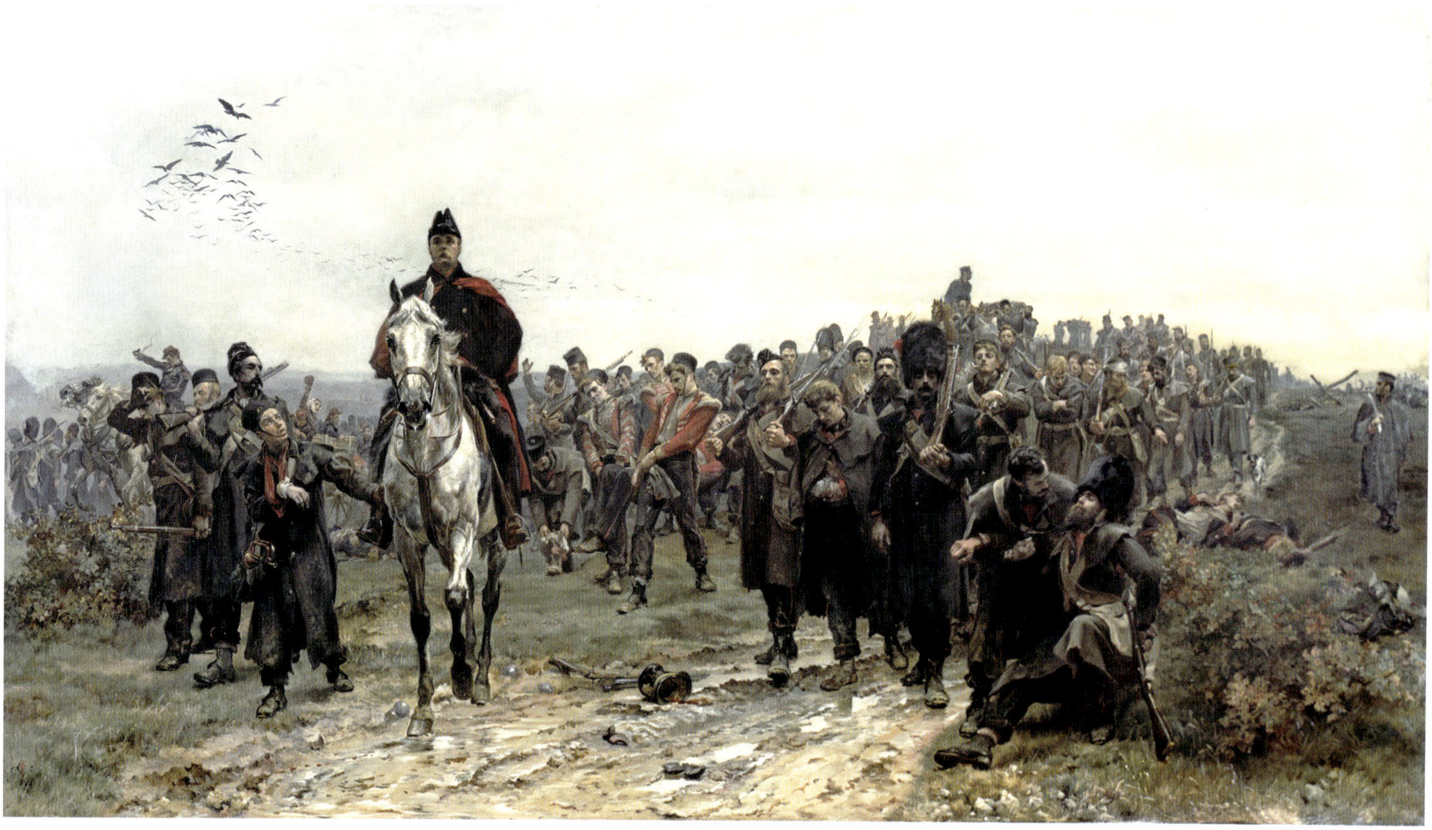

19 *The Return from Inkerman*, 1877. Oil on canvas, 104.4 x 185.6cm. Ferens Art Gallery, Hull. Bridgeman Art Library.

Although *Inkerman* was, Winfried Baumgart notes, 'a victory for the Allies', it was for the British a 'Pyrrhic one' as it underlined the inadequacy of their small army and realization that a long siege was inevitable as they faced the long Crimean winter of 1854–5.[97]

Like *The Roll Call* and *Balaclava* this is a painting of the aftermath of the battle as war-weary soldiers return to the camp of the 2nd Division. Most of the soldiers are from the Coldstream Guards and the 20th Regiment. To the right of the painting near the oak scrub a sergeant gently places a dying comrade on the ground.[98] Russell describes the ground as filled with 'thick scrubby bushes and thorny brakes' and Elizabeth used sketches of bushes that she had prepared in Italy. The next grouping features three soldiers in different psychological and physical states: one looks on in concern at his dying comrade, the middle figure has his head bowed as he clasps a wounded hand while his jauntier companion to his right shoulders his comrade's gun as well as his own (Figure 20). The figure who focuses on his injury recurs across all three of the Elizabeth's Crimean paintings. Such representation provides a perceptive understanding by Elizabeth of psychological trauma – the immediate physical pain provides a buffer to the contemplation of the scenes of battle. Behind this central group is another group of three who parallel the three soldiers in front; one points to dead soldiers on the wayside, drawing the attention of his comrade. To the viewer's left and slightly forward a group of soldiers carry a wounded officer in a makeshift hammock. The mounted staff officer seems oblivious to the surrounding scene; 'his eyes, far away in the memory of the fight, are fixed on vacancy'.[99] Beside him a wearied and wounded bugler stretches his hand towards the stirrup seeking both support from the horse and contact from the officer with his supplicatory gestures. Like the detached Hussar Pennington in *Balaclava*, whose comrades seek to re-engage him, the staff officer does not look down. In the painting's right a French ambulance moves off with its wounded waving at their recent allies in battle. In the painting's left, dejected Russian prisoners trudge wearily beside their captors.

The painting was popular and, like Elizabeth's other paintings of this period, in demand across the country. It was, however, not as extensively reviewed as her earlier Crimean scenes. The exhibition coincided with the Royal Academy exhibition and, as Jenny Spencer Smith and Paul Usherwood suggest, the scene of the return from battle as a 'formula no longer had any novelty'.[100] *The Graphic*, however, praised Elizabeth's vision: 'she makes us feel, above and before all, that they are *men* – men of special types, moods and characters on whom the fever of battle works differently'. It distinguished her work from 'lady-painters' by its 'masculine strength, originality and thoroughness' and she has 'won reputation in a branch of Art that seems to lie so utterly without the pale of womanly power and the range of womanly ambition'.[101] The point underlines the barriers that Elizabeth had to surmount not only as an artist but as an artist working in the traditionally male domain of war.

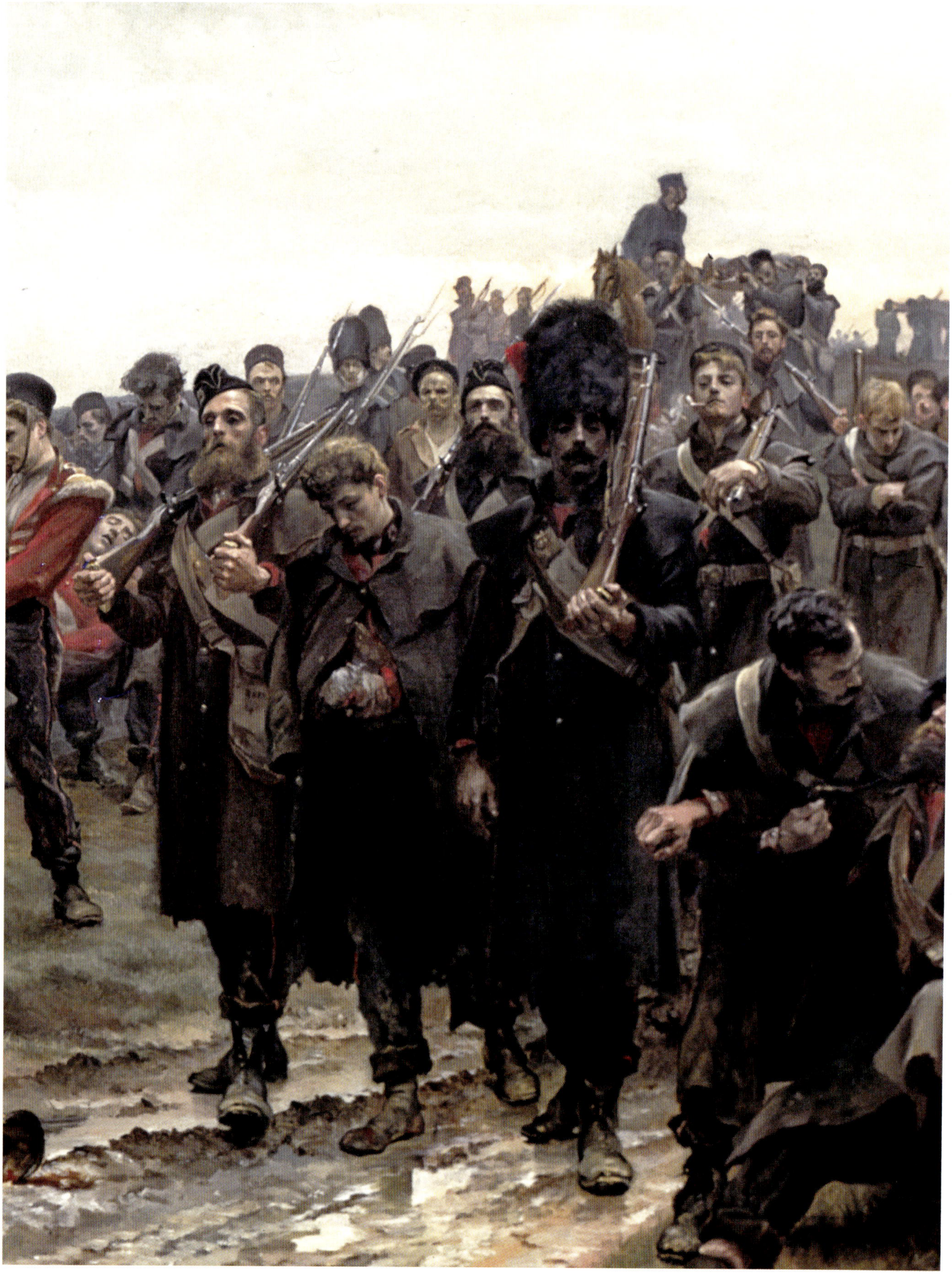

Inkerman was seen as the soldiers' battle, as men with little direction from their superior officers overcame their Russian enemies. In that regard, the painting subscribed to Elizabeth's tribute to ordinary soldiers – it is a patriotic piece. The hyperbolic language of *The Graphic*'s interpretation of the battle, however, leans towards a glorification of war as *Inkerman* 'recorded for England's Gallery of Victories, an achievement that can never be surpassed'.[102] The painting, however, produces an internal conflict: there is no glorification of war in this representation of the return of wearied troops but the painting's frame is more celebratory. At the top of the frame is inscribed the words: 'It was a glorious day for the British Arms' and in a semi-circle above is the French phrase: *Honi Soit Qui Mal Penses* (Shame on him who thinks ill of it).[103] Inscribed along the frame is the list of regiments who fought in the Crimea. Although Elizabeth chose elaborate frames for her work this is a much more detailed frame than either *Balaclava* or *The Roll Call* and suggests an interpretation of the painting as a glorification of war. To become a successful artist Elizabeth negotiated the various strands of British public opinion. Her Liberal sympathies are expressed in the painting's content but a more conservative agenda is suggested by the frame. The frame also offers another way in which the painting might be read.[104] In an 1882 *Times* review about a new engraving of this popular painting, a new tone emerges in the interpretation of the work. Acknowledging that 'war is brought before us in all its ghastliness' in *Inkerman*, the review erroneously sees in the faces a 'proud consciousness that much had been done a few hours previously to maintain the ancient renown of English arms'. The review singles out a soldier of the 20th Regiment, describing him as 'jauntily puffing at a short clay pipe with an expression of profound satisfaction with his own achievements and those of the British legions in general'.[105] The figure returns, as we will see, in different guises in Elizabeth's later paintings, always equipped with his clay pipe.

20 Detail from *The Return from Inkerman.*

None of the reviews use the word trauma in their description of the soldiers' suffering because for the Victorians trauma, as a psychological condition, was not yet understood. One of Elizabeth's great achievements as an artist was to conceive of the effects of warfare a generation before medical discourse came to an understanding of the psychological impact of war on its participants. As Greer argues, Elizabeth was 'an innovative painter not only in her faith in her own observation but in the manner in which she transferred what she saw to canvas'.[106] With *Inkerman* Elizabeth's major phase of Crimean paintings came to an end and a new direction in her personal life and new vistas in art were about to unfold.

CHAPTER FIVE

Painting Ireland, Afghanistan, South Africa and *Scotland for Ever!*, 1878–81

Marriage to William Butler – Connaught Rangers – *Loss of first child – European tour* – The Remnants of an Army – *South Africa – Zulu wars – Begins* Scotland for Ever! – *Commissioned by the Queen – Advice from Millais – Coos is born* – Rorke's Drift – *Plymouth – More children – Death of father* – Scotland for Ever! *and* Floreat Etona!

Elizabeth recounted her honeymoon journey in a letter to her mother in the summer of 1878. Married on 11 June to Major William Butler at the Church of the Servites in Kensington by Cardinal Manning, the couple commenced their travel to Holyhead en-route to Ireland for a 'rustic sojourn in the Hills of Glencar' in County Kerry:

> We did Stratford thoro'ly & I had to sign my new name in 3 or 4 visitor's books 'Elizth Thompson Butler'. The *Telegraph* told the hotel people who we were – consequence, a general sensation & on arriving at this hotel we found everyone on the tiptoe of expectation & Anne [her maid] was forthwith pounced upon by the servants to tell whether it was really Miss E. Thompson. People try from over the way to catch bars of Elizth Thompson Butler at Dinner thro' the venetian blinds.

The letter reveals how Elizabeth enjoyed her fame and cultivated and managed her celebrity: 'I saw so little of our marriage that I shd like a full description from some one. I hope you gave Wilfrid my notes on the dresses, music &c &c'. Wilfrid Meynell, her brother-in-law, was drafted into the role he would play until the end of Elizabeth's life in assisting her to promote her work and public image, particularly as her marriage to an officer necessitated long periods of living abroad, separating her from the London art world.

Unsurprisingly for a new bride, she was effusive in her praise of her husband: 'A greater darling never was there than this Will of mine, & I know that every day he will develop some new excellence'. Will's attraction was his masculinity and bearing; Elizabeth, after all, revelled in painting military bodies: 'Will looks magnificent & is so engaging'. She exhorted her mother to 'Burn this' letter and underlined the command three times as she conveyed to Christiana that 'Will is so considerate & thinks of everything & wont let me be silly & shy'.[1] The intimate details reveal a frank relationship between mother and daughter. Christiana, however, failed to obey and the letter survives as testimony to Elizabeth's fame at this point, her deep physical attraction to her husband, and her feelings on the marriage that would open new vistas for her art but re-establish the travelling patterns of her childhood and adolescence.

William Butler

To all appearance the union of a military painter and a scholarly officer seemed ideal. Certainly, Elizabeth could access first-hand accounts of battle and experience some of the vistas of empire even if the battlefield was, because of her gender, still out of bounds. Ruskin commended the marriage in a letter to William: 'What may you not do for England, the two of you'.[2] William's fellow officers attended the wedding and at the conclusion of the ceremony, Elizabeth's former fellow students of her old South Kensington period gave her a lovely surprise by strewing their path down the church with flowers. She had not even known that they were there. Her union with William wedded art and army in private as well as professional life.

William was a soldier, travel writer and army historian. Born into a minor landlord family from County Tipperary, William, a Catholic, had a formative experience of oppression. In his autobiography, he describes how he witnessed an eviction in which a 'dozen houses were to be pulled down'. The 'weakening effects of the famine were still painfully evident in the people' but the sheriff had the 'miserable inmates of the cabins dragged out upon the road' and their dwelling razed to the ground. '[T]he screaming women, the half-naked children, the paralysed grandmother, and the tottering grandfather were hauled out. It was a sight I have never forgotten'. Although twelve at the time, he claims that if he had a 'loaded gun' he would have fired into that 'crowd of villains, as they plied their horrible trade'.[3] 'There and then', his daughter Eileen recalls, 'he vowed eternal enmity against landlords'.[4] However, the landlord evicting these tenants was, Martin Ryan observes, his own father.[5]

William joined the army under the old system whereby officers had to buy commissions to advance in terms of promotion. Without funds William's early progress in the army was slow until he joined Garnet Wolseley's select group of capable officers. His career coincided with British imperial expansion about which William remained equivocal and outspoken, while playing his part in wars that extended the Empire. He joined the 69th Foot Regiment in 1858 and first served in

Burma and then in India from 1862. Back in Aldershot in 1865, William took some holidays and visited the battlefields of Europe of the Napoleonic campaigns, similar to Elizabeth's tour with her parents at much the same time:

> I had been reading of these places, great hinges of history, graveyards of human glory, for years in all sorts of places, trying hard to transfer their printed names into brain pictures, and now when I came upon them, not in the flesh but in corn ridge and pasture slope and cottage plot, it seemed impossible they could be what the milestones and fingerposts said they were – themselves.[6]

In 1867, William's regiment was sent to Canada due to Fenian unrest. The Fenians, an organization set up a decade earlier in Ireland and amongst Irish emigrants to America, were committed to Irish independence from Britain by physical force. Fomenting trouble on the US-Canadian border was an attempt to start a revolt. William was fighting his fellow countrymen and although he did not subscribe to the Fenian ideals, he did support constitutional nationalism. Fighting enemies with whom he more or less sympathized became a feature of his army career. He was, however, ambitious and advancement through the army ranks was slow. Learning that a military force was being assembled under Garnet Wolseley to Canada's North-West Frontiers in order to suppress an uprising led by Louis Riel and the Métis, an ethnic group living in the Red River Valley, Butler, in contravention of army protocol, telegrammed Wolseley: 'Please remember me. Butler, 69th Foot'.[7] The Métis had lived under the civil authority of the Hudson Bay Company but in 1868 the Dominion and British Governments purchased the Company's territorial rights without consulting the Métis who feared for their traditional way of life. Riel seized the Hudson Bay Company post of Fort Garry and imprisoned some its citizens. William joined Wolseley as an intelligence officer and arranged to meet Riel at Fort Garry. The fort had been flying a flag with a fleur-de-lis and a shamrock, a symbol of the united forces of the Métis and the Fenians who had joined together to challenge a common enemy but the revolt was suppressed by Wolseley. William was then asked by the Lieutenant-Governor of Manitoba, Adam Archibald, to undertake an intelligence-gathering mission across Saskatchewan to the West. William's recommendation on his return shaped policing in Canada by proposing a mounted police force. The North-West Mounted Police was established in 1873.

Canada provided William with literary as well as military opportunities. In 1872, he published *The Great Lone Land* – a travel narrative based on his reconnaissance work. The area covered in the book extended from the Red River to the Rocky Mountains and *The Great Lone Land* was published to critical acclaim. Reviews commended the work, describing him as a 'model traveller, a man of daring even to rashness' but also identified him as a 'figure who sets forth his opinions without hesitation or qualification'.[8] William decried how the 'white world' was 'leagued in a bitter strife against the Indian' as the native way of life was being eroded by settler expansion. The theme was continued in *The Wild North Land* (1872) in which William experiences the tensions between the forces which he was joined to – imperial expansion – and his sympathy for the rights of indigenous peoples. Deploying the invocation – '"The time before the white man came"' – William considers how the 'dweller on the prairie' is 'to us but a savage – the impediment to our progress – the human counterpart of forests which have been felled, mountains which must be trammelled, rivers whose broad currents are things to conquer; he is an obstacle and he must be swept away'.[9] The love affair with natural landscape and the claims of indigenous peoples rest uneasily alongside a figure who, over the course of his career, played a significant part in felling, trammelling and sweeping away human obstacles.

The hero of *Red Cloud: The Story of a Solitary Sioux* (1882) – William's only novel – is born in Glencar, the honeymoon destination of the Butlers. As a young child, the unnamed narrator describes how he envisaged a world beyond his picturesque glen and at the age of ten he gains the summit of the hill behind his home for his 'first view' of the outside world:

> How vast it seemed to me. The glen, my world, lay below, winding away amid the hills. All the streams, all the lakes, were unfolded to my sight, and out beyond the boundary ridge was the great open country. That was on one side – the glen side; but as I turned round to look beyond the mountain I had come up, I saw a sight that filled me with utter astonishment. Below me on that side there lay another glen, smaller than ours; on which I stood; and then, beyond the hill, there spread a great, vast waste of blue water – out – out, until I could see no more, where the sky came down upon it – the end of the world. It was the sea!

And 'From that day forth the glen seemed a small place to me and my mind was ever at work shaping plans for the future'. He consults a 'large old atlas that had maps of every country in the world in it, and in the corner of each map there was a picture of the land, or of some wonderful mountain, or waterfall in it'.[10] This is a boy's adventure romance in the mould of *Robinson Crusoe* (1719). Like Crusoe on his island prison-kingdom, he ascends to the highest point in his locality to survey the territory. Crusoe sees himself as lord and master over his domains; the unnamed young Irish boy seeks adventure in an imperial world. Inspired by an old veteran of the Napoleonic campaigns the boy imagines in the dark evenings outside his cottage 'squadrons' and 'cannon' and the 'pinetops swaying in the storm, were the bearskin caps of the old Guard'.[11] At the same time during his North American travels, Red Cloud, his teacher and 'brother', describes him as 'different from all the white men I have ever met. You seem to love the wildness for its wildness, as a bird loves the air for its freedom'.[12] The story exemplifies the tension in William between the impetus towards adventure, which in the late nineteenth century was imperial in nature, and the desire to preserve threatened civilizations. It reveals his sympathy with indigenous populations threatened by European territorial ambitions. Red Cloud is the last of his tribe as his way of life is consigned to a nostalgic past.

In 1873, William joined Wolseley in Africa for the campaign against the Ashanti tribe in the Gold Coast. Deployed to create a diversionary tactic by invading Ashanti territory, William discovered, however, that his allies, the native Akim forces, were hesitant about attacking their Ashanti enemies. Determined to press on and invade Ashanti territory on the day set out by Wolseley, William and a few of his officers stripped off their clothes and crossed the river separating the territories as the 'Akims stood in groups on the south shore gazing at the white man's doings. The sight was certainly a curious one: three white men and six native policemen carrying luggage had invaded Ashanti'. The account reads like a satire of imperialism. Like Joseph Conrad in *Heart of Darkness* (1899), William reflects on European ignorance of history. Why, he asks, would the tribes have assisted them when previous invasions by the Ashantis into their territories had been devastating?

> Why should they have rushed at our bidding again into a fray which had already proved so disastrous to them? It is a peculiarity with many of our people that they do not know how much they do not know. There is nothing in a land before they came here. History began when the first English traders arrived. Before that event there was a blank. The erection of Smith's shop marks the year one.[13]

At the end of the campaign, William was a 'wreck' and was sent home with a fever to recuperate at Netley Hospital. While convalescing he read the reviews of Elizabeth's *The Roll Call* and joked to his sister: 'I wonder if she'd marry me'.[14] William was sympathetic to Elizabeth's vision of war. Commenting on the Crimean War in his 1889 memoir of Charles Gordon he observes: 'In the absence of staff-organization, transport trains, and efficient machinery of supply, the magnificent veteran battalions that formed the army of the Crimea went for the most part to graves which were dug for them by other agencies than those of the bullets and bayonets of their enemies'.[15] For her part, Elizabeth introduces William in her autobiography as author of the *Great Lone Land*. Wilfrid, keen to assert that marriage did not compromise Elizabeth, wrote an essay on her: 'She learnt to love with even greater fervour the soldier whose humanity she had so intimately understood, and whose sufferings, sorrows, and valour she had drawn with so much power and truth'. However, 'her career is still in its early stages; with every year technical improvement in the methods of her work is observable, and we are certain that if she wields the brush at sixty, as we hope she may do, she will be then, as she is now, and as she desires to be always – a student'.[16]

'Listed for the Connaught Rangers

Elizabeth describes *'Listed for the Connaught Rangers* as her 'first married picture' (Figure 21). It was, perhaps, in acknowledgment of her husband's Irishness that she chose a County Kerry recruiting scene. This new landscape inspired her: 'The deep richness of those typical Irish days of cloud and sunshine had so enchanted me that I was determined to try and represent the effect in this picture'.[17] Her experience of Ireland was that it was 'as much a foreign country to England as is France or Italy'. At a Sunday Mass, she compared the Irish men to Tuscans – 'rough-looking' in 'homespun coats'. The girls, 'so nice in their Bruges-like hoods', were 'very fresh and comely'.[18] However, the political tensions were evident. Limerick Junction was a 'nucleus of Fenian nebula' and in this 'Terrible Tipperary' the 'stalwart constabulary' whom she 'greatly admired' had a 'grave significance'; 'finer men than those she had never seen'.[19]

The picturesque landscape of 'Irish bogs with their rich black and purple peat-earth and bright reedy grass' yields to a description of the landscape's inhabitants who live in 'stone heaps' which are 'scarcely distinguishable' from the land. Her 'contentment' with the beauty of the scenery was, however, 'dashed by the sight of the dwellers in his poor land which yields them so little. Very strange, wild figures came to the black doors to watch us pass'.[20] The Glencar backdrop to William's *Red Cloud* exhibits no such poverty. In that idyllic landscape the narrator grows up in a 'small thatched house, with plenty of June roses and white jessamine'.[21] In front of the house holly bushes 'merged into open mountain, heather-covered and sprinkled here and there with dwarf furze-bushes' and this is the place where his father, whenever he could get leave from his regiment, visited for the 'lakes held plenty of trout, and the mountains had snipe, woodcock and grouse upon them'.[22]

While William's novel sees the Glencar landscape in terms of adventure that shapes his narrator's perspective of foreign topographies, Elizabeth describes the scenery of Glencar with a painter's eye. 'Carran Thual', a mountain in Glencar was 'on fire with blazing heather, its peaks sending up a glorious column of smoke which spread out at the top for miles and miles, and changed its delicate smoke as the sun sank lower'. 'Our glen', as she describes her destination, 'gave the "Saxon bride" its grandest illumination ... Wild, strange birds rose from the bracken as we passed' and the journey ended in a 'brilliant *finale*' as a herd of young horses on their path, careened before their carriage and these 'shaggy, wild things' with their 'manes flying out wildly' joined by a herd of cows escorted them into Glencar. The 'depth and richness of the Irish landscape colouring' provided a new direction for her art and she describes how 'the moisture of the ocean air brings out all its glossy depth. Even without the help of actual sunshine, so essential to the landscape beauty of Italy, the local colour is powerful'.[23] Millais, she explains, described to her the 'same deep colouring' of Scotland by using the simile of a 'wet pebble'. 'Take a grey, dry pebble on the seashore and dip it in the water. It will show many lovely tints'.[24]

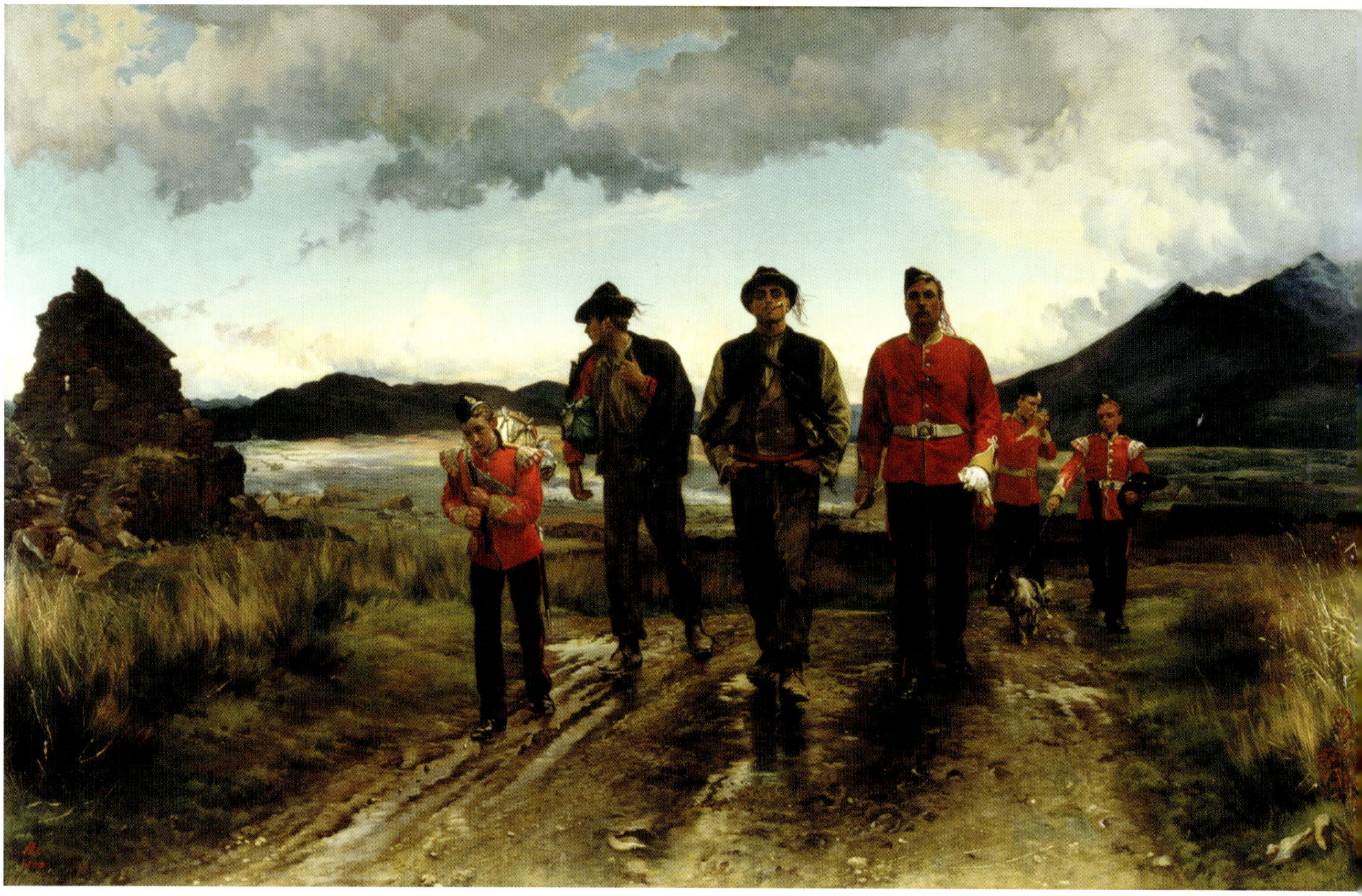

21 *'Listed for the Connaught Rangers: Recruiting in Ireland*, 1878. Oil on canvas, 107 x 169.5cm. Bury Art Gallery and Museum. Bridgeman Art Library.

This was the backdrop to *'Listed for the Connaught Rangers: Recruiting in Ireland* (1878). As she explains, the painting 'was a departure from my former ones, the landscape occupying an equal share with the figures, and the civilian peasant dress forming the centre of interest'. Significantly, 'it was a joy to realize this subject' because she had access to 'variety as to local colour' which was 'denied' her in her other paintings. The Crimea was a landscape researched and imagined, but the Kerry recruiting scene was realized on location. This is a powerful contemporary painting. The viewer is forced into a direct encounter with the new recruits as they are 'marched out of the glen by a recruiting sergeant' to imperial wars. The men are also accompanied by two drummer boys and what Elizabeth describes as a '"decoy" private' – a soldier deployed to draw recruits to the regiment. In this case it is the 88th Foot Regiment, commonly known as the Connaught Rangers, one of eight Irish regiments. In 1881 the regiment amalgamated with the 94th Foot Regiment to become formally known as the Connaught Rangers. In 1877, when Elizabeth was executing the painting, the regiment was still the 88th and the soldiers wore 'the yellow facings' of the period. The models for the Irish recruits were cousins called Foley and they 'wore their national dress, the jacket with the long, white homespun sleeves and the picturesque black hat'. The 'black, white and brown colouring' of the men's clothing, with the 'four red coats and the bright brass of the drum' gave Elizabeth an enjoyable combination with the blue and red-purple of the mountains in the background, and the sunlight on the middle distance of the stony Kerry bog-land'.[25] The *Essex Standard* notes another significant departure in Elizabeth's work as she has 'refrained from showing her power in horse-drawing' and has chosen a 'singularly quiet scene'.[26] Henry Blackburn in his *Academy Notes* describes the 'wet road and brilliant effect of sky after rain, an effect often seen in Ireland amongst the hills'. He commends a 'powerful picture, full of movement and reality'.[27]

Elizabeth avoids political commentary in her scenic description but this can only be read as a political painting. However, it simultaneously occupies two contradictory positions. On one level, it can be interpreted as a patriotic painting portraying an Ireland, which despite its social and political problems and Fenian activity, still provided soldiers for the British army. At the same time, the ruined cottage on the painting's left interposes as a reminder of destitution and loss. The second recruit looks back over his shoulder at a glen in the distance that is his home. His gaze, which takes in the ruin, is suggestive of an uncertain future for him and for the Irish family he leaves behind (Figure 22). Like the figures in Butler's Crimean paintings, the six are individuals and each engages differently in the moment. At the same time each of the three pairings reflect aspects of each other. This is a feature of Butler's Crimean paintings as the soldiers respond to each other's body language while they individually process the aftermath of battle. The recruit's backward glance in *Connaught Rangers* is paralleled by the drummer boy's preoccupied expression as he looks down at the road. The movement of their lower bodies is similar as the left leg

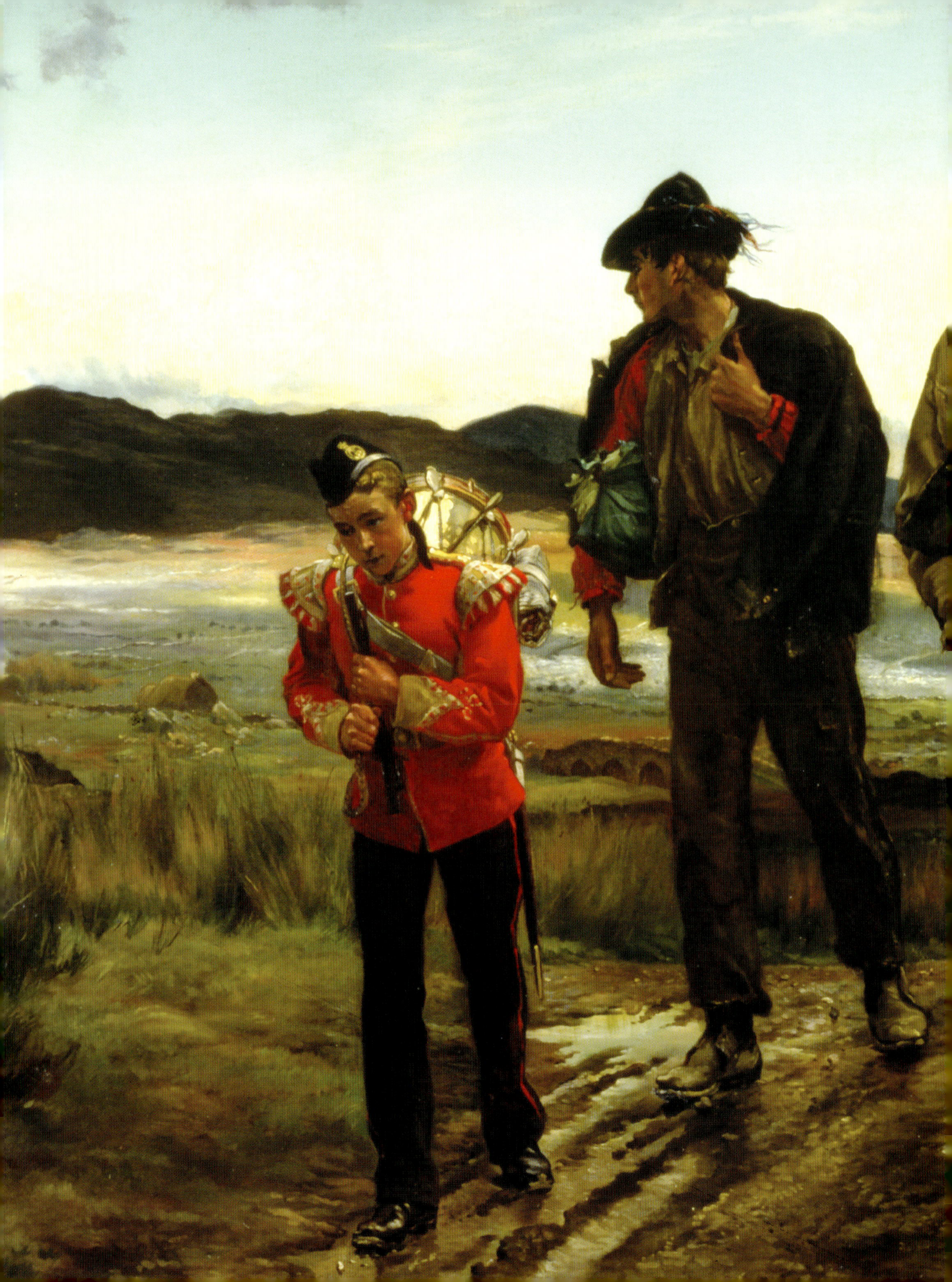

of each figure is thrown back. The other recruit, paired with the sergeant, is slightly off centre. The ruined cottage in the painting's left pushes all the figures toward the right of the frame, demanding attention in its own right. This central recruit, exuding both defiance and nonchalance, has a deadened expression in his eyes, and a clay pipe in his mouth. His left heel is lifted towards the viewer as if he is ready to march through his audience. This figure has his counterpart in *Inkerman* in the pipe-smoking soldier marching alongside Russian prisoners. As we have seen, *The Times* reads the figure in *Inkerman* as 'experiencing profound satisfaction' with himself and with his comrades. Read alongside *Connaught Rangers* one can question this 'profound satisfaction' and alternatively read it as disengagement. With hands in pockets and thumbs exposed, the recruit in *Connaught Rangers* expresses resistance. The body language of the recruiting sergeant conveys military discipline and training, although the *Essex Standard* suggests that he has 'a touch of half-remorse on his face'.[28] Both young men have recruiting ribbons in their hats which also fly from the sergeant's cap. They have been marked for war. The 'decoy private', his duty done, pauses behind the group to light his pipe and another young soldier is considering his dog.

In her travel journal, *From Sketch-Book and Diary* (1909), Elizabeth describes the central recruit as having the 'finer physique' of the two because he was 'reared on herrings', whereas his companion had lived far from the sea. Her own interpretation of the painting is patriotic: 'I wish we could get more of these men into our army'.[29] William was simultaneously preparing an essay for publication entitled 'A Plea for the Peasant' for *Macmillan's Magazine*. Here he deplores the Highland clearances in Scotland and the unjust system of land tenure in Ireland that deprived the army of valuable recruits. An army can only emerge from 'people planted upon the soil', William suggests, but the people were displaced.[30] The rights of the indigenous populations, a theme which recurs across William's work, is evident here. Forthright in his 'plea' for land for the peasant, William's goal, however, is recruitment for the army.

22 Detail from *'Listed for the Connaught Rangers: Recruiting in Ireland.*

In a letter to Alice, Elizabeth extolled her time in Ireland: 'The life Will & I are leading is one quite after our hearts – away from civilization & amongst scenes of natural beauty not to be surpassed in these islands'. She recorded that if she had her 'usual strength' she would 'think this life perfection during this glorious weather, so still & sunny' which she compared to 'Northern Castagnola Vintage weather'. Lacking 'usual strength' is a euphemism for pregnancy. A 'half a mile floor[ed]' her. Fortunately, the 'backgrounds and foregrounds' for her picture were 'all round the corner or out of the window' for their 'little inn' was 'popped down right in the middle of this great round of Glen, & by turning [her] head six side to the right & six to the left' she could see '12 magnificent scenes for pictures'. All she had to do was 'shift' her 'chair round & repeat the movement' of her head and '2 more' appeared.[31] Glencarragh, with its 'streams, bogs, old stone bridges, its peasants, goats and shaggy cows', as well as the 'infinite changes of sun & shadow in mountain & rich bog land', yielded a variety of 'materials' for the artist. The honeymoon journey continued into County Clare which she compares with Portofino: 'Here was the simplest and severest colouring – dark, green, almost amounting to black; light green, cold and pure; foam so pure that its whiteness had over it a rosy tinge, merely by contrast with the green of the waves and that was all; whereas the sea around Porto Fino baffles both painter and word-painter with its infinite variety of blues, purples, and greens'.[32] In a letter to Alice, whom she addresses as 'Dearest Little Matron', she praised the virtues of their respective husbands: 'I suppose Wilfrid is near matchless as a good husband, but allow me to place this beloved Will of mine by his side … I cannot tell you how utterly dear he is & how successful altogether'.[33] They left Ireland on 15 July but returned to Kerry in late September after a trip to London. Christmas was spent with her parents and in the early months of 1878 she was back in her studio.

Her next trip, as she records in her autobiography, was to France. The 'tour was well advised' as she had lost her first child, Mary Patricia. It brought the 'first sorrow' to the marriage and the Butlers visited the Catholic site of pilgrimage at Lourdes. '[T]he send-off from Lourdes gave me the initial impetus towards recovery of which, though I say little, I am very sensible'.[34] It must have been difficult to witness Alice's pregnancies at this time but Elizabeth offered her a 'bercetto' as 'my poor little darling's will do for your babe'. Alice gave birth to her first child, Sebastian, on 19 October 1878. Courageously, Elizabeth claimed to be recovering:

> I verily believe I am Mimi again: I date my steady improvement from my last visit to the grotto at Lourdes. I went back to work yesterday & hope soon to polish off the big picture & knock off a trotting Lancer for the Oil Dudley. I should like to know how you feel & whether the milk has made its appearance. These things interest me tho' they are melancholy to me at the same time.[35]

Alice experienced her own loss of a child, a boy called Vivian, in March 1887. She describes in one of her essays on childhood the 'unique intimacy' of a mother nursing a baby at night which she describes as a 'profound retreat, an absolute seclusion. It is more than single solitude; it is a redoubled isolation more remote than mountains, safer than valleys, deeper than forests, and further than mid-sea'. The loss of a child, Alice argues, is 'something we have to forgive God for' as God 'prodigally overdoes and exaggerates the love in a mother's heart and then forces her to watch a child's long agony'.[36]

Meanwhile, the grieving Elizabeth's letter to Alice continues by enthusing about her trip to Amsterdam and Rotterdam, which succeeded the visit to Lourdes. She had particular praise for the 'Dutch school' which she saw as 'admirable in colour, expression & the "laying on the paint".' She averred: 'I don't think any painters understood & relished "quality" so much as the old Dutch. There is a room in the

Amsterdam gallery devoted to modern Dutch pictures & cruder painting does not exist than in these degenerate paintings'.[37] En route on 8 August Elizabeth visited Claremont where she was born: 'a lovely dwelling overlooking the lake, and facing the snowy ridges of the Dents du Midi. Looking at that house "all my mother came into my eyes" as I thought of her that November night long ago'.[38]

The Remnants of an Army, Jellalabad, January 13th, 1842

The painting that Elizabeth was 'knock[ing] off' as she described it in her letter to Alice was *The Remnants of an Army, Jellalabad* (Figure 23). In her autobiography, she relates how 'invigorated and restored' she 'set to work on an 8-foot canvas' on a subject which had been in her 'mind since childhood'. When she was a child her father had related the story that had 'profoundly moved England in the year 1842' and 'laughingly encouraged' her to paint it when she was older.[39] The subject was the First Afghan War and the painting focuses on an army surgeon, Dr William Brydon, who was then believed to be the last survivor of the British army who had occupied Kabul but were forced into retreat by the Afghan forces, to reach safety at the fort at Jellalabad in 1842. Despite being promised a safe passage by the Afghans the retreating force under Major-General Elphinstone came under constant attack and were wiped out.

The Afghan theme was topical. In 1878, Britain was again at war in Afghanistan when the Disraeli administration launched another imperial war to attempt to secure India from Russian incursions. While Elizabeth attributes the initial idea of the painting to her father, the influence of William was apparent. In an essay, 'Afghanistan and the Afghans', William describes the exodus from Kabul in 1842 in emotive terms:

> Four thousand five hundred fighting men and three times that number of followers turned their faces towards India, beginning the most disastrous movement recorded in English history. This retreat lasted seven days, and measured in distance about fifty-five miles. In those seven days every horror that human misery counts in its catalogue was enacted. The enemy and the elements were alike pitiless. Through driving snow and bitter blast the long column wound its way through stupendous cliffs ... Seven mornings dawned on masses of men frozen as they lay – grim bivouacs of death. At length there were no more to die. Of all these thousands one solitary man passed out from the terrible defile of Jugdullock – he was all that remained of the army of Cabul.[40]

While William is critical of mismanaged ventures that wasted lives and money, Elizabeth's response is on the human level. As Alison Smith argues, the painting, featured in the 2015 exhibition 'Artist and Empire' at Tate Britain, invites 'sympathy'.[41] Possibly the most famous of Elizabeth's paintings today in view of NATO engagement in Afghanistan, the painting is a sombre reflection on the effects of

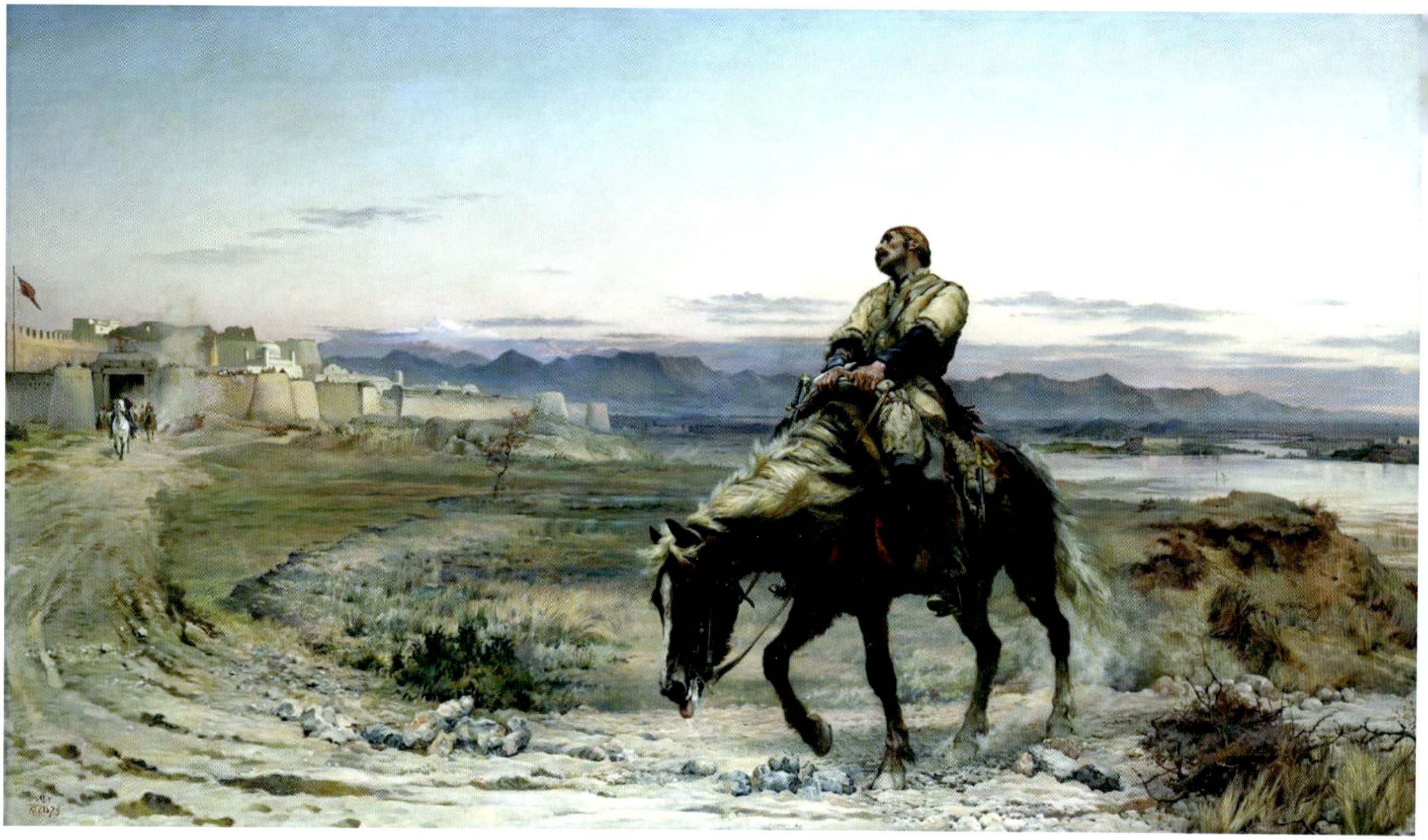

23 *The Remnants of an Army: Jellalabad, January 13th, 1842*, 1878. Oil on canvas, 132 x 234cm. Tate Gallery London.

imperial expansion. In a departure from her peopled paintings of the Crimea and *Connaught Rangers*, this picture is remarkable for its attention to a single wearied figure and pony set against the arid landscape of Afghanistan. The detail of the pony is the painting's most remarkable feature (Figure 24). With water streaming from its eyes and its veins showing through its face and tongue protruding, the pony with its arched back is both malnourished and exhausted. In the distance emerging from the fort is an officer on a sturdy white charger accompanied by mounted native troops and crowds of soldiers are looking out over the fort's walls at the desolate figure, whose exhausted body is angled towards the fort and safety. This is a powerful painting of loss – implicit in the image of the single figure is the thousands who did not make the journey. The landscape – unique in Elizabeth's oeuvre – is almost empty with the solitary fort far in the distance. Looking at the image today the fortification – rendered miniscule by the artist – in this challenging landscape is prophetic in its reflection on the unconquerable nature of this territory.

The artist, more sensitive than her husband, avoids direct political commentary, portraying the suffering bodies of horse and rider to underline the trauma of war. As a Victorian woman, she was licensed to express feeling, and she uses feeling to open a debate on war. While feeling may be seen as a conservative response to social issues, it is important to remember that when Elizabeth exhibited at the Royal Academy in 1879 women in Britain did not have the vote and the 1870 Married Women's Property Act only allowed married women limited control over their own property and earnings. Three years after the painting was exhibited the Act was extended to enable married women to have control over all their property. The power then to generate feeling becomes a political act.

For the 1879 Royal Academy Elizabeth had two paintings to exhibit. *Connaught Rangers* had been commissioned by John Whitehead. This was her first Academy exhibition in three years. Her Studio Sunday was crowded and she describes how her studio was 'got up quite charmingly with curtains and screens, and with wild beast skins disposed on the floor, and my arms and armour furbished up'. *Remnants* made the artist Elmore cry and she was pleased that both paintings were 'well hung' at the Royal Academy.[42] *Connaught Rangers* was hung in Gallery I and *Remnants* was hung in Gallery VII. *The Graphic* describes the horse's 'broken knees, blood-shot eyes, and distended nostrils'. Now called 'Mrs Butler', the review praises her landscape painting: 'She has never shown herself so good a landscape painter as in this view of the flooded course of the Cabul river, and the far-stretching blue range of the Sufed-Koh'.[43] In *The Magazine of Art* Marion Spielmann notes that Elizabeth pursued 'military art with a healthy energy rare in these days of "exquisite idylls".' The review commends her treatment of Brydon: 'An intense expression, in which there is nothing of the theatre – nothing overstepping the modesty of nature – has been given to the face and action of the man; the spectator feels, as indeed he should feel before such a subject, that he is in the presence of one of the tragedies of the world'. Indeed,

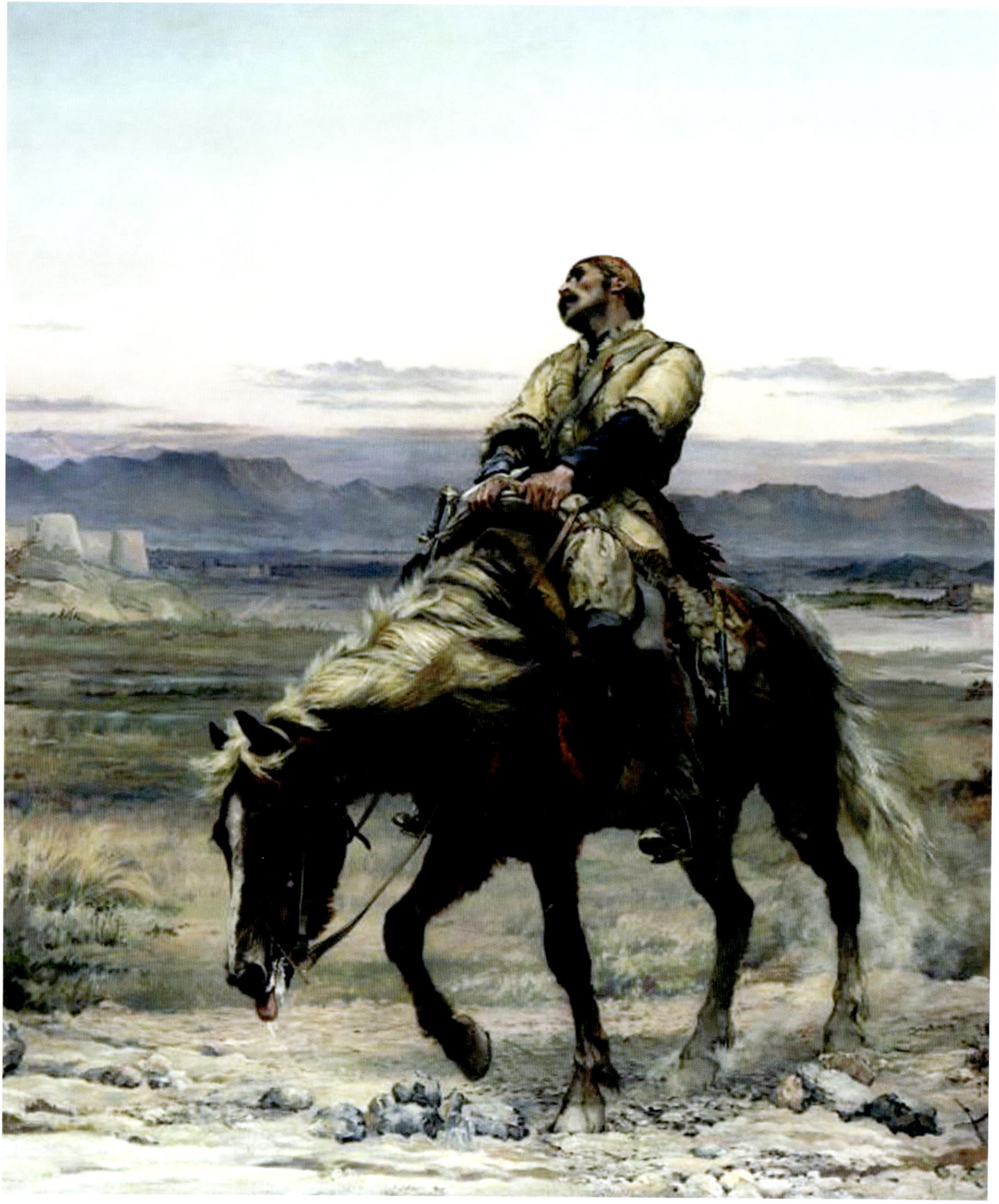

Spielmann draws Elizabeth's two exhibited paintings together in his analysis: *Remnants* shows the 'outcome of war; its beginnings the artist has shown in her Irish recruiting subject'. For Spielmann, the 'two young peasants leave their native glen with a regret which they conceal with masculine reserve; their type and the character of the scenery and of the climate are distinctively Irish; the colour is subdued but intense, and the group marches with steady if somewhat melancholy spirit'.[44]

The Times draws parallels with rider and horse as the rider 'travel-stained, haggard, bleeding, reeling in his saddle, with scarce strength to keep his seat' and the horse, with its 'bloodshot eyes and staring nostrils is scarce able to stumble along the stony track'. Here the artist has 'far outdone anything she has yet accomplished in the way of landscape, and her telling of the story is as impressive in its grim literalness as anything ever put on canvas'.[45] The signature on *Remnants* indicates Elizabeth's transitional status. She uses her ET with the Red Cross between the two letters and her new designation – 18 EB 79 – underneath. *Remnants* was also her largest canvas, and like her husband's travel writings, Elizabeth takes possession of the landscape.

In June she was nominated for election as an Associate Member of the Royal Academy. No woman had to that point been elected. *Punch* championed her cause in May 1879. In their 'Tour of the Academy' they pointed out *The Remnants of an Army* in Gallery VII, noting: '*The* picture of the year. Let us write Mrs. Butler, R. A. – *i.e.*, "Really Admirable!"'[46] It was not to be. The 'difficulties of electing a woman', she notes, 'were great'. The Academy was a male bastion. By 1922 she was no longer challenging their position observing that since her close election 'the door has been closed, and wisely'.[47] Privately, however, she did not forgive the Academy for electing Herkomer instead of her and was equivocal about her rival artist's work. In a letter to Alice she asked her what she thought of 'Herkomer's Veterans', relaying that the painter Marcus Stone 'told [her] he thought their expressions "indicated execration at a condemned malefactor led to execution rather than cheers for the Queen".' 'I do not know', she continues, 'that he is not right to a certain extent – at least you can read the expression in both ways'.[48]

24 Detail from *The Remnants of an Army: Jellalabad, January 13th, 1842.*

However, her popular appeal continued as her work was exhibited regionally. In September, *The Roll Call, Quatre Bras, Balaclava* and *The Remnants of an Army* were in Huddersfield. The *Huddersfield Chronicle* describes *Remnants* as exhibiting 'painfulness'. 'War', it continues, 'is an awful thing we are all accustomed to say; but it is doubtful whether anything other than a painted picture will ever cause the saying to be deeply felt'.[49] As a woman, Elizabeth is licensed to generate feeling but entry into the male bastion of Academy power is denied.

South Africa

While Elizabeth was completing her Afghan painting in the spring of 1879, William had been deployed to South Africa for another imperial war. Defeat of British troops

by the Zulus under the leadership of their King, Cetewayo, at Isandhlwana in northern Natal had caused a furore. This was William's second trip to South Africa; he had been previously deployed at Natal under Wolseley, who had been appointed governor, in 1875. The Zulus were attempting to repulse colonial expansion into their territory. As William had recorded in his diary: 'Thus far the white man's course has been marked with blood, and with blood must it be traced to its termination, either in their own destruction or in that of the thousands of the population of South Africa'.[50] However, the invasion by British forces into Zululand in January 1879 by Lord Chelmsford, a veteran of the Crimean War, resulted in a humiliating defeat. One of the most famous British defences occurred in the aftermath of defeat at Isandhlwana when 139 soldiers from the 24th Battalion of 2nd Foot Regiment fought off a Zulu attack at Rorke's Drift on 22 January. William sailed to southern Africa on 28 February 1879 and was put in charge of troops and supplies. Meanwhile Elizabeth was inspired by Rorke's Drift:

> What magnificent subjects for pictures the defence of Rorke's Drift will furnish. When we get full details I shall be much tempted to paint some episode of that courageous achievement which has shed balm on the aching wound of Isandula. But the temptation will have to be very strong to make me break my rule of not painting contemporary subjects. I like to mature my themes.[51]

The second British invasion of Zululand by Chelmsford was launched on 1 June 1879 and one of its first fatalities was France's Prince Imperial, Eugene Louis Napoleon, son of the deposed Emperor Napoleon III. The Prince Imperial and his mother had been living in exile in England (Victoria was his godmother) and he had joined the British army. The Prince with his small escort were ambushed by Zulus in a supposedly safe territory, and the Prince's body was covered with wounds from Zulu spears. England was shocked by the news. William was charged with the funeral arrangements. Before leaving Natal, however, William, sympathetic to the Zulu cause, performed a service for the defeated King Cetewayo, by bringing rushes from Zululand to him in Cape Town Castle so the king could lie on mats from his homeland. In England, William visited the Empress Eugenie, distraught at her only son's death. Eugenie became a close friend.

While William was in South Africa Elizabeth was busy in Kent making studies of grey horses for her charge of the Scots Greys at Waterloo. She had been inspired to undertake the subject after viewing 'unwholesome productions' of the Aesthetes at the Grosvenor Gallery:

> I felt myself getting more and more annoyed while perambulating those rooms, and to such a point of exasperation was I impelled that I fairly fled and, breathing the honest air of Bond Street, took a hansom cab to my studio.

There I pinned a 7-foot sheet of brown paper on an old canvas and, with a piece of charcoal and a piece of white chalk, flung the charge of 'The Greys' upon it.

When she returned from Kent, she resumed her work in her studio on the painting until she was interrupted by Sir Henry Ponsonby, the Keeper of the Queen's Privy Purse, who had been sent by Victoria to commission a painting of a contemporary war. *Scotland for Ever!* had to be momentarily 'put aside'. It is at this point that there is an indication of a disjunction between Elizabeth's vision of war and the mood in Britain, which was becoming increasingly jingoistic towards the end of the century. Rorke's Drift, she notes, had been celebrated as a new Waterloo and her friends but not, she emphasizes, her parents had urged her to represent the battle. It was, however, 'against her principles to paint a conflict'.[52] With *Scotland for Ever!* the enemy was not shown, but the proposed imperial subject would show British soldiers 'at grips with the foe'. The subject that she 'felt and saw in her mind's eye most vividly' was the 'finding of the dead Prince Imperial and the bearing of his body from the scene of his heroic death on the lances of the 17th Lancers'. It had been the subject of a sombre painting by the French artist Paul Alexandre Protais, whose *Finding of the Body of the Prince Louis Napoleon* featured the prince being carried on a bier of lances and blankets by the 17th Lancers, with his face and hands visible. The bier is flanked by mounted troops of the King's Dragoon and 17th Lancers. The Queen, however, demurred, as she was concerned about the suitability of such a sensitive subject and Elizabeth was 'compelled by clamour to choose the popular Rorke's Drift'.[53] For the painting's subjects, Elizabeth had the 24th Regiment at Portsmouth at her disposal and a re-enactment of the fight took place so she could reproduce the event 'as nearly to life as possible' but from the private soldier's viewpoint. The Zulus presented a greater difficulty and Dr Pollard got her a 'sort of Zulu model from a show in London'.[54]

In a letter to Alice in February 1880 Elizabeth told her how 'The Prince & Princess of Wales paid me an unexpected visit in the midst of my model & stayed a long while this morning'. And attentive to managing her publicity, she asked: 'Do you think it might be put in the papers?'[55] She also recommended an Irish nurse to Alice who was then expecting her second child, Monica. In a subsequent letter, Elizabeth informed her how Millais had come to her studio: 'Millais came & we had a very gratifying interview. He went over the picture thoro'ly & found all the faults he could but they were few & his opinion was that 4 days plucky work ought to turn out the picture grandly. "Be as plucky as blazes" was his advice. He was much struck with its originality. I was in great spirits after he left.'[56] The letter about work is interspersed with matters of childbirth – in 1879 Elizabeth had given birth to her second child, Elizabeth (known as Coos), 'who came to fill the place of the sister who was gone'.[57] Interspersed with information on art matters, Elizabeth told Alice,

another full-time working mother, that she would 'send the flannels & with them every wish for your having a good time. It is very probable that you will be let off very easy this time after so severe an "opening".' She promised that she would 'look round after work' and would 'tell her a lot' depending on whether Alice was 'still perpendicular'[58] Alice gave birth on the 24 March. In an undated letter, most probably relating to Alice's first pregnancy with Sebastian (born October 1878) Elizabeth asked her sister: 'Do you wear a belt? It is time you should if you feel a weight. You will be thankful after the event for having worn one. I am just as tho' nothing had happened as regards figure & I daresay my belt had something to say about it'.[59] These letters reveal the lives of women who appear very modern in balancing their careers with childbirth and child rearing, and in their concerns about their figures.

Summoned to Windsor to show *Rorke's Drift* to the Queen, Elizabeth saw Disraeli – the architect of Empire at this period – bending over it. The Queen 'placed her plump little hand' in Elizabeth's and 'showed so much emotion' as Elizabeth pointed out the soldiers' wounds.[60] *The Defence of Rorke's Drift, January 22nd, 1879* (Figure 25) was exhibited at the Royal Academy in the summer of 1880. Although a success with the Queen and the public, the painting was badly hung in the dark lecture room and press reviews were not complimentary. The *Birmingham Daily Post* on 30 April 1881 found the painting disappointing and 'certainly not equal' to her previous works, comparing it unfavourably with De Neuville's painting of the same scene the previous year. De Neuville had exhibited his painting at the Fine Art Society in Bond Street.[61] The *Daily News*, however, accurately predicted that Elizabeth's painting was 'sure to attract crowds'. A 'daring Zulu' seizes the barrel of a gun but 'only a few of the enemy are distinctly made out'.[62] However, *The Glasgow Herald* reckoned that she 'had minimized a great national event' and the story was not 'forcibly told'.[63] *The Times* had praised De Neuville's work as 'impressive' and as a 'representation of hot and heady fight'.[64] However, its review of Elizabeth's painting was critical: 'one who looks at this picture [will see] that the English are by no means inferior in numbers to the Zulus'. Implicit here is the notion that the obstacles facing the soldiers from the Zulu onslaught are not shown and therefore the soldiers' courage under overwhelming odds is not commemorated. The difficulties facing Elizabeth in depicting this scene are evident – she did not have access to Zulu warriors and she was reluctant to paint scenes of actual combat. The review commends her as an 'excessively clever painter', but declares that was not a 'battle painter at all, but a delineator of the *entourage* of battles: of the glee with which English lads fought at Waterloo, of the sorrowful effect of war as seen on the morning after the battle, and so on through the whole range of picturesque or emotional incidents which she can fancy as accompanying war. Her power is individual and personal rather than general'. It compares her unfavourably in this regard with her rival Richard Caton Woodville. It argues that his Afghan painting of the 92nd

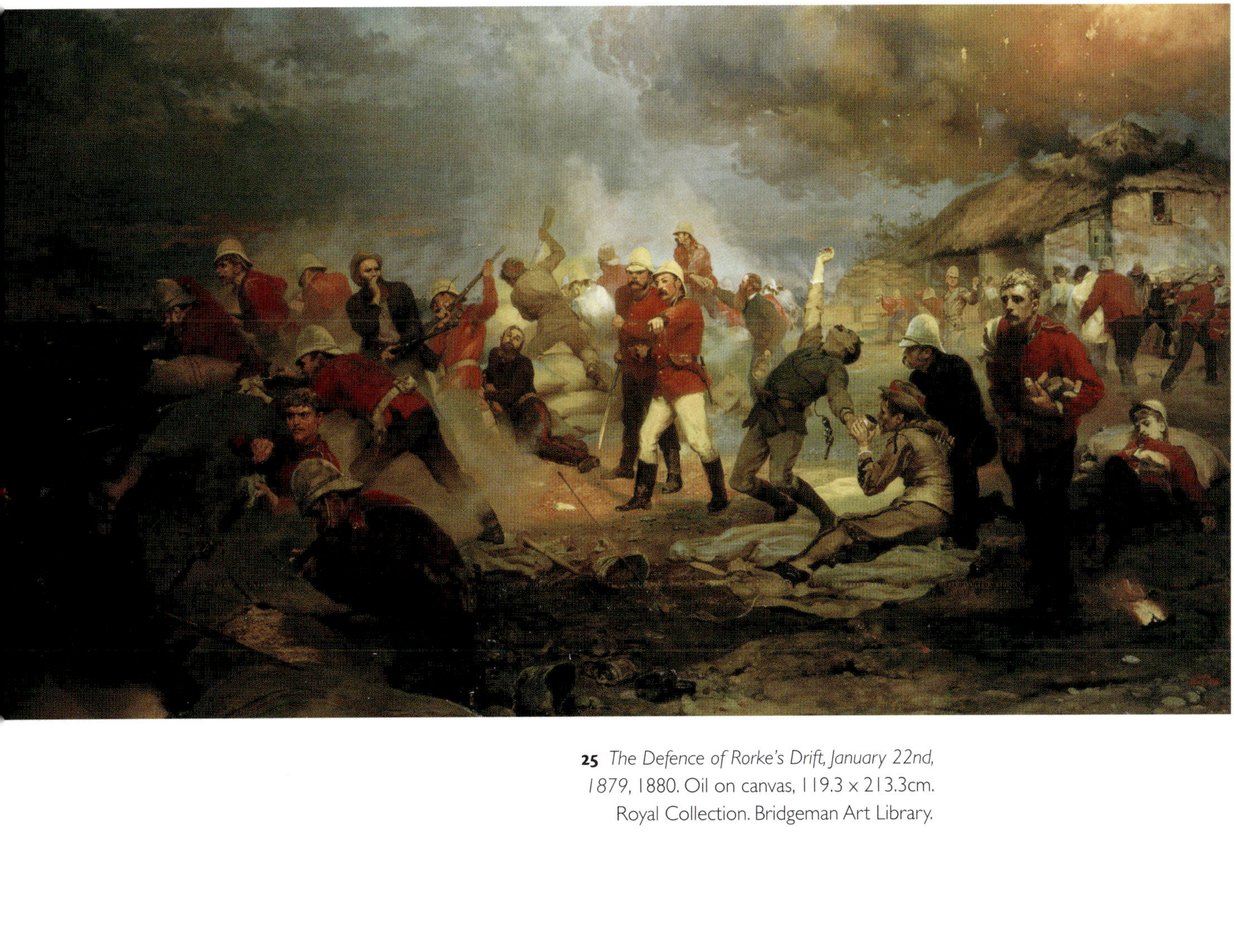

25 *The Defence of Rorke's Drift, January 22nd, 1879*, 1880. Oil on canvas, 119.3 x 213.3cm. Royal Collection. Bridgeman Art Library.

Highlanders and 2nd Goorkhas, which was adjacent to *Rorke's Drift* in the lecture room, 'gripped the scene as a whole'.[65] By contrast, Marion Spielmann argues that Elizabeth's painting was 'more distinctively masculine' than De Neuville's painting of the scene and praised her for her realism.[66]

Despite her fêting by the Queen, Elizabeth's lack of enthusiasm for the painting may have accounted for its lack of critical success. This is a conflicted painting – at one level Elizabeth commemorates victory by ordinary soldiers against impossible odds, but, at the same time, there was an uneasiness about imperial expansion in the Butler home. William, who was extending empire as a soldier, was unambiguous about the territorial rights of the Zulus and critical of the Boers. He notes in his essay collection, *Far Out: Rovings Retold*, that no one thought about the Zulus and their king until they 'suddenly crossed a river'. Then the 'excitement instantly becomes intense. Everybody has something to say about this black king … The illustrated papers immediately produce the very blackest pictures of this black king …. What is called the "popular mind" of the nation is educated into such a becoming frenzy of hostility against black kings as a principle'. In an astonishing indictment of imperial expansion by a serving officer, William continues:

> It does not matter much whether the black king has crossed the river into our territory in an attempted rectification of some wrong which he has suffered at our hands, or whether we have crossed the river into his territory upon the clearest and most conclusive testimony that his property and that of his subjects would be vastly benefited by being transferred to our hands.[67]

'In nine times out of ten', he continues, 'we have taken, or bought, or tricked his land from him'. An ardent Catholic, William nonetheless deplored how the conversion to Christianity sealed the native convert's place in the imperial order because when the native

> adopts the teachings of Christianity, he also adopts the social custom and social standards of what we call civilization … He has been told a hundred times that this new religion meant brotherly love; that before God colour vanished and race was not known … [but] this beautiful theory of the white man's love and brotherhood and charity … means the actual existence of a barrier between him and the white race more fatally opposed to fusion, more hostile to reciprocity of thought, mutual friendship, or commonest tie of fellowship, than that which lies between civilized man and the dumb dog that follows him.[68]

When William returned from South Africa, he was given the post of Adjutant-General at Plymouth. It had been originally intended that William would take up the post of private secretary to the Marquis of Ripon who was being posted to India as Viceroy. Ripon, however, was Catholic and Gladstone vetoed the appointment of

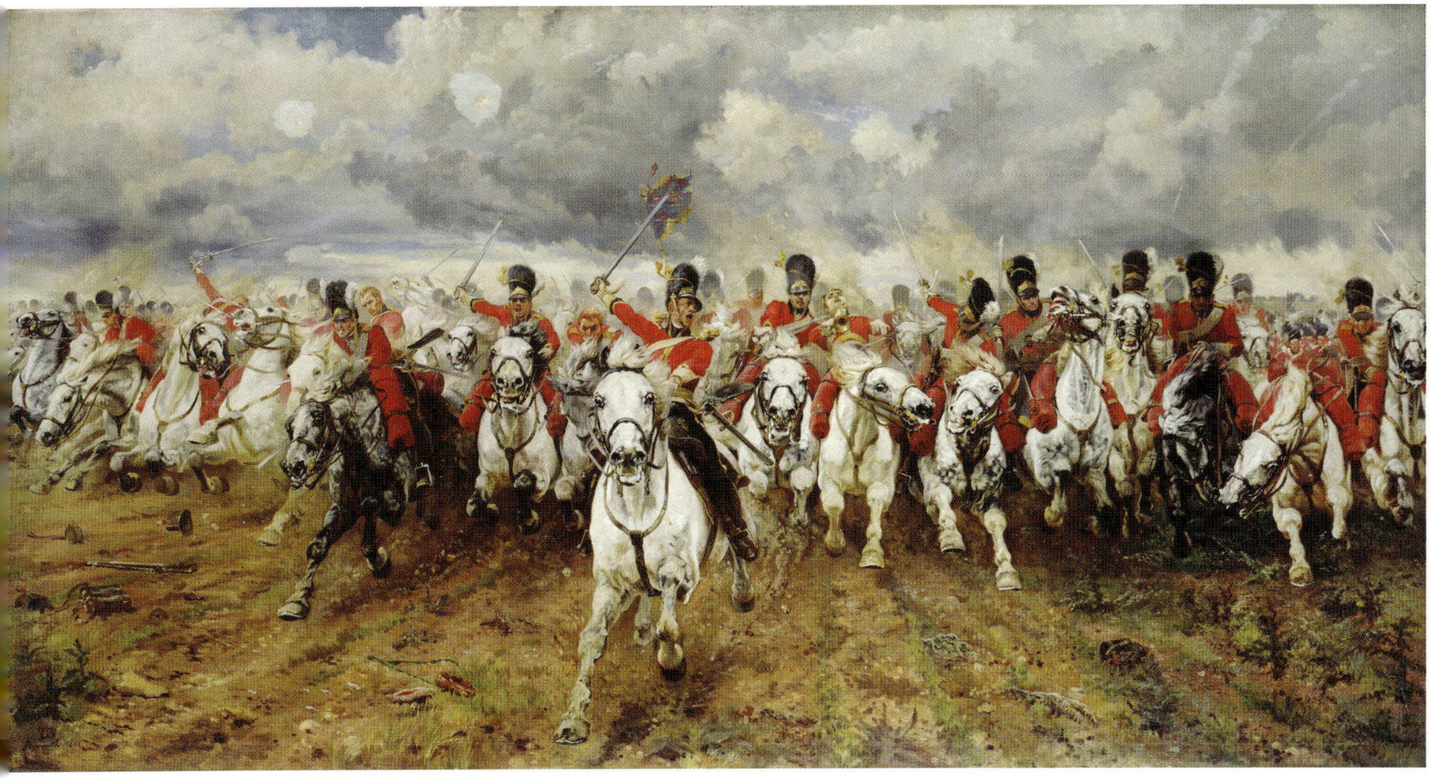

26 *Scotland for Ever!*, 1881. Oil on canvas, 101.5 × 193cm. Leeds Art Gallery. Bridgeman Art Library.

William believing that a 'Catholic viceroy in India was sufficiently experimental without further endangering the position by the appointment of another of the same creed to a subordinate but still influential post'. The loss cost William a considerable amount in terms of remuneration. As Assistant-Adjutant General of the Western District William's pay was £600 but as the Viceroy's private secretary he would have earned between £3,000 and £4,000 pounds. It was at Plymouth that the couple's second child Patrick was born and two more children, Richard and Eileen, were born in quick succession. It was also here that Elizabeth completed *Scotland for Ever!* In Plymouth she had the benefit of clear skies for light and not the 'brown fog' of London as well as 'any amount of grey army horses'. To her great disappointment, however, she was prevented from exhibiting the painting at the Royal Academy as she had wished, describing how she was denied having her 'white and grey *hippogriffes* bounding out of the Academy walls'.[69] The problem arose when she sold the copyright of the painting to S. Hildesheimer who wanted it exhibited at the Egyptian Hall. Butler created further difficulties because she had made an agreement with the Fine Art Society that her next painting after *Connaught Rangers*, unless painted by Royal Command, should be offered to them first. This resulted in an injunction against her with the matter being settled out of court with William issuing a cheque for £500.[70] Elizabeth is reticent in her autobiography about the episode: 'It was exhibited alone. It is quite unnecessary to burden my readers with the reason of this … There was a law suit in question, and there let the matter rest.'

27 Detail from *Scotland for Ever!*

In May her 'beloved father died'. Thomas had made a late conversion to Catholicism and was 'comforted with the heartening rites of the Church.'[71] She took comfort in faith for her loss of her mentor.

The highly dramatic *Scotland for Ever!* is also a painting of loss and the suffering of war (Figure 26). It positions the viewer in front of the charging horses, taking up the position of the enemy, forcing a confrontation with the consequences of war. The painting celebrates Scottish valour in its focus on the famous victory of the Scots Greys against the French forces in the Waterloo campaign. The brochure accompanying the painting advertised the 'GRAND NEW PICTURE' by 'Mrs. Butler' and the moment of action: '*As the Regiment broke into the Charge the men raised the cry of* "SCOTLAND FOR EVER!" which was then taken up by the Highlanders, who followed the "Greys" into action'. This was accompanied for the viewer by an eye-witness account by James Armour, Roughrider to the Scots Greys:

> Orders were now given that we were to prepare to Charge. We gave our countrymen in front of us three hearty huzzas, and waving our swords aloft in the air: several swords were struck with balls while so doing. The Highlanders were then ordered to wheel back; when they had, and were wheeling back imperfectly, we rushed through them, at the same time they huzzaed us, calling, '*Now, my boys, Scotland for Ever!*'

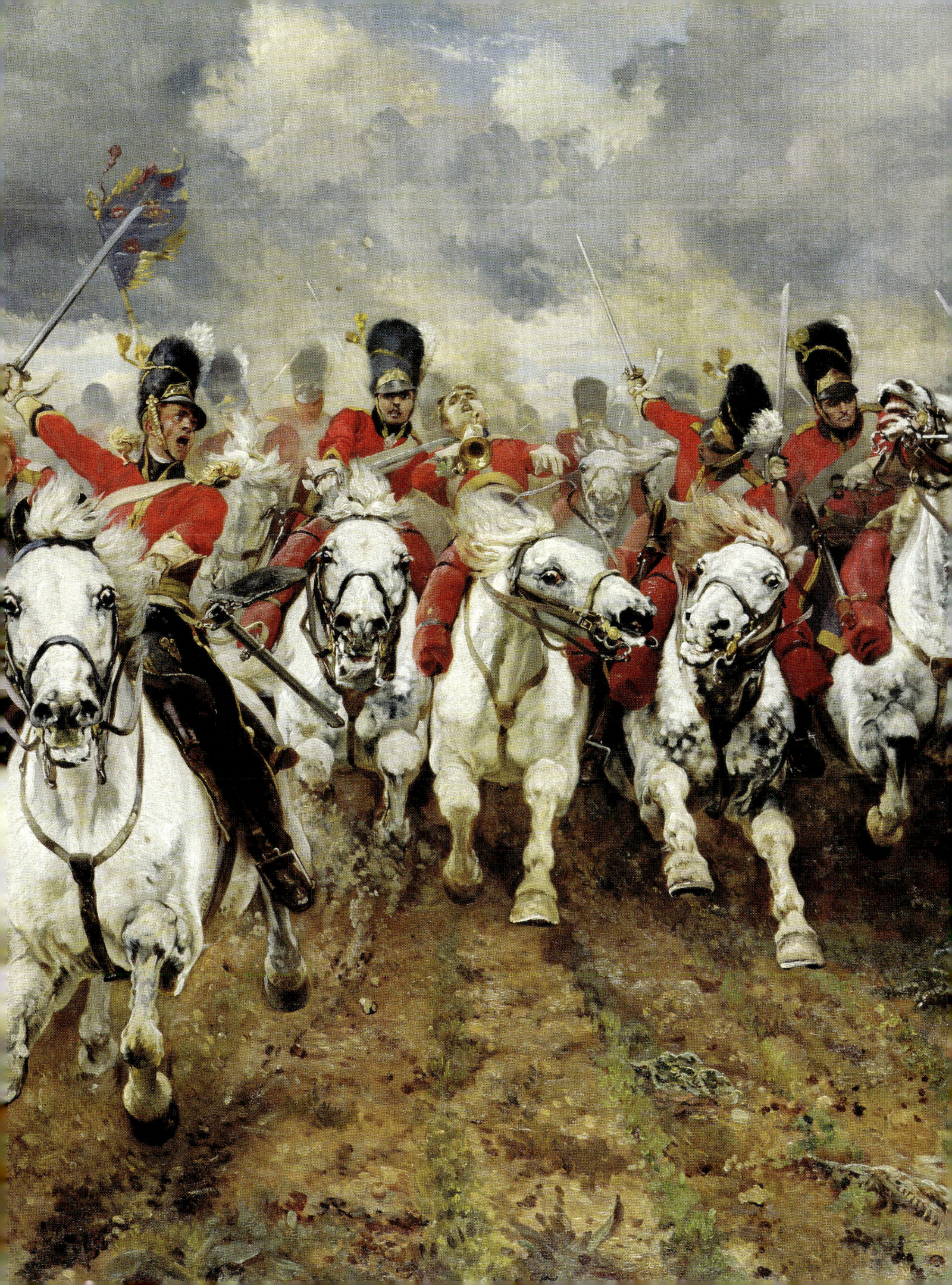

But the exhilaration of battle is tempered by the information that the 'Regiment was almost annihilated in this Charge'. The painting's action is further described:

> The officer in front is the Squadron Leader; his Trumpeter's place should be at his left hand, but the horse of the Trumpeter, feeling his rider reeling, has wavered, and immediately become engulfed in the front rank. The Trumpeter's comrades encourage him to go on. He has hardly finished sounding the 'Charge' when struck. This casualty has caused a pressure of horses to the (spectator's) right of the front rank. Most of the men have already given their shout of *'Scotland for Ever!'* and have come down to the Charge with their sabres lowered.[72]

With its mixture of pathos and patriotism, Elizabeth returned to her earlier Crimean preoccupations (Figure 27). Marion Spielmann observes in his review that the painting represented her 'chief work up to the present time. In it her extraordinary mastery of movement is more fully displayed than in any of her oil-pictures, though several early water-colours showed her capacity in this respect'. Furthermore, 'every face is that of a separate, individual, and distinct man – none are generalities, and none are repetitions of one model's head. An equally conscientious variety is to be found in the heads of the horses, for Mrs. Butler has studied the unit of the horse as closely as the unit of the soldier'.[73]

The painting was a critical and popular success. The magazine *Fun* describes the historic event as 'powerfully and dramatically treated' and playfully continues that it 'shows the mind and hand of a "master," but the thorough management of the "Mrs" and the dexterous efficiency of the "Butler".'[74] Exhibited at Liverpool in 1882, the Liverpool *Mercury* observes: 'So vigorously is the action of the officer commanding depicted that he seems leaping out of the frame' and it becomes more dramatic because 'the enemy is not seen, but the spectator is supposed to be among them, which gives one the idea that he is participating in the action, and gives far greater force to the picture'.[75] The horses are charging into the enemy, some with wild-eyed terror across a ground that is littered with the debris of war. With this painting Elizabeth answered *The Times* critic of *Rorke's Drift* because in this painting she has 'gripped the scene as a whole' and produces a distinct and powerful rendering of an historic incident, without compromising her reluctance to show actual scenes of battle. The painting also subtly returns to a key theme in her battle art: the suffering of war. While the charge was a success, the Greys and Highlanders, seen in a gap on the right of the picture, were routed on their return and many were annihilated.

With *Floreat Etona!* (Figure 28) Elizabeth returned to a contemporary theme: the war in South Africa between the British and the Boers. The outbreak of war was described by William as the 'long pent-up animosity of the Dutch Boers' which 'had suddenly broken into active revolt in the Transvaal, and repeated disasters to our arms were taking place'.[76] Often called the First Boer War, the Boers had declared the

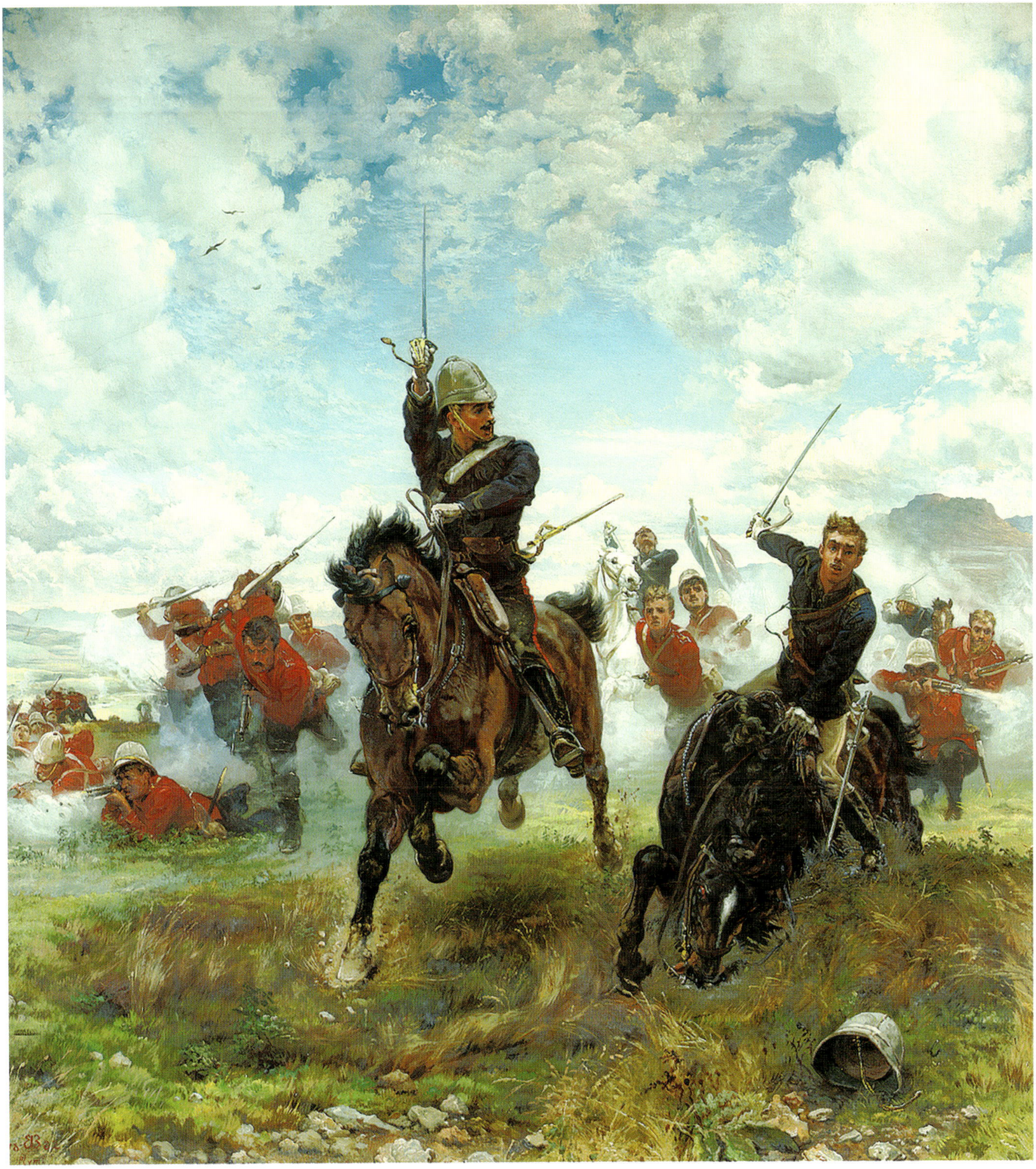

28 *Floreat Etona!*, 1882. Oil on canvas, 84.4 × 78.1 cm. Private Collection. Bridgeman Art Library.

independence of the Transvaal, which had been annexed by Britain in 1877, and the British fought to regain control resulting in a series of defeats culminating in the disastrous defeat at Majuba Hill during which one of Wolseley's 'Ashanti Ring', Major General Sir George Colley, British High Commissioner to South Africa, was killed. After three months of war, the Treaty of Pretoria was signed in August 1881 by which Britain recognized the independence of the Transvaal. An earlier battle, Laing's Nek, was commemorated in Elizabeth's painting. As she notes in her autobiography, 'The Boer War with its terrible Majuba Hill disaster, had attracted all our sorrowful attention … and I chose the attack on Laing's Nek for my subject'.[77] Here Colley led the 58th Regiment up to Laing's Nek. After suffering significant casualties including the loss of most of the regiment's officers, the British abandoned the attack and retreated. Elizabeth's painting and the incident is taken from an eye-witness account, as one of the officers led the 58th Regiment up the hill to their deaths against the Boers. Robert Elwes, a Lieutenant in the Grenadier Guards, was charging towards the Boer defences when he called to another Eton boy, an Adjutant of the 58th, whose horse had just been shot, 'Come along, Monck! Floreat Etona! ['Let Eton Flourish'.] We must be in the front rank!' After uttering his Eton motto, Elwes was shot dead by the enemy. Here Elizabeth commemorates the annihilation of the officer class, while focusing on an incident of war. It covers the same terrain as *Scotland for Ever!* in depicting a charge but, unlike the earlier painting, features the two mounted figures of Elwes and Monck, with the 58th Foot Regiment on the ground firing at the enemy from behind them. The officers are wearing their blue patrol jackets and have their swords drawn, even though Monck's horse is buckling under him. Elwes is looking back as he utters the motto. Like *Scotland for Ever!* the viewer occupies the position of the enemy. This was also the last battle in which military colours were displayed as the Queen's colour can be seen in the painting's background. Despite the courage of Elwes and Monck, celebrated by the painting, Laing's Nek was a defeat by a force which, with its guerrilla tactics, was more adapted to the terrain.

Elizabeth, too, was losing ground to her rivals and her discomfort with the rising mood of jingoism affected her ability to represent imperial warfare. Although she would not have intended it as such, the painting, John Laband argues, represents

> war in transition, the clash of an outmoded British military culture and a fading construction of public school masculinity, based on the ethos of 'Play up! Play up! and play the game!', in collision with the more appropriate Boer adaptation to the realities of modern warfare. If the battle of Waterloo was won on the playing-fields of Eton, then by the same token the battle of Laing's Nek was lost on the identical location to an opponent who did not abide by the rules.[78]

Elizabeth would return to South Africa in the coming years but the expansion of empire in the East and the events of 1882 drew her to a new country: Egypt.

CHAPTER SIX

Egypt, 1882–6

Egypt and Arabi Pasha – Tel-el-Kebir – William's views on Egypt – Birth of Eileen – After the Battle *– A challenging painting – Garnet Wolseley – Reviews of* After the Battle *– Sudan – Charles Gordon – Elizabeth's illustrations for* The Campaign of the Cataracts *– Elizabeth in Egypt*

By 1882, Elizabeth was in need of new experiences. Despite her extraordinary success since 1874, the critical mood had turned against her work. The public wanted paintings that glorified war as Britain extended its Empire in the East. Britain was moving its military to war in Egypt. On 5 August, William departed with Wolseley to suppress the nationalist rebellion led by Colonel Arabi Pasha. Despite her husband's involvement Elizabeth's political sympathies lay with 'poor old Arabi and his "rebels"', although the departure of William from Liverpool was the 'most trying ... of all the many partings, because of its dramatic setting'. It was easier to 'bear up' on a 'crowded railway platform' but the Egyptian campaign left by ship from Liverpool and Elizabeth had the 'sickening sensation' of possibly becoming a 'widow'.[1]

Egypt was a site of European interest since Napoleon's brief incursion into the country in 1798. In the early nineteenth century, its modernizing leader, Muhammad Ali Pasha, forged close ties with Europe. In his 1840 travel account of the country, William Wilde observes how European engineers were procured by Ali Pasha 'to explore the different parts of his dominions' and he sent 'Egyptian boys to Europe, to be instructed in the different arts and sciences, many of whom were educated in British universities', to become 'teachers in their own'.[2] The opening up of Egypt to Europe had significant consequences. Over the course of the century, the country's Pharaonic past and antiquities were desired by museums and private collectors and tombs were often recklessly plundered. During his visit to Saqqara, for instance, William Wilde describes how 'for miles' the ground was 'strewn over with the sacking of the tombs' including the bones of humans and animals, linen, broken mummy cases and blue crockery. The day before his arrival a French man had a mummy raised, opened its case and discarded its contents. His object was 'for the mere purpose of seeing it opened, and for the sake of the ornaments it might contain'.[3]

Egypt was part of what Edward Said defines as the Orient, the region extending from North Africa to Asia occupying the territory of the Ottoman Empire, which became inscribed in European consciousness in the nineteenth century as a site of desire and difference.[4] Egypt was of particular interest both historically and geographically to European powers. The discoveries of ancient tombs were graphically represented in the *Illustrated London News* and popular novelists such as Conan Doyle and Rider Haggard published 'mummy' fiction. Egypt had come into Britain's imperial purview in the 1870s. Part of the Ottoman Empire, its Khedive Ismail Pasha's ambitious and exorbitant plans for modernizing Egypt in the mid-nineteenth century and extending his regional influence by colonizing part of the Sudan, as well as the building of the Suez Canal, had left the country in severe financial debt. European creditors became anxious and Britain sent Sir Evelyn Baring (later Lord Cromer) to the country in 1874 to protect British financial interests. In 1875, Britain purchased Egypt's shares in the Suez Canal for the 'bargain basement price of four million pounds'.[5] In Ahdaf Soueif's historical novel, *The Map of Love* (1999), the events are succinctly described by one of the characters:

> 'We were part of a dying Ottoman Empire. Our Khedive Ismail loved modernism and Europe and – le spectacle. He likes the Suez Canal project and so he borrows money. He is not careful where he borrows. He borrows from Europe – from Britain and the Rothschilds and France. At the same time – you see, here is the conjunction'. The index fingers of his two hands come together. 'Europe is strong and moving outwards' a huge expansive gesture with the arms – 'colonialism is the spirit of the age. Their old enemy the Ottoman Empire is dying. So they use the Khedive's debts to expand into our part of it. Into Egypt. The rest is history.'[6]

The Butler story with Egypt coincides with this moment in 'history'. Ismail was replaced by his more malleable son Tewfiq in 1879. For William, the Egyptian campaign was motivated by monetary factors and the soldier of his day, he argues, went to war for the 'Stock Exchange'. The Egyptian peasantry, the fellaheen, bore the enormous burden of taxation, and when an officer in the Egyptian army, Arabi Pasha, mobilized resistance to Tewfiq's rule he found support amongst Egyptian soldiers and fellaheen. Britain intervened to stabilize the Khedive's rule and the British bombardment of Alexandria on 11 July destroyed the city's forts and other parts of the city. However, William argues that the destruction of Alexandria fuelled 'the determination of the Egyptians to resist intervention in their internal affairs'. Consequently, Britain had to put together an 'army of invasion' to the Delta where Arabi had mobilized his troops.[7] This was the army that Elizabeth waved off at

Liverpool. After some skirmishes, the major British offensive against the Egyptians took place at night in the desert at Tel-el-Kebir. Wolseley decided to attack at night and the Egyptians were unprepared. Despite this, William records:

> There is one thing which I should like to put on record regarding this battle of Tel-el-Kebir. Complete surprise though it was to the Egyptian soldiers behind their entrenchments, they nevertheless fought with the greatest determination against overwhelming odds. Not a moment was given them to awake, form up, prepare, or move into position ... The leaders in whom they could trust were, like themselves, fellaheen; few among them knew anything of war, its arts, manoeuvres, or necessities ... yet they fought stoutly wherever ten or twenty or fifty of them could get together, in the works, in the angles of the lines, and in the open desert between the lines. The heaps of dead with and across their rifles facing the up-coming sun bore eloquent testimony to that final resolve of these poor fellows. Peace be to them, lying under these big mounds on the lone desert – ten thousand, it is said. No word should soldier utter against them; let that be left to the money-changers. They died the good death. Dust to dust. They did not desert the desert, and Egypt will not forget them.

The Egyptian military campaign was over on 13 September and the British casualties amounted to 80. By 15 September William was in Cairo, billeted at the Abdin Palace. William was beguiled by Egypt and in his published writings military occupation is mixed with sightseeing. From the roof of the Abdin Palace, he commanded a view of Cairo just as Britain now commanded the country: 'looking westward across the palm groves that fringed the great river one saw the Pyramids changing from grey to rose-pink in the growing light – vast and clear-carved as though they had been finished yesterday'.[8] There is a self-awareness of his position as part of an occupying force:

> 'If you make the canal from Suez to the Mediterranean you will bring the English into Egypt', said Mehmet Ali in his old age, as he sat in the window of his little palace in the citadel looking out upon that wondrous scene below. Well, they made the Suez Canal, and the English came to Egypt by it, and their bugles are now sounding the reveille from the camp and quarters in the city; nevertheless, somehow these giant sentinels standing erect in the desert, who began their watch six thousand years ago, seemed as they reddened in the sunrise to be even smiling at the thought that this new invader of the Nile Valley was to be the last they were to look at.

For William, the Egyptian people lasted because they had 'rubbed out' the 'invaders [who] have swept this Delta', by absorbing them. In the features of contemporary Egyptians, he sees 'the face and form of the type which you find graven on tombs and

temples that were built many thousand years ago'.[9] The point is emphasized in his earlier writings: 'In the mummies of men and women, king and queen and priest mummies taken from the Theban hills, or found at Memphis, can be read the undoubted proof that those who till and toil to-day were once the ruling race on earth'.[10] William's point is contrary to the views of many nineteenth-century travellers' accounts of contemporary Egyptians which suggest that the Egyptians were not the inheritors of their country's past, thus enabling an ideological agenda to dispossess the country of its antiquities.[11] In the meantime, the deposed leader of the revolt, Arabi Pasha, was sent to the Abdin Palace to await trial. William observes that the Circassian and Syrian officers surrounding the Khedive wanted to assassinate Arabi or court-martial him and have him sentenced to death. When Arabi arrived at the palace a 'large group of officers had gathered on the verandah' to see him. 'He was brought under escort in a carriage. He alighted, and began to ascend the steps as one tired and weary. When he saw the group of officers he pulled himself together, drew himself up, and saluted us with dignity'.[12] However, only General Drury Lowe, the commanding officer, and William, returned Arabi's salute.

Politically, William was influenced by the Arabist Wilfrid Scawen Blunt. The Sussex-born Blunt, who was a close friend of the Meynells, had estates in England and land in Cairo. He retired from a career in the diplomatic service after marrying Byron's granddaughter. The couple travelled extensively in the Middle East and Anne Blunt published travel narratives. Blunt dedicated his life to nationalist causes: Egypt, India and Ireland. Albert Hourani argues that Blunt was a 'pre-imperialist' rather than an 'anti-imperialist' who did not 'think it necessary to the interests or honour of England to extend her rule' and who disliked the 'new Imperial spirit, the product of the new England of the urban middle class … and was shocked by the vainglory, the arrogance and the brutality of its exponents'.[13] Blunt's resistance to imperialism coincided with the position of the Meynells, whose Catholic periodical, *Merry England*, was anti-imperialist.[14] Wilfrid's male friends, his daughter Viola argues, were 'men of strong independent views, not afraid to be the exception … To be in a minority was after all the English climate for a Catholic, and one which must have suited him well enough since his affinity was with the anti-imperialists, Home Rulers, Boer War dissentients, and extreme social reformers'.[15] Wilfrid initiated the friendship with Blunt by sending him copies of the Catholic journal he edited, the *Weekly Register*, in August 1882 and informing him that the journal had been following his leadership on the Egyptian Question. Blunt met Arabi in late 1881 and tried to act as an intermediary between the Egyptian nationalists and the British government. He warned Arabi that if an invasion was to take place then the British would attack from the Suez Canal, but his warning was ignored. In the aftermath of the conflict, Blunt used all his diplomatic and financial power to ensure that Arabi would have a fair trial. William's dislike of the war is recorded in the letter Wilfrid sent to Blunt: 'My brother-in-law, Colonel Butler, who is out in Egypt on Sir Garnet Wolseley's staff,

has, you may be surprised to hear, read all that you have written on the Egyptian question, & with entire agreement';[16] William also shared Blunt's concerns over Arabi's welfare. When Tewfiq was brought back to Cairo under the protection of British troops, the 'fate of Arabi hung in the balance'. Writing in 1910 William notes that 'putting to the death of Arabi under the shelter of Khedival authority was an idea perfectly agreeable to persons in very high ministerial positions in England' and its 'frustration' was due to the intervention of Blunt. In the autumn of 1882, however, William was unaware of Blunt's intervention on Arabi's behalf as he was 'immersed' in his work with the troops in Cairo but in the officers' mess the Egyptian leader's fate was a frequent topic of conversation and he was anxious because the 'tide of opinion was flowing strongly against the prisoner'. In contravention of army protocol, William wrote a letter to the Chief of Staff, Sir John Adye, who was returning to London, urging him to exert his powers to prevent the execution of Arabi. 'You may ask', he comments, 'why I, holding a subordinate position on the staff of this expedition, should take up a question removed from the class of work I have hitherto done in this campaign'. William explains his appeal for clemency: 'the wounds inflicted in war, no matter how deep they may be, soon heal compared to those which are left in the memory of a people by the work of the scaffold'.[17] Although he would have had no influence on the decision, his intervention demonstrates an individual with independent and often heterodox views. In the end, Arabi was sentenced to exile in Ceylon.

After the Battle *(1885)*

In England, Elizabeth was preparing her painting of the aftermath of the battle of Tel-el-Kebir. At the end of April 1883, she wrote to Alice from Plymouth to ask her to help her find a suitable studio in London. Alice and Wilfrid, despite their busy lives, and launch of their new publishing venture, *Merry England*, were often called upon to assist Elizabeth: 'Please let me know about a studio as soon as possible as I must utilize my time immediately on getting to London & not have to waste it looking for one'.[18] There may have been greater urgency as Elizabeth was pregnant. When Eileen, the couple's fourth child, was born in Plymouth in October 1883, William wrote to Alice: 'I have never seen Mimi so well, thank God, & she is very happy to have it over with. "Coose" has now a little sister'.[19] Her art work continued as did her problems with studios. In December 1884 she wrote to Alice asking for a studio for March. Her requirement was for a studio 'with plenty of light, partly from the top'. She acknowledged: 'You will have trouble finding one for that month. I might make February do but wd prefer March, as my picture, wh. I would bring with me for business transactions as well as for little last & beautifying touches, wd go direct from the Studio to the Academy if I had the Studio up to Sending-in Day'.[20]

After the Battle (1885) commemorates British victory in the battle of Tel-el-Kebir and focuses on Wolseley and other officers, including William, at the moment of victory. Wilfrid Meynell describes the event:

> The Commander-in-Chief (Wolseley) reached the bridge almost as the forefront files of the Gordon and Cameron Highlanders gained that point; and, dismounting on the short causeway leading to the drawbridge, he there dictated the order for pursuit of the cavalry and Indian Division, and the despatch home that was to announce a victory for England.

The moment Elizabeth chooses is just before Wolseley has dismounted: 'It is the moment of the decision of the victory, and the slight frame of the General has not relaxed from the long strain of watchfulness and command'.[21] Elizabeth describes how she gave a 'long period' of her 'precious time' into preparations for the painting. William, however, was not 'very enthusiastic' about her choice of subject matter and she notes how he observed that 'To beat those poor *fellaheen* soldiers was not a matter for exultation' as the 'capture of Arabi's earthworks had been like "going through brown paper".' He objected because the 'theme was unworthy' and hoped that she would 'drop the idea'. Elizabeth remained firm, however, and seeing her 'bent on it' he 'did all he could to help [her] realize the scene'.[22] The painting coincided with the public mood of the 1880s. When Wolseley returned with his troops to Britain in 1882, their review on 18 November was celebrated with jingoistic fervour. Wolseley's biographer describes how Londoners would 'not soon forget the brilliant spectacle' which was a 'triumphal procession'. The 'crowd' gathered 'to see what manner of men were they who had overrun the land of the Pharaohs in a few weeks'. Two days later Wolseley was given a peerage, the title of which was 'Lord Wolseley of Cairo, and of Wolseley in the County of Stafford'.[23]

Elizabeth found the painting challenging. Although she had 'crowds of Highlanders' at her command and 'went in for the minutest rendering of the equipment', she was unsatisfied and she admits that she was 'never so long over a work'. 'Depend upon it', she argues, 'if you do not "see" the thing vividly before you begin, but have to build it up as you go along, the picture will not be one of your best'.[24] Elizabeth was again looking for a studio.

For *After the Battle*, Wolseley, she records, 'gave her a fidgety sitting at their house in London, his wife trying to keep him quiet on her knee like a good boy'.[25] This infantilizing of one of the leading military figures of his generation is pointed. Wolseley died in 1913, nine years before Elizabeth's published memoir. However, in 1922 Wolseley's letters were also published and feature a letter to his wife written in October 1890 in which Wolseley expresses his exasperation with William's political viewpoints:

> Anything that will tell against what I prize the most – namely, the honour and reputation of our Empire – [Butler] loves to dwell upon; anything that can be twisted into the glorification of the Celtic race is made to perform on his stage and lauded by a magniloquent chorus.[26]

But in his 1903 autobiography, the Dublin-born and educated Wolseley praises William as a soldier, noting that 'in genius and inventive power, as it can be employed in all the various phases of war, he is second to none' and that his 'imaginative faculty … marked him out pre-eminently'. Here he is more tolerant of William's political opinions: 'A loyal subject of the Crown, yet he always entertained a heartfelt sympathy for those whom he believed to be of a down-trodden race'.[27] Although recognizing William's abilities as a soldier by drawing him into his 'ring' of talented officers, Wolseley was an ardent imperialist and his politics differed greatly from those of his subordinate.

Punch lampooned the depiction of Wolseley in *After the Battle* during the painting's exhibition at the Royal Academy. The horse in Elizabeth's painting was foreshortened and Wolseley was presented as standing up in his stirrups. The result was a figure who was top heavy: 'It is supposed to be Lord Wolseley on horseback, and might be entitled, – "Not quite up to his weight".'[28]

The painting was exhibited in Gallery IX. Henry Blackburn's *Academy Notes* describes it:

> Arrival of Lord Wolseley and staff at the bridge of Tel-el-Kebir at the close of the action, ELIZABETH BUTLER. Mrs. Butler (best known as Miss Elizabeth Thompson, the painter of *The Roll Call*), sends an important war picture, a scene from the battle of Tel-el-Kebir – the arrival of Lord Wolseley and his staff, who have galloped up to the bridge at the close of the action. There are portraits of Sir Redvers Buller, Colonel Butler, Sir John Adye, and others of the staff. The Highlanders are cheering, others are seen firing at the enemy in the distance; early morning light on the group, and distant heights of Tel-el-Kebir.[29]

The painting was recognized as an 'important' piece. What is interesting, however, is how by 1885, Elizabeth is still defined by *The Roll Call* and by the name by which she achieved her fame. The exchange of 'Miss Elizabeth Thompson' for 'Mrs Butler' had professional consequences, as the artist, despite having used her married name for seven years, required introduction to the public.

Elizabeth's correspondence with Wilfrid regarding the painting also underlines that art was a commercial activity for her. In reply to a letter from Wilfrid regarding the sale of the painting, Elizabeth reveals her skills in the marketplace:

> The price of the copyright of *After the Battle* wd depend upon the length of time the holders wd require to possess the picture for purposes of engraving & Exhibition. If for a short time, including or not including, the period of its Exhibition at the Liverpool Walker Gallery to which the picture is pledged during the Autumn, the price wd be lower than for a long period such as I parted with the Scots Greys for vis. 4 years. If the intending purchasers will say the time they wanted it for please let me know. I must know, of course, who the individual is I am to transact business with if the matters are to proceed.[30]

Although subscribing to the popular mood of the 1880s, *After the Battle* was exhibited almost three years after the conflict. Pregnancy and childbirth would, of course, have slowed down the work. The war artist, Richard Caton Woodville, who had been in Cairo with the army in the aftermath of Tel-el-Kebir, produced his painting a year earlier. He also describes Cairo in 1882 as a having a 'festive air, owing to the many visitors of all nations who were flocking in to see a British army occupying Egypt' and 'Shepheard's was then *the* hotel, and to it flocked the *haute volé*. The terrace in front of it was always gay with ladies, civilians and officers in the uniforms both of the English and Egyptian services'.[31] Unlike Elizabeth at this point, Caton Woodville had the advantage of being able to sketch on location. He recalls that while 'at work at Shepheard's, doing some studies of our men in their discoloured, war-worn and stained uniforms',[32] he was visited by the Marquess of Dufferin and Edward Malet, the Consul-General, with a telegram from the Queen's private secretary commissioning him to paint the Duke of Connaught and the guards under his command at the battle of Tel-el-Kebir as a riposte to the 'many people of the time who depreciate the Duke of Connaught's position during the battle';[33] the Duke was the Queen's favourite son. *The Guards at Tel-el-Kebir* (1884) represents the Duke in a prominent position at the front of his troops issuing orders as a shell bursts near his mount. The horse is poised in a commanding position looking over the field of battle in contrast to the officers' horses immediately behind the Duke's who are frightened by the explosion. Notably, Elizabeth's painting also features the Duke slightly behind the figures of Wolseley and Adye, to the viewer's left of William.

Ultimately dissatisfied with the work Elizabeth notes that *After the Battle* enjoyed 'moderate success'.[34] *The Athenaeum* notes that 'the touch is not so crisp as Miss Thompson's used to be, it is firmer and the local colours are clearer; the draughtsmanship, too, is better than Mrs. Butler has given us for some time past. There is a good deal of true energy in several of the figures, and much has been made of an unpromising subject'.[35] In *Merry England*, Alice drew attention to Elizabeth's image of Wolseley: 'The artist has made us feel the tension of intelligence and command in every line and muscle of the light figure, rising in the stirrups, with a tight grip of the knees, as the hind quarters of the horse give way under the sudden rein' and, while remarking, the 'irresponsible enthusiasm in the worn but excited

faces turned to cheer the chief', she observes that Wolseley has the 'shadows of thought over his still watchful eyes'. Alice also observes the 'group of Arab prisoners, with their whites and blues in the pure morning light' and how they make a 'fine passage of colours'. As the painting was 'studied entirely out of doors' it is 'invested with clear and perfect daylight'. The models were 'veritable soldiers' with 'some of them painted immediately after their return from the campaign in Lower Egypt'. As 'usual' with Elizabeth's work, 'it is in the individual face, character, and action of the men that lies her sympathetic and comprehensive power'.[36]

The *Academy* praises the drama of the painting:

> There cannot, indeed, be claimed for the artist the merit of having produced what, from a technical point of view, is a good picture; for the colour is hard and "tea-boardy," atmosphere is insufficiently suggested, and the too symmetrical arrangement which together compose the picture leaves the eye unsatisfied. But, for all that, the work shows evidence of one very precious quality, rare indeed in English art, the true dramatic, as distinguished from the melodramatic gift.

The review continues by focusing on the representation of the Highlanders:

> The figures of the young Highlanders who with almost delirious enthusiasm acclaim their victorious leader are such as few but the painter could have imagined; the faces of the younger lads bear unmistakably, through all their enthusiasm, the stamp of a past physical fear, such as seizes upon even the bravest in their first encounter, controlled though it may be, by intellectual courage and military ardour.[37]

The description of the Highlanders is important in two respects: the effect of battle is represented in the men's faces and the *Academy* review, as well as Alice's review, provides a record of the portion of the painting that is now lost. Only a panel of the painting remains in existence today focusing on the central figure of Wolseley and half of Adye to the viewer's left with Connaught behind and William to the right. The painting was cut up at some point and it is likely that it may have been done after the death of William, given that he disliked its subject matter. The *Academy* review focuses on the human element of Elizabeth's painting and contrasts *After the Battle* with fellow military artist, William Croft's painting of William III at the Battle of Landen. Despite its technical 'superiority' Croft's 'battle-piece' is a 'conventional performance, lacking the inspiring human element which is the secret of Mrs. Butler's success'.[38] Although it is a painting which celebrates an imperial victory, there is, through focus on the 'human element' of the experience of war, a continuity with Elizabeth's Crimean art and her artistic philosophy. Hichberger argues that the 'absence of violence' in this and other paintings 'was a deliberate strategy, designed to accommodate the conflicting ideologies of anti-imperialism and pacifism as well as patriotism and militarism'.[39] A few months after the exhibition of *After the Battle* Elizabeth had her first encounter with Egypt but other events had occurred in the meantime. Although Arabi's revolt was suppressed, as William observes in his biography of Charles Gordon, the 'Soudan, that vast region of unrest, had still to be reckoned with'.[40]

The Campaign of the Cataracts

In the early 1880s a revolt swept through the Sudan which was an Egyptian colony. The Sudanese mobilized under a charismatic leader who proclaimed himself the Mahdi, the successor to the Prophet Mohammad. Unrest in the Sudan was precipitated by the abolishment of slavery (a traditional way of life in the Sudan) and punitive taxation from Egypt. For William, 'two things' had come to the Sudanese – 'a leader to give unity to their efforts, and a knowledge that they were in every way better men and braver soldiers than the race [Turco-Egyptians] which had so long ill-treated them'.[41] When the Mahdists annexed Western Sudan, Tewfiq sent an army of 10,000 and modern equipment under the command of the British General Hicks to recapture the region but they were massacred by the Dervishes (as the followers of the Mahdi were called) in the desert in November 1883. The Mahdi, venerated among his followers, quickly mobilized support and now had the advantage of military equipment captured from his victory. William describes how to 'his friends he was a genius, a guide, a Mahdi; to his enemies an impostor, a villain, a fanatic' but to 'history he will be a man who proved his possession of a great genius by the creation of empire out of nothing, and by the triumph of his revolt of Islam over the highly disciplined efforts of the most powerful of European nations'.[42] For the modern historian, Michael Asher, this was the 'dawn of the Mahdist state in the Sudan, the first radical Islamic realm'.[43]

The Sudan presented a problem for Tewfiq, Egypt's nominal ruler, and for the British, Egypt's *de facto* rulers. Although Tewfiq wanted to maintain his Sudanese colony, Gladstone had no interest in the Sudan. The policy imposed on the Khedive was to evacuate Egyptian garrisons and civilians from the Sudan as quickly as possible. However, this was not easy to implement with many garrisons under siege from the Mahdists. The compromise to full-scale intervention in the Sudan was to send General Charles Gordon to Khartoum to evacuate the garrisons and civilians. Gordon was a venerated figure in Britain. Unconventional and non-conformist, Gordon was sympathetic to the plight of the suffering and the oppressed and for him 'integrity did not mean kowtowing to the hierarchy of the British Empire, but remaining consistent with his own deepest intuitions'.[44] In Gordon, William found a hero. In his biography of Gordon, William notes that he was a 'man who made of the whole world of his life a vast cathedral in which prayer and good work and sacrifice were ever going on' and he was a 'strange mixture of mysticism and measurement ... of the spiritual and the matter-of-fact'.[45] Gordon, however, became entrenched in Khartoum and under pressure from the public Gladstone's government eventually decided to send a relief force and Wolseley was given the task to mount a rescue operation in August 1884. Given that so much of the Sudan was controlled by the Mahdi or by his sympathizers, Wolseley planned to use the Nile. William was set to work to commission several hundred boats similar to the ones previously used by Wolseley in Canada and Canadian boatmen were employed for their expertise to accompany the expedition. Supporting the Nile mission was a specially trained unit, the Camel Corps – a military innovation. William published his account of this unusual rescue mission as *The Campaign of the Cataracts* (1887) with illustrations supplied by Elizabeth.

The jacket to the publication features an Arab figure, presumably the Mahdi, astride a horse with his arm outstretched raising a flag. The Mahdist flag is described by William as a 'cross with Arabic prayers combined'.[46] The image is also reproduced to open chapter 4 on the history of the Sudan conflict. Elizabeth's frontispiece features the Mahdist army traversing the Sudanese landscape under the title 'The Revolt of Islam'. A vista of empty and mountainous land stretches out before an army that is presented as disciplined and in formation. Prominent figures in the group are naked from the knees down and holding spears and shields, whilst one of their comrades holds their flag aloft. The mounted central figure, with his spear drawn and a shield on his back, is charging his horse towards a ridge looking over the landscape beyond. The birds flying beyond his field of vision suggest there is carnage in the valley below. This is an 'after the battle' scene with the focus on a native army. The next full-page illustration shows the British garrison post at Merawi in the Sudan on the left bank of the Nile. An array of army tents stretches out behind the fort, which is itself isolated within an empty landscape. A native figure with camels under a palm tree outside a makeshift fence securing the compound establishes its exotic setting (Figure 29). The third full-page illustration features the river column making its way down the Nile from Sarras. The point that Elizabeth highlights was William's anxiety that the boats might not be able to withstand the Nile currents: 'Moving off in succession from the shore, the boats put out into the stream; for a moment there was a pause ere oars had got good hold of the water, and sails were set, and sheets made fast; and then, slowly but steadily the white-winged flotilla began to move up the great river'.[47] William's text is a combination of travel writing, adventure and military enterprise, and this is reflected in the accompanying images. The opening of chapter 8 features a British soldier from the Camel Corps. 'Incessant camel-bumping', William observes, brought much 'discomfort' to British soldiers.[48] The next full-page illustration features William's crew pulling their boat over the cataract at Dal. The passage seemed impenetrable at this point until an elderly Arab accompanied by a small boy showed them a way through.

Soon a little passage hidden by islands was revealed to us; this opened into wider waters, and following them we found ourselves by noon at the foot of a great rapid – a rush of water more formidable than anything we had yet faced on the river. That the boat could live through this torrent was certain enough, but had we the strength requisite to haul her up. The two Indians must remain on board. Would our crew of nine with the addition of the old Arab and the two small boys (a second had joined us *en route*), be sufficient to drag the boat over this cataract?[49]

Elizabeth's next full-page illustration features the ruins of the temple at Agoulai in the foreground with the expedition boats in the distance. This part of the Nile, 1200 miles from the Mediterranean, is 'glorious' and the 'ruined temple' on the west bank 'seems left to tell what this region of Sukkôte must once have been ... There are no squalid hovels as in Egypt, built among the ruins or standing near them. Alone in sand-swept space ten or twelve lofty columns of red sandstone stand out against a sky whose blue is deepened by the clear atmosphere of this lofty desert'. Here the travel writer takes over from the soldier:

Nowhere else in this land of time and space have I seen age and distance deeper marked than here. A hundred temples stand upon the shores of the great river; broader and loftier than these lone columns and their shattered surroundings, but no temple arises amid such majesty of river and plain, and not in all those 1,200 miles of Nile is there to be found a spot where the desert wind, rustling through the ruins finds deeper voice to tell the story of ended time and endless solitude.[50]

The boats in the background of Elizabeth's illustration remind the reader that this is a 'rescue' mission. Very little of the urgency of the situation in Khartoum is evident in William's musing at this point or of his frustrations regarding the slowness of the enterprise. However, a single shot heard during the night reveals how other soldiers experience the Sudan campaign because when the party reaches their next post they discover that the English commandant has taken his own life: 'there are many English dead lying along the Nubian Nile ... but in all that long line of graves ... I know no sadder resting-place than that which marks where this young life was laid'.[51] Another soldier, Ian Hamilton, from the river column recalls how soldiers struggled up the Nile in 'small row-boats' in this 'vague and typically British adventure'. They felt like a 'party of boy scouts, dressed up as Red Indians and let loose in a flotilla of canoes' and while 'the tale had a ring of glorious adventure' much of their time was spent 'waist-deep in water' with 'broken nights', 'bad food' and drinking sand and water which resulted in scurvy, all of which 'wore health and nerves to fiddle-strings'.[52]

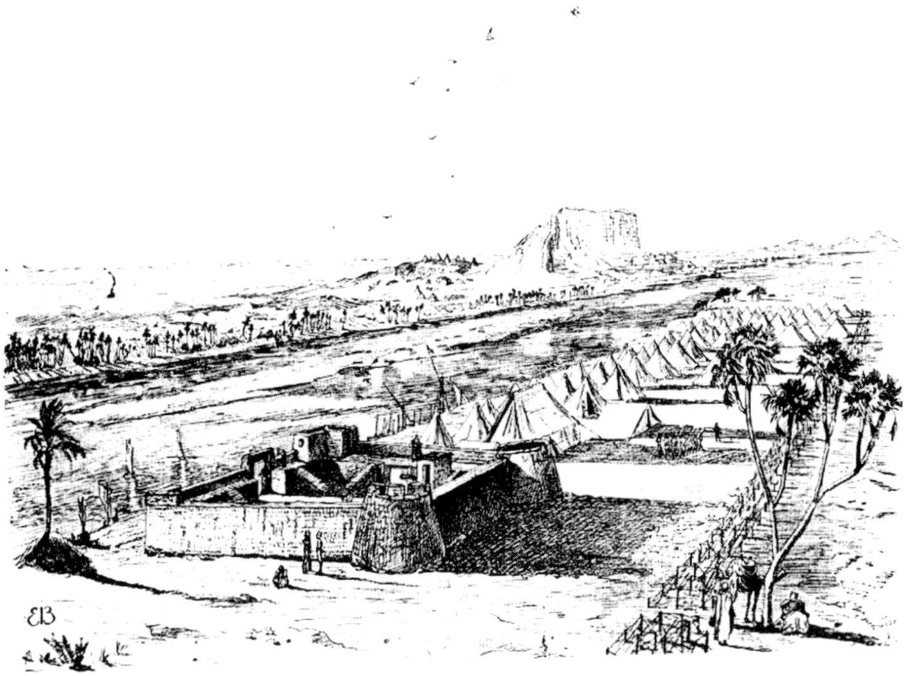

29 'The Frontier Post at Melawi' from *The Campaign of the Cataracts* by William Butler (1887).

The organization of the campaign was mired by delays and the incompetence of one of the Wolseley Ring, Redvers Bullers, who mismanaged the supply chain. Moreover, Wolseley distrusted William's individualism and what he perceived as his inability to work in a team. The mission was further complicated by Wolseley's decision to send the Camel Corps over the desert to shorten the route to Khartoum. When William reached Korti on 4 January the Camel Corps had departed for Metemma where they were supposed to meet with Gordon's steamers. William asserts that the river column, though it would take longer as the Nile bends after Korti, rather than the overland approach, was the right one in desert conditions. One of the great difficulties of an overland route was to maintain water supply for the troops. However, Khartoum, besieged, starved and disease-ridden, was running out of time. Elizabeth's subsequent full-page illustration features a line of the Camel Corps with their pith helmets and rifles. It would later become the subject of a major painting by the artist. The Corps were recruited from the best soldiers in the regiments. In conception, they were, Asher notes, an early incarnation of army special forces.[53] They were, however, comprised of soldiers with no experience of camels and it was a risky experiment. Hamilton, with a prejudiced eye, perceived the desert column as a distraction from the concentrated efforts of the river column to rescue Gordon: 'the pressure of the Ring; the urge to do something for his pals; the picturesqueness of the idea of putting London society on camels and marching them over the desert … was too much for [Wolseley]'.[54] Despite this the Corps encountered and defeated the enemy twice but lost their commanding officer, Herbert Stewart. The river column also encountered Arab resistance at Kirbekan. William devised the battle strategy

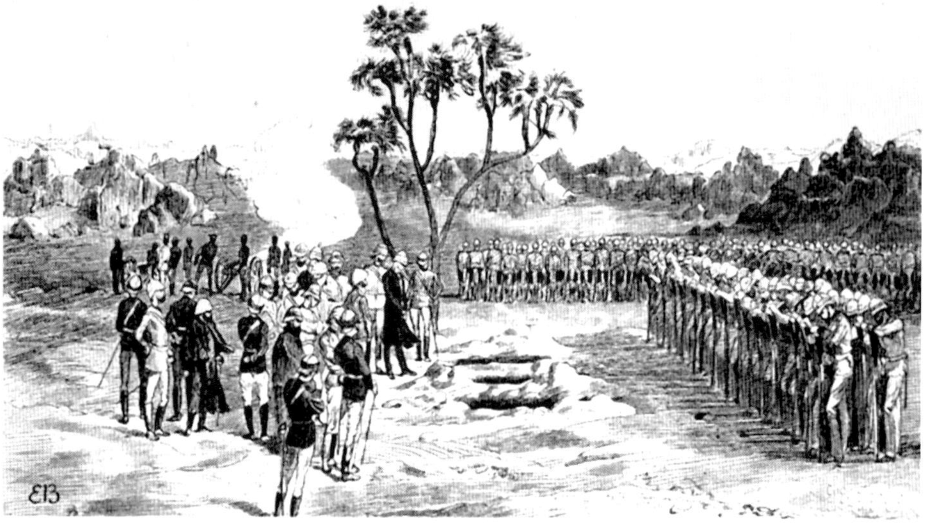

30 'The Burial of General Earle and Colonels Eyre and Coveney at Kirkeban' from *The Campaign of the Cataracts* by William Butler.

under the command of General Earle. The victory was swift but Earle was killed, 'costing the River column its best life'. Later two other bodies were brought in to camp: 'Eyre, the colonel of the Stafford Battalion – Coveney of the Black Watch'. Before the battle, news had filtered through that Khartoum had fallen. Lives were lost in the realization that there was 'no Khartoum' and 'looking at these three lifeless forms which a few hours earlier had moved out of this camp, the best among our little band, they whose presence through all the long road we had travelled, memory linked to a hundred scenes of service to our lost cause, given without stint of labour, it was impossible not to regret that such bootless victory had cost such brilliant lives'.[55] Elizabeth's final full-page illustration shows the burial of the three officers (Figure 30). The opened graves near a large palm tree are flanked by soldiers in formation on the right and to the left the officers are haphazardly gathered. Smoke from the gun carriage indicates that the salute has just been sounded. 'At sunset we laid them in their sleep. In a small spot of green, within sound of the waters of the great river they lie side by side in their long rest. A solitary dom-palm alone marks the spot … It was twilight when all was finished and the guns began to thunder out their last tribute over a darkening solitude'.[56] A letter to Alice on 21 February 1885 reveals Elizabeth's fears about the campaign at the time: 'My anxiety is very great and constant. I scarcely know why, but my heart has grown fainter since the news of Stewart's death. Not even the death of poor Earle under whom Will was fighting gave me such a shock … We have a terrible war before us. I think it was madness to undertake fighting the Mahdi at all, in a practically limitless desert'.[57]

On 26 January, Khartoum fell to the Madhists, thirty-two hours before the rescue mission, the Camel Corps, was within sight of the city. In his biography of Gordon, William describes how at the Church of the Austrian Mission, Gordon and a handful of troops made their last stand: 'For a moment the two parties stood almost face to face, then a volley of musketry fire flashed out at a close range, in the yet uncertain light, the bravest and noblest soldier of our time was no more'.[58] 'The Campaign of the Cataracts was over ... The man we had "come to seek in this desert" was gone, and only the echoes of his "voice crying in the wilderness" reached us through the darkness'.[59]

In recognition of his services, Wolseley appointed William to the command of Wady Halfa, which formed the border between Egypt and the Sudan and William was promoted to the temporary rank of Brigadier-General. First, he returned for leave on 30 June and Elizabeth secured rooms at the Army and Navy Hotel in Westminster, decking them with roses from a Plymouth friend, Sophy Collier. She described how William looked in a letter to Christiana: 'tho' greyer, looking splendid, & is nicely slim & sunburnt. Oh! how thankful I am for his good health & safety!'[60] By mid-August William had departed: 'Poor Will is gone again. He feels leaving me more & more each time. No one knows what a good dear he is to me'.[61] Elizabeth followed him to Egypt with her two eldest children, Patrick and Coos, and her friend, Sophy Collier, in mid-November 1885.

Elizabeth in Egypt

Elizabeth's detailed accounts of her Egyptian travels, related in letters to Christiana with a view to later publication in *From Sketch-Book and Diary* (1909), demonstrate her interest in the landscape, the people, the British military, and the Pharaonic past as witnessed above ground. On her visit to the Pyramids in Cairo Elizabeth described her journey along an 'acacia-shaded road' running 'a long distance in an imposing straight line to almost the very base of the great Pyramid', her eye drawn to the 'mighty Pyramids & Sphinx & tombs' and the 'ever-interesting groups of men, women & children & animals which we passed'.[62] For Elizabeth human interest combines with interest in antiquity. With Sophy she took a stroll to the Sphinx, resting in its 'broad shadow'. The 'face was very impressive, especially the "calm eternal eyes" that have been looking for over 4000 years across the plain. I had a consciousness of awe the whole day which was with me for days afterwards'. They then climbed to the entrance in the north face of the Great Pyramid where they had an 'exquisite view of Cairo in sun & shadow under a sky of most beautiful cloud-forms & up the left the lovely pearly & rosy desert stretched away into the grey & golden West'. Light and colour, typical of an artist, define her relationship with what she sees. 'One feels the stupendous size of the Pyramids most when standing rather close to the centre of the faces rather than at the angles'. These are contrasted with quotidian life. The 'shepherds guiding their flocks along the road & carrying tired lambs on their shoulders' and the 'buffaloes & oxen & ploughmen going home from their work in the soft mysterious light' seemed incongruous with the suburbs where

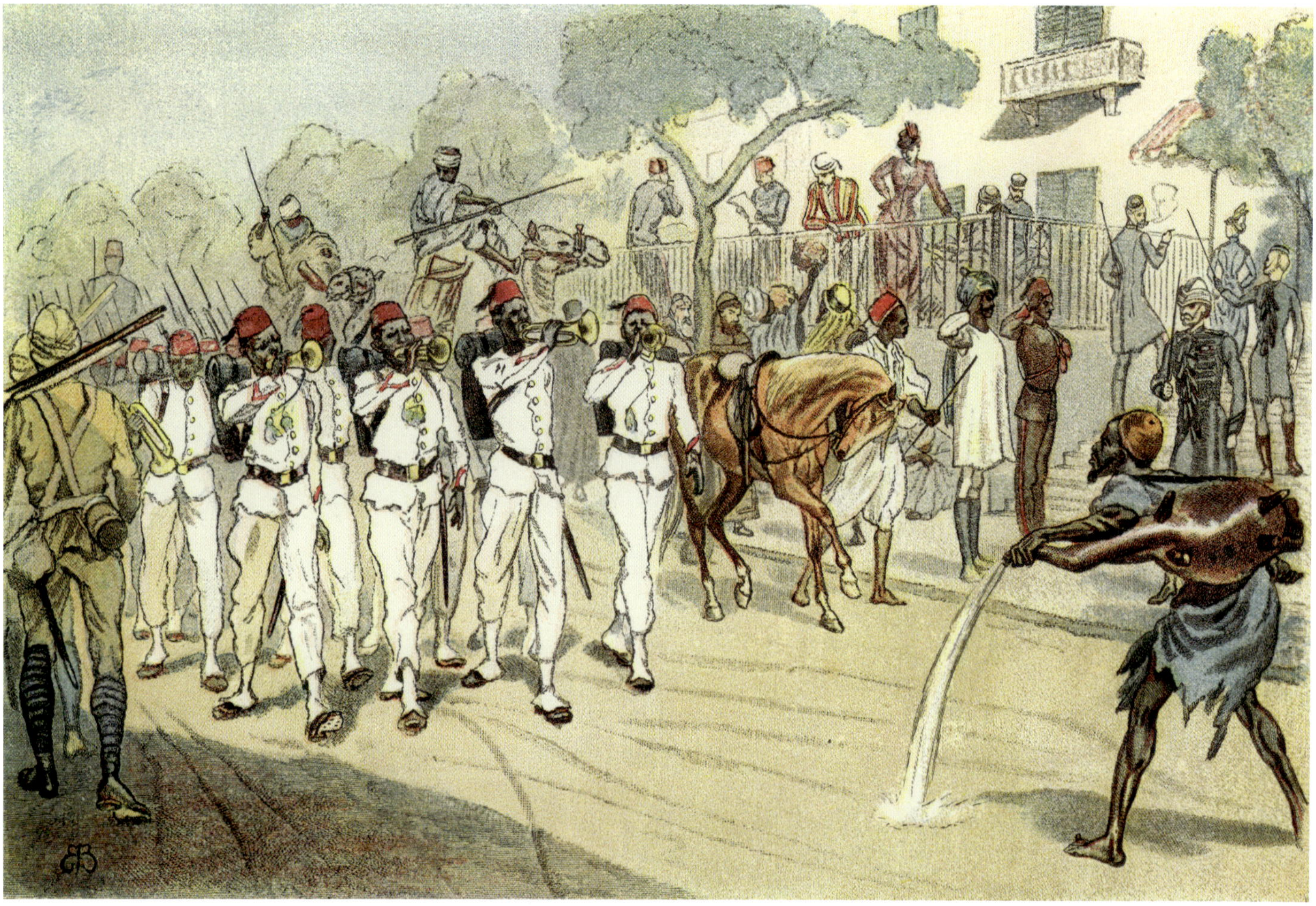

31 *Life at Shepheard's Hotel*, colour litho.
Private Collection. Bridgeman Art Library.

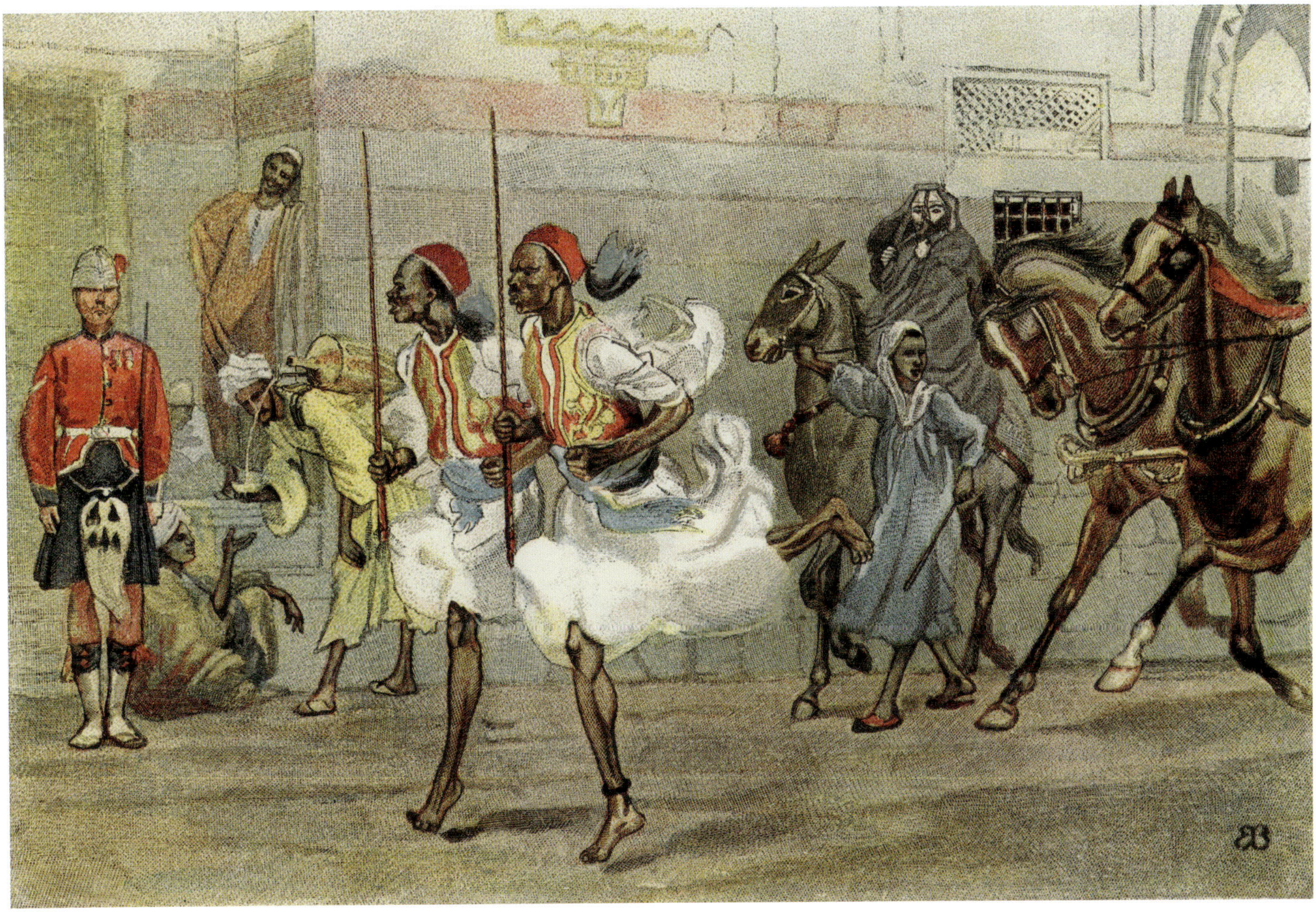

32 *The English General's Syces*, colour litho. Private Collection. Bridgeman Art Library.

'Tommy Atkins was about, & British officers coming in from riding & the cafés were full & noisy in this Parisianized quarter of Cairo', leaving the visitors feeling that they had 'leapt back into today by crossing an iron bridge which spanned 4000 years' while their 'thoughts lingered behind amongst those most ancient, most pathetic part & most solemn monuments of the pre-Christian world'.[63] Elizabeth produced sketches of the Cairo streets in which there is a strong imperial military presence (Figures 31 and 32).

It is the backdrop of military conflict that makes her accounts unique. For a while the travellers linger in Cairo and Luxor because they were 'in daily expectation of a serious fight at the front'. As Elizabeth noted: 'I do not know when I shall be able to join Will [sic] no ladies are allowed to go at present to Wady Halfa'. However, 'if all [went] well at the front', she hoped to venture to Luxor and 'paint a little picture there'. Meanwhile, Cairo surpassed her expectations, but despite its 'perfectly pleasant weather' they had to be very careful of the water which was 'dangerous, a chill equally so, & diet must be carefully taken'. Sophy was excellent at managing their finances. Aside from the practicalities,

> Nothing could equal the picturesqueness of Cairo. The colours of the peoples dresses are endless in their beauty & the buildings are infinite in lovely outline, colour & detail. All is full of light; the reflected light here is in its glory ... Oh! I revel in types & costumes here from morning to night.[64]

On 22 December, Elizabeth wrote to her mother from Luxor where they waited for a dahabiyeh that William was planning to send down for their use and the purpose of which was to house the party at Wady Halfa. Conflict intervened: 'alas! the fighting has broken out again, Will is 100 miles beyond Wady Halfa & the whole army is probably going to fight its way back to Dongola & we women are not allowed to go further than Assouan!' They intended to use the boat at Luxor instead to save on hotel bills. Meanwhile there was 'no chance' of Elizabeth seeing 'Will for a long time' as he had a position of 'great responsibility'. Meanwhile, Luxor offered a 'deep calm' compared with 'busy & commercial & military Cairo'.

A visit to the tombs of the kings made on donkeys reveals Elizabeth's sense of humour and her lack of constraint:

> We crossed over the fast-flowing Nile in a ferry boat & found our black, white & grey donkeys with scarlet & blue saddle cloaks awaiting us in the mud near the waters edge on the other side. We had to be taken to land on men's shoulders & deliciously funny was it to see the ladies being hurried thro' the water in the arms of the swarthy Arabs, some of whom were almost entirely naked. Mrs Collier & another stout lady made the men groan, beneath them good-humouredly. One acid old maid with a Mother Hubbard hat & blue spectacles clung like a monkey to a Nubian giant whose few rags flew behind

> him in the morning breeze & allowed his figure to appear below her skirts in the frankest way. I fell with laughter. We mounted our donkeys & scuttled over the dry mud with a troop of shouting Arabs whose free walk & gloriously developed muscles & polished skins of different shades of bronze distracted my eyes often during the day from the arid Lybian mountains, the awful tombs, the magnificent views.

The landscape and the people interested Elizabeth more than the tombs while the military occupation of Egypt by the British 'Tommy', as well as the ongoing hostilities, form the backdrop to her thoughts. This is a traveller and painter who does not in this landscape stray far from her military preoccupations:

> We rode 7 miles over sand & stones & rocks of rosy & yellowish grey, full of golden reflected light up to the unspeakably arid mountains where rain never falls & which are pierced from base to summit with sepulchres four or five thousand years old. After going thro' three of the most important of these, namely that of King Rameses IV & Rameses IX & Seti I had enough of paintings & hieroglyphics & horrors of sepulchral air & was glad to come out into the sun again. After lunch at the entrance of a filled up tomb I sketched some Arabs & then we climbed to the very top of one mountain & I had one of the epoch-making views of my life. Nile valley, opposite mountains, silver river flowing winding away, away towards Assouan & on to the regions of the mysterious Soudan where so many of our countrymen lie at rest.[65]

Her companion, Sophy Collier, was painted by the Pre-Raphaelite artist, John Collier, a couple of years before her visit to Egypt with Elizabeth. Reclining on a chesterfield in a dark dress with a white collar at the neckline, Sophy is surrounded by three children who peep across at her over the back of the chesterfield. While Sophy grasps the hand of her little girl, an older girl views her mother through a gauzy material which is lying on the sofa. The family's interest in the Orient can be seen in a carved Oriental coffee table. The image, though capturing the muted yellows and browns of a Victorian room, nonetheless evokes John Frederick Lewis's reclining Eastern women from his Egyptian paintings.[66] Elizabeth conveys a less complimentary representation of the 'Amazonian' Sophy going over the desert on a donkey: 'Too delicious is the now familiar figure of dear old Sophy in a dark blue cotton frock apparently running along on 4 legs, with a tail projecting rigidly & energetically from her skirt & a sinewy Arab or two pursuing her with sticks over the desert'.

Karnak, by moonlight, inspires the artist: 'I cannot describe the ponderous & colossal aspect of these masses of ruins & standing pillars so as to convey to you the feeling one has while standing amongst them. As to the beauty of colour at the afterglow when the moon rose, it was beyond words'.[67] At the same time, 'English

33 'Sketches of Life and Character in Egypt' from *The Graphic*, 16 February 1889.

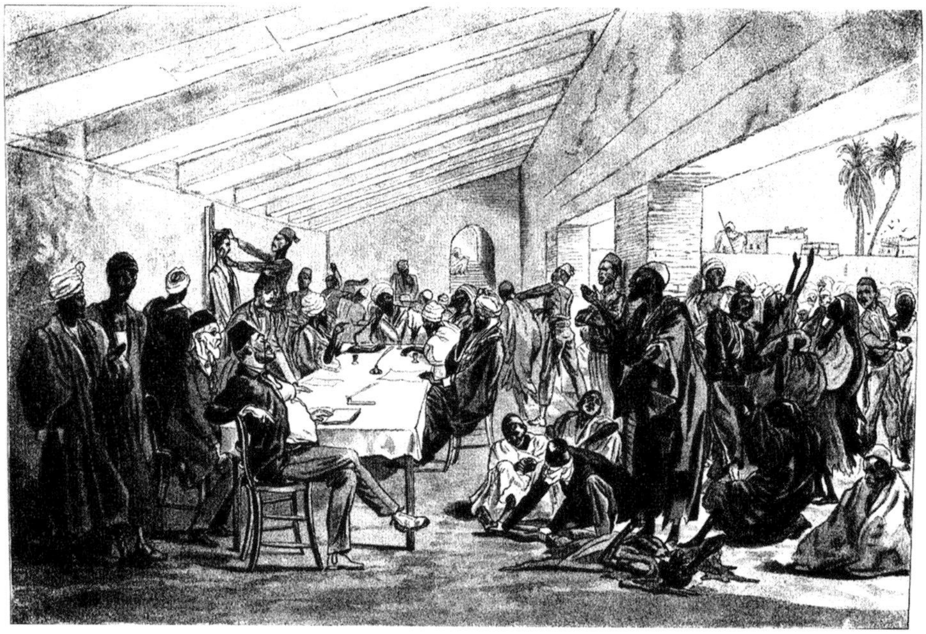

troops are passing her almost daily for the front & stop here for an hour or so for provisions. I thus saw several friends yesterday at the landing stage'. Christmas Eve brought memories of her deceased father:

> Oh! my Sweet Mamma, how much I thought of you & my beloved Father last night. I never go out here without thinking in an especial manner of him for he used to read so much to us of Egypt, both of its old history & of its scenery. Oh! what I owe to him! My dearest Mamma I hope you will spend tomorrow at Alice's & not be lonely. You must feel so lonely sometimes. Thank Heaven, you have your sweet music to think of & the blessed Church to comfort you.

Egypt offered a series of contrasts between painted temples and the 'ragged people & broken pillars & arid mountains'. Poverty was evident: 'Nothing could be more wretched than the mud villages of the Arabs amongst these scorched rocks & mountains'.[68]

One of her most important experiences was her attendance at the conscription of new recruits into the army – a scene later described in *From Sketch-Book and Diary* (Figures 33 and 34):

> We went thro the village to the courtyard where this curious transaction was going on, the English consul leading the way. We had to fight our way to the door of a very dirty alley which was crowded with the female relatives of the wretched youths inside, some of these women were the most ghastly old hags you conceive – hardly more sightly than mummies we had seen at Boulak Museum which had died 4000 years ago. These hideous hags were wailing

something like the Irish, but in a clacking way as tho' their faces were really only skulls & their skinny arms worked like the arms of marionettes. I think, indeed, they were worse than mummies, for the poor mummies at least were quiet & these poor creatures were going thru' antics to express their grief ... At a rickety table sat the officials & the sheiks of the villages from which the young men came – splendid men in elaborate turbans & silk robes. The doctor sat a little aside & as each proposed conscript in his miserable one garment of camel's hair was pushed up to the table the doctor examined him. His eyes, teeth, hair &c & if he passed him two gendarmes seized upon him cuffed & hustled him to the Standard where he was measured. If he was below the minimum he was pushed roughly back to his lamenting people, if his height was as required he was thrust by the nape of the neck by the gendarmes into the group of already chosen conscripts .... What a back-view, a seamy-side view this gave us of the Egyptian army: what material to make soldiers out of! No wonder they are scattered like sheep, as soon as a determined enemy comes among them. I was glad to witness this scene for this Registration only takes place one in 5 years. It was a very painful spectacle altogether & I left the surging mass of unfortunate humanity rather sick & sad, tho' as I say it was an experience I would not have wilfully missed.[69]

By New Year's Eve, which she spent at Luxor, Will informed her by telegram that the 'Arabs [had been] driven from all positions with loss of their guns & standards God be praised'. Elizabeth assured Christiana: 'Will is safe! This telegram is all I know of the battle. Every town in England had the details to-day & you know far more about it than I do here!' While the battle was going on Elizabeth was 'peacefully painting on the terrace here ... Will sent the telegram at 6 last evening – probably from the battle field. Good soldiers always send their earliest messages to their wives'. Incorporated into this letter are her impressions of Cairo:

[O]ne has the feeling that everyone is acting a part in a stage as he walks, strolls drives or rides & that this is a wonderfully well got up play or pageant for the amusement of the denizens of Shepheards' as they sit on the terrace in the delicious shade & watch what passes before them. Men of all shades of colour pass to & from on ambling donkeys; these men are dressed in every variety of Eastern garment & headdress. Veiled women in black, blue & white 'yashmaks' go by riding astride of their donkeys. Then a string of camels will move as it were across the stage, & then a British Hussar orderly will clank past the slow-moving beasts on his wiry little Syrian horse & a cab will follow full of jolly kilted Highlanders out for a spree.

The pageant of Cairo's streets reveals the Empire in Egypt. Elizabeth was, of course, aligned to the British military presence in Egypt.[70]

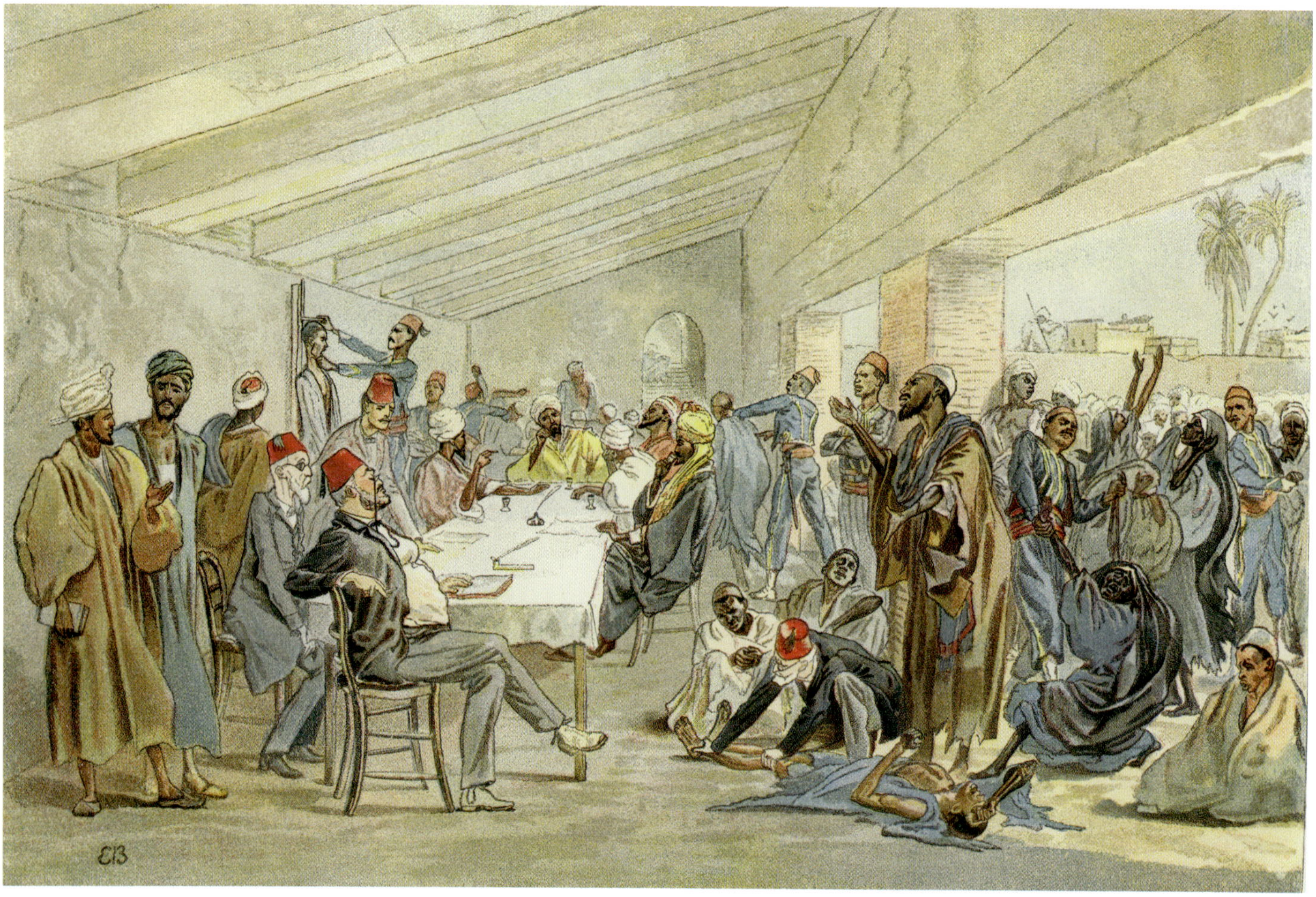

34 *Registering the Fellaheen for Military Service*, colour litho. Private Collection. Bridgeman Art Library.

While as an artist she revelled in the colour of the streets, her views of the people reveal her as a conventional Victorian traveller with her air of cultural superiority. Despite her unorthodox career, she often subscribes to racial stereotyping and exhibits less empathy than William for indigenous peoples:

> Of course, the people are nothing but savages & one sinks in hopeless helplessness at the idea of trying to get them up to a Christian level of thought. Where can one begin? Education is, of course, the only thing & slowly I suppose it will leaven the masses but it will take centuries to become effective. The little Catholic mission here has 80 scholars in its school – Christian Coptic & Pagan – all who wish to come, & it is wonderful how well they are taught by the 'Christian Brothers' ... Three or 4 languages are taught, geography, Botany, History, Natural History & the 3 R's & I was surprised when I visited the school to hear the ragged Arab boys say their lessons in excellent English & to see their beautiful French writing. The priest at the head of the school is an Italian Capuchin.

The 'ragged Arab boys' learning their lessons undermines her argument that it would take 'centuries' to educate the population.[71]

On 9 January, the party left Luxor on the dahabiyeh *Fostât* enroute for Wady Halfa: 'How placid a way of travelling this is, but with no wind it is very slow. Sometimes the sailors get out & haul the vessel from the bank, sometimes they push her with long poles from the deck & as I write they are hauling her along by means of ropes & grappling irons, singing in monotonous cadence whilst over them hang the crescent moon & Venus, both making long reflections in the oily water'. There were ongoing concerns about the position of the enemy: 'Can it be the enemy are threatening to turn on left, & come behind & take us in near Korosko by the desert route. If so of course we must recall all troops advanced far out & concentrate all our forces at the threatened point'. William sent them his Syrian interpreter, 'an arrant coward & I suppose as great a rascal as all these shady so-called Christians are'.[72] On 12 January she wrote from Esneh which was 'celebrated for being the healthiest place in all Egypt, for the wonderful Temple, or rather part of the Temple discovered there, & for its dye works – which dye cloth the beautiful Indigo & other blue which the people wear so much'. They were greeted by the Egyptian consul from Luxor with the post boat: 'This really most obliging man – how very civil these Egyptian officials are to us people in possession – run down to us to salaam & shake hands & we all landed & made at once for the Post Office to post our letters'. Then there was the usual sightseeing 'escorted by the Pasha's orders, by an officer & 4 or 6 Gendarmes who cleared the way for us thro' the crowd, aided by our Syrian Interpreter & the Pasha's "Cawass" with whips'. After dinner the

> Pasha came to pay his respects on board & I had to order the crew to give him a befitting reception with tom-toms & singing. He is a great swell – the

governor of so large a Province … He could not speak a word of French or English & the consul interpreted all our platitudes & florid speeches. Oh! the grinning, the humbug, the Blarney that went on … Oh! I was in good humour. I gave the Pasha & Consul excellent Extra Dry Monopole – finest coffee & Maraschino, & when we went on deck I smoked with the two fezzed individuals in the starlight … When our guests were gone the presents from the Pasha arrived – eggs in hundreds, vegetables, turkeys & a sheep – all very welcome, for living higher up the river is very dear & everything, animal & vegetable very scarce. I have live stock on board for a month.

However, the Pasha lost favour the next morning when he came to see Elizabeth's children: 'As with all these women-despising heathens he took but little notice of Coos & lavished his caresses & compliments on the General's son'. Although he sent his servant to attend to them on their onward voyage Sophy 'shrewdly' suggested that he only did so because he wanted a 'free passage' for him to Aswan. 'As to the presents, alas! they cost the Pasha nothing – these things are all tribute in kind to the fat villain from the fellaheen'.[73] However, on their arrival at Edfoo they found that the Pasha's servant was 'valuable' after all 'for he walked ahead of us with his wand & kept the crowd away & looked a very respectable individual'. At Aswan, they stayed in a hotel as their dahabiyeh was being hauled over the first cataract and they joined it again by railway.

Hurrah! About 3 miles from Assouan we beheld our armed steamer hasting towards us. I was dressing in my best bib & tucker in case Will should be at landing stage. I saw a stalwart figure on the 'bridge' of the steamer waving a handkerchief – no one wd believe me when I said it's Will, it's Will! I was first dressed in time to receive him on board the *Fostât*, & his armour-clad little steamer towed us in half an hour to Assouan. He is looking magnificent.[74]

On the 21 January, she described Aswan as a 'place teaming with historical interest but whose old-world quiet is ploughed up & tossed hither & thither by the British occupation'. Aboard the *Fostât* again they anchored near to Philae but

It took a little from the sentiment of this exquisite place to have a British camp in the fore-ground & to hear the railway whistle & see so many wooden shanties & coal offices &c amongst the palms – but, when the English go, all will speedily melt into perfect harmony again. When we got on to the Fostat all these unsightly & unseemly sights & sounds were shut out & I feasted my eyes on the beautiful island & its ruined temple which lay opposite our moorings. We went on the Island next day – a day of perfect calm – followed by so warm a night that I enjoyed a moonlight promenade by myself on deck

> in my nocturnal garment & dressing-gown. Unfortunately the day following we had a sandstorm, a very ugly & exasperating phenomenon, & my attempts at oil sketching on Philae island was a failure, for after persevering with one eye open at a time & sand thickly mixed with my paints my panel was hurled to the ground on its buttered side as for the moment I turned to answer a remark of Sophy's.[75]

Korosko was 'desolate & strange' and 'sad with regretful memories of Gordon. This was his starting point as he left the Nile to travel across the desert to Khartoum, never to return'. While Elizabeth sketched from the boat Sophy climbed a steep hill from 'whence she could see to the remote horizon the black & ashen landscape which lonely Gordon travelled'. She was, however, forced to retreat rather quickly as 'about 20 wild women came about her & pawed her from head to foot, & their close proximity was too much to stand'. Landing on the opposite side of the Nile at Philae the women were surrounded 'by old shrivelled hags & wild young women with nose rings & anklets & whose hair was plaited in hundreds of little tails reeking with castor oil & each tail ending in a little lump of mud'. Then

> Sophy asked those amongst them whose heads were covered to display their unattractive locks & in return she let down her own hair & stood on it to 'astonish the natives' & they danced & wailed in slow uncanny cadence to express their astonishment & admiration. The picture the rosy, fresh Englishwoman made with her golden chestnut hair trailing on the sand, & surrounded by little half naked brown & black barbarian women & quite naked imps of children, with, for background, a ruined temple, huge wild rocks was one of rare point.[76]

The scene is related in *From Sketch-Book and Diary*. By February, she was experiencing the extreme heat of Wady Halfa:

> I had a most impressive ride into the appalling desert to the East of Wady Halfa the day before yesterday with Will and his Aide de Camp. Gordon said of this desert that it was the most terrible he had ever known & well he might say so! ... It was a dead land – lying dead & unburied, like the many dead camels which lay about withering away in the sun till they had become grey fragments of skin & bleached bones ... Our return from the desert ride ended with daylight & mournful was the scene in the short twilight as we re-crossed the plain, for in the midst of the sad experience with its unburied dead things tainting the wind in rear of the English Camps which border the wholesome Nile appeared the English cemetery now thickly filled with crosses, whither daily are borne the remains of our fast-dying soldiers.

Elizabeth echoed William's views on Wady Halfa: 'If our army is kept here much longer it will be an outrage to our men. Our legislators at home do not take much account of the lives of our soldiers unless lost in battle. Will says he cannot let me & the children remain after the middle of March. How long he will be kept here who can say? What on earth is the army here for now?'[77] On 10 March Elizabeth and the children left Wady Halfa and returned to England via Alexandria. In her autobiography, Elizabeth notes that to 'Plymouth we returned, leaving the General to drag out the burning summer at Wady Halfa'. Meanwhile with her oil sketches made on location she prepared her next Academy painting, *A Desert Grave*. Now lost, the picture, she laments, should have been 'more poetical'. An insight into the painting is provided in her description of the desert graves: 'The Upper Nile had these graves of British officers and men all along its banks during that terrible toll taken in the course of the Gordon Expedition and after, some in single loneliness, far apart, and some in twos and threes'.[78] Lloyd's Weekly notes that she treated the subject 'very skilfully'.[79] Although this paining no longer exists she returned to other versions of desert graves later and her illustration for *The Campaign of the Cataracts* suggests how the subject was handled by her. Elizabeth's encounter with Egypt reveals a figure who is aware that she was one of the 'people in possession', but being in possession enabled her to draw and to take possession of Egypt as an artist.[80] Equipped by the privilege of class she fails to empathize with the Egyptian people, while those in positions of authority repel her. Although she was, like her husband, ambivalent about the imperial enterprise, her culture was permeated by the cult of empire. Cultural encounters with the Pasha, the Syrian interpreter or the women who marvel at Sophy's hair on the banks of the Nile provoke confused responses from her. As always, she mediates her world through her art. She would return to Egypt four years later but in the meantime Elizabeth's next move was to Dinan in Northern France, a move which challenged her personally just as Egypt challenged her artistically and politically.

CHAPTER SEVEN

Dinan, Delgany and Alexandria, 1887–93

Birth of Martin – The Campbell divorce case – Dinan and painting – To the Front – *Delgany, County Wicklow – Charles Stewart Parnell –* Evicted – *Alexandria – Travel writing and illustration – Delgany again – The Holy Land – Napoleon's battleground –* Halt on a Forced March – The Camel Corps

> How happily you and I get thro' our little troubles. My accouchement was almost peasant-like in its dimensions & most happily I had only the sage femme, the doctor arriving long after the baby, as he was away in the country when we sent for him. So I escaped the mortification & violence to my feelings which render the doctor the worst part of these affairs. Never have I been so delicately and quietly handled by a doctor as I was by that excellent sage femme.
>
> The little fellow is a big fat & very intelligent baby. I am going on in the most natural manner, except, of course, that I am not nursing. Is it not a pleasure to introduce the little Papoose to the other children? To watch their expressions of wonder? ... I am thankful for any scrap of art news. We see the *Graphic* and the occasional Irish paper & the W. Register only for we don't get day London news.[1]

Elizabeth wrote to Alice after the birth of her last child, Martin, in Dinan in northern France in the spring of 1887. The escape to this rural setting where Elizabeth gave birth attended by a 'sage femme' and her joy at introducing the 'little Papoose' to its siblings obscures the difficult period that the Butlers were experiencing at this time. Dinan was an escape. When he returned from Egypt on sick leave in July 1886, William discovered at the War Office that he was to be put on half-pay with the rank of lieutenant-colonel. He had angered his superiors in Britain complaining about the conditions of his men in Wady Halfa. Wolseley, from whom he sought advice, counselled him that his conduct to his commanding officer, General Stephenson, 'a most easy man to get on with', bordered on insubordination. 'You must learn to work in a team before you can drive one ... whether you are a follower or a leader you

must pull with a will and not kick at others in the team and refuse to answer obediently to the call that the chief makes on you'.[2]

Elizabeth was also experiencing her own difficulties with William. She had been warned by Alice in 1884 that William was going to be named as a co-respondent in the divorce case of Lord and Lady Campbell. William was in Egypt at the time and Elizabeth replied on the 14 November:

> Dearest Alice
>
> I am, of course, deeply shocked. I can say little now. On receipt of your answer to my telegram I shall wire to Will. He shd be informed without further delay if the thing is really coming off, but I cannot but think Lord C. mentioned that most honourable & spotless name in a fit of anger & that he will not weaken his cause by choosing a man so conspicuous in London for his moral character to shatter his accusations against.
>
> Do you suggest I shd communicate with Lewis in order to represent to Lord C. the mistake he is making? I wish to direct my efforts toward obtaining a withdrawal of the charge, as, altho' I know truth must prevail at the trial, it is better no trial shd take place as regards Will. I tell you nothing of my feelings, the pain is too deep. Please answer by return.
>
> Your loving Mimi[3]

Gertrude Blood, Lady Colin Campbell, had known William since she was a child. As a woman she was beautiful and beguiling and her involvement with the Butler marriage positions her as a *femme fatale*. Giovanni Boldini's painting of her, which was produced in 1897, the same year that Bram Stoker's *Dracula* depicted seductive female vampires, presents a statuesque, ivory-skinned, black-haired woman, dressed in black with a low cleavage, who looks invitingly at the viewer. Her family were Irish landowners from County Clare. Gertrude was also part of the Meynells' literary and social circle. Clever and talented, she was a socialite, published writer and an artist. Elizabeth was on friendly terms with her – an undated letter to Alice encloses an unspecified item for Lady Colin.[4] In another letter Elizabeth thanked Alice and Wilfrid for inviting her friends the Colliers to dinner where they had been introduced to the 'charming people' in the Meynell set. This set included Gertrude and Elizabeth informed Alice that she expected, when she next met him, that Mortimer Collier would 'unburden his soul about you, Mama & Lady Colin, all of whom seemed to have laid him very flat'.[5]

Gertrude had married Lord Colin Campbell after a very brief acquaintance in July 1881. The marriage could not be consummated immediately as Campbell was suffering from syphilis, a highly infectious and life-threatening disease, and one that in its advanced stages is linked to insanity. Before long, the Campbell marriage was failing and Gertrude sought a legal separation accusing her husband of infecting her. Her biographer, Anne Jordan, notes that her symptoms at this point suggest gonorrhoea.[6]

By the summer of 1884 Campbell had Gertrude followed by private detectives and filed for divorce on 6 November on the grounds of adultery, citing three men as co-respondents: a notorious womanizer, Lord Blandford, the respectable head of the London Metropolitan Fire Brigade, Captain Eyre Shaw, and William. Gertrude lodged her own petition just half an hour before her husband lodged his petition, citing his cruelty and accusing him of adultery with his housemaid. Later Campbell added a fourth co-respondent to the list: his doctor Professor Thomas Bird. He did so after the doctor had sued him for the non-payment of his medical bill. During this period the Meynells were Gertrude's 'steadfast friends'.[7] A sketch of the head and shoulders of a demurely dressed Gertrude in side profile appeared in the Meynells' *Merry England* a month after the divorce was filed.[8]

The case against William was based on his visits to Gertrude at her home in Cadogan Place, mostly in the summer of 1883, while Elizabeth was pregnant with Eileen. William met Gertrude at the offices of her solicitors, Lewis and Lewis, in the summer of 1885 and recorded a statement: 'I have not been in love with Lady Campbell, nor have I kissed her'.[9] Although the 'case against Butler was the weakest of the four', and was based on the testimonies of Campbell's nurse and housemaid that William had visited Gertrude alone and had on one occasion stayed for over two hours, during which time her mistress barred other visitors, William refused to take the stand. It was left to his barrister to refute the allegations.[10] During the trial Gertrude appealed to Elizabeth to induce William to appear in her defence, but, in a letter dated 15 December 1886, Elizabeth refused to use her influence: 'Your appeal to me touches me deeply. I would I could help you, but I believe this case to have passed out of our hands and to have gone before a tribunal where human aid is impossible'.[11] The judge in his summing up condemned William for not taking the stand.[12]

On the night of 20 December 1886, the jury returned its verdict that no adultery had been committed by either husband or wife. The outcome of the trial was that the couple remained married, but it was Gertrude's 'hour of victory' as she had 'defended her name against allegations of adultery'.[13] Gertrude, whether innocent or guilty, had, however, become a 'fallen' woman, a figure which regularly appeared in Victorian literature and art in the decades preceding the trial. To further trouble Elizabeth, the foreman of the jury noted that it had been rendered more difficult for them to make a decision by William's refusal to take the stand: 'By not coming forward in the interests of justice, they thought him not worthy of being called an English officer and a gentleman'.[14] During the trial, Wilfrid acted as an intermediary between William and Gertrude's solicitors, with William apologizing to him 'for the trouble I am so often giving you'.[15] On the 21 December, William replied to a telegram from Wilfrid on the verdict. Addressing him as 'My dear Wilfrid', William records his relief: 'One short line to thank you for your telegram which reached me at 10.20 a.m. today. What joy it brought us you & Alice will know'.[16] His refusal to testify at the trial, however, poses questions about the nature of the relationship between

William and Gertrude. Anne Jordan argues that although adultery was unlikely, William was probably attracted to the vibrant Gertrude. In the aftermath of the trial, *Vanity Fair* concluded that William's absence was proof of guilt. Gertrude was incensed and wrote to Wilfrid: 'I am simply foaming with indignation at the article in *Vanity Fair* – read it & you will understand what your precious brother in law has exposed me to! – & then you ask me to forgive him!'[17]

Dinan

For Elizabeth, Dinan was both an escape and a productive environment. In the October before the trial she wrote to Alice asking her for 'art gossip' as they were 'leading an Arcadian life' in the French countryside. She explained how she had taken to 'house keeping' because it was so 'picturesque' and loved 'marketing'. She noted: 'the different women who come daily to the old-fashioned kitchen bringing their different provisions are all so nice in the crêpe white caps & nice warm shawls, neatly & becomingly folded over their broad, strong chests, with their short dark blue dresses well out of the mud'. She revelled in the market:

> Will & I bought a pig the other day. I found it hard work bargaining amongst scores & scores of struggling & squeaking pug-a-wugs & chattering men & women. The pig market was under the old ramparts, shaded by lime trees & close to the old gate of St Louis, with its images & pictures of Saints hanging in frames over the archway. A most beautiful picture the whole made.

It was also a time of reflection on their Italian childhood: 'Oh! what sums of money wd have been saved in Italy if we had pursued the system Will & the natives here employ. And living here is not only cheap but everything is so good – meat, poultry vegetables, fruit & butter & bread & wine'. The farmhouse was 'very cosy – the walls are thick'. Furthermore

> Will is very happy in this little patriarchal abode & can write well in so sweet & peaceful surroundings. I find the place healthy & invigorating, so that I can walk much. It is not the season for outdoor sketching so I will finish up already-begun work indoors. I am sure Sebastian Lepage must have worked much here. The green orchards, white cows & blue & white women, with distaffs, minding the cows remind me so much of him.[18]

In a letter of 23 January, she was concerned about Alice's silence, and although the Campbell case is not mentioned, the subtext is clear: 'I have felt your silence very much & have often spoken sadly of it to Will. Mamma's letters ... have been the kindest & most truly sympathetic I have received of late'. Her work had been affected

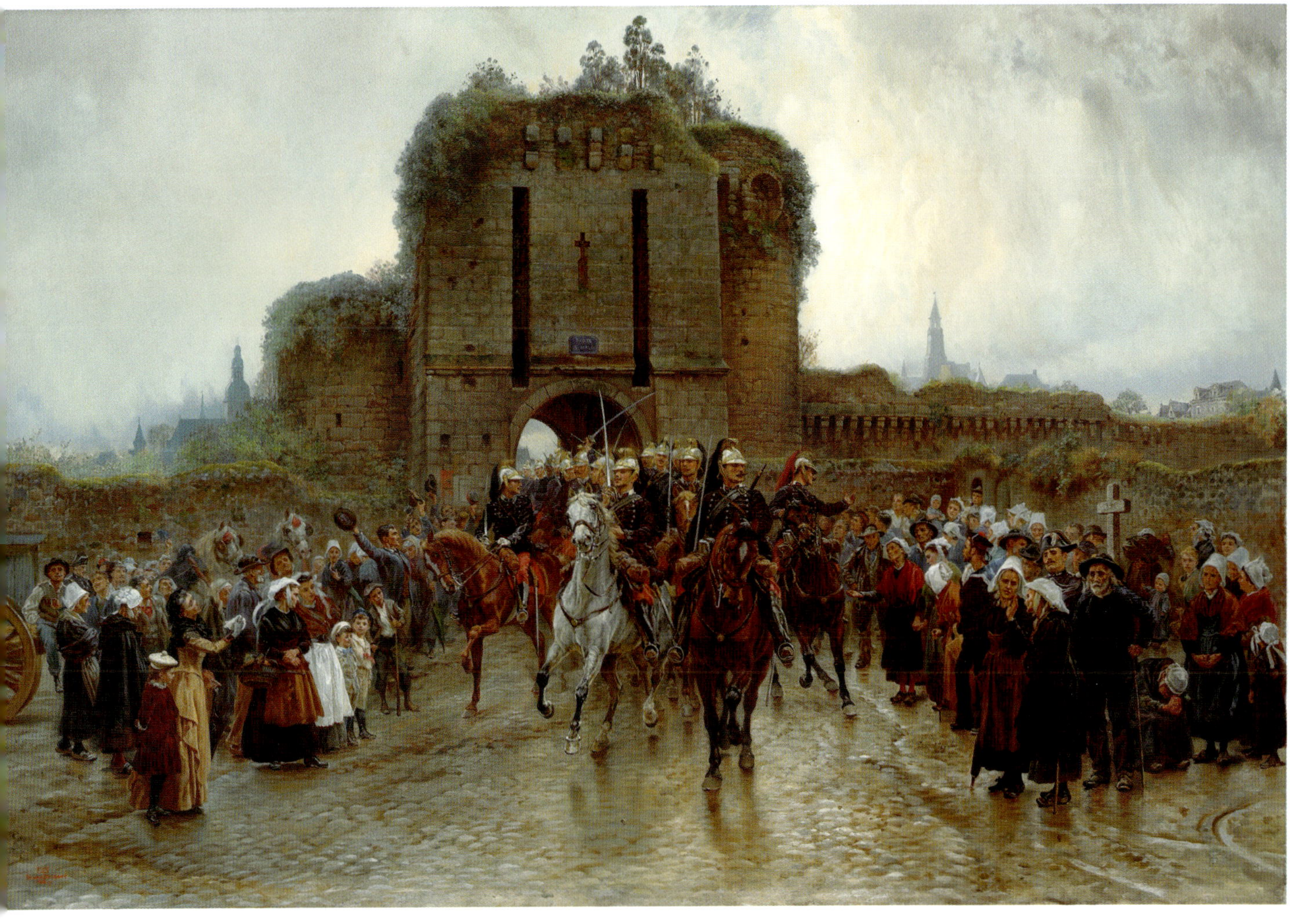

35 *To the Front: French Cavalry Leaving a Breton City on the Declaration of War*, 1888–9. Oil on canvas, 112 x 164.8cm. Private Collection. Bridgeman Art Library.

due to her pregnancy: 'I have not touched my Soudan desert picture for more than two months'.[19] However, she was turning her attention to the French army: 'Will & I are much impressed by the new French Army. All the old Napoleon III "chic" has vanished – that glittering delusion. The privates are horribly untidy & unshaven & ill-set-up, but how hard & workmanlike. Ugly to look at, but fit for long marches, rough bivouacs & fighting. The officers are serious & quiet & determined'.[20] On the 28 February, she put aside her painting for 'nearly 3 months' because of pregnancy but 'long[ed] for her emancipation & visit to the Art World of Paris'. Alice was also pregnant: 'If you are still perpendicular', Elizabeth wrote, 'do send me a line. It is such a pleasure to see your handwriting'.[21]

The Butlers' working arrangements at Dinan were described in idyllic terms:

> My dear old man is working too, well & contentedly & I am grubbing away in the room next to his & hope to make something of the subject which forms the Frontispiece of the 'Campaign'. Oh! if I could only paint that desert as I saw it from the burning heights behind Wady Halfa. I will try hard, but upon my word, it seems more satisfactory work to describe such a vision of lonely & forsaken grandeur in writing than to put it on canvas. I think good word painting of landscape can suggest more than paint-painting.[22]

36 Detail from *To the Front: French Cavalry Leaving a Breton City on the Declaration of War.*

The frontispiece of *The Campaign of the Cataracts* features the Mahdist army, but the painting that Elizabeth describes here failed to materialize. By August, she was consoling Alice on the death of baby Vivian: 'When I think what it wd be to lose our little bright & gentle baby Martin it makes my heart bleed for you. But who would recall an innocent soul to this earth? That epidemic of cholera was terrible in London amongst children'.[23]

Elizabeth's next major painting, *To the Front: French Cavalry Leaving a Breton City on the Declaration of War* (1888–9), provides an interesting study of the artist's psychology (Figure 35). This is a scene of French Dragoons emerging from the semi-ruined Porte St Malo in Dinan to the Franco-Prussian War, and cheered on their way by the locals. It is, as Alice notes in her review in *Merry England*, one of the painter's 'favourite side-scenes of war, the before and after of battle'. Here Elizabeth populates the crowd with women, drawing them in the manner in which she described the Breton women in her letter to Alice in their 'crêpe white caps & nice warm shawls' and 'short dark blue dresses'. This, as Alice confirms in her review, 'is the first time that this artist, who has so complete a hold of masculine character, has exhibited a picture containing female figures'.[24] With their swords drawn the dragoons emerge with confidence from the gates, some turning to greet their well-wishers. On the viewer's right, a peasant woman is bent to the ground, her hands clasped in prayer. At the wall is a cross and over the gate the cross-shaped arrowslit in the masonry seeps with a red substance, suggestive of blood. Spencer-Smith and Usherwood quote from

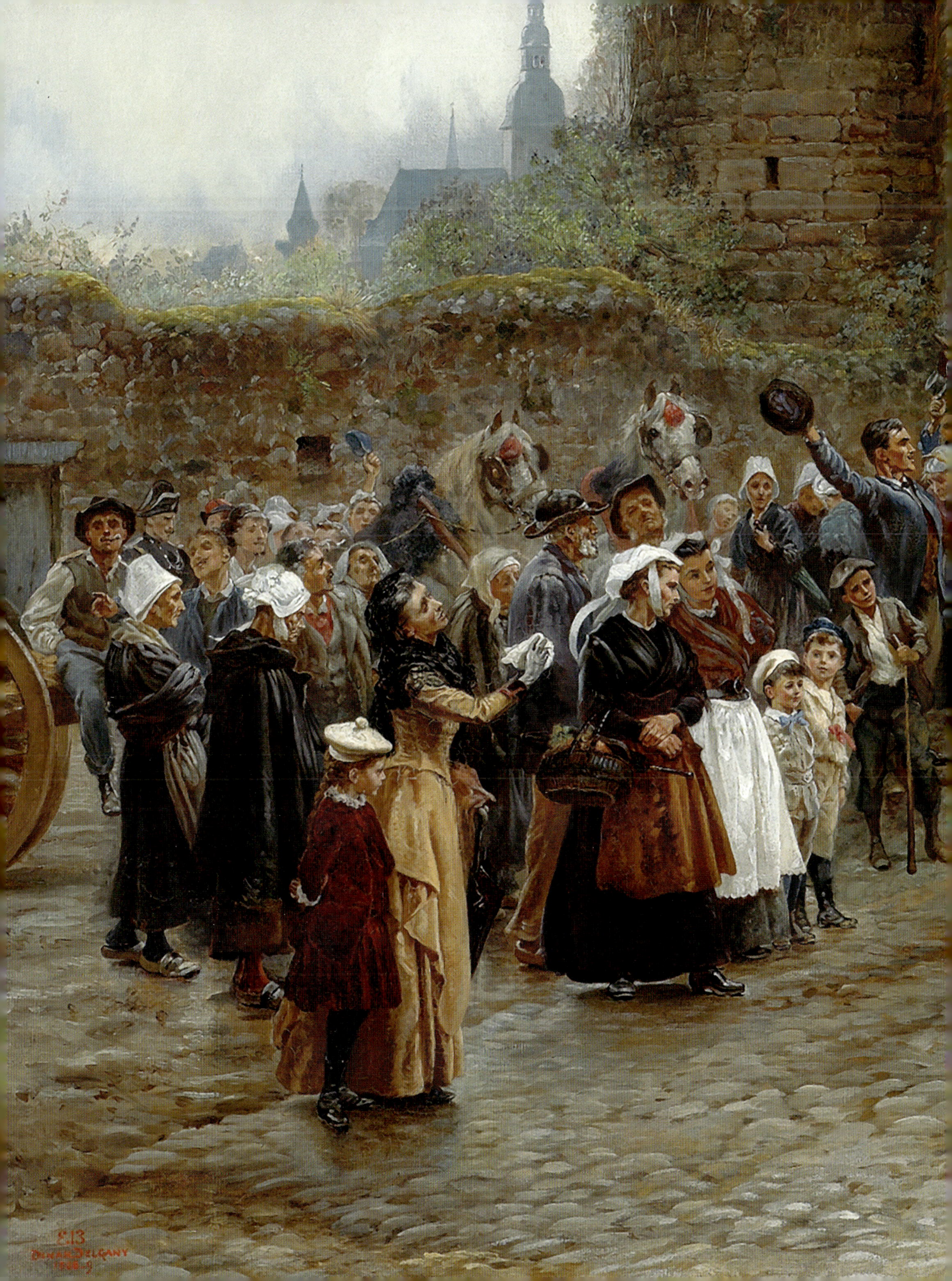

family memory of the painting noting how Patrick recalled dragoons marching in full uniform into the farmhouse to pose for Elizabeth.[25] However, the figures on the painting's left are the most revealing. Here on the extreme left, seated on a cart and smoking a clay pipe, is the same model who poses for the recruit in the *Connaught Rangers*. Elizabeth enlisted her Breton cook to pose as the old peasant with, as Eileen describes, her 'back turned, one hand on the lumbar region, the other supporting herself against a wall'. When at 'long last' she was told she could take a rest from posing, she handed in her notice as cook. 'It was, understandably, "un peu fort ça" – and not even one's face showing itself!'[26]

In the painting, a middle-class woman, clad in a tan-coloured dress, a black shawl over her hair and shoulders, and flanked by a little girl in red with a white beret, waves a handkerchief at the departing regiment (Figure 36). The expression on her face is supplicatory. Two other little boys stand beside some Breton women. The figure is Elizabeth and the children are Coos, Richard and Patrick. The boys, both in berets, wear the colours of the French flag – Richard's bow tie is blue and a red ribbon is tucked into the buttonhole of Patrick's jacket. That this is a family affair is confirmed in a letter to Alice in March 1889 in which Elizabeth informed her sister that *To the Front* was at Graves's for engraving prior to its Academy exhibition and she advised her to go to see it with Christiana: 'I think you will like some of the old women, & please tell me what your impression of the lady is'.[27] By presenting herself and her elder children in this public manner, Elizabeth may have been reminding her husband of the sacrifices of family to war, and of the primacy of family in the aftermath of the Campbell divorce scandal.

Delgany

When the family departed Dinan for Delgany, County Wicklow, Elizabeth took the painting with her to continue working on it there. On 20 April 1888, she wrote to Alice about the trip: 'We arrived here at 9.30 a.m. last Tuesday, having left Dinan at 3 on Wednesday & I must say I was tired. But I think the journey was worthy of record amongst the famous forced marches of history. With 3 small children, 2 new Breton maids & some 27 packages!' Delgany was a 'very clean, thatched, white washed hamlet with none of that feeling of dilapidation & pigs which one has so resolutely to master while enjoying the grand scenery around & beyond the villages of Clare & Kerry'. The house, Monavoe, was a 'most comfortable & bright little box'. However, the separation from the London art world starts to become a regular feature of her letters from this point onwards: 'I am looking forward to my visit to London for, with my love of contrasts, I am quite ready again for the movement of London after the quietude of Brittany'.[28] *To the Front* was sent to the 1889 Academy but was not a success. This was her first Academy painting as Lady Butler, as William had been knighted at the end of 1886.

Delgany drew Elizabeth into the social and political troubles of Ireland, which revolved around land tenure and Home Rule. The struggle between landlord and tenant over the ownership of land was intense. Evictions for the non-payment of rent escalated. The land movement and the political movement for independence were intertwined. This was the era of the charismatic Charles Stewart Parnell, then at the height of his political power. Leader of the Irish Parliamentary Party in Westminster, Parnell's party held the balance of power in the 1886 election. He supported Gladstone who brought a bill on Irish Home Rule to the house but it was defeated by the Lords. In 1886 the Plan of Campaign was launched whereby Irish farmers would withhold their rents from landlords who refused to lower the rent, paying the money instead into a common fund which evicted tenants could draw upon. By 1889, Parnell had been the subject of a series of forgeries claiming that he had played a part in the notorious murders of the Chief Secretary and Under Secretary for Ireland in 1882, known as the Phoenix Park murders. A court case exposed his enemies and Parnell was given a standing ovation at Westminster. However, by the end of December, Captain O'Shea, the estranged husband of Parnell's mistress, Catherine (Kitty) O'Shea, filed for divorce and cited Parnell as co-respondent. Unlike the Campbell case, there was no ambiguity about adultery here. The divorce case split the Irish Parliamentary Party, alienated Gladstone and the Irish Catholic clergy, and precipitated Parnell's collapse and then death in October 1891. He was 45 – only a few months older than Elizabeth.

When the Butlers arrived in Delgany in the spring of 1888, these events were in the future. Parnell had a hunting lodge a few miles from the Butler home and William joined Parnell to shoot grouse. He recalls one outing with Parnell:

> I remember when once out riding with him among the mountains near Aughavanagh we came to a cross roads, at which a group of people had assembled to see him pass. Hat in hand the men stood by the roadside. One among them was more exuberant in his greetings than were the others. Parnell took no notice of the group. He was talking about the possibility of detecting lameness in horses by a certain movement of the animal's ears when the disease was still in its incipient stages. He did not alter his conversation in the least as the curtseying and the cap-lifting went on. When we had passed the group a man who was riding with us whispered to me: "The fellow who was waving his hat so vigorously when the Chief passed has not paid his rent for the last five years." Had he paid his rent five years in advance Parnell would have treated his salutation precisely the same. He did not take off his coat for the farmers who took off their hats, not even for the people who had no hats to take off. It was for Ireland he strove.
>
> He did not tell the Irish people that they were the finest peasantry in the world. He told them … that they had rights.[29]

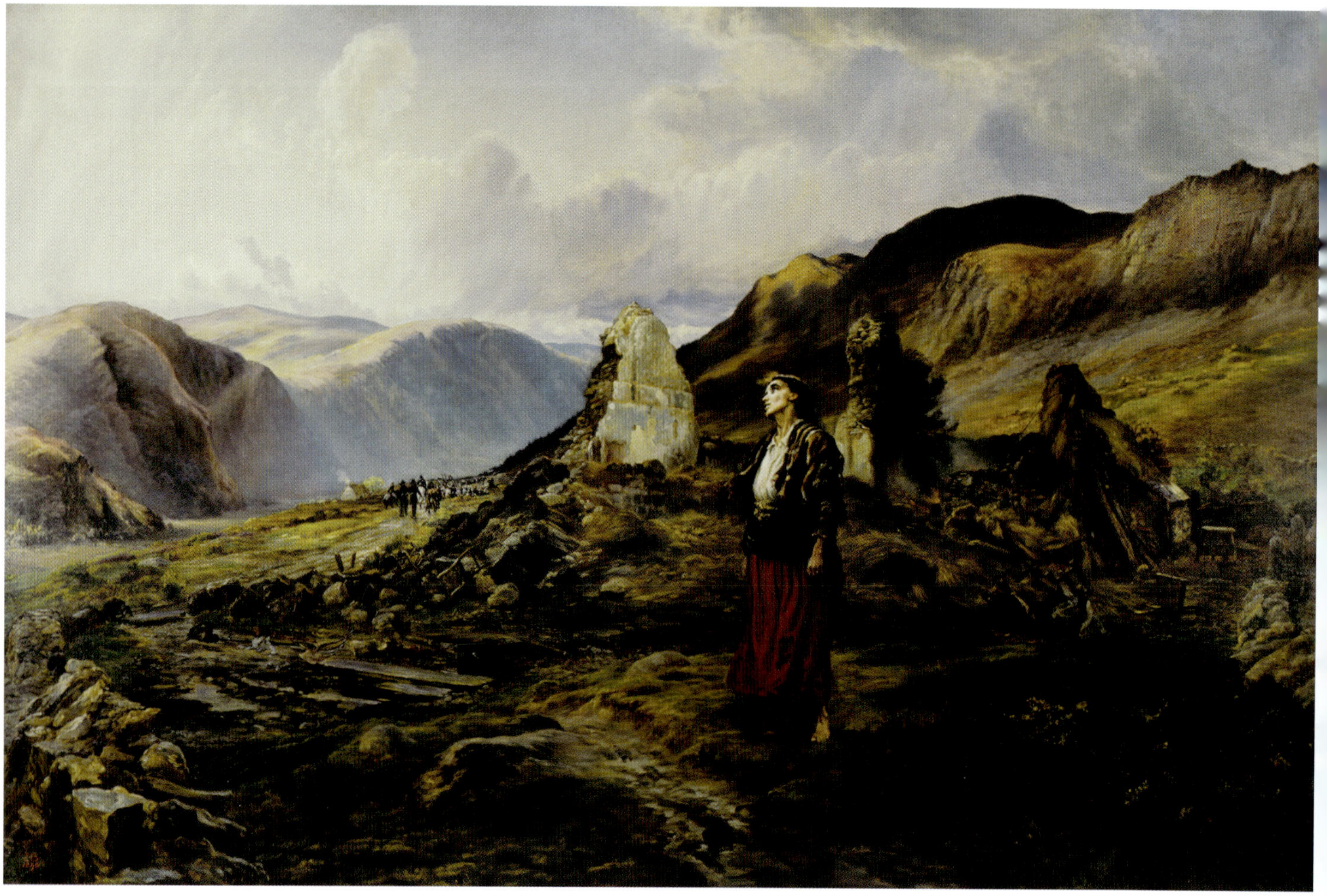

37 *Evicted*, 1890. Oil on canvas, 236 × 177.8cm.
Department of Irish Folklore, University College Dublin.

For William, Parnell was, like Gordon, a hero. In a letter to Wilfrid Meynell in 1893, William castigated the 'miserable mendicants' who betrayed Parnell, describing his fall in terms of treachery.[30] *The Light of the West* (1908) is effusive about the lost Irish leader: 'Rule, Judgement, Daring' were Parnell's qualities in addition to his 'sympathy with suffering peoples ... and rage and anger against injustice' which William identifies as a particularly Irish trait. This quality is 'something of the woman in man. It is a good deal of the God in man. It is the uprising of the human heart and the divine soul against "Man's inhumanity to man".'[31]

Elizabeth was moved by the social conditions of Ireland and, encouraged by William, produced her most political painting, *Evicted* (Figure 37). In August 1889, she wrote to Alice from Glendalough in Wicklow about it:

> I have ample material for my Eviction picture, not only for the landscape but even for the dismantled cabin, as an eviction took place near here a few days ago & I have painted the ruins while still smelling of smoke & almost hot. There are half a dozen evicted houses much nearer our door, but Time has softened with moss & lichen & flower the ugly house of the poor walls & gable ends, & studies of these would have been of little value. A study from right reality is so precious & so strong. It made me a little sick, when after driving along a wild road in search of these poor evicted houses I suddenly came upon them in the deserted hill side.[32]

In her autobiography, Elizabeth recalls how she heard about the eviction, which was nine miles away from Aughavanagh, where William was shooting. She took an 'outside car' and set off 'armed with her paints'. En-route she encountered the 'police returning from their distasteful "job", armed to the teeth and very flushed'. The 'evicted woman came to search among the ashes of her home to try and find something of her belongings intact. She was very philosophical and did not rise to the level of my indignation as an ardent English sympathizer'.[33]

The painting features the lone figure of this 'philosophical' Irish woman standing in the foreground, with the gable walls of her otherwise dismantled cottage framing her. Barefoot and in a red skirt (the traditional ensemble of the Irish peasant woman in nineteenth-century painting), her masculine face is inclined towards the sky and her face and form are illuminated by the setting sun. The stones of the cottage are strewn along with the debris of furniture on the ground. The retreating police can be seen in the distance departing along the road (Figure 38). Another thatched cottage with smoke coming from its chimney can also be seen far away. The scene of devastation is set against what Elizabeth describes as the 'mountain beauty' of Glendalough.[34] The painting, which she completed at Delgany, evokes *Connaught Rangers* but while the earlier picture can be read as both a protest and a patriotic painting, the political message of *Evicted* is unequivocal. Indeed, it speaks to the earlier painting as the eviction party marching down the road recall the Irish recruits marching to war. The hesitant recruit's backward glance in *Connaught Rangers* is towards cottages barely distinguishable in the valley beyond, similar to the scene in *Evicted*. The gable walls of the ruined cottage in *Connaught Rangers* hints at an eviction. This is rendered unequivocal by the gable walls in *Evicted* and by the departing eviction party. Poignant and dramatic, this painting shows Elizabeth at the height of her form as an artist. Writing in 1922, she observes: 'I seldom can say I am pleased with my work when done, but I am complacent about this picture'. In the 1920s, her daughter Eileen was less complacent about it, noting that she could not hang it in her marital home, Gormanston Castle, as it 'would hardly have been congruous on the walls of a landlord's house'.[35]

Alice reviewed the painting in *Merry England* during its Academy exhibition in May 1890. It captures, she argues, the evicted woman at a moment of 'impassioned sorrow'. The woman's 'whole body is eloquent, and speaks by its very simplicity of the solitude and spoliation which make the motive of the picture'.[36] *Evicted* was, however, wilfully misinterpreted by Lord Salisbury, the British Prime Minister, who 'was pleased to be facetious in his speech at the [Academy] banquet, remarking on the "breezy beauty" of the landscape, which almost made him wish he could take part in an eviction himself'.[37] The *Saturday Review* called it the 'principal political picture of the year' and describes the 'army of minions descending the valley' as 'more attractive than the ferocious harridan who clenches her fists in the foreground'.[38] The comments are both imprecise and unfair – the woman's expression is one of resignation. Pathos is what Elizabeth sought to achieve with her representation and the painting in this regard coheres with her Crimean art. The *Academy* was even more aggressive, while at the same time accusing Elizabeth of being aggressive with her choice of topic: 'What is to be said of Lady Butler's aggressive piece of controversy in paint, styled "Evicted" (993)? It shows, with a theatrical emphasis closely bordering on the ludicrous, a sturdy Irish peasant-wife appealing to the heavens, as she stands in front of a cottage very completely unroofed and disembowelled by the evicting party, which is seen in the distance, slowly retiring through a beautiful narrow pass in the hills'. There is, 'too evident political bias [which] is out of place in a work of art pure and simple'.[39] *The Athenaeum* remarks on how 'cleverly' she can '"pile up the agony" of her subject' but is 'happiest in the scenic character of the background, a mountain landscape, and the fitness of it to the theatrical aspect and character of the single figure'.[40] Land and political agitation in Ireland, as well as the Parnell crisis which was unfolding during the painting's exhibition, can account for the hostility to the work in some of the reviews. The painting remained unsold – Irish eviction scenes were unpopular with the English art public.

38 Detail from *Evicted*.

Although she can be accused of 'aestheticizing' the horrors of eviction by choosing a picturesque landscape – Glendalough was an important Victorian tourist destination – *Evicted* remains an important interpretation of Irish social distress in

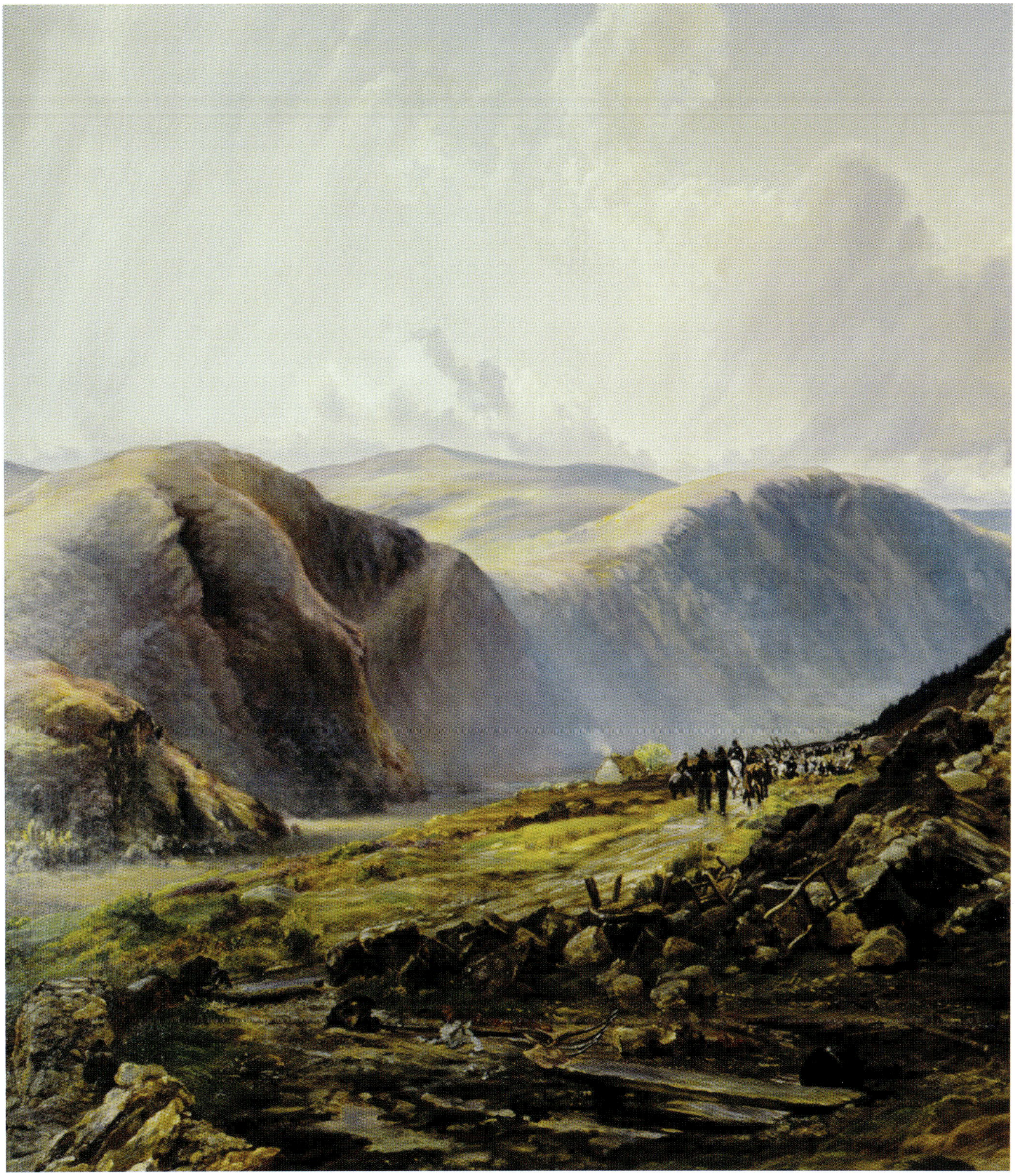

the late nineteenth century. Writing to her niece, Olivia (Alice's daughter) in 1929, Elizabeth tells her that she had been 'induced & "specially invited"' to send her 'picture of "An Eviction in Ireland, in the 'eighties", painted in 1890, to the Irish R. Academy'. The political climate changed dramatically in the intervening years, as Elizabeth observed:

> I don't know what sort of a reception, politically, it will receive, but I hope these things happened so long ago that the subject has become simply historic. I painted it from sketches made on the spot, in a wild Irish landscape. I showed it at our R. A. at the time, & the then Lord Salisbury at the R. A. banquet, while lauding 'the breezy beauty of the sky & Mountains' was pleased to be sarcastic over the subject. The Exhibition opens on the 8th April here. I remember your darling mother's description of the picture in the Press.[41]

Alexandria

Elizabeth did not see the painting at the Academy. By late March 1890 she was preparing to go to Alexandria, where William had been appointed to the command of British forces. Her position, as she gaily notes in *Sketch-Book*, was a privileged one:

> Not least amongst the attractions of an Egyptian command (to Madame!) is the yearly Autumn journey to that country through Italy, with Venice as an embarkation point. Madame knows nothing of the horrors of the summer months endured by the 'man on duty' out there, and serenely enjoys 'the best', without the seamy side ever turning up. She thinks that to spend one's winters on the Nile, and one's summer in the 'Emerald Isle', is as near an ideal existence as this world allows. It is good to be a woman![42]

This breezy persona shields the serious artist. Before she left for Alexandria Elizabeth was 'full of business finishing [*Evicted*] & making arrangements' for the 'colossal journey'.[43] The accommodation at Government House was spacious and 'W. had arranged a good studio' at their 'new post' but she had 'distractions'.[44] She was obliged to undertake official duties and did so with mixed success. Alexandria was less picturesque than Cairo with its confused combination of East and West. Here the British were entrenched at Ramleh and, similar to her 1885 experience of Cairo, she was struck by the incongruity between ordinary Egyptian life and foreign military presence.

A visit to Rosetta near the mouth of the Nile revealed an impoverished country as Elizabeth encountered 'miserable villages' with 'poor graveyards at their sides' with people living in 'mud hovels a few feet high'.[45] The metropolitan life on a Friday evening on Alexandria's 'Rotten Row' on the Mahmoudieh Canal contrasted with

Egyptian life on the other side of the bank: 'I really felt a qualm every time I saw a *fellah* over the way turning his back to the Western sun (and to us) to pray, in absolute oblivion of our silly goings-on'. Because on 'our side was Worldliness running up and down' Rotten Row, 'on the other, the repose of Kismet'.[46] The comparison to Rotten Row is a deliberate reference to the excesses of British life under the Regency in the early nineteenth century.

On 24 May, they celebrated the Queen's birthday: 'Will, mounted on a powerful chestnut, did look a commanding figure as he raised his plumed helmet and led the ringing cheers for the Queen'. The dinner that evening to heads of departments was 'solemn' and 'difficult'. To avoid the duties imposed on her, Elizabeth went out sketching in the morning: 'I should have been at my post all day on such an occasion, I confess. Will said I was like Nero, fiddling while Rome was burning'.[47] Elizabeth found social encounters awkward, particularly due to her hearing difficulties. At the end of May, the Khedive, 'our puppet' as Elizabeth describes him, arrived at his Alexandrian palace. Here the Vice-Reine, in her European dress, presided on a divan in a vast hall with ladies in waiting and girl slaves dressed in the 'funniest frocks' which were supposed to be European, but appeared 'frumpish'. Elizabeth experienced difficulties in conversing in the harem as she was so bad at 'small talk':

> I upset the Vice-Reine's equanimity by telling her (which was quite true) that I had heard that she was taking lessons in painting. *'Moi, madame?!!! Oh! Je n'aurais pas le courage!'* It was as bad as when I told her, in Cairo, how much I liked poking about the bazaars. *'Vous allez dans les bazaars, madame!!!'* So I relapsed into talking of illnesses, which subject I have always found touches the proper note of a harem.[48]

Here Elizabeth subscribes to a stereotyping common to the Victorian female traveller in their encounter with the harem. While in the eighteenth century, Lady Mary Wortley Montagu revelled in the Turkish baths and enjoyed the company of Turkish women, by the nineteenth century the female traveller was keen to establish herself as an active figure compared to the indolent female of the harem. In such encounters, Elizabeth is more akin to Florence Nightingale who was horrified by the inactivity of the women of the Turko-Egyptian ruling class in Egypt, than to Lady Mary, who was able to view herself through the eyes of Turkish women. While Nightingale wanted to send a 'cup and ball' into the harem so the women could better occupy themselves, Montagu perceived that the Turkish women in the baths viewed her English attire, comprising a 'cumbersome bodice and stays', with pity, believing that she was 'locked up in that machine' by her husband.[49] Elizabeth's response to these other women is both conventional and disappointing. She knew the limitations placed on women's lives and was, after all, refused entry to the ranks of the Academy; perhaps her own challenges made her conventional in other ways.

Her responses are often contradictory, exposing different positions and identities. The text of *Sketch-Book* is often conventional and self-effacing. The images are more revelatory. In one illustration, Elizabeth projects a careful self-image of 'Madame' enjoying the Alexandrian life. 'Madame's "At Home"' focuses on the exterior view of Government House showing its portal with Egyptian servants outside. 'Madame' is not to be seen.[50] Though happy to reveal her interpretation of the lives of others, Elizabeth shields herself. While the unpublished letters home describe the incongruity of British and colonial soldiers in Egypt, *Sketch-Book* emphasizes her patriotism as the section concludes with a description of the 'Suffolks or Surreys ... marching from Mandara Camp to the sound of that drum which we like to remind ourselves "beats round the world".' The text is accompanied by a sketch of four British soldiers beating on their drums. The Alexandrian section and, indeed, the whole Egyptian section of *Sketch-Book* concludes with an image of the British infantry.[51] At the same time, the frontispiece of *Sketch-Book* features an image of a solitary Arab figure at prayer on the banks of the Nile. The caption is entitled 'The Hour of Prayer, A Souvenir of Wady Halfa' (Figure 39). But this is also a partial image, as Wady Halfa was the Nile outpost under William's command in the aftermath of the Gordon Relief Expedition. It is this 'collision' of images which makes her work significant and requires her reappraisal in the context of Orientalist art. She produces a type of 'military Orientalism'. Her Egyptian scenes are peopled, comprising native and foreign civilians, military and ruling figures from the Khedive to the native Camel Corps to British and imperial troops. They are busy and active. Only the Nile scenes and the scenes of ancient monuments are less peopled and more serene. The image of Philae is devoid of figures and two miniature figures are seen at the base of the Sphinx. Ancient Egypt, it seems, defies possession.

Elizabeth returned to Delgany in June where the children remained and departed again for Egypt in October 1890. In January 1891, she learned of Anna Dickens's death from Christiana: 'Poor Anna! I have been thinking ever since I got your letter of the unspoken, solitary anguish of mind that she must have suffered in her long, hard solitude. No doubt her mental distress for so many years brought the disease that has ended her unhappy life ... My last little help came too late, of course. You give me no details. Will you put the £3 I sent you the other day towards my contribution to the expenses of the funeral?'[52] She was adamant that Christiana would not have to pay for her sister's funeral and offered to share the expenses with Alice.

In the spring of 1891, Elizabeth and William visited the Holy Land. Her diary entries and letters from the trip were later published in her illustrated travel book, *Letters from the Holy Land* (1903). As she explains in the preface, 'A four week's leave just allowed of our accomplishing the whole tour' and the time of year was chosen by William to avoid any religious celebrations 'so that we should be spared the sight of that distressing warring of creeds that one regrets at Jerusalem more than anywhere

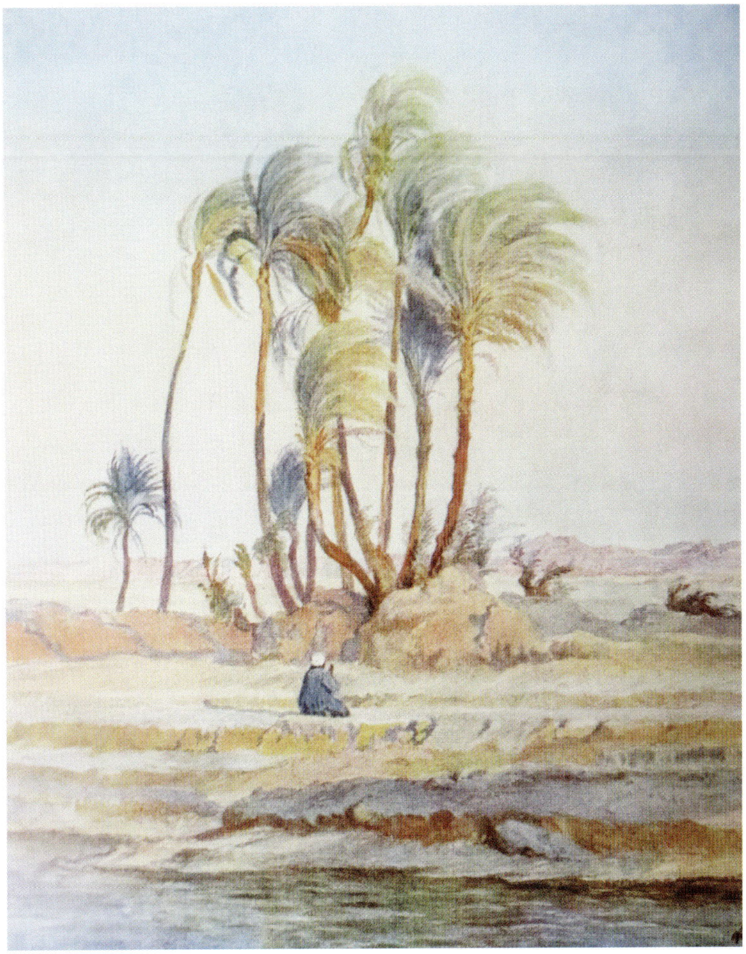

39 'The Hour of Prayer' from *Sketch-Book and Diary* (1909).

else'.[53] On 10 April, she was sketching in Gethsemane: 'I would have preferred a moonlight sketch of that garden, but I had to be content with a very hot daylight one. It was blissful sitting there undisturbed under the old olive trees whose trunks were as hard as stone, and I pleased myself with the idea that they might be offshoots of offshoots of the trees that shaded Our Lord'.[54] Her sketches are largely devoid of human or animal life and she notes how she was committed to focusing on 'scenes connected with Our Lord's revealed life'.[55] She avoided what she describes as the 'indulgence of elaborately sketching the people and animals that seem to call out to the artist at every turn'.[56] Devoid of human or animal life, the images are static and oddly disconcerting as if this is a landscape without inhabitants. This empty landscape is presented as a spiritual one. Without the intrusion of humans, the pilgrim can reimagine it as the landscape of Christ. During her journey, she collected various plants and sent them to Christiana – pansies and olive leaves from Gethsemane as well as flowers from where St Peter fled to after he had denied being a follower of Christ, after Christ's arrest by the Romans in the Garden of Gethsemane. Elizabeth's first foray into travel writing was welcomed with some excellent reviews of her work. The *Dublin Review* responded favourably to the volume, describing it as a 'treasure to rejoice over both from a devotional and an artistic point of view' and 'while she does not obtrude her piety it colours all she writes, and is the unspoken inspiration of her thoughts'.[57] *The Speaker* praises her as a travel writer: 'The true mission of the travel writer is not so much to make a book as to act for eyes for the people who have to stay at home. That is the task these letters fulfil'.[58]

She left Alexandria again in June 1891 with William. She wrote to her mother about the birth of Alice's eighth child: 'Had we been told when she was a girl – so delicate & apparently fragile – that she would have 8 children it wd have seemed the wildest idea. I feel quite mean at my own performance of which I used to feel rather proud'. Before departing, she visited the Vice-Reine and gave her a sketch of a Cairene scene – 'Waiting for the Khedive'.[59] On the return trip via Venice, the Butlers visited the Napoleonic battleground of Arcole. Here Napoleon had been saved from drowning in a marsh early in the battle. 'Between the little bridge and the spot where he sank Napoleon raised the obelisk which we see to-day. Thus do I like to realize the interesting events in history.'[60] Her youngest daugher Eileen had been ill but Elizabeth reassured Christiana on 22 June that she was 'better than we expected'. Delgany was 'looking exquisite – so rich & green' and they were enjoying the 'health & pleasures of such a lovely country as this'.[61] Elizabeth was inspired by the visit to Arcole to return to a Napoleonic theme for her next painting, *Halt on a Forced March*. In October 1891, she was working on the painting in Delgany and then she transported it to Alexandria, accompanied on this occasion by Eileen. On 7 October 1891, Elizabeth wrote to Christiana about the painting and her travels:

> I am working away hard at my picture *Halt on a forced march, Retreat to Corunna*. I should so much like to finish it before I leave to join Will but if I can't, I must take it out to Alexandria to finish there. That will be rather a hazardous undertaking with such a change of light & surroundings as I shall have there. I have fixed, as far as one can fix anything in this life, to leave Venice … sailing on the 6th Dec. & most probably I shall have Eileen with me, as we are anxious to avoid the cold which sets in here after Christmas, & which might give her a chill on her still-delicate chest. My Alexandria maid, Amalia, is a good creature, used to nursing children & she will be the right person to mind Eileen, but on the journey to Alexandria I shall have to look after Eileen myself.[62]

The subject of *Halt* is the retreat to Corunna. The British army (23,000) were overwhelmed by French forces, which exceeded 200,000. The French harassed the British in their retreat and conditions were desperate for army, horses and camp followers. Sir John Moore, the Commander of British forces, was killed in the retreat in January 1809. Moore became a celebrated figure for his bravery. Rather than focus on a general, however, Elizabeth chooses to focus on the suffering of the ordinary soldier and of the horses. This is a sombre painting with the horses in an advanced state of fatigue. She had plenty of time to complete it in Alexandria because in January 1892 the Khedive Tewfik died suddenly. Flu was suspected and all festivities were halted. 'I had ample time to finish my *Halt on a Forced March* in this long interval, so boring and depressing to Alexandrian society' and then 'things returned to pleasantly normal conditions' but by this stage the painting was completed and Elizabeth 'went in wholeheartedly for the amenities' of her 'official position'.[63] She arrived back in England in June 1892 in time for the Royal Academy and sent a postcard to her mother on 15 June: 'Arrived safely ... Tremendous journey. Find it so cold here. It was hotter in Genoa than in Alexandria'.[64] On 20 June 1892, she was in London for the Royal Academy and arranged to meet Alice in room one where *Halt on a Forced March* was exhibited. She knew, however, that her 'quiet picture could not make anything of a stir'.

She returned to Delgany with Eileen 'well provided with a good stock of studies of camels and Camel Corps troopers' which were for her '8-foot picture destined for the next Academy'.[65] Her first experience of a camel ride took place a few months previously in the desert outside Alexandria. On this occasion, she was on the 'finest-bred camels' which 'belong[ed] to the Camel Corps, & they were very velvety in their action'.[66] She 'stalked' camels about the desert in Ramleh to observe their 'mannerisms in movement'.[67] On 14 July, she was working on the 'Camel Charge' in Delgany: 'I am deep in my Camel Charge & have great hopes of it'. In her autobiography, she notes how she had already undertaken a watercolour drawing of the Camel Corps on her previous visit to Cairo:

> I was indebted to the then General commanding at Cairo for the facilities afforded me to see, at close quarters, a charge of the native Camel Corps, which impressed me indelibly. I had driven out of Cairo to the desert, where the manoeuvres were taking place, and getting out of the carriage opposite the saluting base, I placed myself in front of the advancing squadrons, so timing things that I got well clear at the right moment. I wanted as much of a full-face view as possible.[68]

On her last trip to Egypt she took Coos with her and she brought the picture to finish it on its 'native sands'. Here she had the 'richest choice of military camels, arms and accoutrements, and a native trooper or two, as models'. She refused to use a camera, finding that 'quick sketches done unbeknown to the sketchee and a good memory serve much better'.[69] However, despite her efforts the painting was not hung on the line at the Royal Academy. By contrast she observes that in 1893, it enjoyed 'all the appreciation' she could 'desire' when it was exhibited at the Paris Salon.[70]

40 Illustration of *The Camel Corps* from *The Graphic*, 9 February 1889.

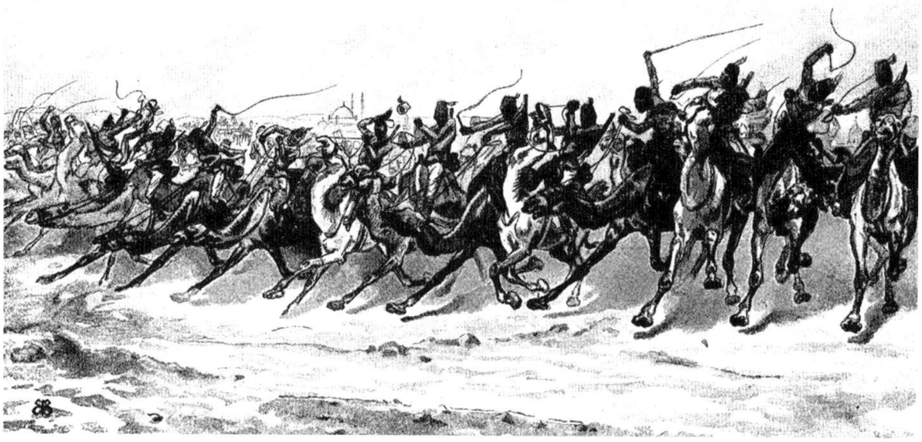

France produced more Orientalist art than Britain so the audience would have been more attuned to such scenes. In *Merry England*, Wilfrid Meynell, writing under the pseudonym of Francis Phillimore, reviewed *The Camel Corps*:

> Lady Butler's picture is of the Camel Corps charging at a review at Alexandria. The strange cavalry in such action present an altogether new subject for draughtsmanship. Shape, attitude, movement are a novelty and a surprise ... The value in the strange group is in the observation after the fact. Lady Butler is not in her method an impressionist, but she has the spirit of impressionism in her instant and insistent grasp of the passing fact ... Lady Butler's picture would be a remarkable one anywhere; it should command particular attention in an Academy where hardly another figure is doing anything but standing stock-still, whether by the artist's intention or not.[71]

The painting, which did not sell either in London or in Paris, was damaged during the Irish Civil War when the Butler home in County Tipperary was occupied by Free State soldiers. It has since disappeared, presumably destroyed, but a sketch of it appears in *Sketch-Book* and in Wilfrid Meynell's short biography of Butler in the *Art Annual* in 1898. In 1889, *The Graphic* produced Elizabeth's sketch of the Camel Corps (Figure 40). It also published an article describing the camel cavalry: 'The Egyptian Camel Corps is a very picturesque body. The men in their red tarbushes are not, according to our Western notions, comely. But ... they look the business with their blue uniforms, brown cartouche belts and their rifles where Moore's "Minstrel Boy" slung that wild harp which he so unnecessarily destroyed'. The image is romanticized. However, 'camels are the most supercilious and gruesome animals' and the 'speed of the rider has to depend on the lash ... Lady Butler shows that the men of the corps, or camelry ... use the lash; but she also shows that the brutes need it'. Her image shows how 'one of the gaunt creatures has fairly turned tail; most of them are in a state of suppressed rebellion, a few are making the best of the situation, having experience probably that the pace cannot last long'.[72] Having had Egypt to her 'heart's content', Elizabeth returned to Delgany in the summer of 1893. William's next two postings were in Britain. She notes: 'Our Irish home under the glorious Wicklow Mountains, broke up, and I was to become acquainted with life in the great English camp'.[73] Before she left Ireland, she started work on her next Academy painting – a return to the subject of the Scots Greys, but this time on the morning of Waterloo.

CHAPTER EIGHT

Aldershot, Dover, Cape Town, Devonport and Bansha, 1893–1909

The Dawn of Waterloo – *Cult of Waterloo – Empress Eugenie and Prince Louis Napoleon – Dover* – Steady the Drums and Fifes! – *Victoria's Diamond Jubilee – Historical paintings – Studio at Dover Castle – Alice's career flourishes – The Boer War – Elizabeth in South Africa – Return to England – Family problems – Royal Academy* – Rescue of Wounded, Afghanistan – *County Mayo – William retires – A new home, Bansha, County Tipperary – International exhibitions of her work* – From Sketch-Book and Diary

In 1993, the writer Beryl Bainbridge contributed to a volume in which women writers wrote about their favourite painting by a female artist in Tate Britain. Bainbridge chose Elizabeth's *Remnants of an Army*. However, the first painting by Elizabeth that she had seen was *The Return from Inkerman* after her uncle, imprisoned in 'one of the Japanese hell camps' during the Second World War, had sent her a postcard of it. Although Bainbridge is inaccurate when she notes that William fought in the Crimean War, her observations on *Remnants* are precise:

> The painting, oil on canvas, depicts the remnants of the Guards, the 20th Division and odds and ends of infantry returning from the battle. Extremely realistic and superbly grouped, with a horseman off centre and a flock of birds rising into the colourless sky, it has none of the static quality of a photograph. If anything, the ranks of men, some walking proudly, some sagging to the ground, are as full of movement as the chorus line in a ballet.[1]

As a child, Bainbridge imaginatively recreated the scene in *Remnants* – Brydon's journey to Jellalabad – by balancing a suitcase on a humpbacked trunk and tying a string to the handle, by which means she found she could 'sway' herself to Jellalabad 'on a dying nag'. Bainbridge comments how she liked 'the way sky and landscape merge, and the way the meandering stagger of the wretched beast echoes the curve of the dusty track to safety'. Although 'less dramatic' than some of Elizabeth's other paintings, 'its mood is faultless'.

Bainbridge interprets the highpoint of Elizabeth's career in the tussle between Galloway and Victoria over possession of *The Roll Call*. 'I feel sorry for her after this because nothing could quite ever match that first national success'. And although she 'went on being famous and lauded' for another 'twenty years', the 'First World War was just round the corner'.[2] Certainly, by the 1890s the popular decline had already set in. While *The Roll Call*, and her other works of the late 1870s and early 1880s, filled columns of press reviews, by the late 1880s and 1890s, Elizabeth's paintings received little attention.

Elizabeth worked on her next 'big picture', *The Reveil in the Bivouac of the Scots Greys on the Morning of Waterloo – Early Dawn*, in Delgany (see Figures 41 and 42 for sketches). As she states: 'I was able to make all my twilight studies at home, all out of doors, not a thing painted in the studio ... I pressed many people into my service as models, and I think I got the light on their fine Irish faces true to nature'. She even got 'an Irish dragoon home on leave in the village whose splendid profile' she realized 'would be very telling'.[3] But, as she wrote to Christiana, the move to Aldershot, 'played havoc' with her 'painting time' and she could not get it completed in time for that year's Academy. Again, she emphasized how it was a '"plein air" & all studied at twilight, with a great variety of types in it'.[4] Unlike Alexandria's splendid quarters, at Aldershot the Butlers were accommodated in a wooden bungalow. Elizabeth made her studio in the 'old court-martial hut' after 'four skylights' were placed in it for her. She painted Aldershot's soldiers in this 'unconventional workshop' (Figure 43) and this was where she finished *The Dawn of Waterloo*.

Elizabeth was confident that the painting would be one of her important pictures. Here is another sombre scene as soldiers wake up on the morning of the battle of Waterloo. The painting is strikingly reminiscent of Detaille's *Le Rêve*, and the return to French military art for inspiration may have been a reaction to her previous change of direction in art with *Evicted* and *The Camel Corps*. *Le Rêve*, exhibited at the Salon in Paris in 1888, shows young conscripts asleep on a field. Military service for all young Frenchmen became law in July 1889. Her son Martin, born in Dinan, would have been eligible for military service if he had remained in France. In Detaille's painting, the young soldiers have a collective dream of battle or, more specifically, of the future glory of battle as they dream of successful campaigns of the past. The vision features Napoleon and the heroes of the Revolution. The desire released in the dream is to avenge the army's defeat in the Franco-Prussian War. The vision is projected into the sky over the recumbent soldiers in their bivouac. This deeply nationalistic painting was enormously successful in France and widely reproduced.

British interest in Waterloo had not abated by the end of the century. At London's pre-eminent theatre, the Lyceum, Britain's leading actor, Henry Irving,

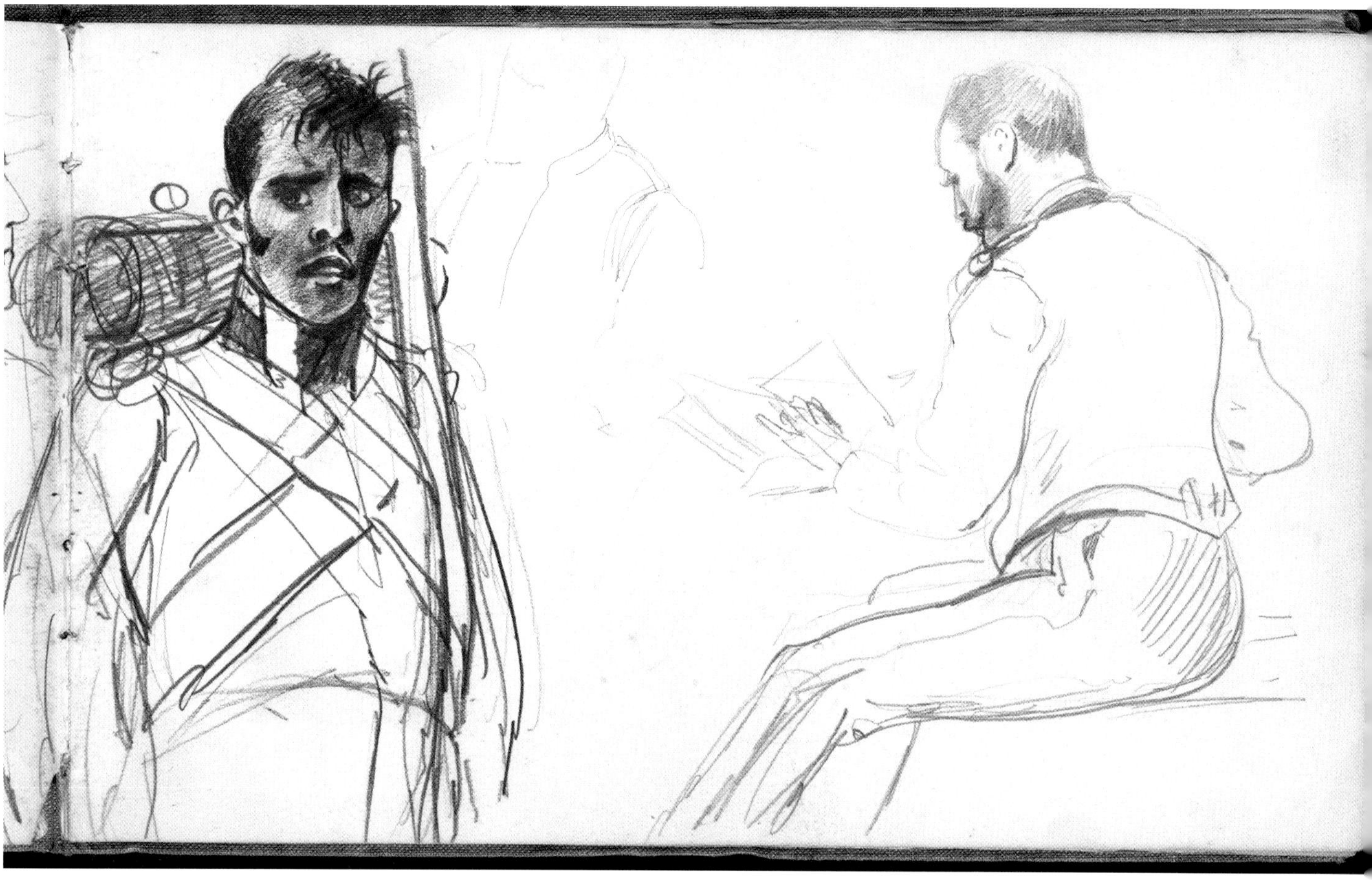

41 'Study for *The Dawn of Waterloo*', 1893. Pencil on paper. National Army Museum, London. Bridgeman Art Library.

played the part of a dying old veteran reminiscing about the battle. This nostalgic piece, which was written by Conan Doyle, and which premiered in Bristol in September 1894, was immensely popular. Bram Stoker, Irving's business manager recalls: 'The play met with a success extraordinary even for Irving. The audience followed with rapt attention and manifest emotion, swaying with the varying sentiments of the scene'.[5] This deeply patriotic play seemed to 'touch all hearts always'.[6] At the Royal Academy in 1891, Ernest Crofts exhibited *The Morning of Waterloo: Napoleon's Headquarters*. In 1894, the historical artist, Stanley Berkeley, exhibited *The Sunken Road at Obain: An Incident in the Battle of Waterloo*. Crofts' *Napoleon's Last Grand Attack: Waterloo* was exhibited in Gallery VII in 1895, with Elizabeth's painting exhibited in Gallery XI. Crofts and Berkeley had been inspired by Elizabeth's pioneering foray into the field of war art, but did not, as Hichberger points out, subscribe to her 'anti-violence' stance. With *The Dawn of Waterloo* Elizabeth painted 'melancholy foreboding' as the soldiers awaken on the morning of battle. Hichberger sees it as a 'dramatic anti-war study', but it can also be seen as a poignant reflection on the nature of war.[7] These Scots Greys, who awaken on the morning of Waterloo, are the same group of troopers who would later storm

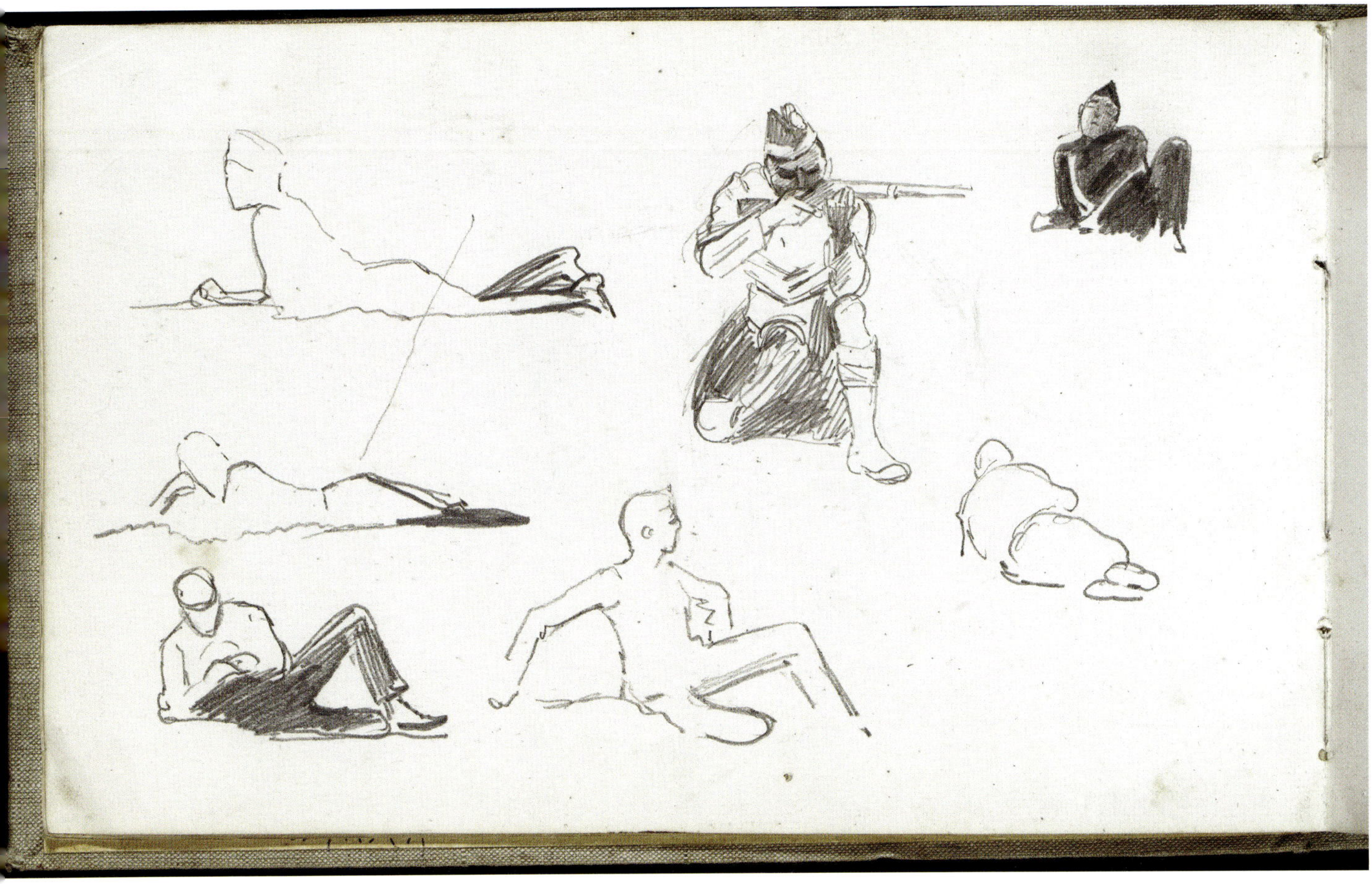

42 'Possible study for *The Dawn of Waterloo*', 1893. Pencil on paper. National Army Museum, London. Bridgeman Art Library.

the French lines with disastrous consequences. This charge, of course, was commemorated in *Scotland for Ever!*[8]

M.K. O'Byrne, who was tutor to Elizabeth's grandson at Gormanston Castle in Ireland, recalls seeing the painting at the castle:

> Dawn is just breaking, a pearly light of a subtle quality steals over the horizon, suffusing the form of the soldier awaking from sleep. The longer one gazes at it, the brighter appears to become the light, growing more brilliant with each second. The effect is to make the scene intensely alive, one almost expects to hear the silvery notes of the Camp réveillé.[9]

Blackburn's *Academy Notes* describes how the 'foreground group is composed chiefly of officers, in whom the regiment lost heavily that day. Part of the line of horses is shown picketed to the left, and beyond is the bivouac of the 1st Royal Dragoons'.[10]

Its reflective nature was a problem for reviewers. The *Western Mail* describes it as 'another of this talented lady's battle pieces', but interesting only because of its 'associations' with her earlier work, and not likely to be 'viewed with pleasure' by

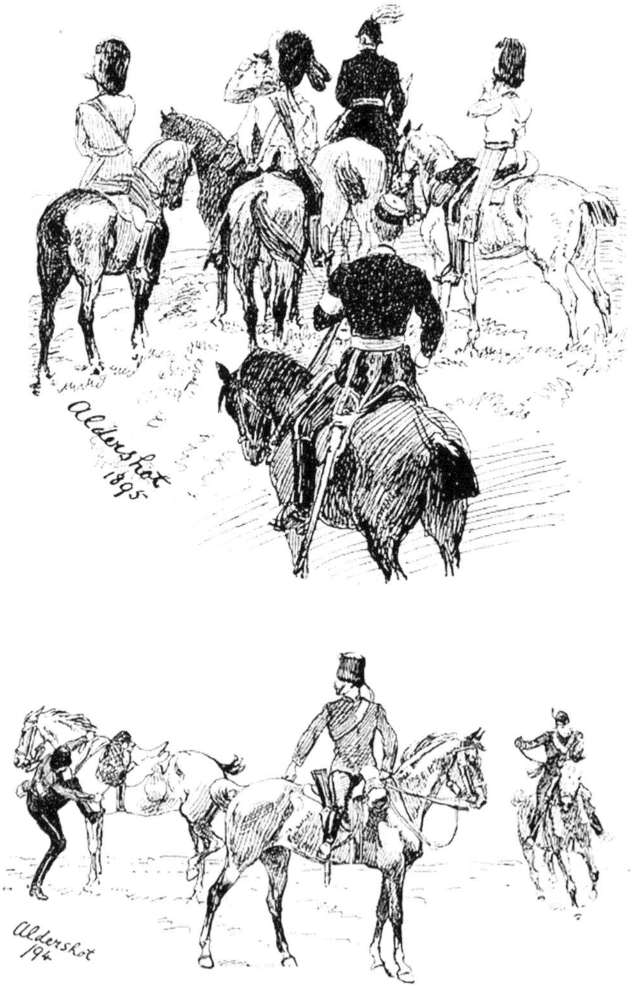

43 'Aldershot Manoeuvres' from Elizabeth Butler, *Autobiography*.

those who remembered *Quatre Bras* and *The Roll Call*. In an insight into the prevailing mood of high imperialism, the review commends Caton Woodville's *Charge of the Light Brigade*, exhibited in the same room, as 'more vigorous and dashing'.[11]

Elizabeth blamed Aldershot society in the previous year for the lack of progress with her painting, but she also revelled in aspects of society. The highlight of Aldershot was its proximity to the Empress Eugenie at Farnborough. William had become friendly with the Empress after arranging the Prince Imperial's funeral in South Africa. In January 1894, Elizabeth attended a memorial service to mark the death of Napoleon III in the Empress's private church. After the service the congregation went down to the crypt to the tombs of Napoleon III and the Prince Imperial. The Empress, 'shrouded in black', was kneeling 'motionless', a 'solitary figure' for whom Elizabeth felt 'a very deep respect'.[12] In a window in the hall of her residence, the Empress grew the tall grass that was taken from the spot where her son

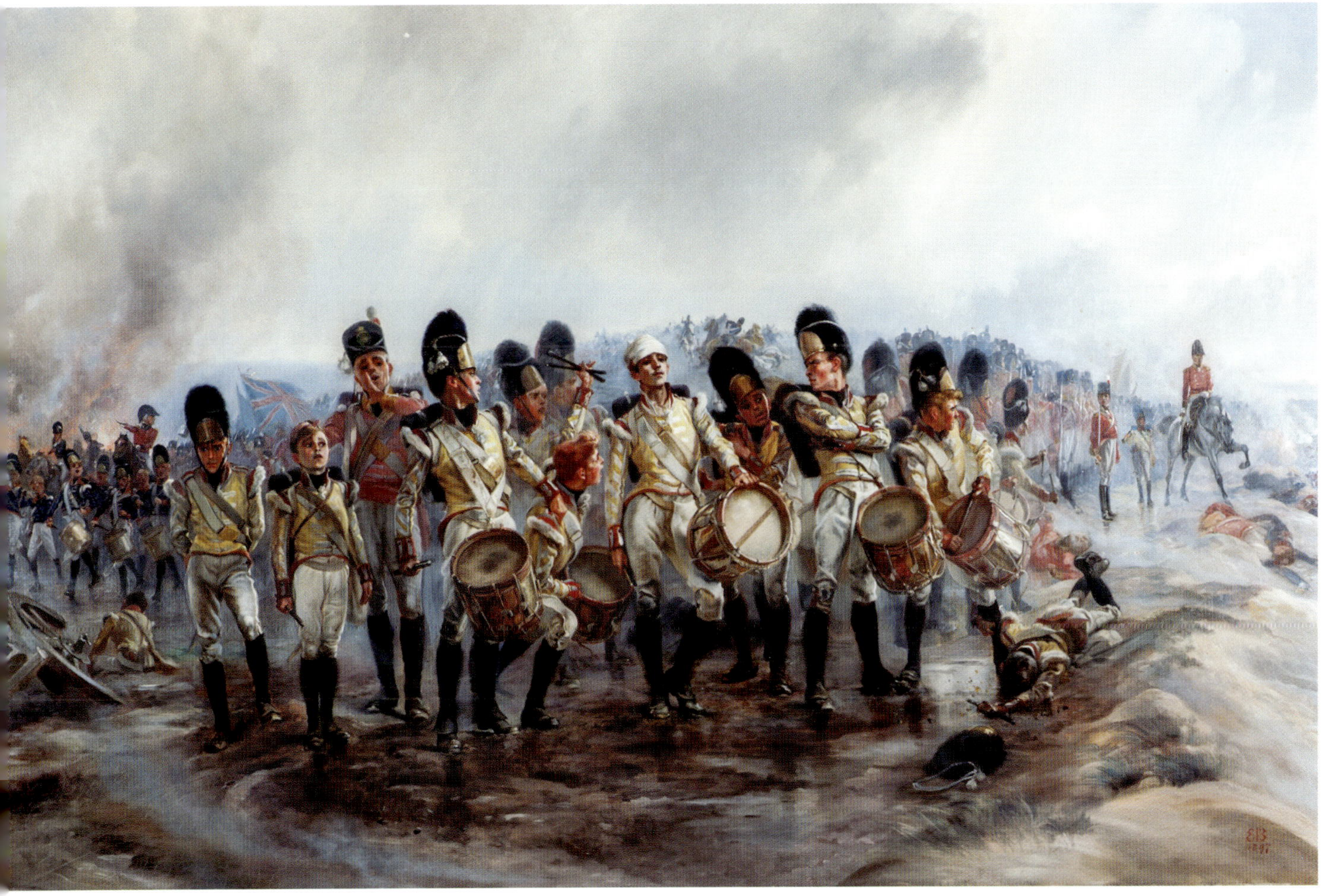

44 *Steady the Drums and Fifes!: The 57th (Die-Hards) Drawn up Under Fire on the Ridge at Albuera*, 1897. Oil on canvas, 127 × 180.4cm. The Princess of Wales's Royal Regiment. Bridgeman Art Library.

was killed by the Zulus.[13] The German Kaiser also visited Aldershot, and Elizabeth's observations on his visit in August 1894, recorded in her autobiography, are interesting:

> I was at once presented to H.I.M., who talked to me, like a good boy, about my painting and about the army which he said he greatly admired for its appearance. He is just now a keen Anglo-maniac (*sic*)! We shall have him dressing one of his regiments in kilts next.[14]

Before sending *The Dawn of Waterloo* to the Academy, she exhibited it at the Club House in Aldershot, and although she was anxious about dust on the wet paint, she experienced the thrill of having crowds go to see it, 'from the generals down to the traditional last drummer'. While Elizabeth's work remained popular with the army, the 'Academicians were again unkind in the placing of picture' and a trip to Paris was required to recover her spirits.[15] On 30 May, Elizabeth was at the Queen's Ball at Buckingham Palace, at which the son of the Ameer of Afghanistan was the chief guest. Although she was 'much complimented that night' on *The Dawn of Waterloo*, it 'was inadequate to salve [her] wounded feelings'.[16] At Farnborough in June, she met Prince Louis Napoleon who was a colonel in the Russian cavalry. He informed William that he had seen an engraving of *Scotland for Ever!* in a shop window in Moscow and had purchased it for the mess of his cavalry regiment, but he had 'little expected so soon to meet the painter of that picture'.[17] Louis later came to her studio where she was undertaking an oil painting of the Scots Greys at manoeuvres, *Right Wheel!* In 1896, she avoided the Academy, exhibiting instead at the New Gallery. She was still smarting from the Academicians' 'unkindness in placing *The Dawn of Waterloo* where they did the preceding year'.[18] It was becoming clear to Elizabeth that her glory days were in the past. *The Dawn of Waterloo* remained unsold in Elizabeth's lifetime and hung alongside *To the Front* in the dining-room of Gormanston Castle, where Elizabeth lived with Eileen in the later stages of her life.

45 Detail from *Steady the Drums and Fifes!: The 57th (Die-Hards) Drawn up Under Fire on the Ridge at Albuera.*

Dover

After a holiday in Italy, the Butlers moved to Dover in 1896. William had been offered the command of either Colchester or Dover and left the choice to Elizabeth. Dover Castle was the attraction and Elizabeth had her studio, complete with balcony, over the moat and drawbridge. She notes: 'The Castle was the very ideal, to me, of a residence. Here was History, picturesqueness, a wide view of the silver sea, and the line of the French coast to free the mind of insularity'.[19] It was here she accomplished a 'creditable picture' as she had 'many advantages'. The painting was *Steady the Drums and Fifes!* and was accorded a 'place of honour at the Academy' (Figure 44). It depicts drummer boys from the 'old 57th Regiment' waiting under fire for the order to

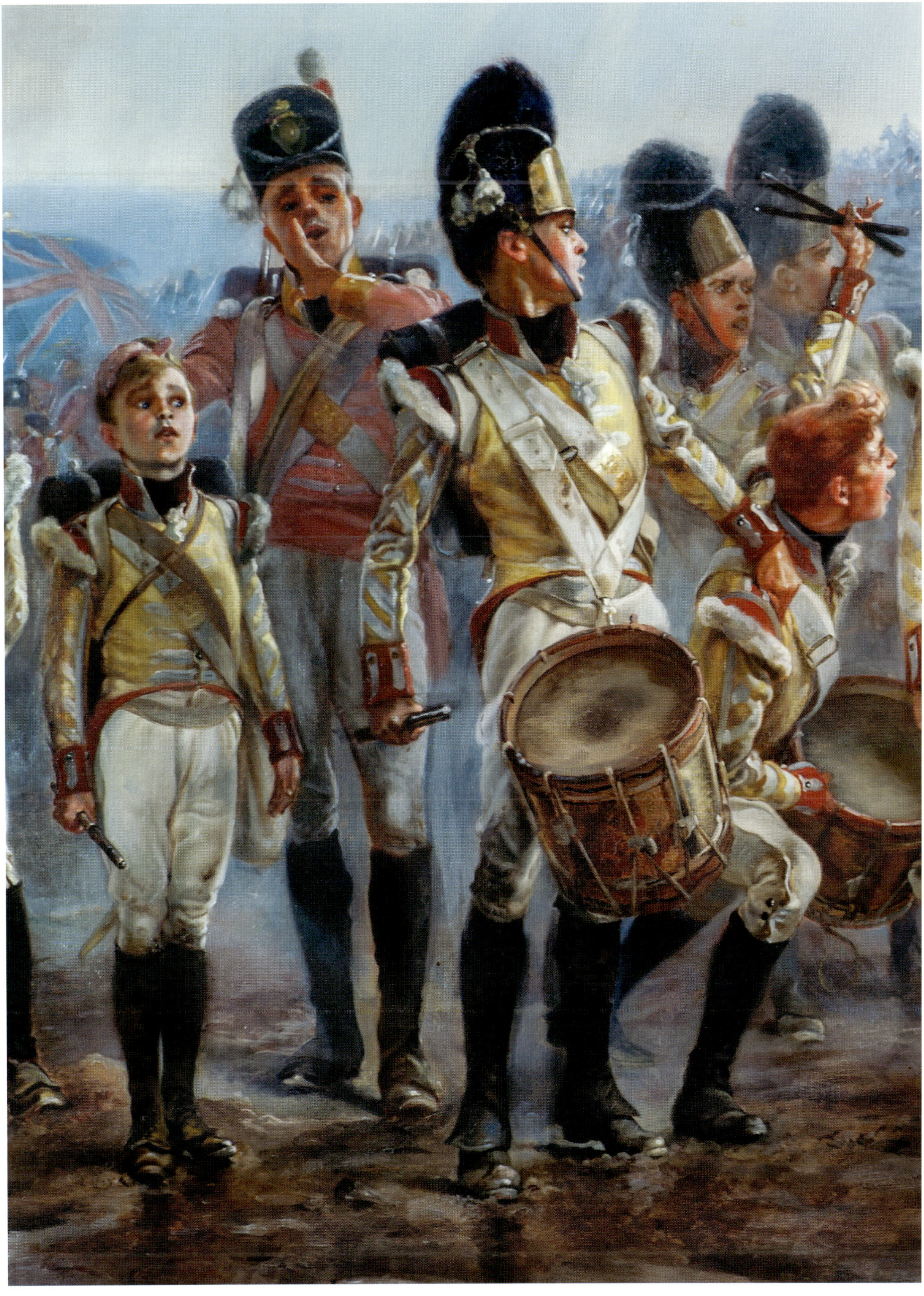

sound the advance at the Battle of Albuera on 16 May 1811. It marked one of the bloodiest battles of the Peninsular War, as Wellington and his Portuguese and Spanish allies defended Lisbon against French forces. Elizabeth relates that the order to advance had been delayed so the drummer boys and the regiment 'had to bear the supreme test of endurance, the keeping motionless under fire'. As she recalls: 'I had had the vision of those drummer-boys for many years before my mind's eye, and it is a very obvious fact that what you see strongly in that way means a successful realization in paint'.[20] The role of the drummer boy was to transmit signals on the battlefield. By the end of the nineteenth century, the drummer boy in combat was increasingly becoming obsolete; with the advent of technology his role became ceremonial.[21] At Dover, Elizabeth had the benefit of 'well-drilled lads, and my own boys were sufficiently grown to be of great use, though, for obvious reasons, I could not include their dear faces in so painful a scene'.[22] Eileen recalls that Dick (Richard), 'partly because of his good looks and figure but more because of his good nature', was her mother's most 'frequent choice' of model. He was required to 'stand by the hour, with short intervals of rest' to pose as a drummer boy.[23]

46 *On the Morrow of Talavera*, 1923. Oil on canvas, 76.2 × 63.8cm. Private Collection. Bridgeman Art Library.

As an artist, Elizabeth was inspired by the colours of uniforms, writing in her autobiography: 'The yellow coatees, too, were a tremendous relief to me after that red which is so hard to manage'. She recalls asking Detaille if he ever thought of painting the British army but he told her he was 'frighten[ed]' of the red. Elizabeth's careful research for her painting revealed that the facings of the regiment were 'canary yellow', which was an 'unexpected treat'.[24] The drummers are young. The youngest, called Drummer Holloway, was only eleven at the time of the battle. In the painting, he looks straight ahead (Figure 45). Like the soldiers in *The Roll Call*, the musicians are individualized as each one processes the conflict in his varying way. Confusion, fear and defiance are featured in the faces. In the right-hand corner of the painting, we see how one of their number has fallen, still clutching his baton. The regiment came to be known as the 'die-hards' after their commanding officer urged them to 'die hard' at Albuera.

Wilfrid argues that the painting is 'at once a picture of war and a picture … of childhood' which makes a 'poignant combination'. He continues:

> For her example of high courage and control the painter has taken boys – the most excitable and impulsive, new to terror, quick to violence – and shown them drawn up under fire on the ridge of Albuera, thus confronting their youth with death, their impulse with discipline. It is from one of Cardinal Manning's *Pastime Papers* that the artist took her quotation for the Academy Catalogue of 1897 in praise of the valour of endurance. 'The highest courage of the soldier', he wrote, 'is said to be the standing still under fire without returning it' … To look from one to another of the band of boys with their various characters and tempers as they face the bullets and are forbidden even

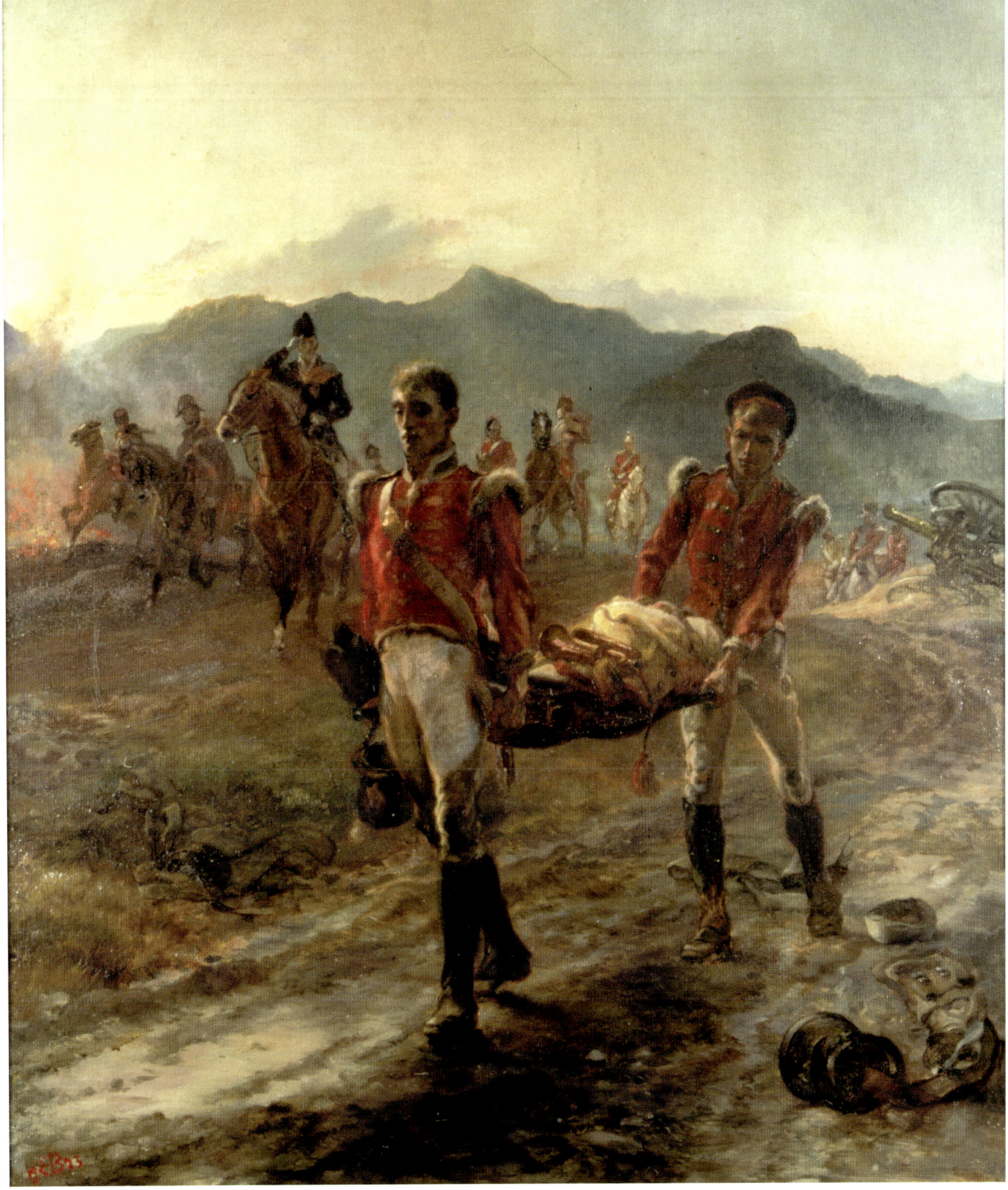

> the action of their instruments (for the music is hushed) is to go through the drama of a boyish life. The artist has not shrunk from the too great pathos of a child of nine or ten consciously shaken by the fear of death and yet proud of his disciplined attitude; nor from the brutality of a much older lad inclined to bully his comrades into quietness; nor from the writhing death of the boy whose hand clings round a little comrade's ankle.[25]

Elizabeth wrote to Alice on 21 March to inform her that she was 'showing the picture to Dover Society with great éclat'.[26] The painting was described as a 'characteristic scene of soldier heroics' in the *Liverpool Mercury*'s Academy review.[27] However, the influential art critic, Marion Spielmann, castigated it as 'a mere travesty of a painting'.[28] But *The Athenaeum* praised it as 'incomparably the best battle piece of the season', far surpassing the productions of her rivals, Crofts and W.B. Wollens. 'It has the advantage of a compact and moving incident, instinct with personal elements which appeal to our common humanity' as the 'thin line of bandsmen stationed on a height at Albuera [were] so exposed to fire that when a comrade or two fell or died at their feet it was not wonderful they lost their heads and made more noise than was required to overcome the screams of the wounded and groans of the dying round them'. But when the command that is the title of the painting came they 'pulled themselves together'.[29] On 15 July 1897, Elizabeth wrote to Christiana: 'The sale of my picture is still in abeyance. I think the 57th Regt. will be the ones to get it, & then I hope I may send you your birthday present'.[30] That Elizabeth was oblivious to the outside world while painting is revealed in a letter to her sister at this time. Alice, concerned by news reports of a fire at Dover Castle, contacted her sister, but Elizabeth reassured her: 'to think that those wretched evening papers shd have given you such a fright ... The fire was in the Artillery mess & I knew nothing of it, but was placidly painting in my studio'.[31]

The summer of 1897 was Victoria's Diamond Jubilee and Elizabeth revelled in the festivities. From her viewpoint in the courtyard of the Horse Guards, Elizabeth saw Victoria, 'a little woman, seated by herself ... with an expressionless pink face, preoccupied in settling her bonnet'.[32] In the diary extract published in her autobiography, she notes how she avoided thinking about impending trouble: 'We won't think of the ugly look of India just now and all the nasty warnings of the bumptious Kaiser'.[33] In 1898, Khartoum had fallen to the British and Kitchener arrived at Dover, 'with all the prestige of his new-won honours shining round him'. William had a 'guard of honour (Highlanders) with the regimental colour ... drawn up at the pier head'.[34] With new military technology, notably the Maxim machine gun, Kitchener had annihilated the followers of the Mahdi at the Battle of Omdurman in September 1898. Possibly to avenge the death of Gordon in 1885, Kitchener was brutal in his killing of the wounded enemy. He looted Khartoum and threw the Mahdi's exhumed skeleton into the Nile but temporarily kept his skull.

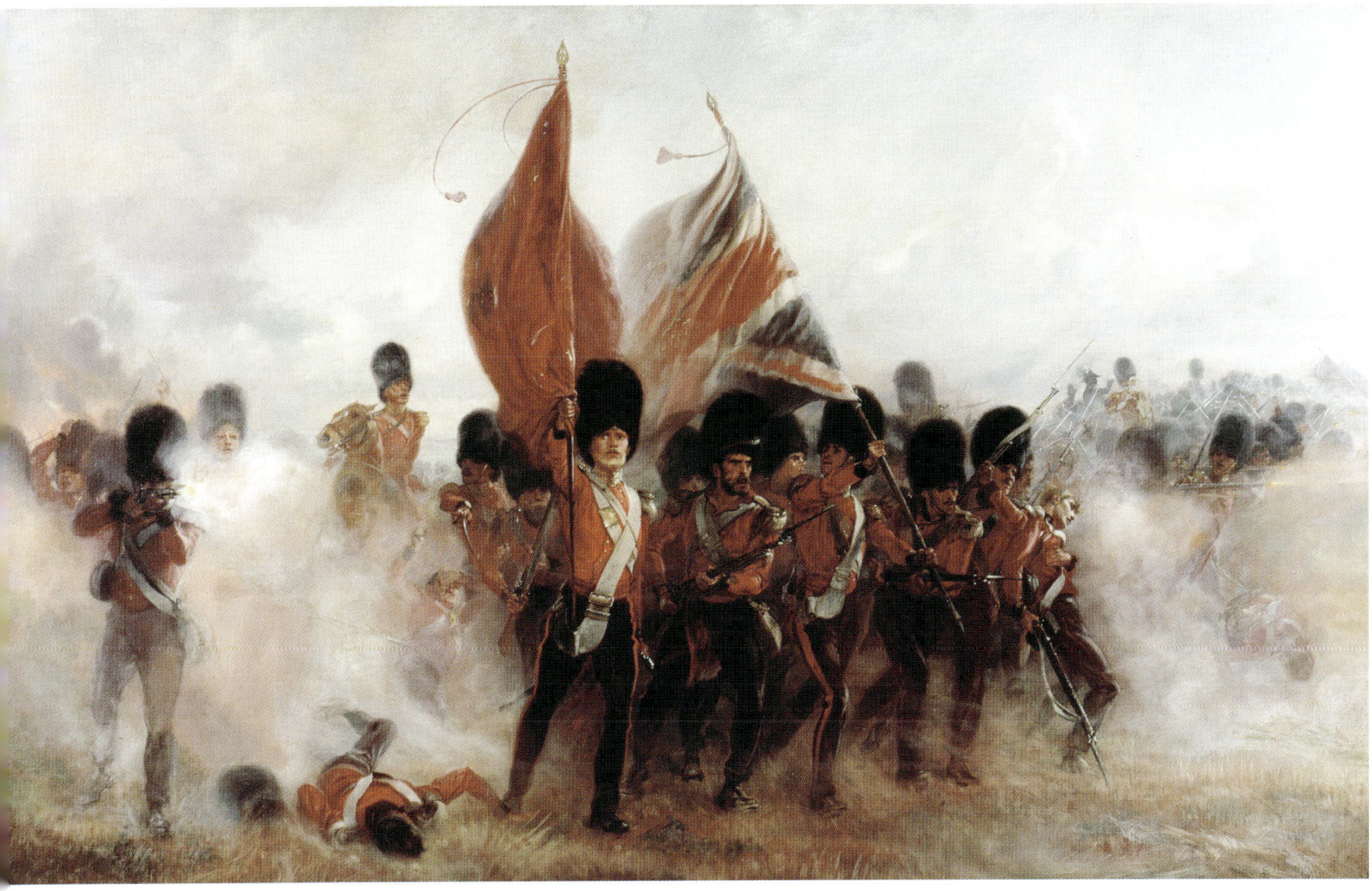

47 *The Colours: The Advance of the Scots Guards at Alma*, 1899.
Oil on canvas, 98 × 155.6cm. Private Collection.
Bridgeman Art Library.

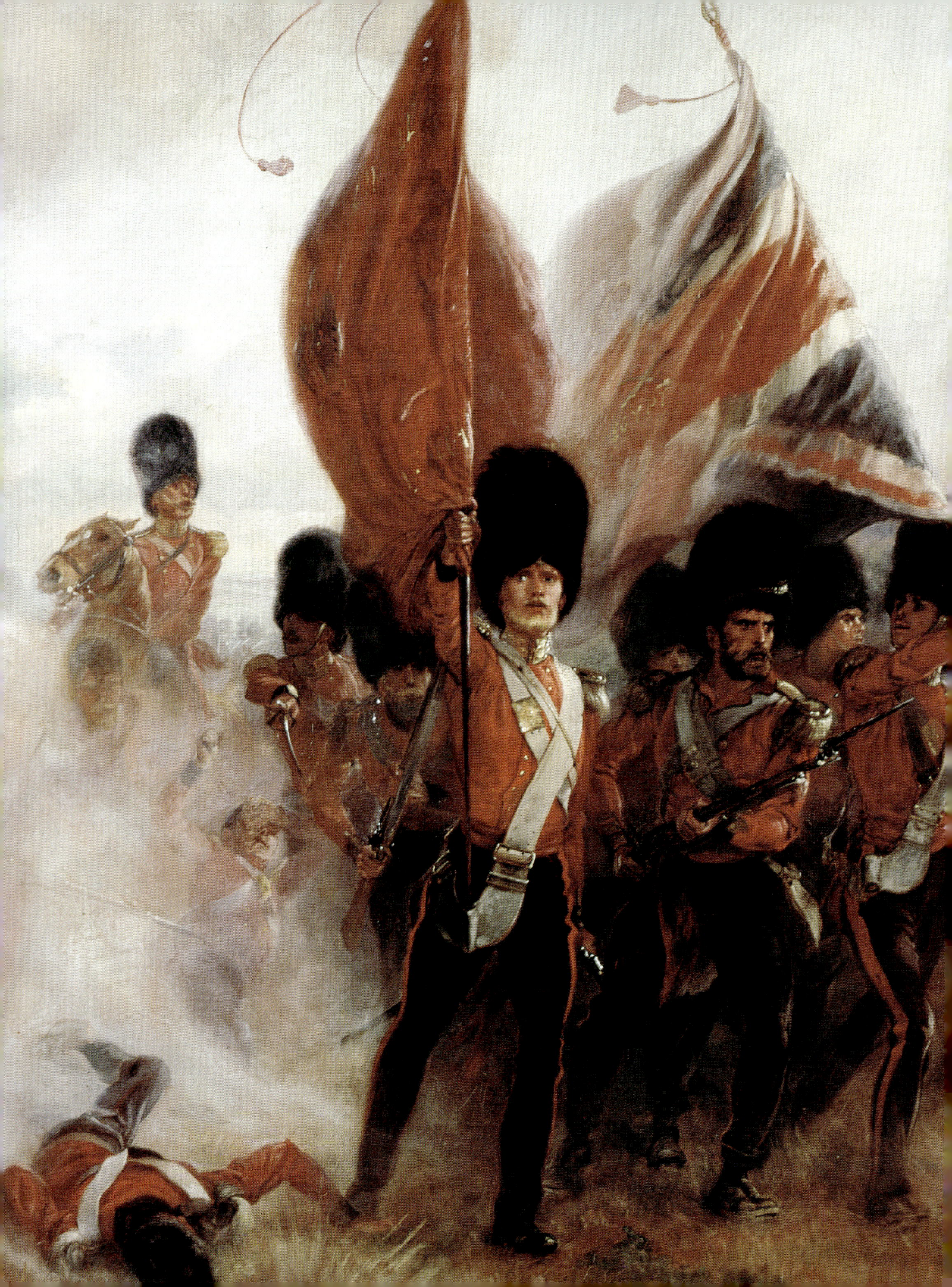

Jingoism was at its height and Elizabeth had never before seen such enthusiasm amongst the crowd who gathered to greet him. Blunt, who was deeply opposed to the conquest of the Sudan, which represented another extension of the British Empire, records a different side to William's reception of Kitchener. In his diaries, he remarks that Wilfrid informed him of William's comment to Kitchener when he disembarked at Dover: '"Well, if you do not bring down a curse upon the British Empire for what you have been doing there is no truth in Christianity."'[35] In Soueif's semi-historical novel, *The Map of Love*, William's alleged remark is quoted as the heroine tries to understand how her soldier husband's experiences in the conquest cause his psychological distress and slow suicide after his return from the Sudan.[36] Blunt, however, as Viola Meynell points out, 'sometimes went astray from accuracy' when he reported on what Wilfrid had said to him.[37] Certainly, Elizabeth's account of Kitchener's visit and his reception demonstrate no evidence of William's hostility. Rather she quotes William prophesying that Kitchener would become a Field-Marshal. However, despite public jubilation, Kitchener had his critics. Winston Churchill, who was a war correspondent in the Sudan campaign, contrasted him with Gordon: 'Revenge may be a good inspiration for soldiers in action. It is not, however, an incentive to which Gordon would often have appealed, nor is it a dignified emotion for a great people to display'.[38] William would have agreed with Churchill's point.

Elizabeth's battle art at this period eschewed contemporary imperial themes in favour of historical battles. She exhibited *On the Morrow of Talavera* in 1898. This oil painting is now lost but she reproduced it in 1923 (see Figure 46). It focused on the aftermath of Wellington's first victory in the Peninsular War. The body of a bugler is being carried in a litter by two soldiers and Wellington is seen in the background on horseback saluting the dead bugler. The painting, which drew attention to Wellington's sympathy for his troops, failed to garner any notice at the Academy. For the next Academy, Elizabeth returned to the Crimea. The subject of *The Colours: The Advance of the Scots Guards at Alma* (Figure 47) was an incident in the battle. On 20 September 1854, the Scots Fusiliers were advancing to support the Royal Welsh Fusiliers when the Russians broke through the Welsh lines. This caused disarray amongst the Scots Fusiliers until Captain Lindsay, standing 'firm with the colours, which were shot through and through and the staff broken', managed by his example to restore order.[39] The scene captured in the painting is of Lindsay holding the colour aloft (Figure 48). 'I wanted', Elizabeth notes, 'to show the colour party of the Scots Guards advancing up the hill of the Alma in their full parade dress – the last time the British troops wore it in action'. When Lindsay, by this time Lord Wantage, heard of the project, he took Elizabeth to the Guards Chapel in London and 'there and then had the old, dusty, moth-eaten Alma colours taken down from their place on the walls, and held the Queen's colour once more in his hand' so Elizabeth could study it. She notes: 'I made careful studies at the chapel, and restored the fresh tints which he told me they had on that far away day'.[40]

48 Detail from *The Colours: The Advance of the Scots Guards at Alma.*

In the *Art Annual* in 1898, Wilfrid produced an extensive overview of Elizabeth's career. The lengthy article was filled with her sketches, paintings and photographs of Dover Castle. In a tribute to Elizabeth's life of travel, Wilfrid observes: 'Wherever Lady Butler has pitched her tent she has taken her palette with her. The homes which her husband has made have been made under the stress of military duty'.[41] In the studio, 'a sketch or a relic lying here or there … recalls distant scenes and carries her mind upon far travels'.[42] Elizabeth was a mobile artist. In one of the photographs, Elizabeth is at her easel in her 'improvised studio in the Constable's Tower'. As Wilfrid describes:

> It is the studio of a hard worker rather than that of a *petit-maître*. About her she has gathered her art-trappings, and each one of them has its history or its use. On the business-like walls are no evidences that she has ever given herself to the subtleties of *bric-a-brac*; no pieces of precious colour droop from screens; no stuffed peacocks stand gaily on guard, and no orange trees in flower tempt you to linger. It is an ascetic work-place rather than an aesthetic show-room.[43]

Here he is setting Elizabeth up in opposition to the Aesthetic movement in art which flourished at the *fin-de-siècle*. Her studio featured a 'grim row of old uniforms – relics of the Peninsula and Waterloo'. 'Relics of later fields' were also seen in the room, including a 'bundle of assegais and spears, a Zulu's shield pierced through and through with bullet-holes'.[44] He quotes Elizabeth's maxim that the 'essential' was to 'seize the heart of a thing. When this mental effort has been made with success, there is never any mistake about it, and no violence of movement, no noise and no attitudes can make amends for the lack of it. The seizing of the very heart and centre of an action is as vital a matter of necessity in art as it is in literature'.[45] However, the comparison he makes between Elizabeth's work and Kipling's has tended to misrepresent her for future generations as an imperialist. 'Lady Butler', he argues, 'has done for the soldier in Art what Mr Rudyard Kipling has done for him in Literature – she has taken the individual, separated him, seen him close, and let the world so see him'.[46] Certainly, both individualize the soldier, but Kipling, by the end of the nineteenth century, was an arch-imperialist. In the coming conflict in South Africa, the painter and the writer would occupy radically different political positions.

William was posted to the Command of British forces in South Africa and sailed on 12 November. Four days later Elizabeth wrote to Christiana that she feared that she would be 'turn[ed] out of the Castle sooner' than she had 'hoped'. Despite the many advantages and luxuries of her lifestyle, there was also insecurity that impacted on her art: 'I fear I shall have to take rooms in Dover & finish my picture somewhere in the town. It is very disconcerting to be turned out like this'.[47] By 15 December her departure was still uncertain: 'I hear such contrary rumours as to the date of my

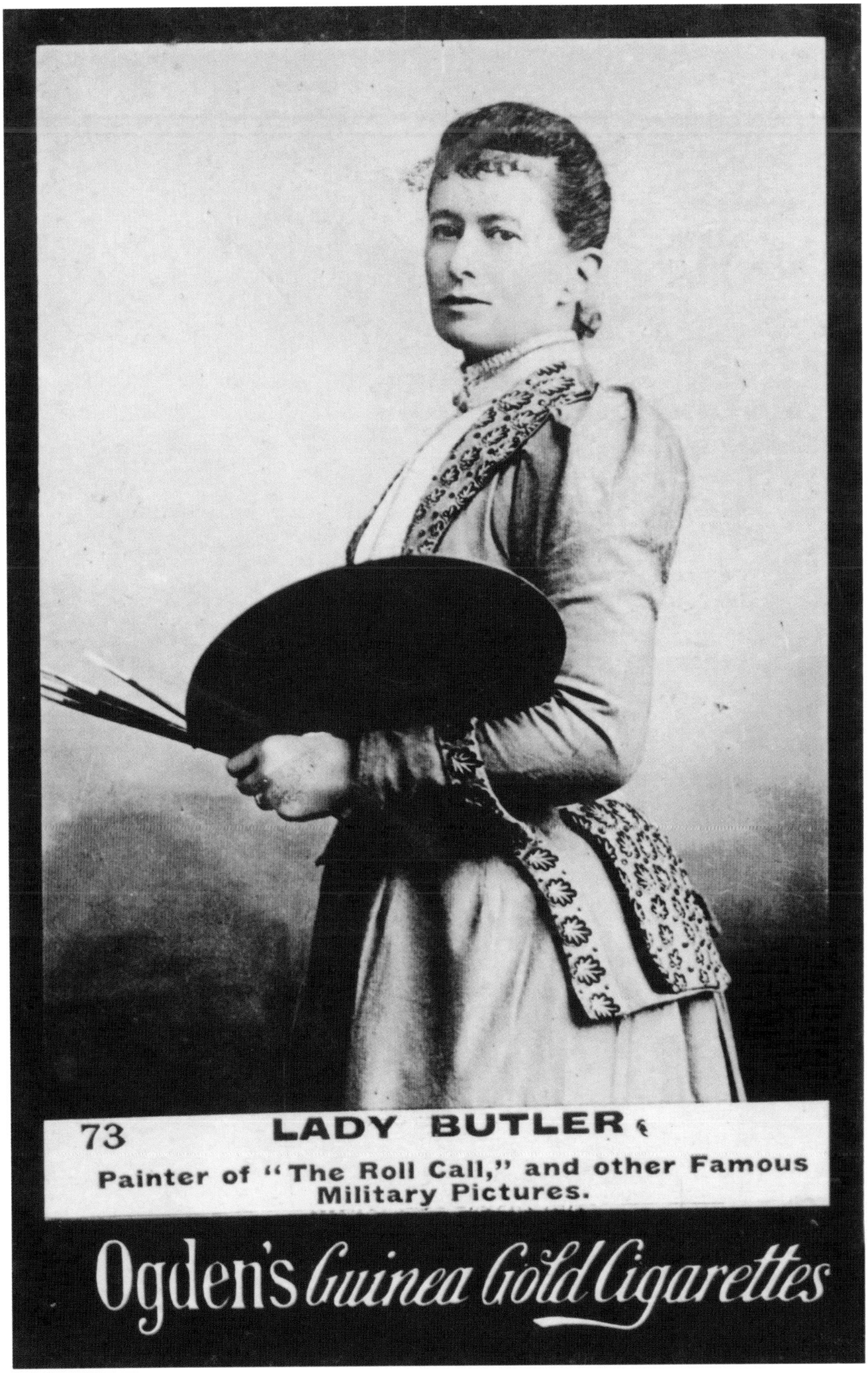

49 *Elizabeth Southerden* (née Thompson), Lady Butler, c.1894–1907. Ogden's cigarette card. National Portrait Gallery.

being expected to leave here. It is very uncomfortable. I can only go on working as hard as I can on the chance'.[48] When her Alma painting was exhibited at the Royal Academy in May 1899, Elizabeth was in South Africa. The painting received moderate reviews. *The Antiquary* reviewed it in conjunction with Wollen's *The 21st Lancers at Omdurman*, observing 'there is nothing specially noteworthy about either, save that they offer a striking contrast as to the way in which troops of the past generation and of the present enter upon the practical warfare of engagement. The Alma was the last battle of the old order, the Guards going into action in full regimentals, with colours flying, and band playing' whereas the uniforms and accoutrements in Wollen's painting were 'dull to paint, and unattractive, but eminently practical for the purpose of actual strife'.[49] Omdurman was a popular theme in the late Victorian climate of jingoism. The *Fortnightly Review* supplanted Elizabeth as Britain's leading battle artist in favour of Crofts, observing that her painting was 'weak and rather theatrical'.[50]

The end of the century produced reflection in the press with regard to the previous century with the *Daily Mail* noting that the 'laurels in painting go to Lady Butler, who as Miss Elizabeth Thompson made so great a fame with her Academy oil picture, *The Roll Call*'.[51] 'Women in the Queen's Reign' features an illustration of Elizabeth's head, alongside Florence Nightingale, Elizabeth Barrett Browning, Christina Rossetti and George Eliot. The article remarks that '*The Roll Call, Balaclava, Inkermann, The 28th Regiment at Quatre Bras*, and *Evicted* are Lady Butler's most famous pictures. Her favourite subjects are battle scenes and cavalry on the march'.[52] While Nightingale, Barrett Browning, Rossetti and Eliot are household Victorian names today, Elizabeth, who shared their pedestal at the end of the nineteenth century, has almost vanished (Figure 49).

Certainly, the highpoint of Elizabeth's career had passed by the turn of the century. By contrast, in the 1890s Alice's career flourished. A review of her essay collection, *The Colour of Life*, describes her 'luminous clearness' and 'rare concentration', remarking, however, that her work was only known to 'the discriminating few [rather] than to the devouring many'. Her association with Elizabeth also defined Alice in the press: 'She and her sister, Lady Butler, the well-known painter of *The Roll-Call* occupy foremost places among the gifted women of the day'.[53] In 1895 Alice was nominated for the position of poet laureate. In 1893, she published her first collection of poems since *Preludes* in 1875. The collection was, in effect, a reissue of *Preludes*, with some new poems added. Visiting her sister at Dover, Alice records the luxury of their surroundings, which offered a respite from Alice's gruelling schedule of writing and publication. Constable's Tower, she informed Wilfrid, 'makes a splendid house. There was a dinner party last night in the Judgement Hall, with the armour all round and the arms of the Constable and the Generals'.[54] However, their departure to South Africa brought the Dover years to an end and marked a turning-point in the Butlers' lives.

The Boer War

William Butler should never have accepted the command of British forces in South Africa. Tensions, which had been mounting in southern Africa since the discovery of gold, were accelerating by the end of the century. The control of this part of Africa was the subject of the argument between the British and Boers. The Boers envisioned a united Boer South Africa and the British envisaged the joining of the two Boer republics – the Transvaal and the Orange Free State – into a British-controlled South Africa. The possibility for incredible wealth creation caused further problems as foreigners flocked to the Transvaal after 1886 in the hope of becoming rich. Paul Kruger, President of the Transvaal, was in direct opposition to the imperialist aims of Alfred Milner who was Governor of Cape Colony and High Commissioner of British Colonies in South Africa from 1897. 'Boer and Briton were on a collision course, both committed to their nationalist aspirations of a united South Africa, one under the Vierkleur, the other under the Union Jack'.[55] The other dominant figure was Cecil Rhodes. Having acquired a fortune in the Kimberley gold mines, Rhodes' ambitions turned to politics, and by 1895 he was Prime Minister of Cape Colony. His desire was to take control of the Transvaal, a sentiment he shared with Joseph Chamberlain at the Colonial Office and Milner. He focused his argument on the political rights of the 'Uitlanders', mostly English gold diggers who had been lured from Europe by the prospect of incredible wealth. By the 1890s the Uitlanders were threatening to outnumber the Boers in the Transvaal. Kruger attempted to contain their power by levying heavy taxes on them and by denying their full rights as citizens. The Uitlanders campaigned for the extension of their rights and in 1895 this resulted in an armed rebellion led by Leander Starr Jameson who invaded the Transvaal with a force of 470 mounted men on 29 December. It ended in fiasco, and Rhodes, who was revealed as the arch-plotter, was forced to resign his premiership. Chamberlain, who was well aware of what was happening in South Africa, managed to extricate himself through political obfuscation. This event, William observes, was 'the point of cleavage, social and political, in the entire fabric of life and politics in South Africa'.[56] The Uitlander question remained unsettled. The fear facing Kruger and the Boers was that they would be outnumbered in their own country, and that their control of the Transvaal would cede to the Uitlanders, paving the way for British imperial ambitions.

In November 1898, William arrived in South Africa to assume not only the command of British forces but to act as temporary High Commissioner in Milner's absence. William and Milner occupied radically different political positions. When he accepted the dual post, William argues in his autobiography that 'nowhere was any hint given' to him that 'war with the Dutch Republic was a probable contingency'.[57] Either William wilfully disregarded the situation or he was politically naïve. The posting, of course, was a prestigious one. On his voyage out, he found awaiting him in Madeira a letter left by Milner enroute to England informing him that South Africa was '"fairly calm"' with nothing that should cause him '"serious embarrassment"'.[58] When he arrived in Cape Town, William was greeted by the recently appointed Prime Minister of Cape Colony, W.P. Schreiner, whom he liked. Both shared similar views on harmonizing relations between the British and Dutch.[59] Schreiner was also the brother of the novelist Olive Schreiner. What William immediately encountered was hostility toward the Boer Republics in Cape Colony: 'There was an acerbity in political and journalistic life, a seeking for causes of offence, a girding and goading at the Dutch in and beyond Cape Colony'.[60] On 17 December, he made a speech at the opening of an exhibition at Grahamstown, where he pronounced that South Africa needed 'peace, progress and the development' which were 'only possible through the union of many hearts and the labour of many hands'.[61] The speech put William in the anti-war camp. At this stage, however, he had no idea that Milner was secretly planning for war. His next action inflamed Uitlander feelings. On the 18 December, a drunken Englishman, Thomas Edgar, assaulted a fellow Englishman in the Transvaal, resulting in the latter's death. When Edgar was pursued by police, he put up resistance and was shot dead. The Uitlanders were outraged and organized a petition calling on Victoria to protect them in the Transvaal. William could see the machinations behind the agitation and telegrammed the Colonial Office: 'Present agitation in Johannesburg is prepared business', and was designed to foment trouble in South Africa. William pointed the finger towards Rhodes, without actually naming him.[62] The policy, as he informed Chamberlain in a subsequent letter, would produce 'a war of the races'.[63] It had become clear that William and Milner were ideologically opposed. The situation between them would become increasingly difficult in the build-up to war. Meanwhile the crisis between Milner and Kruger came to a head in early June. At the Bloemfontein Conference in the Orange Free State (31 May–5 June), the Uitlander question was debated, and Kruger conceded to a period of seven years of residency for Uitlanders to claim voting rights. Milner wanted it reduced to five. When this was refused, the conference was aborted.

War was inevitable. Milner wanted William to prepare his forces for war, but William, following directions from the War Office, looked at border defences, rather than preparing for an offensive operation. The *Daily Mail*'s correspondent in Cape Town observed that '[m]uch uneasiness' was being felt at William's 'pro-Boer sympathies'.[64] When the War Office sent him a communiqué about supplies for the army and asked if he had 'any observations', William seized the opportunity to express his political position: 'I believe that war between the white races coming as a sequel to the Jameson Raid … *would be the greatest calamity that ever occurred in South Africa*'.[65] Milner was incensed; William had gone beyond his duties as Commander-in-Chief of the army by making a political statement. He told Milner that his comments were made in 'the highest interests of the British Empire and for the honour of Her Majesty's Army'.[66] William had to go. The Assistant Under-Secretary at the Colonial Office observed that Milner was rushing Britain into war: 'there is some danger of our being "rushed" by the party in So. Africa which, while its sympathy with the Uitlanders is genuine, has for its chief aim … the speedy annexation of the Transvaal'. '[P]ossibly Sir A. Milner is being carried as rapidly away in one direction as Sir Wm. Butler is in the other'.[67] William resigned his post on 4 July 1899. The *Daily Mail* observed that his departure was 'widely regarded as tantamount to a recall', and though acknowledging William's 'distinguished' career as a soldier and writer, 'owing to his extreme bias', he was 'not the general for South Africa in this hour'.[68] On 11 October 1899, war broke out between Britain and the two Boer Republics of the Transvaal and the Orange Free State.

Elizabeth joined William in South Africa in March 1899. She left Waterloo station with Coos, Eileen and Martin. Christiana saw her off. In her 1909 *Sketch-Book and Diary*, she focuses on the experience of travel. On their voyage out to the Cape, they docked at Madeira, described by Elizabeth as an 'enchanted island'.[69] A 'wine merchant prince' escorted them on their sightseeing tour and in his house, Elizabeth found an engraving of *The Roll Call*. In this magical place, she felt she might 'be dreaming, and would wake, with tears, in Sloane Street'.[70] Back on board ship, the crew and guests celebrated crossing the Line with a fancy-dress ball. The children dressed up for the occasion: Coos 'made up from some Eastern muslins a very coquettish Turkish costume with a little cap', Eileen looked like a 'typical "duck" in a poke bonnet' and Elizabeth 'buckled up little M. in a colonial cavalry "rig" with a "slouched hat".'[71] In a singular allusion to the political situation in South Africa, Elizabeth recounts how her Danish cook 'with the blood of generations of bellicose Vikings coursing through her veins' emerged from the 'saloon stairway – as though rising from the waves she rules – Britannia'. She was dressed in 'a high brass helmet with scarlet crest, then a trident held in one hand, a shield in the other, and the folds of the Union Jack draping her commanding form. She stepped on deck'. The effect was sensational:

> 'I say', said a voice, 'this is *the* success of the evening; who is it?' 'Who is it?' you heard on every side. 'Who is it?' asked Lady — turning to me. 'My cook', I faintly answered. The last speaker knew her South Africa, and all the possibilities of the future might have spoken in my face to judge by the choking laughter that caused her precipitate withdrawal. Each time she ventured back within sight of my smileless face the fit seized her again.

Meanwhile, Britannia was enjoying dancing with Lancers and was 'hand in hand' with a Marchioness.[72]

South Africa was disorientating for Elizabeth. When she saw the Pole Star for the last time on her voyage out, she lamented: 'I shall not feel content, no matter how beautiful I shall find the Southern heavens, till the joyful night when the captain of the Homeward Bound tells us we shall see thee rise'.[73] At that point, Elizabeth expected that her stay in South Africa would last for two or three years. The experience of Rosebank, her new home, was also unsettling: 'Strange land; strange birds with startling cries; strange flowers; strange scents ... Where am I? *Where* are the points of my compass?'[74] At the same time, the landscape had qualities of 'light and colour' that she never saw anywhere else. 'Incredible altogether are the colours at sunset, but all so fleeting. And there is no after-glow here as in Egypt and Italy; the instant the glory of the setting sun is gone all is over and all is grey.'[75] Table Mountain rose 'square and precipitous' above their garden, looking 'like an altar in the pure white light that falls upon it from the Milky Way'.[76] She shared William's sentiments on South Africa: 'Would that all the evil brought to South Africa by the finding of gold could be gathered together and burnt on that altar as a peace offering!'[77] In *Sketch-Book*, she also criticizes the colonial settlements. The colonial house comprised 'corrugated iron' and 'barbed wire fence', and offered a stark contrast to the Dutch 'farmhouses with white walls, thatched roofs, and rounded Flemish gables', which harmonized with the landscape. She notes: 'We talk so much of the love of the beautiful, and yet no people do so much to spoil beauty as we do wherever we settle down, all the world over'.[78] Cape Town had 'glaring streets' lined with 'American "Stores" with cast-iron porticoes' and the outskirts were populated with 'corrugated iron shanties'. Such accommodation sprung up due to the gold rush. She observes: 'No one cares for poor Cape Town as a town. The adventurer is essentially a bird of passage'.[79] The wealthier British settlers were also criticized: 'Our sophisticated life, too, is out of place in this unfinished country, and we ought to live more simply, as the Dutch do, and not feel it necessary to carry on the same ménage as in London. Liveried servants in tall hats and cockades irritate me under such a sun, and the butler in his white choker makes me gasp ... The native servant in his own suitable dress, as in India and Egypt, does not exist down here'.[80] The Boers, she felt, were more sympathetic to the landscape than the foreign intruders. The 'wise Dutch' planted 'dense forests' and instituted a law whereby if a pine was cut down, two saplings had to be planted to replace it. 'We are doing a great deal of the felling without the planting'.[81] At the same time, she realizes her own limitations in identifying with the landscape in contrast to Olive Schreiner, an 'Africander born' who 'expand[ed] into heartfelt home-fervour when returning to the red soil and atmospheric glamour of her native veldt'.[82] In her autobiography, Elizabeth confirms that although she admired the beauty of the South African landscape, she 'never felt the happiness which Italy, Egypt or Palestine' had given her. For her South Africa was 'melancholy' because of the way William had 'suffered' for his 'honesty and devotion to the honour of the Empire he served'.[83]

Elizabeth had little time to paint in South Africa. Her duties as the wife of the commanding officer over the course of five months kept her busy with calls and her planned sketching expeditions with a Dutch artist 'never came off'. This particular artist had 'battled with snakes' and 'sustained the stone-throwing of baboons who made a target of her as she sat at work'. Elizabeth declares: 'I was willing for the baboon bombardment, and even would chance the snakes, as one chances everything, to wrest but a poor little water-colour from nature'.[84] At the Queen's Birthday Review in May she remarks how a 'prophet might have seen the War Spectre moving through the ranks of red-coats' behind William. Her experience of South Africa was brief. The Butlers departed on 23 August 1899. The day was one of 'blinding rain' which, as the ship moved off, 'drew like a curtain across that country which I felt we were leaving to a fast-approaching trouble. The war cloud was descending. It burst in blood and fire a few weeks later and deepened the sense of melancholy with which I shall ever think of that far-away land'.[85] Four days into the voyage home, a consumptive governess was buried at sea. The burial of the lonely governess deepened Elizabeth's despondency, as she describes it as the 'forlornest thing' she had ever witnessed. This governess, who had been travelling alone, 'must have been far too ill to be put on board ship'. The passengers knelt beside her body which lay on a bier covered with the Union Jack. She was a Catholic, so William read the prayers and the Captain read the responses. As her body fell 'with a loud splash into the black ocean', the flowers which had been placed on it, scattered into the sea and 'were soon left behind to sink and disappear'. William attempted to console her: '"Christ", he told her, "walks the waters as well as the land".'[86]

Devonport

Trouble awaited them at home. William was given the Command of the Western District. The *Daily Mail* criticized his lack of preparation for the war and asked why he was being placed in charge of an 'important home command' and invited to take part in a reception for the Queen in Bristol.[87] The 'general public ... will not tolerate incapable or anti-English British officers'. Due to the outcry in the press, William was told to stay away from the Queen's visit to Bristol, in case trouble would ensue. The liberal press rallied in his defence. *The Speaker* criticized the vilification of William's reputation, calling it a 'disgraceful crusade'.[88] In the Afterword to William's autobiography, Eileen comments how her father was described as 'the best abused man in England'. She observes how he was subjected to 'persistent attacks' by the pro-war press and that the 'repeated reverses' to British forces in the war were 'attributed to his neglect of warning the Government during his late command'.[89] Immediately after their return home, William, as Elizabeth notes in her autobiography, was faced with a 'campaign of calumny' that had begun in South Africa and the press 'was letting loose all the poison with which it was being supplied'. Elizabeth had to intercept the 'vilest anonymous letters, many of them beer-stained missives couched in ill-spelt language from the slums'. His 'offence had been a frank admission of sympathy for a people tenacious of their independence and, knowing the Boers as he did, he knew what their resistance would mean in case of attack. He was appalled at the prospect of a war, not against an army but against a people, involving the farm-burnings and all the horrors which our armies would have to resort to'.[90] William, she comments, favoured diplomacy over war and he 'employed the utmost vigour ... to warn those in power of the necessity for enormous forces in order to ensure success. Some of his dispatches were suppressed'. The 'campaign of calumny' was due to a report that Britain's early defeats in the war 'were owing to [William's] wilful neglect in not warning the directing powers of the gravity of their undertaking'.[91] When Redvers Buller was sent to South Africa, William was given the temporary Command at Aldershot, alongside Devonport. With British losses to the Boers, Buller was stripped of his command in December 1899 and replaced by Lord Roberts in early 1900. By January 1901, Buller returned to Aldershot to resume his command and William returned to Devonport. Roberts instituted the 'scorched earth' policy destroying farmsteads so the Boer guerrilla forces would not be supported by farmers and later established concentration camps.

A trip to Rome in March 1900 with Coos offered some respite for Elizabeth. Here Coos saw the Coliseum for the first time by moonlight. Rome was 'intoxicating' and Elizabeth found her 'rapture about Italy increased, if anything' and Genoa was 'very magnificent'.[92] The Hotel Angleterre in Rome was 'very pleasant', but 'crammed with English & a more hideous lot could not be seen'.[93] From there they planned to go to see Fanny in Florence and visit their old friend, Janet Ross, then living in 'Boccaccio's villa to the south of Florence'.[94] Meanwhile, Alice demonstrated her public support of William's political position on South Africa by dedicating her biography of Ruskin to him. Published in July 1900, the inscription read: 'Dedicated to Sir W.F. Butler' and she used a quotation from Ruskin: 'A British officer who is singularly of one mind with me on matters regarding the nation's honour'.[95]

On 22 January 1901, Victoria died. In the diary entry, reproduced in her autobiography, Elizabeth notes: 'Model wife and mother, how many of your women subjects have strayed away, of late from those virtues which you were true to the last'. The Queen had been a champion of her art. King Edward was a different figure. When he took the oath at the opening of Parliament on 16 February, he incensed her. The oath was anti-Catholic and a throwback to the 'darkest days of "No Popery" bigotry', with its 'lies about "idolatry" and the "worship" of the Virgin Mary'. Elizabeth was not a fan of the new King: 'Could not the King have the strength of mind enough to refuse to insult his Catholic subjects?' Yet, she tempers her anger: 'I know he must have deeply disliked to pronounce those words'.[96]

The war continued to dominate their lives. Roberts was due to visit in early September, and Elizabeth told Christiana: 'How carefully I shall have to avoid the burning subject of the War, for I shd certainly say most unsuitable things otherwise!' She also provided her with updates on her art: 'My Tent pegging is well on – neck broken – & my "Last moments of the Brave" (Highlanders, not waving the white flag, in a deep kloof, surrounded by invisible Boers)'.[97] The Roberts' visit was again discussed in her letter to Alice: 'I shall feel very conscious when I look at him with the feeling uppermost in my mind that he said the War was over last October! My conversation during dinner will be studiously oblivious of the War'.[98] Buller was scapegoated for British military failures, as Elizabeth wrote to Christiana: 'Poor Sir Redvers Buller is disgraced & has been deprived of the Aldershot command. I think his punishment too cruel ... If Will had been offered [the command] he wd have declined under the painful circumstances of his poor friend's misfortune'.[99] It was better news for William who had been appointed by Roberts to a commission to enquire into the operation of a War Office Department that was responsible for supplying the war with horses and mules. This necessitated him being in London on a regular basis, enabling Elizabeth to visit her mother in Guildford. By December 1901, Elizabeth confided to her mother: 'The war seems more hopeless than ever. I don't think it is possible to beat a people flat to the Earth who are fighting for, & on, their own soil. We have spent over £200,000,000 already in this shameful war. Unless this Government goes out of office no terms can be made. What is to become of this country? What state will England be in by the time the Coronation comes off?'[100] On 29 March 1902, she wrote to her mother to tell her that she and Will had been invited to the Coronation, which was later postponed due to the King's illness: 'I repeat their words with unction several times a day. If it can be managed I mean to come to London for the Varnishing Day & to meet Alice on her return & if I can get time will run down to see you ... . Is it not a striking fact that the prime author of the War, Cecil Rhodes, should have died now. If Milner & Chamberlain could also disappear from at least the active world we might have peace'.[101]

On a visit to Devonport in March 1902, King Edward spoke to Elizabeth in a 'confidential tone' about William. What he said was 'kind' and he regarded him as a '"splendid soldier"' and 'had in mind the painful trial Will had gone through'.[102] Eileen records a slightly different impression, with Edward observing:

> 'Your husband is a very fine soldier, Lady Butler, but it is a *pity* he takes so much part in politics.' The royal steps retreated a few paces and then approached again, and the one emphatic word '*Pity*' was repeated.[103]

Due to the rules of military service, William was prevented from stating his position or offering any description of his undertakings in South Africa until a war commission was established after the war and he was exonerated. 'Although', Paula Krebs argues, 'few British statesmen came out against the war, by the war's end the rest of Europe vehemently denounced the British cause and fighting methods'.[104] Despite being on the right side of history, William's South African experience dogged him for the rest of his life.

The new century saw the older Butler children make decisions about their future. Patrick joined the Indian army, with Elizabeth writing to Alice that Patrick 'passed the Army exam brilliantly. He had no cramming & no influential lifts'.[105] Dick prepared to become a Benedictine priest at Downside Abbey in Somerset. Quoting from a diary entry of June 1901, reproduced in her autobiography, Elizabeth notes: 'It is inexpressibly touching to me to see my son where he is. A hard probation, for the Benedictine test is long and severe'.[106] However, Coos presented a problem as she had fallen in love with an unsuitable man. Coos had met Captain Randolph Kingscote at Devonport. In a divorce case that was richly detailed in the press, Kingscote divorced Louise Boehm, daughter of the sculptor, Sir Edgar Boehm, on the grounds of adultery, in March 1902. Elizabeth knew Edgar Boehm who had, in 1875, advised her on her 'bounding' horse during her painting of *Quatre Bras*.[107] Boehm had died suddenly in 1890. His son-in-law, Kingscote, discovered that his wife of eleven years was having an affair with a Captain Anderson, after she had taken a sleeping draught and spoke about Anderson in her sleep. When he challenged his wife, she informed him that she 'much preferred living with Captain Anderson to living with him, and that she intended to act accordingly'.[108] At some point during this period, Coos had fallen in love with Kingscote who had been stationed at Devonport in 1901. Elizabeth sent her to stay with Alice and Wilfrid in London in an attempt to separate the couple. Elizabeth wrote to Alice thanking her for accommodating her, remarking: 'May she find happiness ere long, poor wayward child'.[109] The Butlers were not happy with Coos's relationship. Elizabeth asked Alice to speak with her as she feared that Coos intended to meet Kingscote after an appointment with her dentist in London in January 1903.[110] In the previous month Coos told Wilfrid that she hoped to get a dispensation to marry Kingscote:

> I think we have done all we can to meet the wishes of the Catholic Church – & if she remains obdurate we shall have to be married quickly in July in town, & in his Church. All his people highly approve – & have written very kindly to us … I am afraid you will not approve of what we are determined to do – but we have both of us gone through too much to throw away our chances of happiness on account of a priest begotten law.[111]

To his credit, Kingscote recognized the difficulty of their position. He wrote to Wilfrid to thank him for a meeting: 'In the position in which I am placed there are not many who would have left their door open to me and I am deeply sensible of the kindness of feeling which prompted such trust'.[112] Yet again, Wilfrid found himself in the position of mediator in Butler family difficulties. All attempts to get Kingscote's marriage to Louise Boehm annulled proved fruitless. The Butlers had to 'nerve' themselves for the marriage of their daughter.[113] Coos informed Wilfrid that she had a long discussion with her father about her plans, with the date settled for 24

July. As strict Catholics, her parents did not attend the marriage ceremony but Wilfrid agreed to act as a trustee for Coos.[114]

Christiana was also presenting difficulties. Much of the correspondence between Elizabeth and Alice during this period concerns their mother's nomadic lifestyle. Christiana's frequent changes of residence were often accompanied by unpaid bills. On 20 July 1902, Elizabeth wrote to Alice:

> Mama wants a house with a garden & she will have a house with a garden, & as usual we will mop up the unexpired rent of the last one ... One lady told me I was considered 'very hard' at Aldershot to let my mother want clothes & even food. I sent her coals when I heard she was borrowing them from her neighbours & clothes when I heard a lady had given her a mantle. I will never again send Mama money, but in future will help her in kind, alone. ... What wd we think of Lady Audry Buller if we thought her mother was living at Farnboro' in want?[115]

Several months later Elizabeth informed Wilfrid, after yet another move by her mother, that 'this constant changing' had 'become quite a monomania' with her.[116]

During the Devonport years, Elizabeth recalls how she 'carried on her painting "through thick and thin" and did well on the whole at the Academy'. She had the '"consuming zeal" – a very necessary possession'.[117] She had, as Eileen records, to manage 'conflicting duties':

> The matter of returning calls, as the G.O.C.'s wife, for instance, was seldom up to schedule. How *could* she so waste the precious daylight until she had finished wrestling with the difficulties of the foreshortening of a rearing horse? Or until she had completed a rough drawing of her new picture? One morning, at Government House, Devonport, when my mother was at her easel, and I, home for the holidays, was making a copy by way of lesson of one of her watercolours in a corner of the studio, the A.D.C. entered with a notebook in his hand. 'Well, Captain Clifford, what is it?' asked my mother, impatiently tapping with her mahl-stick. The unfortunate man had brought a list of calls, the most urgent names underlined in red ink, which, he knew from complaints that had reached him, would brook no further inattention. My mother realized that for the afternoon her work must be laid aside.[118]

Work was invariably resumed. *The 10th Bengal Lancers Tent-pegging* was exhibited at the Royal Academy in 1902, capturing horses and riders galloping towards the viewer. Elizabeth was pleased with it when she saw it at the Academy, but lamented that it was in the last room, 'where the public looks with "lack-lustre eyes," being tired'.[119] Her South African painting, *Within Sound of Guns*, was exhibited at the 1903

Academy. At Government House, she had horses trot up and down in the grounds for her 'study of movement'.[120] When she returned from a trip to France, she found her picture of the 'yeomanry cantering through a "spruit" in the Boer war ... admirably placed this time at Burlington House'. 'I had', she remarks, 'greatly improved in tone by this time. Millais' remark once upon a time, "She draws better than any of us, but I wish her tone was better," had sunk deep'.[121] The painting, however, was not kindly reviewed, with the *Art Journal* remarking, 'Lady Butler scarcely keeps up her reputation with her picture of a South African incident'.[122] As Elizabeth told Alice, the 'yeomanry picture' was 'simply a frolic'. *Stand Fast Craigellachie* (1903) was a more serious affair for her: 'My picture *Stand Fast* was painted simply to record deep admiration of the devotion to duty of our young officers – sacrificed so often by the Generals in their blunderings'.[123] Commemorating a military engagement of the 2nd Battalion Seaforth Highlanders on India's North West frontier in 1895, the painting depicts a young Highlander in a kilt with his sword in his hand standing defiantly in a mountainous terrain as his dead comrade lies prostrate at his feet. Its dramatic pose evokes that of Pennington in *Balaclava*.

The publication of *Letters from the Holy Land* launched a new dimension to her career. Although the volume, as noted in the previous chapter, was well reviewed, she, nonetheless, felt that an anti-Catholic sentiment biased some critics. To Wilfrid, she wrote: 'I have only seen the *Daily News* & Westminster notices so far – all praise for the sketches but ill-repressed dislike of the tone of the letter-press. No wonder. I suppose a good sprinkling of sneers wd be to their taste, & chronicles of our breakfasts & lunches wd appeal'.[124] She wrote in a similar vein to Christiana: 'the Catholic tone of the book no doubt annoys some critics, but the sketches are universally liked. As to our Catholic friends, they find the book altogether "fascinating". I have sent a copy to dear Fanny'. The success of her illustrations inspired her to go 'in for a series of water colours, much encouraged by the chorus of admiration in the Press of my Palestine sketches. What would they say to the originals!'[125]

In January 1905, she told Alice that she was 'grinding away at *Rescue of Wounded, Afghanistan* as Will wd much sooner I finished it here & 'a done with it. But I hanker after a few touches at it in London. You know us artists!'[126] The painting pleased her. It was exhibited in Gallery III of the Royal Academy. 'I have just heard', she informed Christiana, 'that my picture is in the big room at the Academy, on the line, of course. As Will is going to the Banquet he may chance to sit opposite to my picture for the dinner is always held in that room! I think I shall have success this year'.[127] And in a second letter on the same day, she gave her more information on its precise location:

> I hasten to tell you that my picture is in a post of honour at the top of the big room & looks more brilliant, more in motion & altogether more striking than ever it did in the Studio. It is a strange thing that the 3 pictures I painted at Government House <u>in a sidelight</u> have all appeared better at the Academy than

> at home – a most gratifying fact, as usually artists are shocked at the change for the worse when they first confront their pictures on Varnishing Day. I was much complimented on that occasion by artists, & from what I hear, I believe the picture is going to be a success. I prefer Patrick's going with Will to the Private View today to going myself & I shall hear all about it at tea. I think it is time the R. A. bought one of my works from the Chantry fund.[128]

'I wish', she later told Christiana, 'you could be transported into my little crowd at the Academy. Eileen & Patrick took the place you used to occupy in front of my work & they tell me the remarks were most enthusiastic. They went there two days & it was always the same – a regular press to see it like before my Drummers'.[129] Although critical interest had waned, public interest in her work continued, with *The Camel Corps* and *The Dawn of Waterloo* drawing crowds at the Bristol exhibition. Neither, however, had sold. 'I wish', Elizabeth wrote to Christiana, 'the Bristol niggard ruffians would buy one of these pictures for their permanent gallery'.[130]

In May 1905, Elizabeth commenced work on a new Academy picture in Mulranny in County Mayo, in the West of Ireland. In *Sketch-Book* she describes how '[y]ou travel right across Ireland, getting a very informing vista of the poverty and stagnation of those Midland counties till your eyes greet the glorious development of natural beauty on the confines of the sea-girt Western land'.[131] Farther on, 'one-day's journey from Mulranny, poignantly melancholy in its beauty and remoteness', was Achill Island. One place on the island captured her attention – a deserted village: 'It is Achill's mournful little Pompeii, a village of the dead, on a bare hillside which we passed one day on our way to an unfrequented part of the island'. This long-deserted village looked 'more heart-breaking' with the 'bright sunshine' on its 'roofless cabins' than it 'might have done in dismal rain'. And here the artistic vision comes to the fore: 'I wish I could have made a sketch of it as I saw it that day – a subject strongly attracting the attention of the mind rather than the eye. Pictorial beauty there was none'.[132] In this part of Mayo, the women and girls were still wearing the 'head-shawls and white caps and the red petticoats' that had 'charmed' Elizabeth on her honeymoon in Kerry in 1877.[133] The country, however, was 'ebbing away' with its deserted cabins. It was here she encountered an Irish peasant woman, while doing studies of sheep:

> I was sketching sheep for a contemplated picture, in the evenings on the lovely marshes by the sea, and one evening a widow, left completely lonely in her little cabin on the heights above by the departure for America of her last child, came down to fetch home her solitary sheep from amongst the others, and I told her I thought these creatures were leading a very happy life. 'Yes', she answered, pausing for a moment and looking down on the flock, 'and they are without sin'.[134]

Her studies, however, of 'wild mountain sheep on the marshes came to an abrupt close' in late July when, as she was waiting 'for the sunset and its after-glow, to get final precious notes of colour upon the fleeces', her favourite model, a three-legged sheep called Pacer, appeared on the edge of a rock over her head: 'But what had happened to "Pacer's" neck? Good gracious! I jumped up and beheld a shorn "Pacer" and all the flock in the same lamentable condition. It had all happened in twenty-four hours'.[135]

She wrote to Christiana about preparations for the painting: 'It is to be that lovely Cistercian Shepard bringing in his sheep on the hill side', a study she had begun in Henley in 1871.

> Everything is here for it – sheep, sky, landscape & every evening a radiant afterglow. This is a very wild and beautiful coast & it seems so strange to be in an hotel of the most modern comfort in the midst of such scenery. The dress of the peasant women is most picturesque – the deep rich red of their petticoats is made of a dye which they extract themselves from the roots of the heather. Many of them wear the white cap on Sundays & all have the shawl over the head. Such nice people to talk to![136]

In June, she wrote that she was 'still learning sheep'. Chasing them with 'block and palette all over the place' was 'healthy work'.[137]

Meanwhile, William's army career was coming to an end. Before his retirement, he had been appointed to chair a committee into the squandering of £6.5 million by the Army Stores Department. William's 1905 report pointed the finger at the highest levels of the War Office. For Elizabeth, William's appointment to head the enquiry was a vindication. Writing to Christiana, she noted:

> he has to conduct a commission at the War Office which has to enquire into the mismanagement of stores in S. Africa after the War! To think that they shd have to come to <u>him</u>, of all men. What a compliment. They want a straightforward clear-headed, honest man, of course, they come to him. It is the old story 'Get all you can & <u>give nothing</u>'. They will, as usual, give him nothing for this task. It is a Herculean one.

In the same letter, she informed Christiana that William had been approached by the Liberal Party to stand as an MP in Leeds: 'Will is to stand for East Leeds at the next election!! The Liberals are confident of his carrying the seat with a handsome majority. It is at present held by a conservative who had a majority of 600 at the last election, so W. will have first to pull down 600 before a majority becomes possible. The news has created a great sensation'.[138] Unfortunately, William had different views on education than the Liberal Party, resulting in him standing down. 'Will is deep in his work at the War Office. As to Leeds, everything is at a deadlock, as he has to stick to his Catholic principles on the Education question & these principles are not those of the Liberal Party. If they cannot agree, he will withdraw. I am longing for the Liberal government to come into power'.[139] In December 1905 William set off on a fact-finding mission to South Africa, with Elizabeth seeing him off at Waterloo, as well as preparing for a 'one-man' show in London. Meanwhile, Elizabeth was living at her London club but needed a place to paint, asking Alice, 'Can you give me a corner in your drawingroom or elsewhere where I can dab dab for 2 or 3 hours a day?'[140] In April 1906, Elizabeth, Alice and Eileen went to Rome, where they received Holy Communion from Pope Pius X. Elizabeth presented him with a copy of *Letters from the Holy Land* with an inscription: 'To His Holiness Pius X with the profoundest homage of his faithful daughter Ebth Butler'.[141] At the closing of her exhibition, she wrote to Christiana:

> My expenses will be covered, & I have shown the world I can do landscapes & peaceful subjects, & that I love the beauty of nature. There have been more than the usual numbers of visitors to the Graves Galleries & the Press has been most favourable. Had I shown more horses & soldiers I shd have made much more money. People are very like sheep – they all run one way at a time.[142]

Bansha

The Butlers prepared a home in Ireland at Bansha Castle in County Tipperary, not far from William's ancestral home. This was clearly William's choice. Elizabeth wrote to her mother on 12 October 1905 that life at Bansha was 'very quiet & simple' and although they had 'very nice neighbours' they lived 'at great distances' and there was 'not much entertaining'. William, she noted, was due to retire from the army on 31 October, when he turned 67. 'I hope he has many strong years before him of public life. I don't want him to retire from that. The education difficulty has stood in the way of his entering Parliament, as you know. How I wish the Liberals would come in. It would be a good thing for us & wd bring us much to England'.[143]

At Bansha, Elizabeth continued working on her art from a studio in the garden. On 9 December 1907, she wrote to Christiana that she was showing her 'Cistercian to friends & it seems to please exceedingly. The sheep are all alive & moving out of the picture' but she could get no model for her monk's face because she wanted it so 'beautiful & saintly'. She confirmed that '[e]verything has been done from abundant data & hence the real look of the picture – all except <u>that face</u>. But it is very nearly the thing. The after-glow on it is from Martin's face'. Bansha, however, was dull: 'I have nothing else to write about so retired is our life here'.[144] By 17 December she was satisfied with the monk's face, informing Christiana: 'It is very ascetic & thin so the radiant face I did from you would not be suitable'. The reference was to the studies she had done from Christiana's face for *The Magnificat*, which was then hanging in her studio. She was returning to the religious themes of her early days: 'I have nearly finished a watercolour of the monk preaching the Lenten sermon in the Colosseum. You remember the abortive oil I attempted of that subject in Ventnor? I have used it for this very successful watercolour, which I shall exhibit somewhere'.[145] By February 1908 she was longing for Portofino – 'Oh! What scenes of paradise are there'. Ireland was 'deplorably dull'.[146] In March, she sent off her painting to the Academy, but was expecting rejection: 'They will never guess it is mine from the subject'. The Portofino trip did not materialize: 'We cannot afford it. Pazienza!'[147] An extensive wing was being added to Bansha Castle, comprising five extra rooms. At the end of April, she was on her way to the Academy. On 8 May she wrote to Christiana from Langham's Hotel that she was just off to the Academy with Alice: 'My shepherd looks a very gentle, low-toned pastoral in rather glaring surroundings but it is kindly hung with dark canvases immediately around it'.[148] For her, the work on the painting was a joy, but the public was not convinced:

> [T]he public did not want idylls from me at all. 'Give us soldiers and horses, but pastoral idylls – no!' People had a slightly reproachful tone in their comments after seeing my poor pastoral on the Academy walls. Someone said, 'How are the mighty fallen!'[149]

Although Elizabeth envisaged Bansha as a 'dear home for the summer months', it became a permanent residence. Located in the heart of the southern Irish countryside, it isolated her even more from the London art world.[150] It was a twelve-hour journey from London to Bansha by train, via Fishguard. She complained to Wilfrid that she had the 'the greatest difficulty here to paint at all, unless it is landscape, pure & simple!'[151] Despite the decline in critical interest in her work, her public appeal remained strong. Both *The Roll Call* and *Scotland for Ever!* drew crowds at the Irish International Exhibition in Dublin in May 1907.[152] She wrote to Alice: 'I was so very happy at the look of my poor old *Roll Call* & the *Scotland for Ever* at the International in Dublin. It is many a long age since I saw them last'.[153] She was also invited to send two paintings to the women's exhibition in Melbourne in the autumn of 1907.[154] At the same time William was engaged in making speeches in different parts of the country, attempting to 'quicken' in his fellow countrymen a 'sense of the necessity for industry, sobriety, and a more serious view of existence. They did not seem to like it'.[155] Despite his Catholicism, Home Rule affiliations, support for Egyptian nationalism and sympathies with the Boers, William was also a retired army officer and from a privileged class in Ireland, a class which would undergo radical change a decade later.

In August 1908, Elizabeth commenced her next 'literary venture', *From Sketch-Book and Diary*, and was working on a new painting: '"Last wishes: an eve of battle" an officer writing his last wishes in case of its being his last chance, the grey horses of his regiment tethered on the crest of a hill behind him in the wan evening light. But it is really too soon to speak of it'.[156] By November she was making watercolour sketches for her new book and was working on 'night effects', which she was determined to 'master'.[157] It was dedicated to Alice and drawn from her diaries and letters to her mother. Elizabeth was delighted with the quality of the production but regretted having so many landscape scenes when she saw how 'excellently the figure groups' had 'come out'.[158] With chapters on her Irish, Italian, South African and Egyptian travels, it was more broad-ranging and appealing than *Letters from the Holy Land*. It was very well received in the press. *The Athenaeum* notes: 'What we find in Lady Butler is the quick responsiveness which at once appropriates the spirit of a scene, a country, a people; and the gift of carrying the reader along and making him see with almost her own clear eyes and profound sympathy'. Here also there is an echo of Christiana's personality as it is revealed in her travel journals and diaries: 'Always dwelling on a high – some will say – ecstatic plane, she never condescends to petty details of travel, unless they have an aesthetic meaning for her'. At the same time 'there is no lack of enjoyment of the humorous'.[159]

In January 1909, Elizabeth saw her own two paintings which later fired the young imagination of Beryl Bainbridge. *Inkerman* was exhibited at the winter exhibition of the Royal Academy. She told Christiana: 'I was enchanted on seeing it. It is a fine work, I will say. I had forgotten parts of it! It is splendidly hung'.[160] In a subsequent letter, she recorded her views on *Remnants of an Army*:

> I had the great pleasure of seeing another of my best pictures of days gone by this morning, when I saw *The Remnants of an Army* (Dr Brydon) at the Tate Gallery. Hitherto it has been shamefully skied there, but the new keeper, Mr McColl has had all the pictures re-arranged & mine is grandly placed on the line with a great space of dark red wall all round it. It never looked so well, even when first exhibited at the Academy! Oh! I was happy. It has been beautifully varnished & is under glass. The sky is most beautiful. How thankful I am that all my best works are in public galleries & taken such care of – not knocking about.[161]

By 1909, there is a sense of looking back, of re-appraising her artistic legacy and a return to the religious themes of her early career. She also forged new areas with her illustrated travel books. The subsequent years, however, would bring heartbreak, worry and change.

CHAPTER NINE

Wars and beyond: the Irish years, 1909–33

Deaths of Christiana and William – William's autobiography – Dick ordained – Eileen marries – Exhibition at the Leicester Galleries – Preparation for Waterloo centenary – Lyndhurst – Dick signs up – War letters – 'Summer in England, 1914' – Exhibition – Trauma – Exhibition reviews – The London Irish at Loos *–Family and the war –* Eyes Right! *– Another exhibition – Trouble in Ireland – Autobiography – Alice dies – Gormanston years –* The Retreat from Mons *– The End*

On the eve of the First World War, Elizabeth was with her son Patrick in Lyndhurst in the south of England prior to his departure to France as part of the 7th Division of the British Expeditionary Force. In *A Galloper at Ypres* (1920) Patrick describes how on 4 October 1914, he was summoned from the Grand Hotel in Lyndhurst to accompany his commanding officer, General Capper, to the War Office. On the way to his tent where he grabbed his coat and sword, and stuffed his haversack with his few articles, a fellow officer told him that the orders for embarkation had come.

> My mother, who had come over from Ireland to spend the last few days with me, and to whom I had whispered the news, met me on my way down from my tent and helped me to carry some of my things. She and I had all along known that when the summons came it would be sudden, but in such matters the actual happening always takes one by surprise and this occasion was certainly no exception. For all we knew it was to be our final parting, and it was a very brief one.[1]

Elizabeth had arrived from Ireland in mid-September. As Patrick describes, it was a 'most sporting undertaking on her part, and an inexpressible joy to both of us to be together during those last few days'. At Lyndhurst, Elizabeth also had 'ample opportunities for studying a war division coming into being, and amply availed herself of them'. Patrick had acquired three 'fine Irish hunters' and Elizabeth painted portraits of them, which formed the frontispiece of his book.[2] Patrick's descriptions, his particular aptitude for detail, and his focus on the intimacies of war, echo

Elizabeth's art. In a description, for instance, of an open-air Mass which he attended with his mother behind the camp of the Scots Guards, he constructs a 'before the battle' scene:

> The sun shone brilliantly and the thick golden bracken and background of forest trees made a beautiful setting to the scene. There was just enough breeze blowing to threaten to extinguish the two altar candles, so two stalwart privates of the Guards knelt one on either side of the altar and sheltered with raised hands the tiny flames.[3]

The work at Lyndhurst comprised getting the diverse brigades and regiments to work together. 'Nobody', Patrick observes, 'could be more appreciative' than his mother of 'all that she saw'. Moreover, '[l]ittle did those sunburnt men know as they swung past, that the lady in black, who never seemed tired of watching them, was the artist whose pictures had brought home to thousands the pathos and glory of the soldier's calling'.[4] Poignantly, Elizabeth produced a watercolour of Patrick in this final days. Entitled *Patrick, Au Revoir*, it features him on one of his horses.

Eve of War

The years between 1909 and the outbreak of war had brought death. First, Christiana passed away. As late as September 1909, Christiana was unchanged in her responses to her daughter's achievements – she was in 'ecstasies' about *Sketch-Book*.[5] Christiana died when Elizabeth was in Italy in spring 1910. Alice had cancelled her planned trip to Italy and was with her mother when she died at her home in Camberley. In her last letter to her mother, Elizabeth recounted her time in Portofino:

> The traditional citron & myrtle are everywhere and the vineyards are carpeted with large and most fragrant violets ... I lunched with Monty & his nice little wife at their castle yesterday ... Monty showed me a pencil portrait you made of him when he was 25! He is a good bit shrivelled up but his voice is the same ... I thought Fanny looking well. She is so very anxious to know how you are ... YOU have such wonderful vitality, my beloved Mama; I am full of hope that you rallied well after I saw you.[6]

With the death of Christiana on 13 March, Elizabeth lost her most ardent supporter and the person who had cultivated her aptitude in art from toddlerhood. She wrote to Alice from Portofino: 'Oh! Alice, what a wringing of the heart must yours have been by that bedside. It is inexpressibly touching to me to think of her here where I remember her in her prime. Her face of those days is as vividly before me as the poor distressed one I last saw, overshadowed by the fast approaching end'.[7]

Then, in June, William died suddenly after a short illness. In an obituary in *The Tablet*, Wilfrid describes William as a man who

> would not be hustled into positions he felt to be false, or flattered into compliances to which his conscience did not subscribe. Such independence of character has its awkwardness both for the man who aspires to it and for his comrades by the way; and they are awkwardnesses which, if only because they fall on others, require from him all the greater fearlessness to face. But SIR WILLIAM BUTLER, firm in his sense of duty, faced them and did not flinch; faced them when, in the case of a war he believed to be unnecessary and therefore criminal, they threatened to overwhelm him.[8]

Another obituary notes that William would be 'best remembered by the public for his Cassandra-like prophecies when sent to Command the Cape in 1898. At the time, like the unfortunate prophetess, he gained nothing but unpopularity for his gloomy forebodings'.[9] Eileen Gormanston describes her father as 'so overdosed with moral courage that to find himself in a minority of one pleased rather than disturbed him'. At home, however, William was a difficult figure:

> What is surprising is that one who, in public life, invariably championed the under-dog should, in his own home, have been a complete autocrat. No one there ever dared dispute my father's will – least of all, my mother, in whom loyalty was an outstanding quality, who detested rows, and who, fortunately for herself, had her studio in which to retreat and there find tranquillity.[10]

Eileen describes Bansha as 'an ideal retreat for my parents in their declining years'. Here William worked in his study and Elizabeth 'spent nearly all the hours of daylight painting in the studio' that had been built for her in the paddock. For Eileen, however, Bansha was lonely, and she often suffered from what she describes as 'Bansha-it is'.[11]

Eileen also had the responsibility for finishing her father's autobiography. Wilfrid and Alice helped her. On 16 June 1910, Eileen noted in a letter to Wilfrid that she had the 'difficult job of finishing the last S. African chapter'.[12] Eileen also grappled with the various publishers interested in it, but eventually settled for Constable who offered the best deal. In a letter to Wilfrid on 23 September, she observed:

> I have worked, heaven only knows how much over it, & worried too – so have mother & Dick; & I do hope now our efforts will be crowned with success. Above all, of course, I want the book to be a <u>great</u> success & widely read.[13]

The book was extensively reviewed in the press, with most focusing on William's revelations on the South African conflict. *The Telegraph* interprets the autobiography as 'a vindication' of William's stance on the war.[14] For *The Star*, it reveals how 'two peoples [were] hurried into wanton wicked war'.[15] The *Daily News* observes the discordance between William's political sympathies and his military role: 'It is odd … that he was nearly always fighting against people in whose cause he more or less believed'.[16]

In the Afterword, Eileen quotes her mother's words on her father's death: 'He taught me how to live, and now he has taught me how to die'.[17] In William's autobiography, however, there is scant reference to Elizabeth. In this regard, William may have been shielding his personal life, but in doing so, he obscures the significance of his wife's contribution to an understanding of war, as well as her fame.

In the spring of 1911, Dick was ordained in Rome. Elizabeth and Eileen travelled to Rome where they were joined by Patrick. Holy Saturday was the 'great day' when Dick 'assumed the chasuble' and became 'officially known as Father Urban'. For Elizabeth, the sight of the young deacons was 'very touching' in their 'white and gold vestments'. Each, in turn, was called by name and 'ascended the altar steps, where sat the consecrating bishop … When Urbano Butler (pronounced *Boutler*, of course, by the Italian voice) was called, how we craned forward! To me the whole thing was poignant. What those boys give up! ("Well", answers a voice, "they give up the world, and a good thing too!")'.[18]

On 26 October, Eileen escaped Bansha when she was married into the Preston family, whose seat was at Gormanston Castle near the sea in County Meath, not far from Dublin. She was married at Brompton Oratory, the church 'so loved' by Christiana and where Elizabeth had been received into the Catholic faith.[19]

During the winter of 1911–12, Elizabeth prepared for an exhibition at the Leicester Galleries. In her autobiography, she observes: 'The King lent my good old *Roll Call*, and the whole thing was a success. I showed many landscapes there as well as military subjects; many Italian and Egyptian drawings made during my travels, and scenes in Ireland'.[20] The calm before the storm was evident in 1912 as Elizabeth enjoyed the serenity of an 'Irish midsummer' with Eileen at Gormanston, telling Alice in a June letter that Eileen led a 'charming, peaceful life' and that she was a 'fortunate creature'. Furthermore, Elizabeth's show at the Leicester Galleries had 'been a wonderful success & the management excellent'.[21] After a trip to Rome with Alice in early 1913, she returned to her art, telling Alice that she was busy 'pushing' on her '"Waterloos" steadily' and that all her days 'resemble[d] each other strongly'.[22] Elizabeth was preparing for the centenary of Waterloo, when the war that would displace Waterloo in the British cultural consciousness, broke out. She was working on an oil painting, *The Cuirassiers' Last Réveil, Morning of Waterloo*. She describes the preparation for the painting in her autobiography:

> I left no stone unturned to get true studies of dawn twilight for the *reveil*, and I got them. At the pretty house of my friends, the Egerton Castles, on a steep

Surrey hill, I had my chance. The house faced the east. It was midsummer; an alarm clock roused me each morning at 2.30. I had modelled a little grey horse and a man, and set them up on my balcony, facing in the right direction, and there I waited, with palette spread, for the dawn. Time was short; the first ray of sunshine would spoil all, so I could only dab down the tones, anyhow; but they were all-important dabs, and made the big picture run without a hitch. Nothing delays a picture more than the searching for the true relations of tone without sufficient data. But it is a truism.[23]

Her dedication to research was unflagging: 'I had any amount of books for reference, records of old uniforms to get from contemporary paintings; and I utilized the many studies of horses I had made for years, chiefly on the chance of their coming in useful some day'. This is not a crowded painting. Four white horses with their four figures, who are sounding the réveil, are isolated against a brown landscape. But before her exhibition opened, war 'burst' upon them. As she notes, 'First, my soldier son went off, and then the Benedictine donned khaki, as chaplain to the forces. He went, one may say, from the cloister to the cannon. I had to pass through the ordeal which became the lot of so many mothers of sons throughout the Empire'.[24]

Elizabeth also describes her time in Lyndhurst with Patrick. Arriving at Lyndhurst, she immediately perceived the difference between this and her Aldershot days: 'This *is war*, and there is no doubt the bearing of the men is different ... There is a quiet seriousness quite new to me'. She records how she had a 'most striking lesson in the appearance of men after a very long march, *plus* that look which is quite absent on peace manoeuvres, however hot and trying the conditions. What surprises and telling "bits" one sees which could never be imagined with such a convincing power' (Figure 50). Like much of her focus in her earlier art, horses draw her attention:

> A team of eight mammoth shire horses drawing a great gun is a sight never to be forgotten; shapely, superb cart horses with coats as satiny as any thoroughbred's, in polished artillery harness, with the mild eyes of their breed ... But I see the German shells ploughing through those teams of willing beasts. They will suffer terribly.[25]

Patrick shared his mother's sensitivity towards horses. His first experience of the suffering of horses is recorded on his deployment to France. A horse was injured on the journey in the crowded conditions of the vessel. The animal, in a 'paroxysm of fear and rage', was being bled to death, as a bullet in those close confines would have been dangerous. Patrick describes the 'drip, drip of blood' as it made its way through the planks. 'It was', he relates in an understated manner, 'not pleasant'. The looks on the men's faces were of 'horror and pity' and the blood became a 'steady outpouring'.

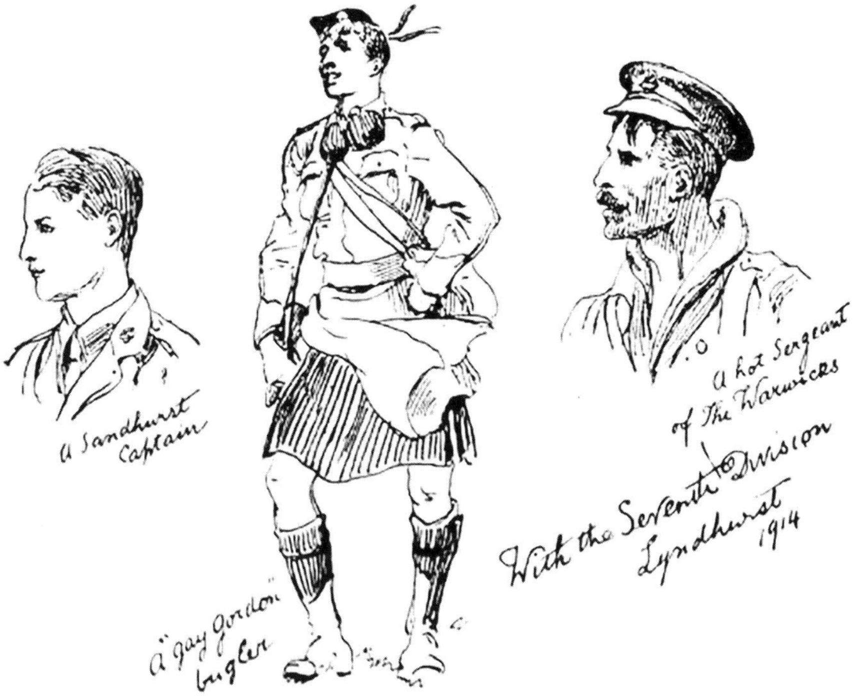

50 Images of soldiers from Elizabeth Butler, *Autobiography*.

'Poor beast', Patrick relates, 'his troubles were over early'.[26] Like his mother's art, which often conveyed in an episode the horror which was about to unfold, Patrick's story of the horse prefigures the slaughter that was to come.

In these early weeks of the war, Elizabeth records the disturbing sight of 'mere boys' arriving from Sandhurst to be given companies to command, captains being 'killed, wounded or missing in such numbers'. The horses at Lyndhurst, she describes as 'superb'. They are, however, 'poor beasts'. 'One daily, hourly, reminds oneself that the very dittoes of these men and animals, are suffering, fighting, dying, over there in France'.[27] Elizabeth studied the scenes with the eye of the artist (Figure 51). One evening Patrick took her at sunset to the high ground overlooking the camp:

> The mellow, very red sun was setting and the white moon was already well up over the camp, which looked mysterious, lightly veiled by the thin grey wood-smoke of the fires. Thousands of troops were massed or moving, shadowy, far away; others in the middle distance received the blood-red glow on the men's faces with an extraordinary effect. They showed as ruddy, vapourous lines of colour over the scarcely perceptible tones of the dusky uniforms. Horses stood up dark on the sky-line. The bugles sounded the 'Retreat'; these doomed legions, shadow-like, moved to and fro. It was the prologue to a great tragedy.[28]

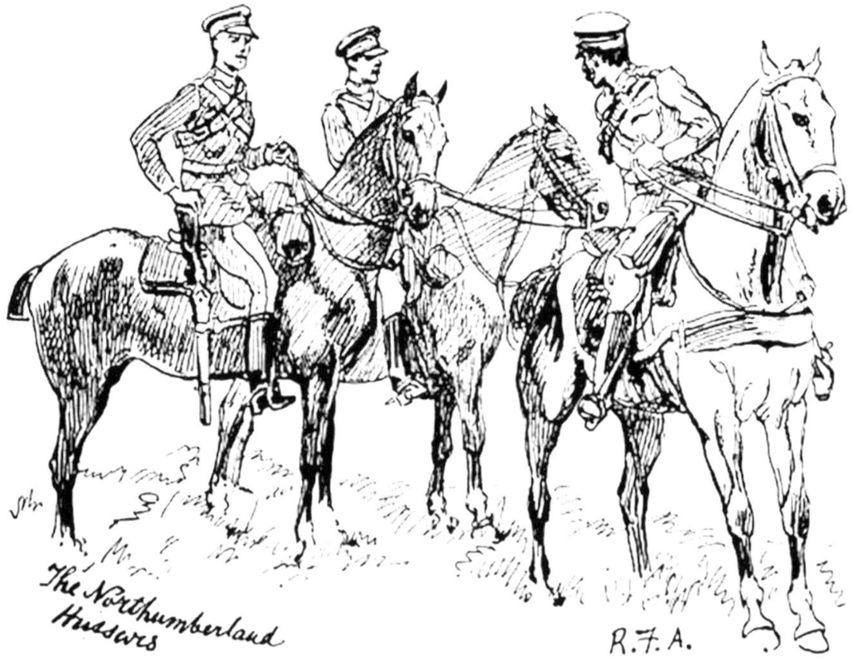

51 'Northumberland Hussars' from Elizabeth Butler, *Autobiography*.

Elizabeth also wrote to Alice about her experience at Lyndhurst. She recounted here, and in her autobiography, the scene at Mass which Patrick describes in his work. The Sunday offered 'repose' amidst the 'week of drumming … marching, fifes, bag-pipes, dust & toil', but it was also a 'hush' during which Elizabeth could hear in her 'minds' ear' the distant guns in France. She went to Mass with Mrs Capper, as well as Patrick. Here in the secluded dell, the 'heather had not been ploughed up as elsewhere'. She continued:

> Guards and Grenadiers were all on their knees as we arrived & the bright green & gold vestments of the priest were relieved very vividly in the strong sunshine against the background of darker green of the forest behind.
>
> The deep soft blue sky was the roof. Quite a little crowd of stalwart guardsmen received Holy Communion, & two of them were sheltering, with careful hands, the candles from the soft warm breeze. You know what I felt with my soldier boy kneeling by my side, in his fighting kit.

Patrick had also made his will, she told Alice, and sent it to Dick. 'He is with me every moment that he can be spared & does all he can to lay up a memory for me & for himself without regrets. Some Belgian friends here photographed us yesterday, sitting together. What a precious moment that little snap-shot will be'.[29] But then Dick also signed up. On 2 March 1914, he wrote to his mother from Downside Abbey: 'Patrick urged often that my place was beside you, but I knew you would not stand in my way when I thought the time had come'.[30] He was, after all, the son of a soldier, as well as the son of a war painter.

In a letter to Wilfrid, Patrick recorded his thoughts on leaving: 'I cannot remember a time when some of you or all of you have not been the very best of friends to me'. The letter has the quality of farewell and Patrick acknowledges it as such. 'There is a baleful tone of "sadness of farewell" about all my letters now. It's this waiting'. His mother's presence was a comfort: it was 'beyond words sweet having my mother here. One's friends go down daily, vide the casualty lists'. Nostalgia and a sense of doom prevailed: 'Let me have your prayers. I get such beautiful letters from the brave little Company of the family, & references to childhood's days together are almost more than one can bear'. He told Wilfrid that he wore a cross of 'much sacredness' from Father Vaughan.[31]

Patrick was injured early in the war and was sent back to Guy's Hospital in November, from where he wrote to Alice thanking her for her prayers: 'there is something infinitely consoling & helpful in the knowledge one has of the prayers & feelings of the best people at home. I know it kept me going on many occasions "down there" in that horrid welter of blood and sorrow'.[32] On recuperation, Patrick returned to war.

The anxieties for her son pervade Elizabeth's letters to Alice. While the letters from Patrick at the front have 'all been enthralling in interest' his last one filled her with apprehension as the 7th Division was bearing the 'brunt of the fighting for many days'. One of Patrick's friends had fallen: 'The Brigade in which poor young Cox was, was the one … as I saw it from a height, that evening in the afterglow, preparing for night operations. You could have written a fine poem on that scene. It was an epic'.[33] In 'Summer in England, 1914', Alice compared this last idyllic summer with the horrors of war. While 'the hay was prosperous; and the wheat' and 'moon after moon was heavenly sweet', 'armies died convulsed'. The wheat standing on the English summer plains contrasts with the 'thousand shattered men/ One wet corruption heaped the plain/ After a league-long throb of pain'. One of the poem's most shocking images is of 'men shot through the eyes'. The poem attempts consolation with the soldiers dying upon the 'kiss of Christ', but it fails to mitigate the human suffering which the 'unpardonable race' has inflicted upon itself.[34] Similarly, in Elizabeth's letters the casualties of war continued to haunt: 'More & more of soldiers I knew are falling!'[35]

In the midst of this total war, Elizabeth opened her private show at the Leicester Galleries in the summer of 1915, which commemorated the centenary of Waterloo. The cheque from the exhibition was donated to the Officers' Families Fund. Elizabeth studiously avoided the horrors of war. Although this was consistent with her career from the 1870s, her reluctance to comprehend or anticipate that the current war would need an entirely new representation accounts for the diminishment of her achievement in war art in twentieth-century thinking about her

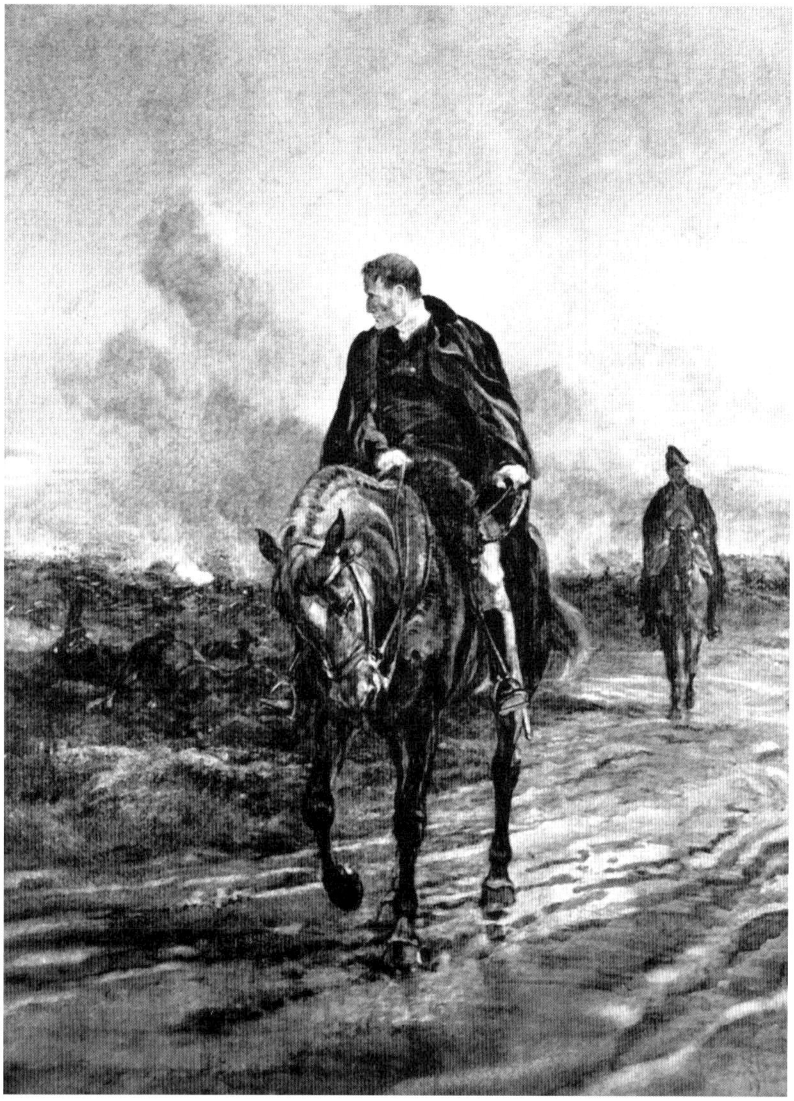

52 *The Waterloo Centenary – The End – Wellington, Illustrated London News,* 12 June 1915.

work. However, such thinking is retrospective and contemporary conceptions of the war have been shaped by the modernist climate of the post-war period. In terms of artistic production, no seismic shift occurred in the early stages of the war. As George Robb points out, the most 'popular and widely circulated war art depicted soldiers engaged in heroic acts of bravery'.[36] The public still favoured paintings and images that told stories and, as James Fox, argues 'popular illustrators ... produced vivid and diverting images of soldiers going over the top at night, cavalry charges, aerial dogfights' and other scenes which were not really 'representative of front-line realities'. Indeed, Fox observes the desire for the theatrical and the melodramatic and 'there is evidence that those involved in war actually preferred melodramatic representations of combat to realistic ones'.[37] Furthermore Fox argues that the cavalry charge remained a popular representation although such charges were rare in this war.[38] It was Elizabeth's charges of decades earlier which artists such as Caton Woodville and the Italian artist Fortunio Matania (born in the same year that Elizabeth exhibited *Scotland for Ever!*) drew upon although her influence was unacknowledged.

Elizabeth confirms how she eschewed the visceral nature of this war. While she understood the change of modern warfare and had two sons at the front who provided accounts of their experiences, she resisted an artistic change in direction. In the midst of her exhibition, 'Pardy', her 'best of sons' was in the 'thick of the fighting near Ypres' and now that her art work was done she felt, she told Alice, a sense of 'loneliness'.[39] Patrick was in the 'hideous pandemonium of the Trenches'.[40] On 10 July, she noted to Alice: 'What [Patrick's] sensitive nerves must be suffering'. Patrick also conveyed the relentlessness and immediacy of death:

> When the other day one of his subalterns came running in to say one of his (Patrick's) friends, & to whom he had just been talking & joking, had been destroyed by a shell, he found him unrecognizable, but, he adds, 'God will recognize him, now he is out of this Purgatory.' What can a man do more to atone for the Past than give up his life? What is so terrible in this war is that the fighting is <u>continuous</u>. In all others you had a good big battle, or now & then a smaller fight, but with intervals between, when not a shot was heard.[41]

Her advice to Alice on how to deal with the writer Shane Leslie who had been invalided out of the Ambulance Corps is significant in terms of the way in which she dealt with the war as a mother. Leslie was from a large Anglo-Irish landowning family in County Monaghan, and a relation of Winston Churchill. He had converted to Catholicism at Cambridge and supported Irish Home Rule. He had come to the Meynells for recuperation. Elizabeth wrote:

> How deeply I <u>sympathize</u> with Shane Leslie! Don't let him talk of what he has been thro'. I can't think of anything better for him than life in your cheery midst, & in such a peaceful place. Your younglings will be the very best companions for him. Tell him, from me, to keep his mind in the <u>Present</u>, as I do, which makes one <u>go on</u>; but this can only be done with the aid of work – congenial work, & his writing is so beautiful.[42]

A friend of a Bansha acquaintance, she told Alice on 26 August, had lost all four sons, 'splendid young fellows highly educated & brought up with the utmost care – healthy, successful young fellows: the mother is going blind from crying'. Alice's son-in-law, Percy, who had been married to Madeleine in 1907, was deployed and later lost his life. 'You will be proud', Elizabeth told Alice when he joined up, 'to have a soldier in the family on active service'.[43] In Italy, Fanny's grandson Edmondo was also in the trenches: 'I hear from Fanny of Edmondo's plucky deed with a bomb that fell in his trench. I understand he chucked it out, & that it burst just as he chucked, &

that, had his spectacles not acted as buffers, he might have been blinded by the explosion'.[44]

The Leicester Gallery exhibition offered some respite from the immediacy of the current war. The 'Ladies Page' of the *Illustrated London News* describes the work in the exhibition as 'remarkable for its spirit and sense of movement'. Interestingly, the article opens with the news that women in Denmark had been given the vote on the same terms with men, and decries the limited opportunities open to women in Britain to undertake war work, despite their capabilities.[45] Elizabeth and Alice supported women's suffrage, although, as Alice pointed out to Wilfrid, after a meeting at which she was a prominent guest, she was '*not* militant'.[46]

The *Illustrated London News* also featured some of Elizabeth's paintings – *The Fugitive* shows Napoleon fleeing the battle on horseback, while *The End – Wellington* features the victor, bareheaded and sombre, surveying the carnage of the battlefield. His horse's bowed head reflects the rider's mood (Figure 52). In the caption accompanying the painting, Elizabeth quotes Wellington's words and William Siborne's history of the war: '"There is nothing sadder than a victory, except a defeat. – WELLINGTON." "The Duke … then continued to ride leisurely towards (the village of) Waterloo … his staff and even orderlies almost all killed or wounded. His only attendant a foreigner attached to his suite." – SIBORNE'.[47] The exhibition also featured *Scotland for Ever!* which was on loan from Leeds. This painting was one of Elizabeth's most famous paintings at this period. Indeed, a Christmas postcard found on the body of a German prisoner is a reworking of it. Here the charging Scots Greys are replaced by Prussian cavalry.[48] The postcard is a propaganda piece to predict the onward rush of the Germans in the New Year. The irony, of course, is that although the original charge was a success the Scots Greys were annihilated on their return. This is a reminder that it is important not to take Elizabeth's art at face value – what might seem a celebration of battle is also a reflection on the human cost of engagement. At the same time, *The Observer*, although acknowledging the exhibition as 'praiseworthy', and observing her 'accomplished and painstaking draughtsmanship, her fine sense of movement in man and horse, and her knowledge of the military accoutrements of the British and French troops in Napoleonic days', opines that her 'art belong[ed] to the past and not to the present hour'. Her work, it suggests, fails to 'arouse our emotions' because she lacked the 'power of complete visualization which Impressionism has taught us to expect from an artist who aims at realistic representation and not at decorative abstraction'.[49]

Elizabeth understood that her Waterloo paintings were redundant in the current climate. She watched a division preparing for the war on 2 October 1914 in Lyndhurst, as General Capper trained men on the use of the sword, which had been rendered obsolete by the experience of combat in the Boer War.[50] As she viewed the men learning to use a 'new arm on the eve of battle' she was 'stirred with the pathos of this sight'. '[M]ounted and drawn up on a long, two-deep line on that brown

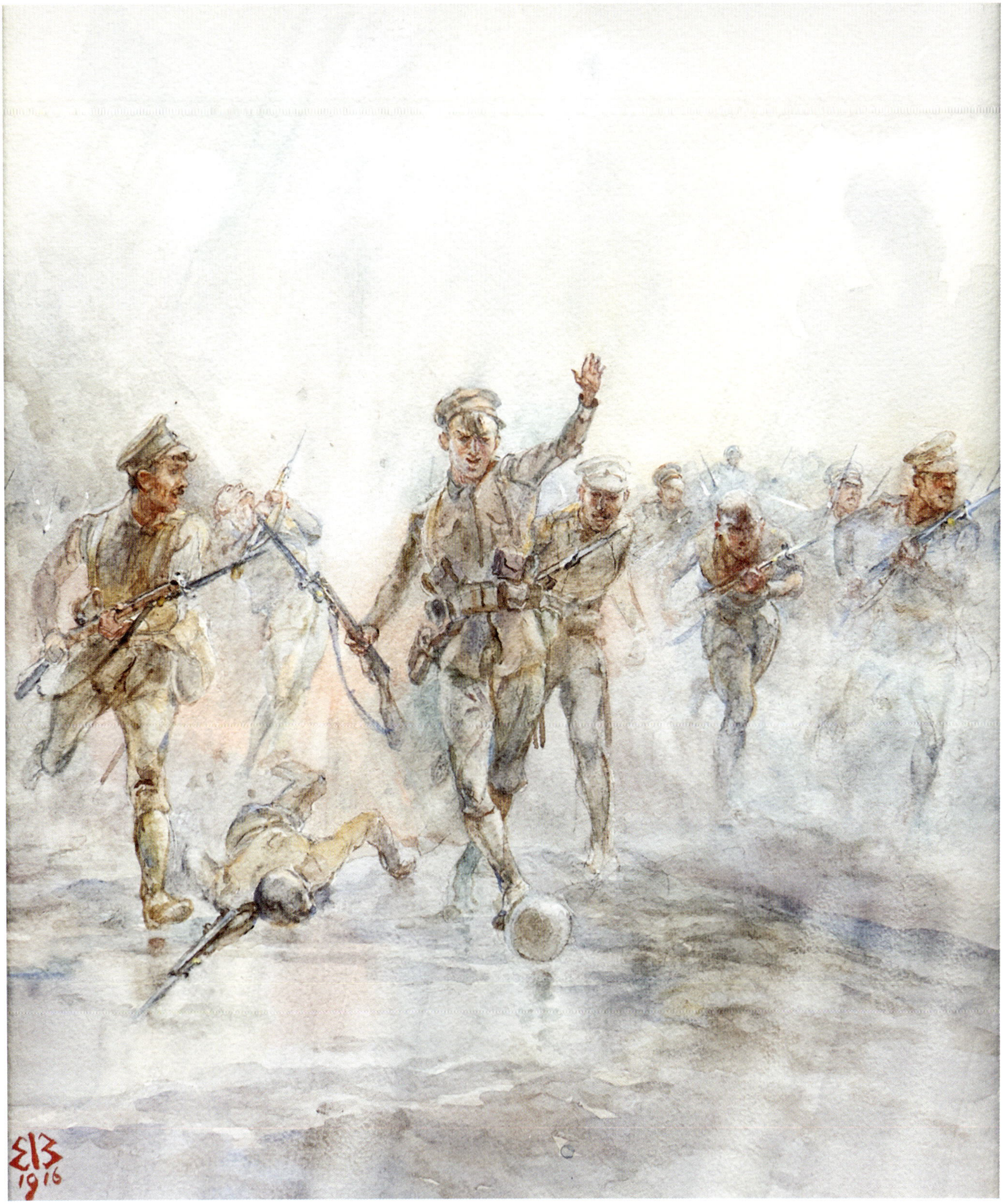

53 *The London Irish at Loos*, 1916.
Watercolour, 30.5 × 25.5cm. London Irish Rifles.

heath, with a heavy bank of dark clouds like mine in "*Scotland for Ever!*" behind their heads', the scene made 'a fine subject'. But she remarks:

> Who will look at my 'Waterloos' now? I have but one more of that series to do. Then I shall stop and turn all my attention and energy to this stupendous war.[51]

Turning her attention to the current conflict, Elizabeth prepared for her next exhibition. She started working on her most well-known painting of the war, *The London Irish at Loos* – a watercolour (plate 53). This, and other war scenes, were undertaken for her 'khaki' exhibition at the Leicester Galleries in May 1917. On 25 May, Butler's private view of her one-man show opened at the Leicester Galleries. The entire proceeds were donated to the Officers' Families Fund. The choice of the famous footballers of Loos testifies to her avoidance of representing carnage. The incident in the painting took place on 25 September 1915, when the British army 'launched its biggest offensive at Loos in northern France'.[52] Football had a strong tradition amongst the London Irish, and many soldiers had footballs hidden in their packs. Although the men had been ordered to deflate their balls, as zero hour advanced the football captain, Rifleman Edwards, re-inflated his ball. He released the ball and it was dribbled and kicked towards enemy lines. The London Irish achieved their goal of the German trenches but spent the next four days consolidating their position and resisting counter-attack.[53] The event was iconic and the regiment became known as 'The Footballers of Loos'. Although the battle was a failure with over 60,000 casualties, the event appealed to Elizabeth and cohered with her dedication to stories and episodes of war which reveal and highlight the individual soldier's experience. Here she celebrates the ordinary soldier. Rifleman Edwards, his right arm aloft and his left hand carrying his gun, dribbles the ball forwards into an empty space, accompanied in the charge by other soldiers. One has just fallen, his body hitting the ground with arm and leg splayed as his bayonetted gun points towards the enemy lines. In the actual charge, the men were wearing gas masks, but Elizabeth removes them, undoubtedly to portray the men's individuality and experience of the event, or, as Iain Adams argues, to 'display their brave and grim goal-scoring determination'.[54] Adams notes that the 'whole picture is lit from above, and light reflects off men's hats, giving an angelic quality, hinting of sacrifice for a righteous cause'.[55] The painting is also reminiscent of *Scotland for Ever!* – the brave charge is successful, but the aftermath unleashes the horror of war. Like the Scottish painting, the viewer is placed in the position of the enemy, facing the onslaught. Elizabeth wrote to Wilfrid about her preparations for it:

> Please to note that the footballer is dribbling the ball (done with the inside of the foot).
>
> I suppose he did not kick it high in the air as in that case he might have lost it in such a scrimmage where men were not running after his ball but after the Bosches! 'Dribble' it he did, according to the reports.[56]

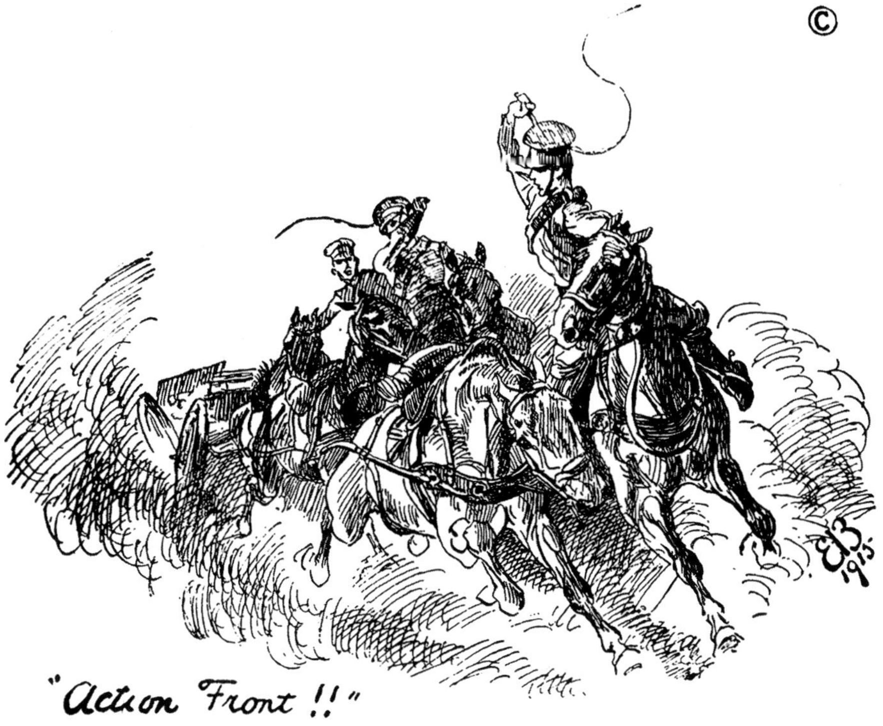

54 *Action Front!* (notepaper for the Red Cross).

Proceeds from Elizabeth's 'Glimpses of the Great War' exhibition were given to the Lord Roberts Memorial Fund Workshops. The Red Cross commissioned her to produce an image for stationery. She produced an artillery gun team, *Action Front!* (Figure 54). John Singer Sargent also designed notepaper. The Anglo-American Sargent, a celebrity portrait painter, who expressed little interest in the war in its earlier phases, was made an official war artist, unlike Elizabeth, whose career had been shaped by war. Sargent was in his early 60s and Elizabeth was 67. His co-option as official war artist was political – America entered the war in 1917. Sargent did produce one of the most iconic paintings of the war, featuring soldiers who had been blinded by mustard gas. *Gassed* was undertaken after a visit to the frontlines at Arras.[57] The exclusion of Elizabeth can be explained by a social climate that still prevented women's full participation in the world.

Elizabeth also exhibited a series of watercolour portraits of soldiers who had been awarded the Victoria Cross. One is of Drummer Walter Ritchie, 2nd Battalion Scottish Highlanders, who won the award for bravery on the first day of the battle of the Somme (Figure 55). Another is supposed to represent an Irish soldier, Lance-Corporal Michael O'Leary, from the 1st Battalion of the Irish Guards, who was awarded the VC for storming two enemy positions near Ypres. O'Leary was promoted to sergeant and was celebrated in England and in Ireland in the summer of 1915. O'Leary's face was used in the recruitment drive of 1915, and it was hoped that this use of the Cork soldier would generate recruitment from Ireland, in particular. The O'Leary of Elizabeth's portrait, however, bears little resemblance to the original; rather the figure is a replica of the central recruit in *'Listed for the Connaught Rangers.*

Her oil painting, *The Dorset Yeomanry at Agagia, 26 Feb. 1916,* was commissioned by the Dorset Yeomanry. The battle occurred in the Libyan desert after a squadron of 180 yeomanry routed the Senussi tribe who had been backed by Turkish forces. The tribe were preparing to attack Egypt. Their achievement was a rare instance of a successful cavalry charge in the First World War and was undertaken by Territorial soldiers, recruited from Dorsetshire.[58] This is an action painting as the soldiers and officers charge a Turkish machine gun and the tribesmen. Some of the Senussi have fallen beneath the charging horses, while the central British officer, Lieutenant-Colonel Souter, charges a group of Senussis, his brown horse collapsing beneath him. Souter was unhurt though and landed to the ground in front of the Senussi chief, Ja'afer Pacha, who surrendered to him. Although Elizabeth chose an actual moment in the action, she was asked to include all the officers in the scene, breaking with historical accuracy. The painting was exhibited at the Academy in 1917 and then toured Dorset. Six thousand people saw it, paying 8*d.* each for the privilege. Elizabeth's work, it would seem, remained popular with her public. She discussed her preparations for the painting with Alice, writing to her on the 24 June 1916, 'I had the colonel of the Dorset yeomanry here today to see my sketch for the proposed picture. He seemed much pleased & gave me his own attitude & that of his horse at the moment I have chosen – just as the poor gee falls shot'.[59] For the Senussis Elizabeth could draw on her sketches from Egypt.

55 *A V.C. of the Seaforth,* 1916. Watercolour on paper, 58 × 43.5cm. Russel-Cotes Art Gallery and Museum, Bournemouth, UK. Bridgeman Art Library.

Transporting a picture from Ireland to Britain for the 1917 Academy was dangerous – German gunboats were operating in the Irish Sea. Its weight was also an issue as she related to Wilfrid: 'I think I can manage to keep its weight down to just below 100lbs. in which case I do not see how I could be hindered in bringing it through, as personal luggage. But do you think its being in a packing case however disguised would be an obstacle?'[60] On 30 April, she wrote to Alice from the Ladies Athenaeum Club describing her experience of the Academy. Although 'pleased' with the placing of her painting, the 'surrounding works, very bad some of them, & very coarse others, tend to overpower the more delicate works of smaller scale'. She praised Lucy Kemp-Welch's *Forward the Guns!*: 'Miss Kemp Welch has a very powerful artillery team. Strange, that the two women, she & self, have sent the only war pictures fit to be seen. The men's efforts are feeble & silly beyond belief'.[61]

Meanwhile her sons were in constant danger. She wrote to Alice on 20 April 1916: 'I hope [Dick] will continue to stand the awful din of those guns & rifles. One may say he has gone from the cloister to the cannon. No preparation such as a soldier has had at manoeuvres & sham fights [prepares him] for the violence of real fighting, no drill, no practice with horses for his long & difficult rides amongst the plunging guns & ambulance wagons'. Dick was 'full of admiration for the rank & file' among whom he moved 'so intimately' – this was unsurprising, given the focus of his

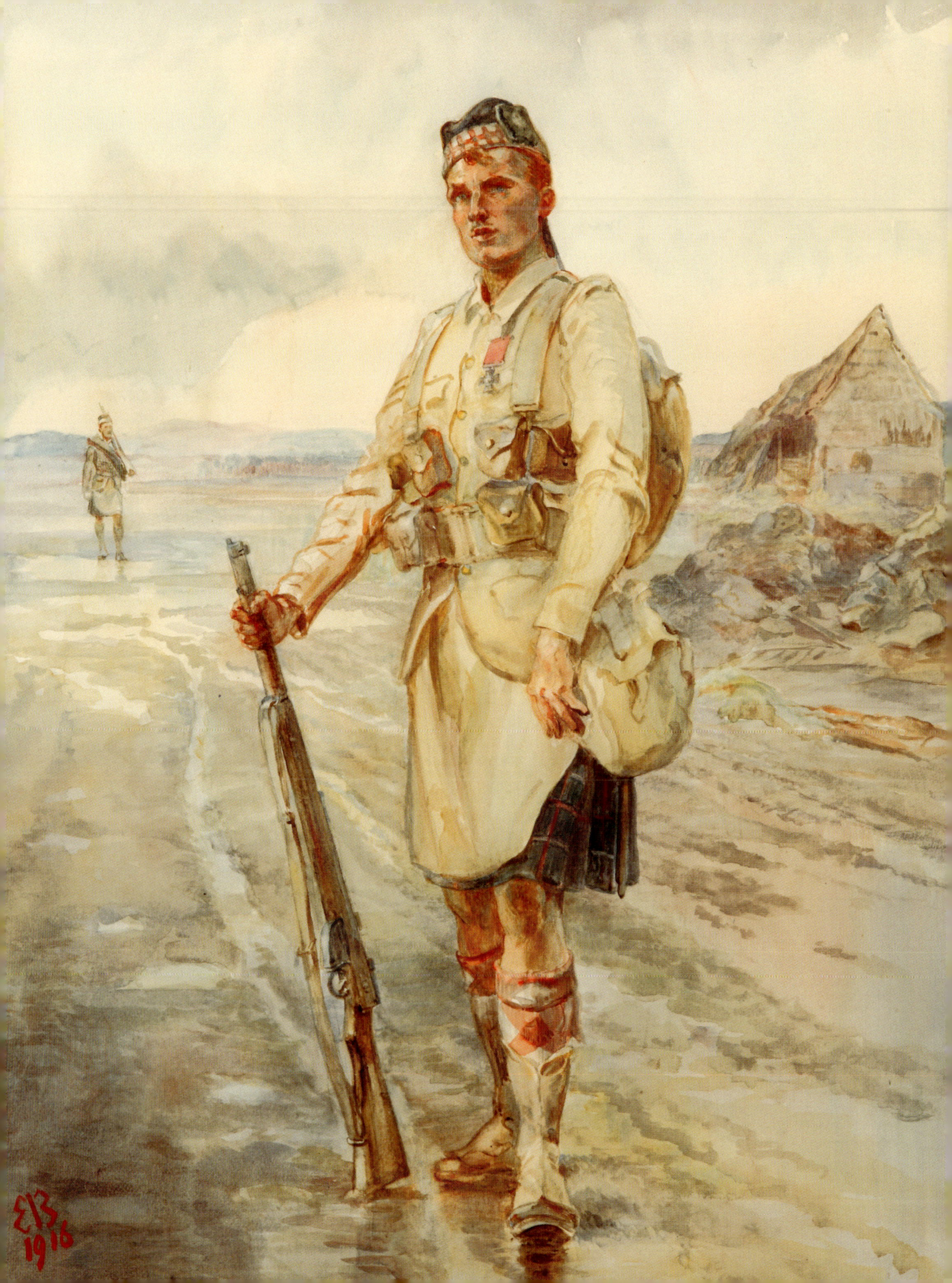
1916

mother's art since 1874 centred on the ordinary soldier. At this point, however, he was in 'greater danger than his soldier brother!'[62] On 24 June 1916, she wrote: 'Dick's leave is "off." They are marching towards the guns, & he says great things are impending'.[63] A letter on 21 November recorded that Dick was 'living up to his knees in mud' while Patrick, who had been promoted to Major, was now being 'buffeted by Balkan blizzards'. She commented on Everard's (Alice's son) work with the wounded: 'What a noble work his will be for those who are not bidden to kill', concluding, 'Poor humanity is getting well drubbed, eh'.[64]

Alice's son, Francis, a conscientious objector, was a 'great puzzle' to Elizabeth. 'How is it', she asked Alice on 7 February 1917, 'that he can't be put to patriotic work quite apart from killing his fellow creatures, like so many C.O.s? – la Patrie en danger! not an able-bodied man can escape now'.[65] Francis's stance also disturbed Alice. Francis had declared himself a conscientious objector in August 1916, but refused a non-combatant role which resulted in his arrest in January 1917. Alice explained her distress in a letter to her son Sebastian: '[Wilfrid] is hurt by Francis involving his family in his conscientiousness. Your father had asked him not to do so. A paragraph is in all the papers today naming his case as that of my son, and I think I shall have to write to *The Times* a line, disclaiming'. After Francis's imprisonment, she became more incensed by his stance: 'a man undergoes [prison] because he is intensely convinced that we ought to have allowed Belgium to be sacked, murdered, tortured and ruined. There is nothing more idiotic than a conscience *can* be'.[66]

Understandably, Elizabeth feared for Dick's safety, in particular, as he was not a trained soldier. Before his deployment with the Cheshire Regiment of the 9th Expeditionary Force to the frontlines as a chaplain, she observed to him that joining the army was 'an act most approved by heaven'. Nonetheless, she urged: 'Dear Dick won't you let the authorities, lay or clerical, know that you are not of the robust type of priest – not the trench type, but far more useful in a base hospital where the wounded are brought in'. She described the war as a 'monstrosity' citing the 'horror of Verdun!'[67] Despite her anxieties as a mother, Dick's experience supplied her with what she would later describe to Alice as 'word pictures' of the war.[68] On 7 July 1916, Dick wrote a detailed account of his experiences of the Somme. Writing from the dressing station in a chateau in the wood near Bécourt, he admitted:

> The horror of that place, in which I have since spent so many hours will live in my mind till my last day. The heat was overpowering, & I could hardly support the awful stench of blood & perspiration … these wounds are an outrage against humanity & I will not offend our feelings by describing what I have witnessed. Was man made after God's image to be torn by hideous machinery.[69]

A pronounced religious vein suffuses family letters during the war. On 12 March 1916, Elizabeth wrote to Dick quoting Alice on his role in the war: '"One must envy the priest more than any other man; whoever may be wrong, he is right. He has the one perfectly good part in the whole war".'[70] Elizabeth's Catholic identity emerges in her letters and war art of this period. She understood the brutality of the conflict, but avoided its overt representation. One of her watercolours from the 1917 exhibition is significant from the perspective of faith. In *Eyes Right!* war-weary soldiers pass a statue of the crucified Christ on their return from action. Roadside crucifixes and calvaries populated the French and Belgian countryside and were frequently represented in the literature and art of the early war years. *Eyes Right!* evokes the 'after the battle' reactions of the soldiers in *Inkerman*. The war-weary men pass the image of the suffering Christ which looms over them on the viewer's left of the painting. Some of the formation have marched beyond the crucifix. Two soldiers at the front are looking out beyond the viewer, one has his arm in a sling and the other shoulders his rifle. Slightly separated from the group, like one of the soldiers in *Inkerman*, a soldier marches with a rifle on his shoulder and in the distance behind him are shady ruins of a building. Of the figures grouped behind, one passes the monument, a pipe in his hand, and his head cast downwards. His comrade, adjacent to him, is bloodied and grey-faced and looks directly at Christ. Behind them, another soldier, part of his head bandaged, tilts his one eye towards Jesus on the cross. A Red Cross ambulance follows the soldiers. Like Butler's earlier war paintings, the soldiers are captured in moments of contemplation, withdrawal, or engagement with their immediate surroundings. The market value of her work had fallen sharply. She sold the copyright of the painting to George Pulman & Sons for the 'ridiculous sum of £30' (equivalent to £1,769 today).[71] Art prices, in general, had plummeted during the war.

Elizabeth's immersion in her faith was her way of coping with two sons at war. On 23 June 1916, Dick sent her a postcard of the shelled basilica in Albert in northern France. On the tower, a statue of the Virgin and Child had fallen into a horizontal position. The famous 'Golden Virgin' remained in this position for three years. Perched on the top of the tower, it shows the Virgin and child leaning over looking at the chaos below them. Paul Fussell notes that the horizontal Virgin was either interpreted as the 'Virgin throwing the Child down into the battle, offering him as a sacrifice which might end the slaughter' or as an 'act of mercy: she was reaching out to save her child, who – like a soldier – was about to fall'.[72]

Dick, in his role as priest, was in a unique position to articulate the suffering of the war. At the start of the battle of Passchendaele on 28 July 1917, he wrote to his mother:

> Sometimes a priest finds his work very hard out here. Last night I walked up & down for nearly two hours after dinner with a very nice young officer in a certain guards battalion, trying to argue for Christianity & the Catholic Church. He longs to become a Catholic from sheer need of religion, but has no faith! What can one do?[73]

On 15 October 1917, he told her what had happened to his friend:

> Our ordeal in the battle was a trying one. I lost my dear young friend whom I told you had expressed his so eager desire to be a Catholic if only he could have believed in Christ. To make matters worse he had just written to propose two days before he fell. I have now seen such horrors & such mind staggering things that I no longer care to write or think about the war.[74]

Between those two letters he described how a fellow priest had been hit by a shell: '[I was] working with him amid the shattered remnants of a village, helping the dying in their last journey ... It has given me more of a shock than anything I have yet experienced ... I have before me another night amidst these ghastly scenes, & the groans of the dying'.[75] For Dick, faith provided the only consolation, but he remained traumatized by what he had seen and experienced years after his service on the Continent:

> It is wonderful how our men know their religion & what is expected of them. The Latin words of the ritual spoken over them when dying seem to awake memories. The fact that the Catholic priest has always a definite thing to do is an immense help, and non-Catholic medical officers appreciate it.[76]

Martin had been the first of Elizabeth's sons to be deployed to France, but with the near-extinction of his regiment, the Irish Guards, in the opening phases of the war, he was redeployed to duties in Ireland. Dick expressed his frustration to his mother after she informed him that Martin was suffering with his 'nerves': 'What do you mean by saying that Martin's nervous system is bad? If the poor fellow could only have got for himself some job, he would have had no time for nerves. I wish he was not a source of anxiety to you. Fancy a young & strong man at a time like this having "nerves" in surroundings such as his ... I am writing this about three thousand yards from the line'.[77] On 6 December 1917, Dick wrote to Elizabeth from a position on the line near Gouvey-En-Artois, behind Arras: 'The officers live in a fine old Chateau, where we make ourselves comfortable & try to forget. That is one of the hardest things about this life. You must carry on, & I think not of the new graves lying out there beneath that ghastly ridge'.[78] Just before Christmas, Dick informed Eileen that he was joining the Tank Corps as a senior chaplain: 'It will be a great wrench to leave the 3rd Guards Brigade in which I have worked so long, but coming as it does now, when death has taken so many friends, it really does not much matter. It is promotion to a higher rank & a wider field of work, but who cares for promotion, & as for further work, I really feel as if I could do with a month's rest'.[79]

While her sons were absorbed in the immediacy of the life and death of war, Ireland was experiencing an event that would dramatically change the course of its relationship to Britain – the Easter 1916 Rising. After a protracted constitutional struggle, Home Rule for Ireland had been passed by the House of Commons in 1912. It was vetoed by the Lords but their veto could only extend to two years. Had the war not intervened, Ireland was facing the prospect of Home Rule in 1914. It was not, however, that simple. Protestant unionists, mostly in the North, started mobilizing to resist, by arms if necessary, the prospect of self-government for the island. Irish nationalists mobilized their own volunteer group and, on the eve of European war, the prospect of civil war in Ireland loomed. Home Rule was suspended for the duration of the war. John Redmond, the leader of the Irish Parliamentary Party, put his support behind the European war. But the nationalists were split. Irish separatists, such as the Irish Republican Botherhood, started to mobilize. Sir Roger Casement, knighted for his humanitarian work in the Belgian Congo, when, as British Consul, he exposed the abuse perpetrated on the Congolese under the imperial administration of King Leopold of Belgium, attempted to land arms from Germany to support the Rising. Casement was arrested after the German gunboat in which he had been travelling was captured off the Irish coast. However, the Easter Rising of 1916 went ahead, when a group of volunteers, led by a school teacher, Padraig Pearse, occupied key locations in Dublin and proclaimed an Irish Republic outside the General Post Office. They held out for four days between 24 and 29 April. Sixteen of the Rising's leaders, including Pearse, were executed and Casement was hanged for high treason. The Rising's legacy mobilized public opinion in Ireland in favour of the executed leaders and their political ideals.

In the immediate aftermath of the Rising, Dick wrote to Elizabeth for information:

> What has been happening in Dublin? Do those poor idiots imagine that they are going to effect anything definite or useful by seizing the post office & killing a few English soldiers, instead of fighting at their sides? It looks as if Germany was tired of keeping Sir R. Casement & forced him to try & redeem his insane promises. I think the criminal lunatic asylum is the place for him. As to the Sinn Feinners, they could do with a taste of German methods to bring them to their senses.[80]

Politically, Butler sympathies lay with constitutional nationalism. John Redmond had urged Irish men to join the war effort in the belief that it would consolidate nationalist claims for self-government. Dick had little sympathy for what would become the dominant political force in Ireland in the years after the war. His views on Casement, a British Consul and the Knight of the Empire, turned separatist nationalist, were, however, consistent with much mainstream opinion. Conan Doyle, for instance, appealed for clemency for Casement, arguing that he was insane. What Doyle and Dick could not understand was that Casement's political U-turn could be read as a response to his experiences of empire in Africa. In any case, the execution of Casement and the other leaders changed the political mood in Ireland. Conan Doyle had warned the British government about the dangers of making political martyrs.[81] He was right. For those Irish soldiers who returned from the war, the south of Ireland had changed irrevocably. Elizabeth would experience the ramifications of that change. By spring 1918, Dick was still unhappy about the situation in Ireland, asking if the country had 'to be given over to complete anarchy? Why can't they be given their Home Rule to make what use they like of it, provided they fight the common foe'.[82] The plea signifies Dick's alienation from the country. He urged his mother to go to Dublin: 'From all accounts there is complete lawlessness in Clare! And to think that this should be going on at the time when England is undergoing the greatest strain of the war'. Not all his clerical comrades shared his view: 'I met the other day an Irish Chaplain out here, who seemed to consider it quite the right attitude for his fellow country-men to take! The cowardly aspect of it never seemed to strike him'.[83] Dick, partly raised in Ireland, and the son of an Irish nationalist, did not seem to regard himself in any way as Irish. On the 16 December 1918, Dick wrote to Eileen from Italy, wishing he was still with the Irish Guards during the 'final trial'. He observed: 'Just four years ago I said midnight Mass in your chapel, with Pat home wounded from Flanders – time seems to have stood still since those early, anxious days'.[84] For Dick, the war seemed to be a period out of time. But time had not stood still and the political, social and cultural ground had shifted.

In March 1918 Elizabeth wrote to Alice about Everard's war work: 'The seeing behind the scenes which poor Evvy is forced to go thro' is horribly disenchanting & almost slackens my arm for the Khaki subjects. Still, I will go on, on the higher level. What he must suffer!'[85] In her autobiography, Elizabeth observes: 'Men who have gone through the horrors of war say little about them, but I have learnt many strange things from rare remarks here and there'.[86] On 11 November Elizabeth was in London for Armistice Day: 'I saw some sad faces, but, of course, such as these kept mostly away'. Elizabeth was amongst the 'smilers' because both her sons 'who faced death to the very end … had survived'. She returned to Ireland on a boat with no 'protecting airship serpentining above us'. Her final words in her autobiography that they 'could breathe freely now' were premature.[87] One month later, Sinn Féin, the Irish nationalist party, won the general election in Ireland, taking a majority of seats everywhere in the country outside Ulster. Sinn Féin declared an Irish Republic and the first Parliament, the Dáil, met in Dublin in 1919. The result was war with Britain.

Gormanston

In May 1919, Elizabeth had another exhibition at the Leicester Galleries with the proceeds going to soldiers blinded in the war. Here her most significant painting was a watercolour of the 'memorable charge of the Warwick and Worcester yeomany at

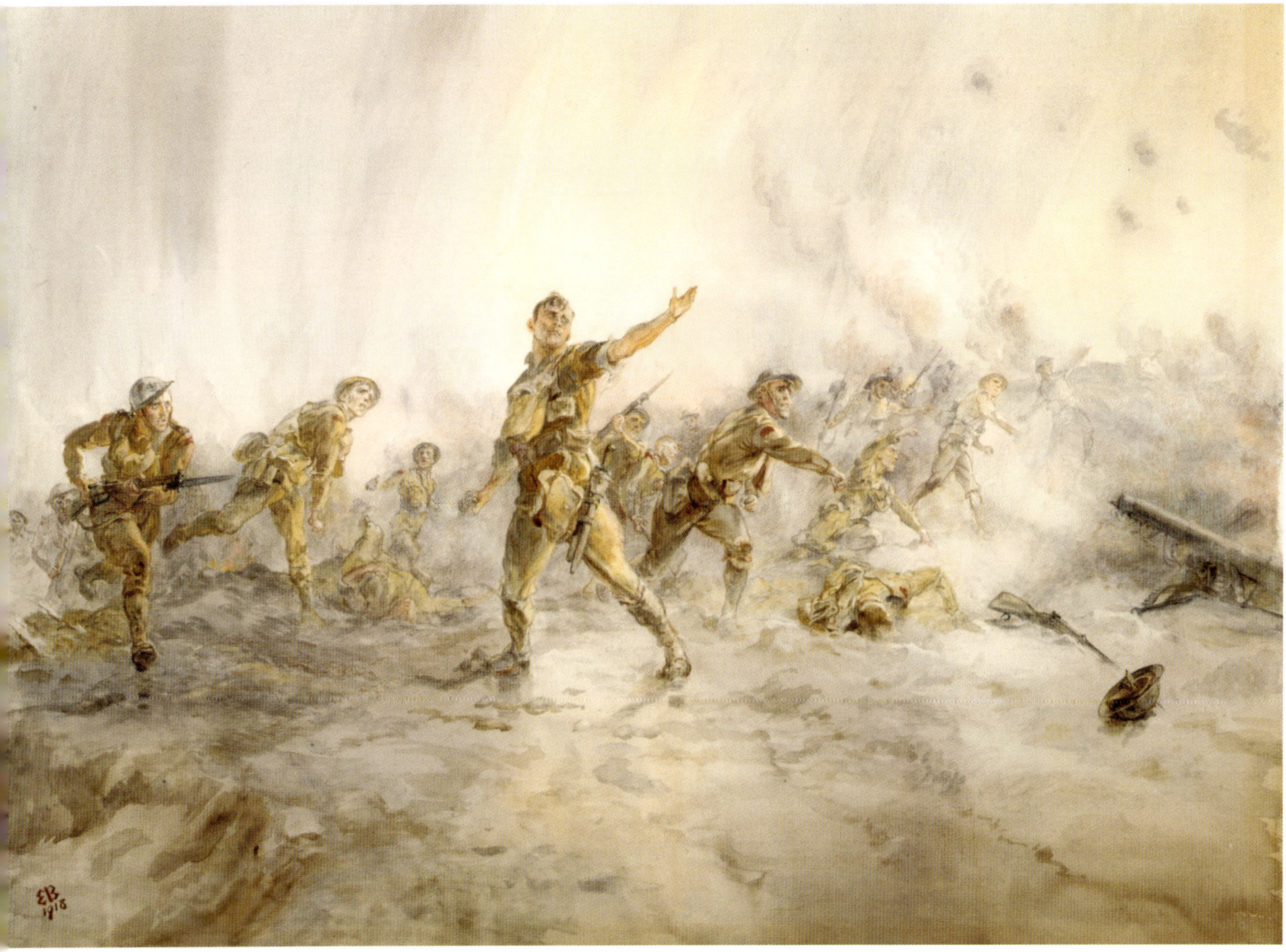

56 *Cede Nullis, the Bombers of the 8th Canadian Infantry on Vimy Ridge, 9th April 1917*, 1918. Watercolour, 80.6 × 60.3cm. Library and Archives Canada.

Huj, near Jerusalem'. She notes: '[this] charge outshone the old Balaclava one we love to remember, and which differed from the Crimean exploit in that we not only captured all the enemy guns, but *held* them'. She recalls how she had all the 'ground plans, description of the weather on that day, position of the sun etc' from an 'eye-witness', Colonel Richard Preston. She called it *Jerusalem Delivered* 'for that charge opened the gates of the Holy City'.[88] Another painting was *Cede Nullis, the Bombers of the 8th Canadian Infantry on Vimy Ridge, 9th April 1917* (Figure 56). This is a dramatic action painting as soldiers charge forward towards an unseen enemy. The central figure has his left arm outstretched and his right hand holds a grenade. Others have just thrown their grenades into the enemy lines as they advance through the dead bodies. A discarded helmet, a trademark of Elizabeth's war paintings since the 1870s, occupies a position on the ground closest to the enemy. Vimy Ridge, fought in April 1917, marked both the bravery and sacrifice of these Canadian soldiers. Vimy became 'a defining moment for Canada, when the country emerged from under the shadow of Britain and felt capable of greatness'. It also became a 'symbol for the sacrifice of the young Dominion'.[89]

She wrote to Wilfrid, who had been instrumental in helping her with the arrangements, about her exhibition in February 1919:

> I am glad to say that the Dorchester County Council are lending me the Charge of the Dorset Yeoman for my show. It will greatly add to the interest thereof, & it also gives me the large, inner room at the Leicester which I so much prefer to the other, by helping to increase the exhibition & well cover the wall space. I am so glad the world will see the picture which was (I had feared for ever) hidden away in the Shire Hall. The Canadian Premier, Sir Robert Borden, has asked the Canadian authorities in London to let it be known to the Canadians that my drawing of their 5th Infantry Regt. storming Vimy Ridge is to be one of the subjects at my show.[90]

Her reflections on war in Ireland are interspersed with her ongoing commitment to her art. She came to London for the Royal Academy in the spring of 1920. She wrote to Wilfrid on 25 April: 'it is a relief to be in London where one is no longer fearing the collapse of a policeman, shot in broad daylight, in the chest. I was in Dublin when the last poor fellow fell, a few streets from where I was shopping'. Ireland was in the midst of a War of Independence. In London, she could turn her attention to the Academy: 'Tomorrow is Varnishing Day at the Academy where I hope to find my picture well placed. It is a much fuller rendering of John Ayscough's fine subject of the Horse Guards' retreat from Mons, a water colour of which you may remember I had at the Leicester Galleries last Spring. You & Viola may be going to the Private View & will see it'.[91] *The Retreat from Mons* is a sombre subject. Like *Inkerman* it features soldiers returning from battle, but unlike Inkerman, Mons was a defeat. She was delighted that the painting was bought for the city of Durban, Natal, as she relished having another of her works outside Britain (*Quatre Bras* was in Melbourne). In early spring, prior to the Academy, she travelled to Italy to see Fanny. On 6 February 1921, she wrote to Alice from Bordighera:

> Three days ago I saw from my window one of the most memorable dawns of my long experiences in travel. In the rich, mysterious sky, slowly brightening, hung the globe of the waning moon with its crescent facing the East, brilliantly gold, & the sea lay calm below, in a dark, soft of purple mystery, a few high clouds beginning to flush into rose colour. The whole globe of the moon looked like a peal in that limpid atmosphere. The whole scheme of colour was exceedingly rich. When later I got up I danced with joy as I dressed. The Cote d'Azur lay below my window in all its blue radiance. To think that from the sadness & mud of poor Ireland, where I was beginning to doubt whether life was worth living, after all, I should feel so soon the joie de vivre! The Riviera is very built up and filled with nouveaux riches and the prices are piled on and the customs are horrible.[92]

Fanny was far stronger than she had expected, but much changed in appearance. She was, after all, 87. But back in Bansha in May, she told Alice that 'Life here is made very gloomy by these daily murders. Such callous ones: & no prospect of their abatement'. She also told her that she was beginning her memoirs: 'Eileen & others are urging me, at long last I have taken up my autobiographical pen. I think I shall warm to it as I go on, & the material is there in plenty … I see the Academy is becoming modern! Have any of you seen it? … I am going along well with the watercolours but have no gallery to send them to. Rather sad'.[93] On 19 May 1921, she wrote to Wilfrid: 'Here we are in the midst of murders. The poor Green Isle is turning red! It is awful to hear shots & to know they cannot mean anything but the loss of someone's life'.[94] A month later, she wrote to Alice:

> You may well call this country unhappy! It could hardly be worse. But one does not like to say much in writing. Spies of both sides are everywhere! We are really in a reign of terror … I myself am none too well in all this nervous condition of things which has come close up to our very doors here … I am happy to know that the direct route to London from here, via Rosslare, will be opened again on thc 4th July, which makes it so much easier for me to run over to London. We are dreadfully cut off. Wires are cut, mails are seized, trains cease running – it is dismal. On oeuvre les lettres. Pas de politique![95]

In September, she wrote to tell Alice that the 'The Police (R.I.C.) came last night to warn us that this house was marked down for the next raid for arms. Such as we have are in the custody of the police even my rustiest old Brown Besses! The Sinn

Fein take everything. I shall just let them search the whole place'.[96] Despite the immediate problems in Ireland, her art remained a key concern. In early August 1921, she wrote to Manchester Art Gallery to enquire into the condition of *Balaclava*, which had been presented to the gallery by John Whitehead in 1898. 'I was aware', she wrote, 'of a certain amount of "wear and tear", at which I was not surprised & considering the great and prolonged ordeal it went through during the period of its exhibition when it first came out, in the Provinces and elsewhere'.[97] The curator, however, assured her that he had taken the picture out of its frame to examine it in detail and 'that although the varnish may possibly have slightly yellowed' there was 'absolutely no signs of any "wear and tear"'.[98]

Wilfrid and Alice were drafted in to help with the writing of the autobiography. She sought Wilfrid's advice on a publisher, telling him that 'money' was 'a consideration'. 'What do you say to the little pen and ink (initial letters), sketches, and tail pieces, out of my contemporary sketchbooks? for some chapters, if not for all? Italian, French, German, Egyptian, Irish &c &c quite small. I want the book to come out next Spring'.[99] Alice organized the material into chapters and advised Elizabeth on expanding some sections and shortening others. On 7 January, she admitted to Wilfrid that she feared that he and Alice were 'having a hard job of it!' but this did not prevent her from asking him or Everard to promote the fact that *The Retreat from Mons* had been bought for Durban: 'I shd be glad if some kind of mention might be made – perhaps in Evvy's "Sketch" – or some other publication? It might suggest to other colonies to follow suit & I particularly want the attention of the colonies'.[100] She was concerned about her legacy.

On 27 January 1922, she told Wilfrid that she was nearly finished with the revised batch of changes to her manuscript: 'As I go along I am more and more struck with the immense pains you and Alice have taken'.[101] On 9 April 1922, she told Wilfrid that Constable was 'delighted' with her 'pen & ink sketches which give that sparkle to the text'. She was to sign the agreement on the next day but in a postscript to the letter she noted how she has just received a letter from Alice: 'I am dismayed at what she says about the price down for the book. I shall postpone the signing. Unfortunately, I thought it better not to insist on a higher price, but did not do more than negatively accept, urging the value of the sketches'.[102] Alice was commissioned with reading the proofs, although Elizabeth promised that there would be little to do. Meanwhile, the post was in disarray: 'You cannot realize what a state of anarchy we are living in, & nothing is safe as a matter of course'.[103] On 13 August 1922 she wrote to Alice from Bansha as concerns were growing about her sister's health: 'How I thought of you going through those always alarming heart-thumps & kicks! I have always been told that these recalcitrant demonstrations are not as bad as the opposite want of animation'. But Alice, who had been suffering with heart trouble for about ten years, was critically ill. The situation in Ireland meant that it was 'too dangerous to trust [the] proofs to the Post' but as Cork had fallen out of Republican hands, she felt that the 'bulk of the trouble' was over. She feared the book might not be popular: 'My only fear about the book is that people will miss the strong flavour (not always very nice) of the modern Autobiography & pungent personalities so much in vogue just now'.

Ireland was undergoing dramatic changes as the War of Independence gave way to civil war. The new Irish state had come together under the leadership of Michael Collins who, with Arthur Griffith, the founder of Sinn Féin, had negotiated the Anglo-Irish Treaty in December 1921. Not all elements of the Irish Republican Army were satisfied with the settlement and civil war broke out:

> We are all feeling very 'sick & sorry' in Ireland. There will soon be hardly any of the gentry left (the 'Quality' as they are called). Their castles & ancestral homes are nearly all in ashes now ... My finances seem to be in a parlous state. Such tenants as I have refuse to pay & I fear some property in Sackville St Dublin is in ashes, too![104]

Alice was sympathetic to her plight, telling her: 'I have received the galleys and pages. And tomorrow I begin to collate. Need I tell you with what pleasure I do this little thing for you? ... Your exile has been long and cruel indeed. Who could have foreseen such things in our time! I think of you constantly, and never without the wish that you were in England'.[105]

Coos, living on the Kingscote estate, Ciamaltha, in Tipperary, was waging her own war with the Republicans. 'Poor Coos', she told Alice, 'has been living in a Republican volcano up in those Limerick Mountains ... Col K has insisted on a holiday for her & her plan is to escort me to Rome'. The unstable situation in Ireland affected Elizabeth's mental health.

> I think one never realizes during dangers how much ones nerves are being shaken. But when there comes a period of comparative quiet one is aware of a change. The Republicans have taken everything portable of value (except furniture) out of Ciamaltha. I may hope, now, that 'Bansha Castle' may be spared. What do you think of the Irish Presidents' uncle being murdered in his sister's public house in Dublin, for money? This happened the other evening in a crowded shop. Of course, as usual, the crowd let the miscreant escape. Coos will take this letter to post in England. One fears the Censor. Do not allude in writing to this. I do think the country is being destroyed by its own children. The two sides are fighting each other with the same animosity as they fought the British with.[106]

By 4 October she felt 'quite hopeless about this poor country' but a few days later arrived in England and wrote to her sister after her house had been requisitioned by Free State soldiers:

I arrived yesterday a fugitive. My home is, I trust, adequately defended by the Regulars but there is no knowing what violence may not achieve, after the 15th inst. when the offer of amnesty to the Rebels expires to lay down their arms. Poor Ciamaltha is wrecked and looted & Coos, who was to have gone with me to Rome, is determined to go back, to be with Col. K. in their extremity. I shall do all I can to prevent her going. She is here. She has had verbal fights with the Republican ruffians up in that utterly undefended home of hers, & I trouble to think how in a moment, during one of their raids, a tragedy may happen in an instant if she 'fires up'. This is your dear birthday. May you spend it in peace. Patrick has gone to Bansha to see what had best be done there before the unfortunate country is made finally impossible after the 15th. I hope he and Martin may be spared so long as the Free Staters are there I have no fear & they are at least 50 strong at my place, & others are in the village & neighbouring towns. My excellent Noone is as brave as can be & insists on remaining in charge. 2 of the maids, poor things, remain, for the present.[107]

A few days later she wrote to Wilfrid to say that the situation had deteriorated and warned him not to tell Alice of her troubles.

On 28 October 1922, the *Daily Mail* reported that Colonel Patrick Butler had to dash to Bansha from his regiment, the Royal Welsh Fusiliers, in order to rescue his mother's paintings from Bansha Castle. The Free State army had come under attack by Republicans at Bansha Castle. 'The Free Staters beat off the attack, but fighting continued for several days, in the course of which one of the pictures – *Charge of the Egyptian Camel Corps* – in the studio just outside the castle was damaged by six bullets'. Patrick, however, was able to get the 'pictures out of their frames and, collecting the plate and heirlooms, set out for Dublin, where after one of the art galleries had refused to take them, Sir Nevil Macready, the British Commander-in-Chief, agreed to take charge of them', just two months before Macready and the final contingent of British troops left Ireland.[108] The report lists the other paintings that Patrick rescued included *To the Front*, which dated from the family's stay in Dinan in the late 1880s, as well as a Waterloo and a Crimean painting, 'two South African studies' and 'two Irish pictures', one of which, although unnamed by the article, was *Evicted*.[109] The episode marked the end of Elizabeth's time at Bansha.

By 14 November she was deeply concerned about Alice. As her sister's condition deteriorated, Elizabeth wrote to Alice's daughter, Olivia:

Your card has plunged me into such grief! But, who, seeing your beloved mother suffering so long, so long, could doubt the possibility of her keeping up the brave fight for very further long? I am trying to brace myself up for the next news. Who is the priest who sees her? Tell her all my thoughts are with her & repeat to her what I told her – my gratitude for all she has done to help me in life, in every way, moral physical.[110]

Elizabeth was devastated by the death of her sister on 27 November expressing her 'deepest love' and her 'profoundest veneration' of Alice to Wilfrid, describing her sister as 'one who combined a powerful intellect with so gentle and devout a nature'.[111] Alice's death came just before the publication of Elizabeth's autobiography and Elizabeth explained to Wilfrid how Alice had requested her to 'reduce, to the simplest possible mention of her name, the many allusions to her which I had included in my little autobiography' and was 'anxious to keep her personality back from the world as much as possible'. She told Wilfrid: 'Half my life seems to have been struck off'.[112] And later:

> What a tribute has come like a flood around her memory! Not alone as a great poetess but as a saintly woman. A triumph of sheer goodness has shown the World what a power that is, even as shining by itself, apart from the radiance of genius. It speaks well for the times we live in! Every paper one opens makes one draw a long breath of satisfaction at the token of her influence. I wonder if she would have approved of it all had she seen it in prophecy.[113]

Her sense of diminishment continued with the loss of her sister: 'When Alice went there went with her half of what was left of me when she was taken'.[114] By late January 1923, she told Wilfrid: 'One tries to cheer up but sometimes the effort makes one worse'.[115] She was, however, delighted with the success of her book, thanking Wilfrid for his review in *The Observer*: 'I cannot tell you how touched I am at seeing the evidence of the time & thought you have given to this review, with the weight of an unparalleled sorrow upon you'.[116] By May, she had intended to sell Bansha, the 'sacred home' that she could never look at again after its 'defilement'. The auction in 1924 was 'floridly advertised' and became a matter of interest 'being the result of [her] expulsion from Ireland'. Keen to make the most of the sale she told Wilfrid that she intended to auction a 'few engravings (Proofs)' of her pictures and a 'few watercolours'. Her 'largest oil', *The Camel Corps*, had 'been riddled with bullets' during the attack on Bansha.[117]

Her grandson's tutor describes Elizabeth's final years at Gormanston. O'Byrne and his charge used to lunch with Elizabeth. 'She was so deaf, conversation was difficult, but he had a wonderful way of making her hear in his clear childish treble'. O'Byrne was invited to her studio where she continued to paint:

> One of the last things I saw on her easel was a water-colour, fresh and vigorous, of an Inniskilling Dragoon. She painted uniforms and accoutrements, of which she had a unique collection, with meticulous regard for detail. She had a tremendous capacity for work. A hard and fast rule of hers was to take exercise every morning before going to her studio and again before luncheon.

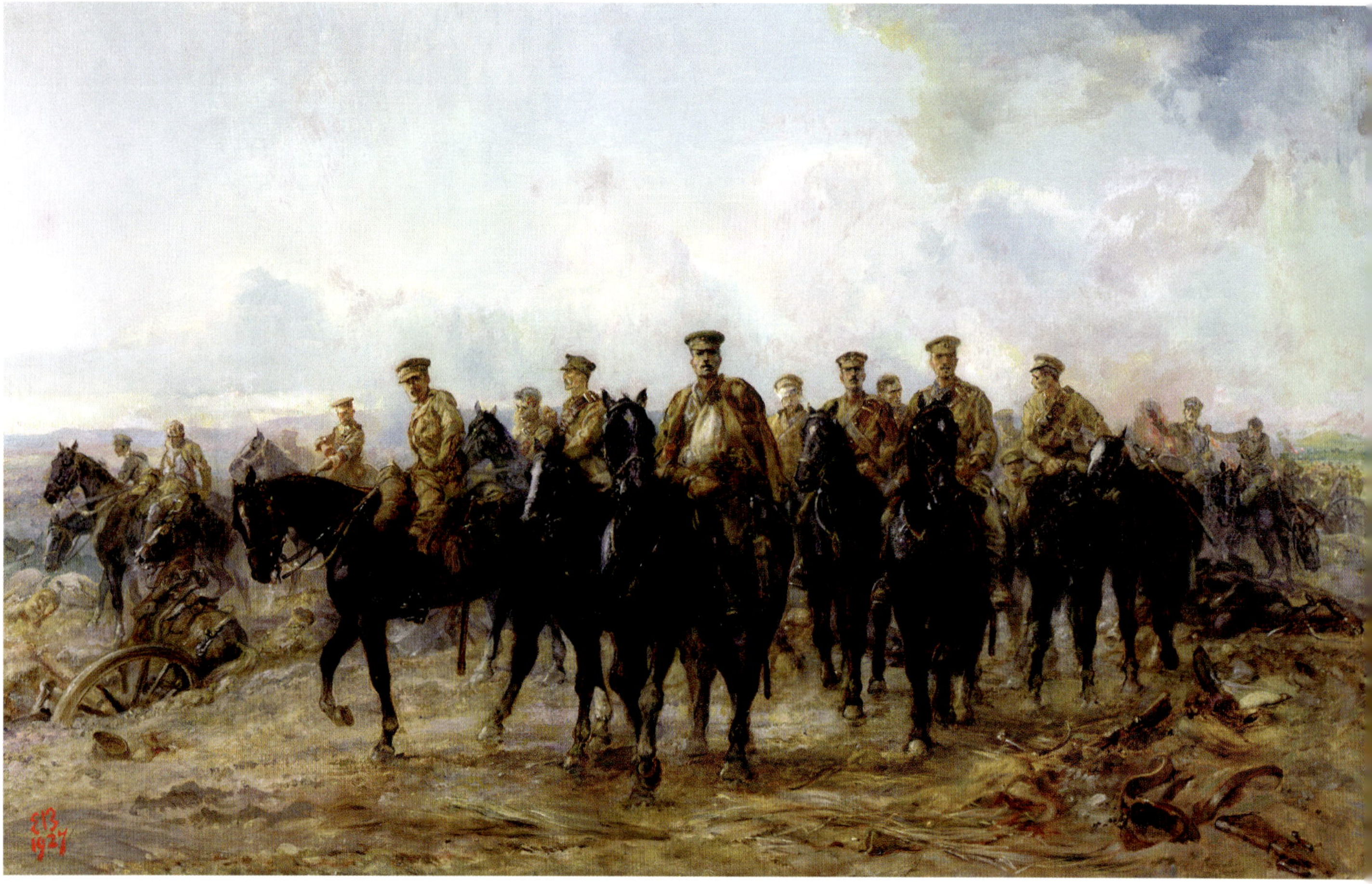

57 *The Retreat from Mons*, 1927. Oil on canvas, 61 × 96.5cm. Royal Hospital Chelsea. Bridgeman Art Library.

At Gormanston, this woman of 'high courage' led a 'secluded life', a 'contrast to the brilliant years of her success as an artist and her role as the wife of an officer of high rank'.[118] In 1925, Eileen's husband died and Elizabeth supported her in her grief. Eileen recalls: 'The days of some of those years she spent with me at Gormanston were dark: but my mother's laughter-evoking powers were little shafts of light'. On one occasion on an after dinner walk her mother urged her to bury her head in wild garlic flowers. She had a 'wonderful', 'adorable knack of making one *laugh in spite of oneself*'.[119] Both were experiencing straitened financial circumstances. On 17 February 1924, Elizabeth asked Wilfrid's advice about the royalties for her autobiography: 'You see I am, like the rest of the "new poor", looking after the pence! The book up to the 31st Dec. has brought £300 in Royalties in England, America & the Colonies, so far'.[120] By 1932, she was in a reflective mood about her finances when writing to Dick: 'Really the want of money is becoming such that we must begin to feel what the Poor feel. Serve us all right'.[121] The previous year she had given Dick her South African painting: 'I send you (& it will be a birthday present) my Boer War Academy picture "Within Sound of the Guns" British Yeomanry starting in pursuit of the enemy on hearing their guns. Of course, I know you can have no property of your own but it is through you for the "general good".'[122]

The Retreat from Mons: the Royal Horse Guards (1927) was a re-working of her 1920 painting and a return to the theme of *Inkerman* and the Crimean paintings of the 1870s (Figure 57). In the foreground is the debris of battle as sombre and wounded soldiers retreat from Mons in one of the war's early campaigns. The central figure, his arm in a sling, looks out into the distance (Figure 58). This quiet painting reflects the trauma of their experiences and, with the hindsight of history, this early campaign is a grim reflection on the suffering that was to follow. She wrote to Wilfrid about its exhibition at Ackermann's Gallery in Bond Street in the spring of 1928: 'The Rear Guard: Household Cavalry coming in at the close of the Mons Retreat is the subject. Not a large picture & perhaps too quietly told to be in the least sensational, but I want you to see mental stress in the mens' faces. I am not a master of effect'.[123] This 'quietly told' painting was followed by her last work, *A Detachment of Cavalry in Flanders* (1929). Here weary troops and horses make their way past a roadside crucifix. The painting is imbued with a sense of redemption as the crucifix is lit by sunlight. Unlike the crucifix of *Eyes Right!*, this one is small and almost insignificant in the distance, and positioned in the corner of the painting. The soldiers, with their backs to the viewer, are seen travelling towards it on their exhausted journey from war. It also reflects Elizabeth's retreat from life.

In the autumn of 1933, Elizabeth's children were summoned to Gormanston. On 1 October, Coos wrote to Wilfrid after the funeral: 'The darling who has left us leaves also a place in the world which can never be filled … I hear the B.B.C. broadcast about her last evening though we did not hear that, & the C. in C. [Commander-in-Chief] wrote so charmingly to Pat on behalf of the Army'.[124] On

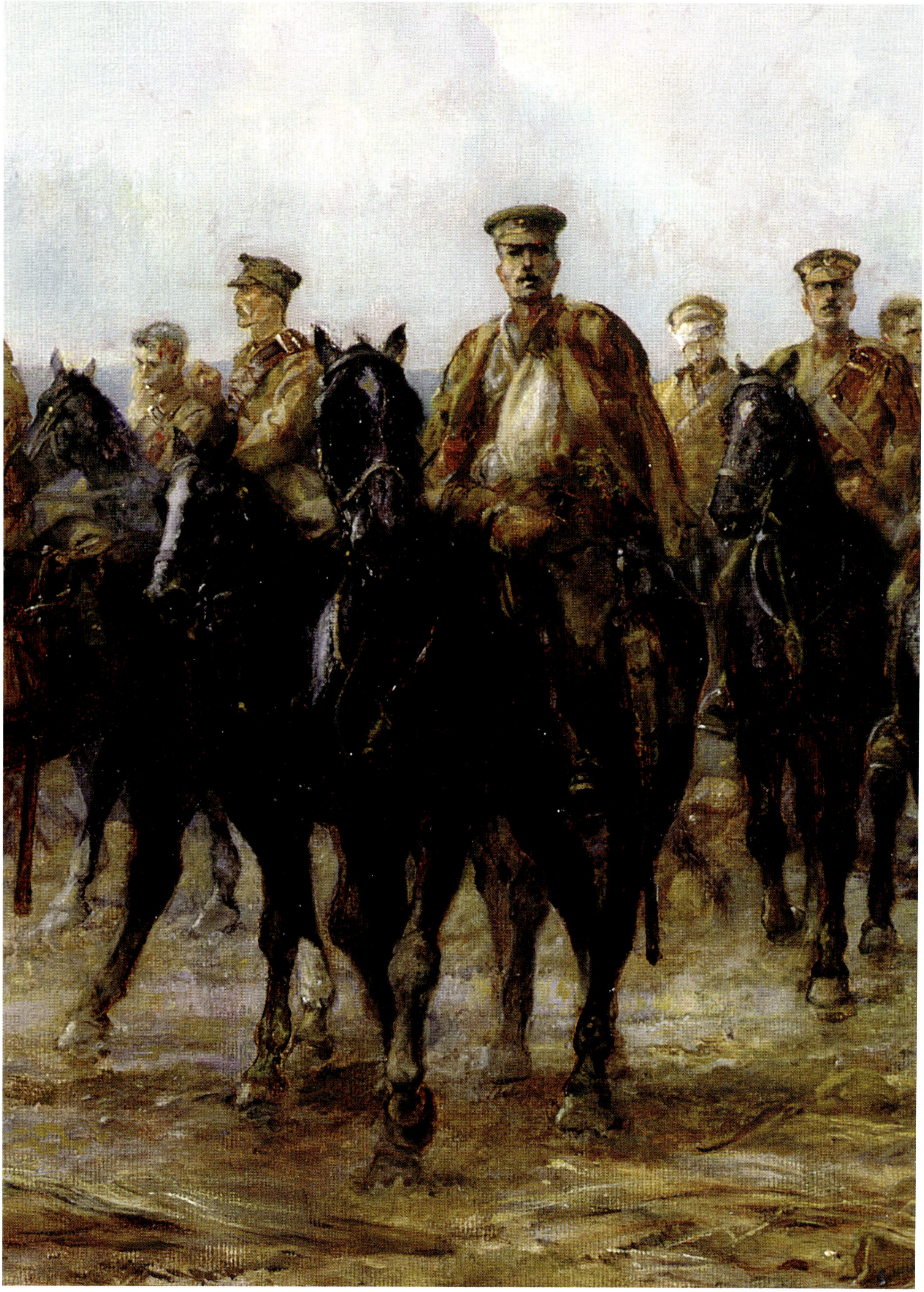

5 October, Patrick wrote to his uncle about his mother: 'We laid her to rest yesterday, on an Irish day such as could only have been made for her'.[125]

Many of Elizabeth Butler's paintings are journeys – journeys to, but more often back from, battle. Her cavalry in *Scotland for Ever!* and her footballers at Loos charge the enemy lines. In *The Return from Inkerman* wearied troops straggle back on foot or are carried; in *Balaclava* the survivors have gained the ridge, with the dead young trumpeter nestled in the arms of a trooper reflecting the human cost of conflict; in *Connaught Rangers*, the Irish road takes the recruits to the wars of empire. This voyage out to far-flung campaigns culminates in *The Remnants of an Army* on the road to Jellalabad. In her two paintings of Mons, mounted grim-faced soldiers retreat from war, yet know that they will have to return to battle.

In a 1925 painting, Elizabeth depicts a Highland regiment on a lonely moonlit march through the desert, carrying the bier of a dead comrade. The painting was based on an illustration from *Sketch-Book* (Figure 59). While she was on the Upper Nile with William in 1886, he told her how the Highland pipes had halted a night of fighting with the Mahdists. The story was so vivid that she claims she 'could see the whole scene' as if she had been present:

58 Detail from *The Retreat from Mons.*

> They were out in the desert, the moon was full; the Dervishes were sniping at long range, when afar off was heard a Highland lament. The sniping ceased all along the enemy's line and dead silence fell upon the night but for the wail of the bagpipes. The Dervishes seemed to be listening. The lament increased in sound, and presently the Cameron Highlanders approached, bearing, under the Union Jack, the body of an officer who had died that day of fever, to add yet another grave to the number that lay at intervals along the shores of the great river.[126]

The incongruous sound of the bagpipes made the enemy pause, as the kilted Highlanders carry their comrade to his desert grave. They are out of place.

Elizabeth Thompson Butler's grave is in a small, nondescript cemetery in the village of Stamullen, near Gormanston Castle. As a woman, painting war, empire and men, she was out of place. In her final resting place, this artist, who spent her life in travel, is also out of place. Dying in a country she was attached to by marriage, she lies under a Celtic cross. There is nothing to suggest that this is the grave of Victorian Britain's finest war artist, who pioneered a representation of the effects of war on combatants, and whose work questioned the human cost of conflict in the remote battlescapes of empire. That this painter was a woman makes her achievement all the more remarkable.

Throughout her career her loyalty to the ordinary soldier remained steadfast. Soldiers, veterans and the public held faith with her long after her critical appeal had vanished. On 15 September 1954, Colonel M. Browne of Inglis Barracks, Mill Hill, corresponded with Dick Butler about *Steady the Drums and Fifes!*, the painting of the young musicians of the 57th Regiment, who are witnessing battle:

> I was not aware that the actual command 'Steady the Drums and Fifes' had been so portrayed in the picture and that was the Drummer you portrayed, who made it. You come into the picture in a great many places and that of The Drummer with the bandage round his head is a splendid one of courage, and steadiness in Battle. Lady Butler gave us a wonderful testimonial to the 57th, and we have always felt that our thanks could never be adequate for the gift of her art. However, she knew all her life, and knows now, that the picture has held our men steady, and fearless ever since, and will always do so.[127]

After the publication of her 1922 autobiography, Wilfrid, deep in mourning for the death of Alice, championed Elizabeth's career in his review in *The Observer*, as Alice would have wanted him to. 'To have achieved all, and more than all, her girlhood dreamed, has been her kind fate'. Yet, 'the letters, "R. A.", which she wrote after her name in an early notebook, are not even now hers. Millais, who said that her draughtsmanship – the masculinity of the phrase almost jars – exceeded that of any of her contemporaries, also told her, when they first met, that he hoped to vote her into the Academy, "an honour thoroughly deserved".' The 'victory [which] would then have been won for women' was not to be. Wilfrid calls for an 'Honorary Membership' to 'put the finishing touches to a career in every other way complete and crowned'; but that was not to be.[128]

59 *A 'Lament' in the Desert*, 1925. Oil on canvas, 76 x 62.5cm. Private Collection. Bridgeman Art Library.

Elizabeth was a product of Italy as well as England. Her early life spent in travel shaped the woman and artist she was to become. When William offered her a choice of posts in Britain, she opted for Dover so she could look out across the sea to France. It was the French military art tradition of Meissonier and Detaille that inspired her and which she imported and developed. She worked on canvases in Ireland and transported them across the Irish sea to the Academy. *Halt on a Forced March*, another of her weary journeys from war, made its own journey from County Wicklow to Alexandria and back to the Academy. The ill-fated *Camel Corps*, conceived and developed in Egypt, became the victim of the Irish Civil War. Elizabeth travelled extensively and her vision was expansive. Her canvases were often, like *Remnants*, large and commanding. To see *Remnants* – one the artist's favourite paintings – at the Tate's 'Artist and Empire' exhibition, surrounded by other inferior paintings, is to understand her greatness and boldness as an artist; one does not have to be a Millais to see her skill. The Academicians, perhaps threatened by her talents, put her back in her place after celebrating *The Roll Call*. Her follow-up painting,

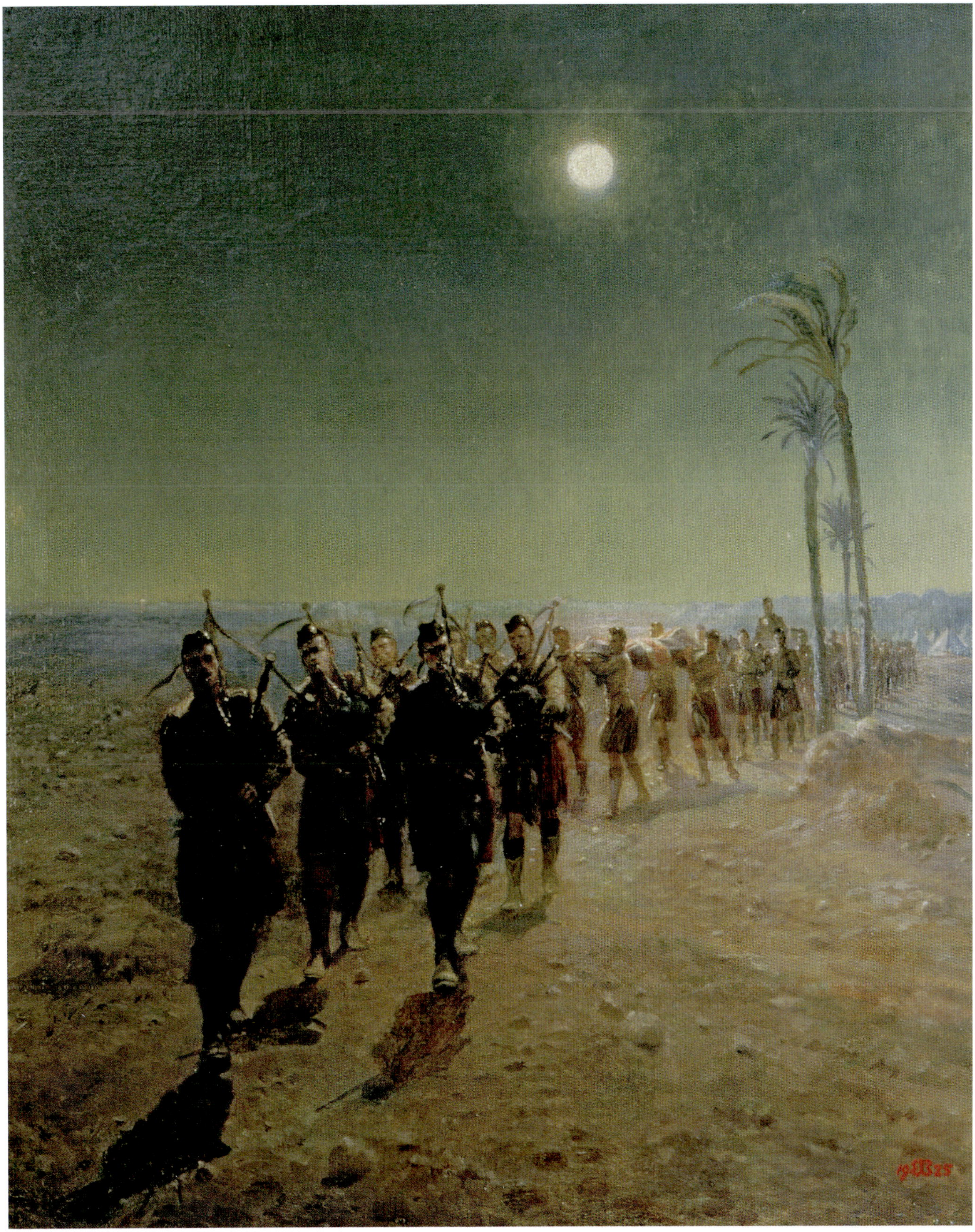

Quatre Bras, was banished to the dark recesses of the Academy's lecture room for the 1875 exhibition. Forty years later, little had changed as Britain's finest living painter of war was not accorded an official role as a war artist during the First World War.

Wilfrid presents Elizabeth as being birthed into a life of art and travel. '[D]uring the winter of her daughter's birth', Christiana 'cultivated her favourite art of landscape painting, and the natural pictures of the snowy mountains and the ice-bound lakes ... were the first objects that caught the child's eye'. Her childhood was 'divided between Italy and England' and '[c]ountry life, with the companionship of a sister, and with the perfect freedom to run about on the hills of Nervi, or in the fields of Kent', provided a 'healthy contrast to the studies which were vigorously pursued' from the ages of five to seventeen under the tutorship of her father.[129] The 'companion of her childhood', the figure who supported her in her career, dedicated a poem about fathers to her sister. It is also a feminist war poem that calls on the world of men to recognize the abilities of women. 'Our father works in us, / The daughters of his manhood'. Alice exhorts the 'million living fathers' who are 'mourning in this crippled world' to 'Approve, accept, know the daughters of men'.[130] Elizabeth Thompson, Lady Butler, should be better known and celebrated. The time has come for her to have her place.

Notes

Prelude

1 All quotations are taken from Christiana's Lausanne Diary (unpublished) from 1846. The Lausanne Diary is in the Meynell Archive at Greatham.
2 Charles Dickens, Letter to Thomas Thompson, in Kathleen Tillotson (ed.), *The Pilgrim Edition of the Letters of Charles Dickens*, vol. 4 (Oxford: Clarendon Press, 1977), p. 652.
3 Elizabeth Butler, *Autobiography* (Seven Oaks, Kent: Fisher, 1993), p. 1.
4 Eileen Gormanston, *A Little Kept* (London: The Catholic Book Club, 1954), p. 40.
5 Elizabeth Butler, *Autobiography*, p. 1.
6 Gormanston, *A Little Kept*, p. 39.
7 Alice Meynell, *Hearts of Controversy* (London: Burns & Oates, 1917), p. 36.
8 Thompson, Lausanne Diary.
9 Elizabeth Butler, *Autobiography*, p. 1.

Chapter One: Liverpool to Lausanne, 1844–6

1 A copy of the poem is in the Meynell family papers (Meynell Archive).
2 'Theatre Royal', *Freeman's Journal*, 5 December 1842.
3 'Philharmonic Concert', *The Liverpool Mercury*, 31 March 1843.
4 'Miss Christiana Weller's Concert', *The Manchester Times and Gazette*, 24 February 1844.
5 'C. Dickens, Esq., (Boz) in Liverpool', *Liverpool Mercury*, 1 March 1844.
6 'Boz in Liverpool', *Preston Guardian*, 2 March 1844.
7 'Miss Christiana Weller', *Musical Examiner*, 15 June 1844.
8 Kate Perugini and Walter Dexter (eds), *Mr & Mrs Charles Dickens: His Letters to Her* (London: Constable, 1935), p. 94.
9 Alice Meynell, 'To O – Of Her Dark Eyes', *Collected Poems* (London: Burns and Oates, 1921), p. 131.
10 Joseph Hatton, *Club-Land: London and Provincial* (London: J.S. Virtue, 1890), p. 30.
11 Alice Meynell, 'A Remembrance', *The Scots Observer*, 9 August 1890.
12 Wilfrid Meynell, *A Dickens Friendship* (London: Nonesuch Press, 1931), n.p.
13 *Letters of Charles Dickens*, vol. 4, p. 54n.
14 Kathryn Sutherland, 'Dickens and Women', *Critical Quarterly*, 25 (28 September 2007), 17.
15 *Letters of Charles Dickens*, vol. 4, p. 69.
16 Ibid., p. 70.
17 Ibid.
18 Rosemarie Bodenheimer, 'Dickens Fascinated', *Victorian Studies*, 48:2 (Winter 2006), 270.
19 *The Letters of Charles Dickens*, vol. 4, p. 70.
20 Ibid., p. 87.
21 Ibid., p. 97.
22 Ibid., pp 99–100.
23 'Miss Christiana Weller's Concert', *The Musical World*, 17 July 1845.
24 Elizabeth Butler, *Autobiography*, p. 2.
25 'Miss Christiana Weller', *The Standard*, 24 October 1845.
26 All quotations come from Christiana's unpublished Journal (1845–6) in the Meynell Archive.
27 Ibid.
28 Ibid.
29 Gormanston, *A Little Kept*, pp 40, 43.
30 Viola Meynell, *Alice Meynell: A Memoir* (London: Jonathan Cape, 1929), p. 12.
31 Thompson, Journal (1845–6).
32 Ibid.
33 James Buzard, *The Beaten Track: European Tourism, Literature, and the Ways to Culture, 1800–1918* (Oxford: Oxford University Press, 1993), pp 159, 160.

34 Thompson, Journal (1845–6).
35 Charles Dickens, *Pictures from Italy* (London: Penguin, 1998), pp 31–2.
36 Martin Willis and Catherine Wynne, 'Introduction' in Martin Willis and Catherine Wynne (eds), *Victorian Literary Mesmerism* (Amsterdam: Rodopi, 2006), p. 3.
37 Thompson, Journal (1845–6).
38 Claire Tomalin, *Charles Dickens: A Life* (London: Penguin, 2012), p. 160.
39 Thompson, Journal (1845–6).
40 Tomalin, *Charles Dickens*, p. 163.
41 Thompson, Journal (1845–6).
42 Ibid.
43 Ibid.
44 Paul-Emile Schazmann, *Charles Dickens in Switzerland*, trans. H.P.B. Betlem (Geneva: Swiss National Tourist Office, 1972), p. 19.
45 Thompson, Lausanne Diary.
46 Viola Meynell, *Alice Meynell: A Memoir*, p. 12.
47 Thompson, Lausanne Diary.
48 Ibid. William James Müller (1812–45) was a landscape and Orientalist painter. He painted European, Turkish and Egyptian scenes before his premature death. His work became more popular after his death. Born in Bristol he was of Prussian descent.

Chapter Two: South of England to the Italian Riviera: the making of an artist, 1847–61

1 Elizabeth von Arnim, *The Enchanted April* (London: Vintage, 2015), pp 54–5.
2 See Maura O'Connor, *The Romance of Italy and the English Imagination* (Basingstoke: Macmillan, 1998), pp 29–30.
3 Elizabeth Butler, *Autobiography*, p. 5.
4 'Multiple News Items', *The Morning Post*, 28 July 1847.
5 'Miscellaneous', *Hampshire Advertiser and Salisbury Guardian*, 14 August 1847.
6 Christiana Thompson, Journal (1848).
7 For a study of Dickens's relationship with his brother, see Gerald G. Grubb, 'Charles Dickens and His Brother Fred', *Dickensian*, 50 (1 January 1954), 123–31.
8 Sidney P. Moss and Carolyn J. Moss, 'Frederick Dickens: From Courtship to Courtroom', *Dickensian*, 90 (Summer 1994), 102.
9 *Letters of Charles Dickens*, vol. 4, pp 400, 401.
10 Christiana Thompson, Journal (1848).
11 Christiana Thompson, Journal (1849).
12 Ibid.
13 Christiana Thompson, Journal (1850).
14 Christiana Thompson, Journal (1851).
15 Ibid.
16 Ibid.
17 Ibid.
18 Elizabeth Butler, 'Notebook', Meynell Archive.
19 See Margaret Denny, 'Framing the Victorians: Photography, Fashion and Identity' in John Potvin (ed.), *The Places and Spaces of Fashion, 1800–2007* (London: Routledge, 2009), pp 45–8.
20 Christiana Thompson, Journal (1851).
21 Deborah Cherry, *Painting Women: Victorian Women Artists* (London: Routledge, 1993), p. 25.
22 Elizabeth Butler, *Autobiography*, p. 2.
23 June Badeni, *The Slender Tree: A Life of Alice Meynell* (Padstow: Tabb House, 1981), p. 4.
24 Elizabeth Butler, *Autobiography*, p. 1.
25 Alice Meynell, Letter to Fanny Edelmann, 9 September, Gormanston Archive.
26 Thomas Thompson, Letter to Christiana Thompson, 2 June 1853.
27 Elizabeth Thompson, Letter to Christiana Thompson, 2 June 1853.
28 Thomas Thompson, Letter to Christiana Thompson, 2 June 1853.
29 Elizabeth Thompson, Letter to Christiana Thompson, 10 June 1853.
30 Ibid.
31 Alice Meynell, 'Agostino', *Pall Mall Gazette*, 19 January 1898.
32 Alice Meynell, 'The Maidservants', *Pall Mall Gazette*, 26 January 1898.
33 Elizabeth Butler, *Autobiography*, p. 2.
34 Charles Dickens, Letter to Catherine Dickens in Graham Storey et al. (eds), *The Pilgrim Edition of the Letters of Charles Dickens*, vol. 7 (Oxford: Clarendon, 1993), p. 178.

35 Elizabeth Shaw, Letter to Christiana Thompson, 10 July 1854.
36 Thomas Thompson, Letter to Christiana Thompson, 13 July 1856.
37 Thomas Thompson, Letter to Christiana Thompson, 19 July 1856.
38 Elizabeth Butler, Letter to Wilfrid Meynell, Palm Sunday 1927.
39 Thomas Thompson, Letter to Christiana Thompson, 18 July 1856.
40 Christiana Thompson, Journal (1856–7).
41 Ibid.
42 Thomas Thompson, Letter to Christiana Thompson, 19 July 1856.
43 Amelia Thompson, Letter to Christiana Thompson, 3 January 1860.
44 Reprinted in Frédéric Lepelle de Bois-Gallais, *Memoir of Mademoiselle Rosa Bonheur*, trans. James Parry (New York: Williams, Stevens, Williams, 1857), p. 59.
45 Quoted in Cherry, *Painting Women*, p. 56.
46 Christiana Thompson, Journal (1856–7).
47 Elizabeth Butler, Letter to Wilfrid Meynell, 3 September 1923.
48 Elizabeth Butler, Letter to Wilfrid Meynell, 3 September 1923.
49 Christiana Thompson, Journal (1856–7).
50 Elizabeth Butler, *Autobiography*, p. 4.
51 For a full account of the marriage breakdown and the legal situation, see Moss and Moss, 'Frederick Dickens: From Courtship to Courtroom', 102–12.
52 Stuarta Yeats Brown, Letter to Christiana Thompson, 6 October 1858.
53 Christiana Thompson, Journal (1859–61).
54 Alfonso Scirocco, *Garibaldi: Citizen of the World* (Princeton and Oxford: Princeton University Press, 2007), p. ix.
55 Ibid., p. 53.
56 Ibid., p. 156.
57 A.L.V. Gretton, *Vicissitudes of Italy, Since the Congress of Vienna* (London: Routledge, 1859), p. 2.
58 O'Connor, *The Romance of Italy and the English Imagination*, p. 91.
59 Christiana Thompson, Journal (1859–61).
60 Butler, *Autobiography*, p. 5.
61 Christiana Thompson, Journal (1859–61).
62 Scirocco, *Garibaldi*, p. 241.
63 Butler, *Autobiography*, p. 5.
64 Christiana Thompson, Journal (1859–61).
65 Scirocco, *Garibaldi*, p. 243.
66 Christiana Thompson, Journal (1859–61).
67 Thomas Thompson, Letter to Christiana Thompson, 15 June 1860.
68 Butler, *Autobiography*, p. 5.
69 Elizabeth Barrett Browning, *Letters of Mrs Browning*, vol. 2, ed. Frederic G. Kenyon (London: Smith, Elder, 1897), p. 398.
70 See Harry W. Rudman, *Italian Nationalism and English Letters: Figures of the Risorgimento and Victorian Men of Letters* (London: George Allen & Unwin, 1940), p. 295.
71 Christiana Thompson, Journal (1859–61).
72 Butler, *Autobiography*, 7.
73 Christiana Thompson, Journal (1859–61).
74 Butler, *Autobiography*, p. 7.
75 Thomas Thompson, Letter to Christiana Thompson, 24 September 1861.
76 The 1861 census reveals that Amelia and her two nieces, Mary and Frances Amelia (1845–1909), were boarders in Paddington in the home of Christiana's sister, Betsy.
77 Elizabeth Thompson, Letter to Christiana Thompson, 6 November 1861.

Chapter Three: Road to fame, 1862–73

1 This painting is in a private archive.
2 Gormanston, *A Little Kept*, p. 55.
3 Germaine Greer, *The Obstacle Race: The Fortunes of Women Painters and the Work* (New York: Martin Secker & Warburg, 1979).
4 Jane Austen, *Emma*, ed. James Kinsley (Oxford: Oxford World Classics, 2008), p. 35.
5 Dinah Mulock Craik, *Olive*, ed. Cora Kaplan (Oxford: Oxford World Classics, 2000), p. 126.
6 Paula Gillett, *The Victorian Painter's World* (Gloucester: Alan Sutton, 1990), p. 138.
7 The painting is *Cloakroom, the Clifton Assembly Rooms* (1817–18). See Kathryn Metz, 'Ellen and Rolinda Sharples: Mother and Daughter Painters', *Woman's Art Journal*, 16:1 (Spring–Summer 1995), 3–11.

8 See Debra N. Mancoff, *Danger! Women Artists at Work* (London: Merrell, 2012), p. 139.
9 Cherry, *Painting Women*, p. 25.
10 Patricia Zakreski, *Representing Female Artistic Labour, 1848–1890: Refining Work for the Middle-Class Woman* (London: Routledge, 2006), pp 65–6.
11 Gormanston, *A Little Kept*, p. 52.
12 Craik, *Olive*, p. 118.
13 Cherry, *Painting Women*, p. 21.
14 Viola Meynell, *Alice Meynell*, p. 27.
15 Vita Sackville-West, Introduction, in *Alice Meynell: Prose and Poetry, Centenary Edition*, ed. Vita Sackville-West (London: Jonathan Cape, 1947), p. 11.
16 Thomas Thompson, Letter to Fanny Edelmann, 29 December 1880. Gormanston Papers.
17 Samuel Smiles, *Self Help* (London: John Murray, 1908), pp 183, 186.
18 Mancoff, *Danger! Women Artists at Work*, p. 7.
19 Charlotte Yeldham, *Women Artists in Nineteenth-Century France and England*, vol. 1 (New York: Garland, 1984), p. 2.
20 Christopher Frayling, 'Design at the Royal College of Art: the head, the heart and the hand' in Christopher Frayling and Claire Catterall (eds), *Design of the Times: One Hundred Years of the Royal College of Art* (Shepton Beauchamp: Richard Dennis/Royal College of Art, 1995), pp 8, 9.
21 F. Graeme Chalmers, *Women in the Nineteenth-Century Art World: Schools of Art and Design for Women in London and Philadelphia* (Westport, CT: Greenwood, 1998), p. 14.
22 John Physick, 'The Government School of Design: foundation, rebellion, investigation, and the triumph of Henry Cole' in Frayling and Catterall (eds), *Design of the Times*, p. 15.
23 Estella Canziani, *Round About Three Palace Green* (London: Methuen, 1939), p. 20.
24 Mancoff, *Danger! Women Artists at Work*, p. 12.
25 Rafael Cardoso Denis, 'Drawing or Design? The development of the National Art Training School' in Frayling and Catterall (eds), *Design of the Times*, p. 22.
26 Elizabeth Butler, *Autobiography*, p. 8.
27 Ibid., p. 9. *The Ransom* (1860–2) depicts a sixteenth-century knight paying ransom for the return of his daughters. The painting was one of Millais's less successful works.
28 Christiana Thompson, Journal (1862).
29 Michael Freeman, *The Undercliff, Isle of Wight: A Geographic History* (Newport: Crossprint, 2012), 7. For a study of Dickens in Bonchurch, see Richard J. Hutchings, *Dickens on an Island* (1970; Freshwater Bay: Hunnyhill Publications, 2012).
30 Christiana Thompson, Journal (1862).
31 Ibid.
32 Elizabeth Butler, *Autobiography*, p. 10.
33 Christiana Thompson, Journal (1862).
34 Gormanston, *A Little Kept*, p. 63.
35 Thomas Thompson, Letter to Christiana Thompson, 3 January 1863.
36 Elizabeth Butler, *Autobiography*, pp 10, 11.
37 Thomas Thompson, Letter to Christiana Thompson, 21 August 1863.
38 Elizabeth Butler, *Autobiography*, p. 11.
39 Elizabeth Thompson, Letter to Alice Thompson, 2–3 June 1865.
40 Elizabeth Butler, *Autobiography*, p. 11.
41 Elizabeth Thompson, Letter to Alice Thompson, 18 July, n.y.
42 Elizabeth Butler, *Autobiography*, pp 14, 15, 18.
43 Ibid., p. 25.
44 Ibid., p. 27.
45 Ibid., p. 28.
46 Quoted in Meaghan Clarke, *Critical Voices: Women and Art Criticism in Britain, 1880–1905* (Aldershot: Ashgate, 2005), p. 8.
47 Elizabeth Butler, *Autobiography*, p. 31.
48 Ibid., p. 32.
49 Ibid., p. 33.
50 Ibid., p. 36.
51 Ibid., p. 39.
52 Ibid., p. 42.
53 Caroline Dakers, *The Holland Park Circle: Artists and Victorian Society* (New Haven: Yale University Press, 1999), pp 178–9.
54 Elizabeth Thompson, Letter to Christiana Thompson, May 1868.

55 Ibid. Still in existence today, Rotten Row, a track running alongside Hyde Park, was a popular meeting place for the upper classes and their horses in the eighteenth century. The artists are objecting to the fashionable horse.
56 Pamela Gerrish Nunn, *Canvassing: Recollections by Six Victorian Women Artists* (London: Camden Press, 1968), p. 166.
57 Elizabeth Thompson, Letter to Christiana Thompson, May 1868.
58 Elizabeth Thompson, Letter to Christiana Thompson, 21 May 1868.
59 Ibid. 'My Loze' was a pet name for her father. Littlehampton is a seaside resort in West Sussex.
60 Elizabeth Thompson, Letter to Christiana Thompson, 30 May, n.y.
61 Yeldham, *Women Artists in Nineteenth-Century France and England*, p. 319.
62 Elizabeth Thompson, Letter to Christiana Thompson, 31 May 1868.
63 Elizabeth Thompson, Letter to Christiana Thompson, 30 May, n.y.
64 Quoted in M.H. Spielmann and G.S. Layard, *Kate Greenaway* (London: Adam and Charles Black, 1905), p. 43.
65 'Miss Kate Greenaway', *Illustrated London News*, 16 November 1901.
66 Alice Meynell, 'Elizabeth Butler', *St Nicholas*, 1 January 1883, 189.
67 Elizabeth Butler, *Autobiography*, p. 43.
68 Viola Meynell, *Alice Meynell*, p. 40.
69 Elizabeth Butler, *Autobiography*, pp 44, 45, 47.
70 Ibid., p. 47.
71 Alice Meynell, 'Elizabeth Butler', p. 188.
72 Elizabeth Butler, *Autobiography*, p. 42.
73 Alice Meynell, 'Elizabeth Butler', p. 182.
74 Elizabeth Butler, *Autobiography*, p. 52.
75 Alice Meynell, 'Elizabeth Butler', p. 189.
76 Elizabeth Butler, *From Sketch-Book and Diary*, pp 69–70.
77 Ibid., p. 170.
78 Ibid.
79 Elizabeth Butler, *Autobiography*, pp 61, 67, 63.
80 Ibid., p. 67.
81 Giles Walkley, *Artists' Houses in London, 1764–1914* (Aldershot: Scolar Press, 1994), pp xxiv, 142.
82 Alice Meynell, 'Elizabeth Butler', p. 189.
83 Ibid., p. 190.
84 'The Dudley Gallery', *The Pall Mall Gazette*, 13 February 1872.
85 'The Dudley Gallery', *The Examiner*, 27 January 1872.
86 'Winter Exhibitions – The Dudley Gallery', *The Tablet*, 30 March 1872, p. 390.
87 'The Dudley Gallery', *The Times*, 11 November 1872.
88 'The Dudley Gallery', *The Pall Mall Gazette*, 5 March 1873.
89 'The Dudley Gallery', *The Examiner*, 8 February 1873.
90 Elizabeth Butler, *Autobiography*, p. 75.
91 Alice Meynell, 'Elizabeth Butler', p. 190.
92 Elizabeth Butler, *Autobiography*, p. 78.
93 E.R. Norman, *Anti-Catholicism in Victorian England* (London: George Allen and Unwin, 1968), p. 14.
94 Like Christiana, Elizabeth kept diaries throughout her life which she used to inform her autobiography. The Paray material quoted in this section is a remaining fragment of her original diary. Diary Manuscript, Gormanston Archive.
95 Elizabeth Thompson, Diary Manuscript 1873, Gormanston Archive.
96 Ibid.
97 Viola Meynell, *Alice Meynell*, p. 40.

Chapter Four: The war path: from *The Roll Call* to *Inkerman*, 1874–7

1 Christiana Thompson, Letter to Fanny Edelmann, 7 May 1874. Gormanston Archive.
2 Elizabeth Butler, *Autobiography*, p. 81.
3 It is difficult to estimate what this is worth in the twenty-first century. However, estimates are provided by the National Archives. See Currency Converter: 1270–2017. The National Archives. http://www.nationalarchives.gov.uk/currency-converter/#currency-result
4 Elizabeth Butler, *Autobiography*, p. 84.
5 George du Maurier, 'Varnishing Day at the Royal Academy', *Punch*, 19 June 1877.
6 Elizabeth Butler, *Autobiography*, p. 84.
7 Ibid., pp 85–6.
8 'Essence of Parliament', *Punch*, 8 August 1874.
9 Robert Wilkinson-Latham, *Uniforms and Weapons of the Crimean War* (London: B.T. Batsford, 1977), p. 7.

10 William Francis Butler, *The Wild North Land* (London: Burns & Oates, 1915), pp 4–5.
11 J.W.M. Hichberger, *Images of the Army: Military in British Art, 1815–1914* (Manchester: Manchester University Press, 1990), p. 76.
12 Winfried Baumgart, *The Crimean War, 1853–1856* (London: Arnold, 1999), pp 215–16.
13 William Plomer (ed.), *Kilvert's Diary, 1870–1879: Selections from the Diary of the Revd Francis Kilvert* (London: Jonathan Cape, 1944), p. 250.
14 Frederic Leighton, Letter to the President and Council of the Royal Academy, 13 May 1874. Royal Academy of Arts Archive, London.
15 Terry Brighton, *Hell Riders: The Truth about the Charge of the Light Brigade* (London: Penguin, 2004), p. 2.
16 Frances Isabella Duberly, *Mrs Duberly's War: Journal and Letters from the Crimea, 1854–6*. Ed. and intro. Christine Kelly (Oxford: Oxford University Press, 2007), p. 94.
17 Matthew Lalumia, 'Lady Elizabeth Thompson Butler in the 1870s', *Women's Art Journal*, 4:1 (Spring–Summer 1993), 11.
18 Elizabeth Butler, *Autobiography*, p. 86.
19 Ibid., p. 87.
20 'Academy Banquet', *The Times*, 2 May 1874.
21 'The Queen and Miss Thompson's Picture', *The Sheffield and Rotherham Independent*, 15 May 1874.
22 W.W. Fenn, 'Echoes from the Royal Academy', *Belgravia*, June 1874, p. 421.
23 Ibid., p. 422.
24 'The Prince of Wales on Hunting', *Jackson's Oxford Journal*, 9 May 1874.
25 'London and Paris Gossip', *Trewman's Exeter Flying Post Or Plymouth and Cornish Advertiser*, 13 May 1874.
26 'Exhibition of the Royal Academy', *The Times*, 2 May 1874.
27 'The Royal Academy Exhibition. Second Notice', *Illustrated London News*, 9 May 1874.
28 'Fine Arts', *The Graphic*, 9 May 1874.
29 Matthew Lalumia, 'Realism and Anti-Aristocratic Sentiment in Victorian Depictions of the Crimean War', *Victorian Studies*, 48:1 (Autumn 1983), 48.
30 *'The Roll Call', The Newcastle Courant*, 23 October 1874.
31 *'The Roll Call', Birmingham Daily Post*, 6 November 1874.
32 'Gossip of the Clubs', *The Lancaster Gazette*, 24 October 1874.
33 Elizabeth Butler, *Autobiography*, p. 91.
34 Patrizia Di Bello, 'Elizabeth Thompson and "Patsy" Cornwallis West as *Carte-de-Visite* Celebrities', *History of Photography*, 55:3 (August 2011), 241.
35 Edward Fitzgerald, *The Letters of Edward Fitzgerald*, vol. 3. Eds Alfred McKinley Terhure and Annabelle Burdick Terhure (Princeton: Princeton University Press, 2015), p. 506.
36 Di Bello, 'Elizabeth Thompson and "Patsy" Cornwallis West', 249.
37 Elizabeth Butler, *Autobiography*, p. 87.
38 Florence Nightingale, Letter to Mr C. Aldous, 4 June 1879.
39 Elizabeth Butler, *Autobiography*, p. 92.
40 Ibid., pp 93, 94.
41 'The Emperor of Russia at Woolwich', *Bradford Observer*, 21 May 1874.
42 Elizabeth Thompson, *'The Roll Call', The Times*, 12 May 1874.
43 Elizabeth Butler, *Autobiography*, p. 95.
44 Elizabeth Thompson, *'The Roll Call', The Times*, 16 May 1874.
45 *'The Roll Call', Daily News*, 19 May 1874.
46 *'"Halt!" A Reminiscence of Aldershot', The Graphic*, 18 July 1874.
47 'Fine Arts', *Illustrated London News*, 27 June 1874.
48 *'Tent Pegging', The Graphic*, 29 May 1875.
49 Currency Converter: 1270–2017. The National Archives. http://www.nationalarchives.gov.uk/currency-converter/#currency-result
50 Elizabeth Butler, *Autobiography*, p. 89.
51 Ibid., pp 89–90.
52 Elizabeth Butler, *Autobiography*, p. 96.
53 Ibid., p. 97.
54 Ibid., p. 98.
55 Ibid., p. 99.
56 Currency Converter: 1270–2017. The National Archives. http://www.nationalarchives.gov.uk/currency-converter/#currency-result
57 Elizabeth Butler, *Autobiography*, p. 100.
58 Ibid., p. 101.
59 Ibid., p. 104.

60 Ibid., p. 102.
61 Ibid., p. 103.
62 Currency Converter: 1270–2017. The National Archives. http://www.nationalarchives.gov.uk/currency-converter/#currency-result
63 Elizabeth Butler, *Autobiography*, p. 105.
64 Ibid., p. 209.
65 Ibid., pp 106, 107.
66 Paul Usherwood, 'Elizabeth Thompson: A Case of Tokenism', *Woman's Art Journal*, 11:2 (Autumn 1990–Winter 1991), 16.
67 Elizabeth Butler, *Autobiography*, p. 107.
68 Ibid., pp 107–8.
69 Ibid., p. 104.
70 Claire Bowen, 'Lady Butler: The Reinvention of Military History', *La Revue LISA*, 1:1 (2003), 132.
71 'Miss Thompson's *Quatre Bras*', *Birmingham Daily Post*, 8 May 1875.
72 'The Royal Academy', *The Times*, 1 May 1875.
73 'Miss Elizabeth Thompson', *The Graphic*, 8 May 1875.
74 Elizabeth Butler, *Autobiography*, p. 117.
75 Greer, *The Obstacle Race*, p. 84.
76 Elizabeth Butler, *Autobiography*, p. 120.
77 Ibid., p. 121.
78 'Miss Thompson's New Picture', *Nottinghamshire Guardian,* 28 April 1876.
79 'Miss Thompson's New Picture', *Daily Telegraph*. Reproduced in *Nottinghamshire Guardian*, 28 April 1876.
80 'Miss Thompson's New Picture', *The Morning Post*, 22 April 1876.
81 George Loy Smith, *A Victorian RSM: From India to the Crimea* (London: Costello, 1987), pp 131–2.
82 'Miss Thompson's New Picture', *The Morning Post*, 22 April 1876.
83 'Miss Thompson's New Picture', *Daily Telegraph*. Reproduced in *Nottinghamshire Guardian*, 28 April 1876.
84 'Miss Thompson's New Picture', *The Morning Post*, 22 April 1876.
85 Elizabeth Thompson, *Autobiography*, p. 11.
86 'Miss Thompson's *Balaclava*', *The Sporting Gazette*, 6 May 1876.
87 Elizabeth Butler, *Autobiography*, p. 122.
88 Ibid., p. 123.
89 Ibid., p. 124.
90 Ibid., p. 125.
91 Viola Meynell, *Francis Thompson and Wilfrid Meynell: A Memoir* (London: Hollis & Carter, 1952), p. 7.
92 Ibid., p. 60.
93 Elizabeth Butler, *Autobiography*, p. 132.
94 Ibid., p. 133.
95 Ibid., p. 134.
96 W.H. Russell, *The War: From the Landing at Gallipoli to the Death of Lord Raglan* (London: George Routledge, 1855), p. 246.
97 Winifred Baumgart, *The Crimean War* (London: Arnold, 1999), p. 138.
98 Russell, *The War*, p. 246.
99 'Miss Elizabeth Thompson's *Return from Inkerman*', *The Graphic*, 28 April 1877.
100 Paul Usherwood and Jenny Spencer-Smith, *Lady Butler: Battle Artist, 1846–1933* (London: National Army Museum, 1987), p. 67.
101 'Miss Elizabeth Thompson's *Return from Inkerman*', *The Graphic*, 28 April 1877.
102 Ibid.
103 See the painting in the Ferens Art Gallery, Hull, UK.
104 For a discussion of the frame, see Christopher Wright, *From Victorian to Edwardian: The Ferens Art Gallery Collection of Victorian and Edwardian Art* (Hull: Hull Museums, 2009), p.18. The painting was purchased for the gallery on 9 May 1913 for 850 guineas. Artist's File, Ferens Art Gallery, Hull. This would amount to approximately £67,000 in today's currency. Currency Converter, 1270–2017. The National Archives. http://www.nationalarchives.gov.uk/currency-converter/#currency-result
105 'New Engravings', *The Times*, 31 May 1882.
106 Greer, *The Obstacle Race*, p. 84.

Chapter Five: Painting Ireland, Afghanistan, South Africa and *Scotland for Ever!*, 1878–81

1 Elizabeth Butler, Letter to Christiana Thompson, June 1878.
2 Quoted in Paul Usherwood, 'Elizabeth Thompson Butler: The Consequences of Marriage', *Women's Art Journal*, 9:1 (Spring–Summer 1988), 30.

3 William Butler, *Sir William Butler: An Autobiography* (London: Constable, 1911), p. 12.
4 Gormanston, *A Little Kept*, p. 21.
5 Martin Ryan, *William Francis Butler: A Life, 1838–1910* (Dublin: Lilliput Press, 2003), pp 1–2.
6 Quoted in Edward McCourt, *Remember Butler: The Story of Sir William Butler* (London: Routledge and Kegan Paul, 1967), p. 29.
7 Ibid., p. 69.
8 'Current Literature', *Daily News*, 24 September 1872.
9 William Butler, *The Wild North Land: Being the Story of a Winter Journey, with Dogs, Across Northern America* (London: Sampson Low, Marston, Low, & Searle, 1874), p. 52.
10 William Butler, *Red Cloud: The Story of a Solitary Sioux* (London: Sampson Low, Marston, 1892), pp 3–4.
11 Ibid., p. 10.
12 Ibid., pp 322, 49.
13 William Butler, *Autobiography*, pp 163, 165.
14 Gormanston, *A Little Kept*, p. 23.
15 William F. Butler, *Charles George Gordon* (London: Macmillan, 1889), p. 17.
16 John Oldcastle [Wilfrid Meynell], 'Our Living Artists: Elizabeth Butler (nee Thompson)', *The Magazine of Art* (January 1879), 262.
17 Elizabeth Butler, *Autobiography*, p. 135.
18 Ibid., p. 136.
19 Ibid., p. 138.
20 Ibid., p. 136.
21 Butler, *Red Cloud*, p. 1.
22 Ibid., p. 5.
23 Elizabeth Butler, *Autobiography*, p. 137.
24 Ibid., p. 138.
25 Ibid., p. 135.
26 'The Royal Academy', *Essex Standard*, 24 May 1879.
27 Henry Blackburn (ed.), *Academy Notes: Facsimiles of Sketches by the Artists* (London: Chatto and Windus, 1879), p. 8.
28 'The Royal Academy', *Essex Standard*, 24 May 1879.
29 Elizabeth Butler, *From Sketch-Book and Diary* (London: Burns and Oates, 1909), p. 14.
30 William Butler, 'A Plea for the Peasant', in *Far Out: Rovings Retold* (London: Isbister, 1910), p. 289.
31 Elizabeth Butler, Letter to Alice Meynell, 8 October 1877.
32 Elizabeth Butler, *Autobiography*, p. 138.
33 Elizabeth Butler, Letter to Alice Meynell, 3 July 1877.
34 Elizabeth Butler, *Autobiography*, p. 140.
35 Elizabeth Butler, Letter to Alice Meynell, n.d.
36 Quoted in Badeni, *The Slender Tree*, p. 75.
37 Elizabeth Butler, Letter to Alice Meynell, n.d.
38 Elizabeth Butler, *Autobiography*, p. 142.
39 Ibid., p. 145.
40 William Butler, *Far Out*, p. 173.
41 Alison Smith, 'Elizabeth Butler' in Alison Smith (ed.), *Artist and Empire* (London: Tate, 2015), p. 110.
42 Elizabeth Butler, *Autobiography*, p. 146.
43 'Royal Academy Exhibition', *The Graphic*, 17 May 1879.
44 Marion Spielmann, 'Pictures of the Year – I', *Magazine of Art* (January 1879), 127–8.
45 'The Exhibition of the Royal Academy (Second Notice)', *The Times*, 12 May 1879.
46 'The Tour of the Royal Academy', *Punch, or the London Charivari*, 24 May 1879, 229.
47 Elizabeth Butler, *Autobiography*, p. 122.
48 Elizabeth Butler, Letter to Alice Meynell, n.d.
49 'Exhibition of Miss Thompson's Pictures', *Huddersfield Chronicle*, 27 September 1879.
50 Quoted in McCourt, *Remember Butler*, pp 121–2.
51 Elizabeth Butler, *Autobiography*, p. 146.
52 Ibid., p. 148.
53 Ibid., p. 149.
54 Ibid., p. 150.
55 Elizabeth Butler, Letter to Alice Meynell [February 1880].
56 Elizabeth Butler, Letter to Alice Meynell, undated [March 1880].
57 Elizabeth Butler, *Autobiography*, p. 151.

58 Elizabeth Butler, Letter to Alice Meynell, undated [March 1880].
59 Letter to Alice Meynell, undated 1878.
60 Elizabeth Butler, *Autobiography*, p. 150.
61 'The Exhibition of the Royal Academy', *Birmingham Daily Post*, 30 April 1881.
62 'The Royal Academy', *Daily News*, 30 April 1881.
63 'The Royal Academy', *Glasgow Herald*, 9 June 1881.
64 *'The Defence of Rorke's Drift', The Times*, 18 March 1880.
65 'The Royal Academy: Fourth Notice' *The Times*, 27 June 1881.
66 Marion Spielmann, 'Pictures of the Year – I', *The Magazine of Art* (January 1881), 304.
67 William Butler, *Far Out*, pp 176–7.
68 Ibid., p. 243.
69 Elizabeth Butler, *Autobiography*, p. 151.
70 Usherwood and Spencer-Smith, *Lady Butler: Battle Artist*, p. 83.
71 Elizabeth Butler, *Autobiography*, p. 151.
72 Brochure, Private Collection.
73 Spielmann, 'Pictures of the Year – I', p. 304.
74 'Exhibitions', *Fun*, 20 April 1881, p. 163.
75 '*Scotland for Ever!*', *Liverpool Mercury*, 1 September 1882.
76 William Butler, *Charles Gordon* (London: Macmillan, 1889), p. 178.
77 Elizabeth Butler, *Autobiography*, p. 152.
78 John Laband, *The Transvaal Rebellion: The First Boer War, 1880–1881* (London: Routledge, 2005), p. 2.

Chatper Six: Egypt, 1882–6

1 Elizabeth Butler, *Autobiography*, p. 153.
2 W.R. Wilde, *Narrative of a Voyage to Madeira, Tenerife, and along the Shores of the Mediterranean*, vol. II (Dublin: William Curry, 1840), pp 13, 14.
3 Ibid., vol. I, pp 369, 370.
4 Edward Said, *Orientalism* (New York: Pantheon, 1978).
5 McCourt, *Remember Butler*, p. 147.
6 Ahdaf Soueif, *The Map of Love* (London: Bloomsbury, 1995), p. 229.
7 William Butler, *Autobiography*, pp 219, 220.
8 Ibid., pp 237, 240.
9 Ibid., pp 240, 241
10 William Butler, *The Campaign of the Cataracts: Being a Personal Narrative of the Great Nile Expedition of 1884–5* (London: Sampson Low, Marston, Searle & Rivington, 1887), p. 98.
11 See Florence Nightingale, *Letters from Egypt: A Journey on the Nile, 1849–50* (London: Barrie and Jenkins, 1987)
12 William Butler, *Autobiography*, pp 241–2.
13 Albert Hourani, *Europe and the Middle East* (Berkeley and Los Angeles: University of California Press, 1980), pp 101–2.
14 Hichberger, *Images of the Army*, p. 80.
15 Viola Meynell, *Francis Thompson and Wilfrid Meynell, A Memoir* (London: Hollis & Carter, 1952), p. 63.
16 Ibid., p. 75.
17 William Butler, *Autobiography*, pp 242, 243.
18 Elizabeth Butler, Letter to Alice Meynell, 28 April 1883.
19 William Butler, Letter to Alice Meynell, 3 October 1883.
20 Elizabeth Butler, Letter to Alice Meynell, 17 December 1884.
21 Wilfrid Meynell, 'The Life and Work of Lady Butler', *The Art Annual* (London, 1898), pp 14–15.
22 Elizabeth Butler, *Autobiography*, pp 153–4.
23 Charles Rathbone, *General Lord Wolseley (of Cairo), A Memoir*, 2nd ed. (London: Richard Bentley, 1883), pp 474–5.
24 Elizabeth Butler, *Autobiography*, p. 154.
25 Ibid.
26 George Arthur (ed.), *The Letters of Lord and Lady Wolseley, 1870–1911* (London: Heinemann, 1922), p. 268.
27 Viscount Wolseley, *The Story of a Soldier's Life*, vol. 2 (London: Constable, 1903), pp 202, 323.
28 'Our Royal Academy Guide – Or Guy'D', *Punch*, 9 May 1885.
29 Henry Blackburn (ed.), *Academy Notes 1885: Facsimiles of Sketches by the Artists* (London: Chatto & Windus, 1885), p. 15.
30 Elizabeth Butler, Letter to Wilfrid Meynell, 17 June 1885.
31 R. Caton Woodville, *Random Recollections* (London: Eveleigh Nash, 1914), p. 53.

32 Ibid., p. 61.
33 Ibid., p. 62.
34 Elizabeth Butler, *Autobiography*, p. 154.
35 'The Royal Academy: Fifth Notice', *The Athenaeum*, 20 June 1885.
36 [Alice Meynell], 'Reviews and Views', *Merry England*, 4:24 (April 1885), 427–8.
37 Claude Phillips, 'The Royal Academy', *The Academy, 1869–1902*, 16 May 1885, 354.
38 Ibid.
39 Hichberger, *Images of the Army*, p. 82.
40 William Butler, *Charles Gordon*, p. 192.
41 Ibid., pp 192–3.
42 Ibid., p. 193.
43 Michael Asher, *Khartoum: The Ultimate Imperial Adventure* (London: Penguin, 2005), p. 1.
44 Ibid., p. 96.
45 Butler, *Charles Gordon*, p. 96.
46 Butler, *Campaign of the Cataracts*, p. 75.
47 Ibid., p. 148.
48 Ibid., pp 169–70.
49 Ibid., p. 189.
50 Ibid., pp 195–6.
51 Ibid., pp 197–8.
52 Quoted in McCourt, *Remember Butler*, p. 170.
53 Asher, *Khartoum*, p. 169.
54 Quoted in McCourt, *Remember Butler*, p. 171.
55 Butler, *Cataracts*, p. 342.
56 Ibid., pp 342–3.
57 Elizabeth Butler, Letter to Alice Meynell, 21 February 1885.
58 Butler, *Charles Gordon*, p. 252.
59 Ibid., p. 368.
60 Elizabeth Butler, Letter to Christiana Thompson, 12 July 1885.
61 Elizabeth Butler, Letter to Christiana Thompson, 7 August 1885.
62 Elizabeth Butler, Letter to Christiana Thompson, 30 November 1885.
63 Elizabeth Butler, Letter to Christiana Thompson, New Year's Eve, 1885.
64 Elizabeth Butler, Letter to Christiana Thompson, 12 December 1885.
65 Elizabeth Butler, Letter to Christiana Thompson, 22 December 1885.
66 The painting, *Mrs Mortimer Collier and Family*, can be seen at Plymouth Museum and Art Gallery, UK.
67 Elizabeth Butler, Letter to Christiana Thompson, 22 December 1885.
68 Elizabeth Butler, Letter to Christiana Thompson, 24 December 1885.
69 Ibid.
70 Elizabeth Butler, Letter to Christiana Thompson, 31 December 1885.
71 Elizabeth Butler, Letter to Christiana Thompson, 5 January 1886.
72 Elizabeth Butler, Letter to Christiana Thompson, 9 January 1886.
73 Elizabeth Butler, Letter to Christiana Thompson, 12 January 1886.
74 Elizabeth Butler, Letter to Christiana Thompson, 13 January 1886.
75 Elizabeth Butler, Letter to Christiana Thompson, 21 January 1886.
76 Elizabeth Butler, Letter to Christiana Thompson, 23 January 1886.
77 Elizabeth Butler, Letter to Christiana Thompson, 13 February 1886.
78 Elizabeth Butler, *Autobiography*, p. 157.
79 'Impressions of the Academy', *Lloyd's Illustrated Newspaper*, 8 May 1887.
80 Elizabeth Butler, Letter to Christiana Thompson, 12 January 1886.

Chapter Seven: Dinan, Delgany and Alexandria, 1887–93

1 Elizabeth Butler, Letter to Alice Meynell, n.d. [1887].
2 Quoted in Ryan, *William Francis Butler*, p. 190.
3 Elizabeth Butler, Letter to Alice Meynell, 14 November 1887.
4 Elizabeth Butler, Letter to Alice Meynell, 20 November, n.y.
5 Elizabeth Butler, Letter to Alice Meynell, 30 June, n.y.
6 Anne Jordan, *Love Well the Hour: The Life of Lady Colin Campbell* (Leicester: Troubador, 2010), p. 52.
7 Ibid., p. 61.
8 'Lady Colin Campbell', *Merry England*, 4:20 (December 1884).

9 Ryan, *William Francis Butler*, p. 137.
10 Ibid., 139.
11 Ibid., 149.
12 Jordan, *Love Well the Hour*, 127.
13 Ibid., p. 129.
14 Ibid.
15 William Butler, Letter to Wilfrid Meynell, 2 November 1886.
16 William Butler, Letter to Wilfrid Meynell, 21 December 1886.
17 Quoted in Jordan, *Love Well the Hour*, p. 129.
18 Elizabeth Butler, Letter to Alice Meynell, 23 October 1886.
19 Elizabeth Butler, Letter to Alice Meynell, 23 January 1887.
20 Ibid.
21 Elizabeth Butler, Letter to Alice Meynell, 28 February 1887.
22 Elizabeth Butler, Letter to Alice Meynell, 26 July 1887.
23 Elizabeth Butler, Letter to Alice Meynell, 27 August 1887.
24 Alice Meynell, 'Views and Reviews', *Merry England*, 13:74 (June 1889), 141.
25 Spencer-Smith and Usherwood, *Lady Butler: Battle Artist*, p. 92.
26 Gormanston, *A Little Kept*, p. 55.
27 Elizabeth Butler, Letter to Alice Meynell, 19 March 1889.
28 Elizabeth Butler, Letter to Alice Meynell, 20 April 1888.
29 Butler, 'Parnell' in *The Light of the West* (London: Methuen, 1909), pp 58–9.
30 William Butler, Letter to Wilfrid Meynell, 10 June 1893.
31 William Butler, *The Light of the West*, p. 54.
32 Elizabeth Butler, Letter to Alice Meynell, 29 August 1889.
33 Elizabeth Butler, *Autobiography*, p. 158.
34 Elizabeth Butler, Letter to Alice Meynell, 29 August 1889.
35 Gormanston, *A Little Kept*, p. 59.
36 Alice Meynell, 'Pictures', *Merry England*, 15:85 (May 1890), 70.
37 Elizabeth Butler, *Autobiography*, p. 157.
38 'The Royal Academy: Third Notice', *Saturday Review*, 17 May 1890.
39 Claude Phillips, 'Fine Art: The Royal Academy', *The Academy*, 24 May 1890, p. 361.
40 'The Royal Academy: Second Notice', *The Athenaeum*, 17 May 1890, p. 646.
41 Elizabeth Butler, Letter to Olivia Sowerby, 18 March 1929.
42 Elizabeth Butler, *Sketch-Book*, pp 77–8.
43 Elizabeth Butler, Letter to Wilfrid Meynell, 12 March 1890.
44 Elizabeth Butler, *Sketch-Book*, p. 79.
45 Ibid., pp 81–2.
46 Ibid., p. 96.
47 Elizabeth Butler, *Autobiography*, p. 156.
48 Ibid., p. 157.
49 Nightingale, *Letters from Egypt*, p. 208. Lady Mary Wortley Montagu, *Turkish Embassy Letters* (London: Virago, 2004), p. 58.
50 Elizabeth Butler, *Sketch-Book*, opposite page 81.
51 Ibid., p. 88.
52 Elizabeth Thompson, Letter to Alice Meynell, 21 January 1891.
53 Elizabeth Butler, *Letters from the Holy Land* (London: Adam & Charles Black, 1903), p. viii.
54 Ibid., p. 29.
55 Ibid., p. 30.
56 Ibid., p. 31.
57 E.M.C. 'Letters from the Holy Land', *The Dublin Review* (July 1903).
58 'Palestine in the Spring', *The Speaker* (April 1903).
59 Elizabeth Butler, Letter to Christiana Thompson, 5 June 1891.
60 Elizabeth Butler, *Autobiography*, p. 178.
61 Elizabeth Butler, Letter to Christiana Thompson, 22 June 1891.
62 Elizabeth Butler, Letter to Christiana Thompson, 7 October 1891.
63 Elizabeth Butler, *Autobiography*, p. 179.
64 Elizabeth Butler, Letter to Christiana Thompson, 15 June 1892.
65 Elizabeth Butler, *Autobiography*, pp 180, 181.
66 Elizabeth Butler, Letter to Christiana Thompson, 21 January 1891.

67 Elizabeth Butler, *Autobiography*, p. 181.
68 Ibid., p. 183.
69 Ibid.
70 Ibid., pp 183–4.
71 Francis Phillimore, 'A Group of Painters', *Merry England*, 21:119 (June 1893), 135–6.
72 'Sketches of Life and Character in Egypt', *The Graphic*, 9 February 1889.
73 Elizabeth Butler, p. 185.

Chapter Eight: Aldershot, Dover, Cape Town, Devonport and Bansha, 1893–1909

1 Beryl Bainbridge, '*The Remnants of an Army* (1879) by Elizabeth Thompson (Lady Butler)' in Judith Collins and Elsbeth Lindner (eds), *Writing on the Wall: Women Writers on Women Artists* (London: Weidenfeld & Nicolson, 1993), p. 2.
2 Ibid., p. 4.
3 Elizabeth Butler, *Autobiography*, p. 184.
4 Elizabeth Butler, Letter to Christiana Thompson, n.d. Unless otherwise stated, all letters are from the Meynell Archive.
5 *Bram Stoker, Personal Reminiscences of Henry Irving*, vol. 1 (London: William Heinemann, 1906), p. 249.
6 Ibid., p. 251.
7 Hichberger, *Images of the Army*, p. 83.
8 Usherwood and Spencer-Smith, *Lady Butler: Battle Artist*, p. 107.
9 M.K. O'Byrne, 'Lady Butler: The Painter of the "*Roll Call*"', *The Irish Monthly*, 78 (December 1950), 592.
10 Henry Blackburn, (ed.), *The Academy Notes 1895 with Illustrations of the Principal Pictures at Burlington House* (London: Chatto & Windus, 1895), p. 23.
11 Parker Hagarty, 'Pictures at the Royal Academy', *Western Mail*, 27 May 1895.
12 Elizabeth Butler, *Autobiography*, p. 186.
13 Ibid., p. 187.
14 Ibid., p. 189.
15 Ibid., p. 194.
16 Ibid., p. 195.
17 Ibid., p. 196.
18 Ibid., p. 205.
19 Ibid.
20 Ibid., p. 206.
21 For an account of drummers, see John Norris, *Marching to the Drums: A History of Military Drums and Drummers* (London: History Press, 2012). Elizabeth's painting is the jacket image of this book.
22 Elizabeth Butler, *Autobiography*, p. 206.
23 Gormanston, *A Little Kept*, p. 55.
24 Elizabeth Butler, *Autobiography*, p. 206.
25 Wilfrid Meynell, 'The Life and Work of Lady Butler', p. 17.
26 Elizabeth Butler, Letter to Alice Meynell, 21 March 1897.
27 'The Royal Academy: Second Notice', *Liverpool Mercury*, 4 May 1897.
28 Marion Spielmann, 'The Exhibition of the Royal Academy. II', *The Magazine of Art*, January 1897, p. 157.
29 'The Royal Academy, Third Notice', *The Athenaeum*, 5 June 1897, p. 752.
30 Elizabeth Butler, Letter to Christiana Thompson, 15 July 1897.
31 Elizabeth Butler, Letter to Alice Meynell, 14 December 1897.
32 Butler, *Autobiography*, p. 212.
33 Ibid., p. 213.
34 Ibid., p. 215.
35 Wilfrid Scawen Blunt, *My Diaries: Being a Personal Narrative of Events, 1888–1914*, Part 1 [1888–1900] (New York: Alfred Knopf, 1922), p. 311.
36 Soueif, *The Map of Love*, p. 31.
37 Viola Meynell, *Francis Thompson and Wilfrid Meynell*, p. 76.
38 Winston Spencer Churchill, *The River War: An Historical Account of the Reconquest of the Sudan*, vol. 2, ed. Col. F. Rhodes (London: Longmans, Green), p. 393.
39 Quoted in Spencer and Usherwood, *Lady Butler: Battle Artist*, p. 112.
40 Elizbeth Butler, *Autobiography*, p. 214.
41 Wilfrid Meynell, 'Lady Butler: Her Life and Work', *Art Annual*, p. 22.
42 Ibid., p. 27.
43 Meynell, 'Lady Butler', pp 22–3.

44 Ibid., p. 23.
45 Ibid.
46 Ibid., p. 31.
47 Elizabeth Butler, Letter to Christiana Thompson, 16 November 1898.
48 Elizabeth Butler, Letter to Christiana Thompson, 15 December 1898.
49 'The Antiquary among the Pictures', *The Antiquary*, June 1899: 170.
50 'The Academy, the New Gallery and the Guildhall', *Fortnightly Review*, July 1899: 103.
51 'The Woman's Century: How feminine influence has effected the golden age', *Daily Mail*, 31 December 1900.
52 'Women in the Queen's Reign', *Daily Mail Queen Victoria's Diamond Jubilee Extra*, 23 June 1897.
53 'Chat about Books', *Daily Mail*, 21 August 1896.
54 Quoted in Badeni, *The Slender Tree*, p. 138.
55 Desmond Bowen and Jean Bowen, *Heroic Option: The Irish in the British Army* (Barnsley, Yorkshire: Pen & Sword, 2005), p. 259.
56 William Butler, *Autobiography*, p. 392.
57 Ibid., p. 385.
58 Ibid., p. 387.
59 Ryan, *William Francis Butler*, p. 172.
60 William Butler, *Autobiography*, p. 392.
61 Ibid., p. 398.
62 Ryan, *William Francis Butler*, pp 174–5
63 Quoted in Ryan, *William Francis Butler*, p. 175.
64 'Sir W. Butler and the Boers: Commander-in-Chief's Transvaal Sympathies', *Daily Mail*, 7 July 1899.
65 Quoted in McCourt, *Remember Butler*, p. 225.
66 Ibid., p. 226.
67 Quoted in Thomas Pakenham, *The Boer War* (London: Abacus, 1991), p. 79.
68 'General Butler's Recall', *Daily Mail*, 16 August 1899.
69 Elizabeth Butler, *Sketch-Book*, p. 93.
70 Ibid., pp 94, 96.
71 Ibid., p. 99.
72 Ibid., pp 100–1.
73 Ibid., p. 102.
74 Ibid., p. 105.
75 Ibid., p. 108.
76 Ibid., pp 108–9.
77 Ibid., p. 109.
78 Ibid.
79 Ibid., p. 111.
80 Ibid., p. 112.
81 Ibid., p. 116.
82 Ibid., p. 113.
83 Elizabeth Butler, *Autobiography*, pp 217, 218.
84 Butler, *Sketch-Book*, p. 119.
85 Ibid., p. 120.
86 Ibid., pp 102–3.
87 'Partly, though not Wholly, Responsible', *Daily Mail*, 6 November 1899.
88 'Sir William Butler', *The Speaker*, 6 January 1900.
89 Eileen Butler, Afterword, in William Butler, *Autobiography*, p. 456.
90 Elizabeth Butler, *Autobiography*, p. 218.
91 Ibid., p. 219.
92 Elizabeth Butler, Letter to Christiana Thompson, 23 March 1900.
93 Elizabeth Butler, Letter to Christiana Thompson, 4 April 1900.
94 Ibid.
95 Quoted in Ryan, *William Francis Butler*, p. 193.
96 Elizabeth Butler, *Autobiography*, p. 226.
97 Elizabeth Butler, Letter to Christiana Thompson, 5 September 1901.
98 Elizabeth Butler, Letter to Alice Meynell, 5 September 1901.
99 Elizabeth Butler, Letter to Christiana Thompson, 24 October 1901.
100 Elizabeth Butler, Letter to Christiana Thompson, 12 December 1901.
101 Elizabeth Butler, Letter to Christiana Thompson, 29 March 1902.

102 Elizabeth Butler, *Autobiography*, p. 230.
103 Gormanston, *A Little Kept*, p. 20.
104 Paula Krebs, *Gender, Race and the Writing of Empire: Public Discourse and the Boer War* (Cambridge: Cambridge University Press, 1999), p. 5
105 Elizabeth Butler, Letter to Alice Meynell, 22 August 1902.
106 Butler, *Autobiography*, p. 235.
107 Ibid., pp 104–5.
108 'Probate, Divorce and Admiralty Division', *The Times*, 21 March 1902.
109 Elizabeth Butler, Letter to Alice Meynell, 20 July 1902.
110 Elizabeth Butler, Letter to Alice Meynell, 25 January 1903.
111 Elizabeth (Coos) Butler, Letter to Wilfrid Meynell, 28 December 1902.
112 Randolph Kingscote, Letter to Wilfrid Meynell, 5 February 1903.
113 Elizabeth Butler, Letter to Alice Meynell, 24 June 1903.
114 Elizabeth (Coos) Butler, Letter to Wilfrid Meynell, 25 June 1903.
115 Elizabeth Butler, Letter to Alice Meynell, 20 July 1902.
116 Elizabeth Butler, Letter to Wilfrid Meynell, 17 February 1903.
117 Elizabeth Butler, *Autobiography*, p. 219.
118 Gormanston, *A Little Kept*, p. 53.
119 Elizabeth Butler, *Autobiography*, p. 234.
120 Ibid., p. 236.
121 Ibid., p. 238.
122 'The Royal Academy', *Art Journal*, June 1903: 175.
123 Elizabeth Butler, Letter to Alice Meynell, 26 March 1903.
124 Elizabeth Butler, Letter to Wilfrid Meynell, 2 April 1903.
125 Elizabeth Butler, Letter to Christiana Thompson, 5 April 1903.
126 Elizabeth Butler, Letter to Alice Meynell, 12 January 1905.
127 Elizabeth Butler, Letter to Christiana Thompson, 20 April 1905.
128 Ibid.
129 Ibid.
130 Elizabeth Butler to Christiana Thompson, 17 March 1905.
131 Butler, *Sketch-Book*, p. 15.
132 Ibid., p. 17.
133 Ibid., p. 19.
134 Ibid., p. 20.
135 Ibid., p. 21.
136 The hotel they stayed in was constructed by Midland Great Western Railways in 1897 to cater for tourists to this picturesque area. It is now the Mulranny Park Hotel. Elizabeth Butler, Letter to Christiana Thompson, 21 May 1905.
137 Elizabeth Butler, Letter to Christiana Thompson, 13 June 1905.
138 Elizabeth Butler, Letter to Christiana Thompson, 5 February 1905.
139 Elizabeth Butler, Letter to Christiana Thompson, 17 March 1905.
140 Elizabeth Butler, Letter to Alice Meynell, December 1905.
141 Elizabeth Butler, Letter to Christiana Thompson, April 1906.
142 Elizabeth Butler, Letter to Christiana Thompson, 30 June 1906.
143 Elizabeth Butler, Letter to Christiana Thompson, 12 October 1905.
144 Elizabeth Butler, Letter to Christiana Thompson, 9 December 1907.
145 Elizabeth Butler, Letter to Christiana Thompson, 17 December 1907.
146 Elizabeth Butler, Letter to Christiana Thompson, 22 February 1908.
147 Elizabeth Butler, Letter to Christiana Thompson, 30 March 1908.
148 Elizabeth Butler, Letter to Christiana Thompson, 8 May 1908.
149 Elizabeth Butler, *Autobiography*, p. 242.
150 Elizabeth Butler, Letter to Christiana Thompson, 14 July 1905.
151 Elizabeth Butler, Letter to Wilfrid Meynell, 8 September 1908.
152 Elizabeth Butler, Letter to Christiana Thompson, 12 May 1907.
153 Elizabeth Butler, Letter to Alice Meynell, 15 July 1907.
154 Elizabeth Butler, Letter to Christiana Thompson, 25 May 1907.
155 Butler, *Autobiography*, p. 244.
156 Elizabeth Butler, Letter to Christiana Thompson, 15 August 1908.
157 Elizabeth Butler, Letter to Christiana Thompson, 3 November 1908.

158 Elizabeth Butler, Letter to Christiana Thompson, 23 September 1909.
159 'From Sketch-Book to Diary', *The Athenaeum*, 15 January 1910: 64.
160 Elizabeth Butler, Letter to Christiana Thompson, 7 January 1909. It is also well hung today at Ferens Art Gallery in Hull.
161 Elizabeth Butler, Letter to Christiana Thompson, 22 January 1909.

Chapter Nine: Wars and beyond: the Irish years, 1909–33

1 Patrick Butler, *A Galloper at Ypres and Some Subsequent Adventures* (London: T. Fisher Unwin, 1920), pp 9–10.
2 Ibid., p. 18.
3 Ibid., pp 18–19.
4 Ibid., pp 20–1.
5 Elizabeth Butler, Letter to Christiana Thompson, 26 September 1909.
6 Elizabeth Butler, Letter to Christiana Thompson, 10 March 1910.
7 Quoted in Badeni, *The Slender Tree*, p. 199.
8 Wilfrid Meynell, 'Sir William Butler', *The Tablet*, 11 June 1910, p. 921.
9 'Two Great Men', Newspaper cutting, Meynell Archive.
10 Gormanston, *A Little Kept*, pp 33, 20.
11 Ibid., p. 36.
12 Eileen Butler, Letter to Wilfrid Meynell, 16 June 1910.
13 Eileen Butler, Letter to Wilfrid Meynell, 23 September 1910.
14 W.L. Courtney, 'Sir William Butler's Autobiography', *The Telegraph*, 2 March 1911 [press cutting].
15 'How the Boer War was Made', *The Star*, 2 March 1911 [press cutting].
16 'Prophet and Soldier: General Butler's Autobiography', *The Daily News*, 2 March 1911 [press cutting].
17 Quoted in 'A Soldier and a Man', *Evening Standard and St James's Gazette*, 2 March 1911.
18 Elizabeth Butler, *Autobiography*, p. 146.
19 Ibid., p. 251.
20 Ibid., p. 251.
21 Elizabeth Butler, Letter to Alice Meynell, 18 June 1912.
22 Elizabeth Butler, Letter to Alice Meynell, 26 December 1913.
23 Elizabeth Butler, *Autobiography*, pp 252–3.
24 Ibid., p. 253.
25 Ibid., p. 254.
26 Butler, *A Galloper at Ypres*, p. 24.
27 Elizabeth Butler, *Autobiography*, p. 257.
28 Ibid., p. 256.
29 Elizabeth Butler, Letter to Alice Meynell, 28 September 1914.
30 Dick Butler, Letter to Elizabeth Butler, 2 March 1914. Downside Abbey Archive.
31 Patrick Butler, Letter to Wilfrid Meynell, 1 October 1914.
32 Patrick Butler, Letter to Alice Meynell, 14 November 1914.
33 Elizabeth Butler, Letter to Alice Meynell, 28 December 1914.
34 Alice Meynell, 'Summer in England, 1914', in *Poems* (London: Burns, Oates and Washbourne, 1921), p. 123.
35 Elizabeth Butler, Letter to Alice Meynell, 20 February 1915.
36 George Robb, *British Culture and the First World War* (Basingstoke: Palgrave Macmillan, 2002), p. 137.
37 James Fox, *British Art and the First World War, 1914–1924* (Cambridge: Cambridge University Press, 2015), p. 102.
38 Ibid.
39 Elizabeth Butler, Letter to Alice Meynell, 8 May 1915.
40 Elizabeth Butler, Letter to Wilfrid Meynell, 10 May 1915
41 Elizabeth Butler, Letter to Alice Meynell, 10 July 1915.
42 Elizabeth Butler, Letter to Alice Meynell, 10 July 1915.
43 Elizabeth Butler, Letter to Alice Meynell, 26 August 1915.
44 Elizabeth Butler, Letter to Alice Meynell, 22 December 1915.
45 'Ladies Page', *Illustrated London News*, 12 June 1915. Although Elizabeth supported female suffrage, no mention is made of this in her autobiography.
46 Quoted in Badeni, *The Slender Tree*, p. 210.
47 *The Waterloo Centenary – The End – Wellington*, *Illustrated London News*, 12 June 1915.
48 See Elizabeth Butler, *Autobiography*, p. 332.
49 'Art and Artists: The Leicester Galleries', *The Observer*, 30 May 1915.
50 Elizabeth Butler, *Autobiography*, p. 298.

51 Ibid., p. 258.
52 Iain Adams, '"Over the Top": Images of the Football Charges of the Great War', *Journal of Sport History*, 43:2 (Summer 2016), 192.
53 Ibid., 195.
54 Ibid., 200.
55 Ibid.
56 Elizabeth Butler, Letter to Wilfrid Meynell, 17 March 1916.
57 David M. Lubin, *Grand Illusions: America Art and the First World War* (Oxford: Oxford University Press, 2016), p. 152.
58 www.dorsetcountymuseum.org/dorset_yeomanry.
59 Elizabeth Butler, Letter to Alice Meynell, 24 June 1916.
60 Elizabeth Butler, Letter to Wilfrid Meynell, 25 January 1917.
61 Elizabeth Butler, Letter to Alice Meynell, 30 April 1917.
62 Elizabeth Butler, Letter to Alice Meynell, 20 April 1916.
63 Elizabeth Butler, Letter to Alice Meynell, 24 June 1916.
64 Elizabeth Butler, Letter to Alice Meynell, 21 November 1916.
65 Elizabeth Butler, Letter to Alice Meynell, 7 February 1917.
66 Quoted in Badeni, *The Slender Tree*, p. 235.
67 Elizabeth Butler, Letter to Dick Butler, 4 March 1916. Downside Abbey Archive.
68 Elizabeth Butler, Letter to Alice Meynell, 17 March 1918. Downside Abbey Archive.
69 Dick Butler, Letter to Elizabeth Butler, 7 July 1916. Downside Abbey Archive.
70 Quoted in Elizabeth Butler, Letter to Alice Meynell, 12 March 1916. Currency Converter: The National Archives. http://www.nationalarchives.gov.uk/currency-converter/#currency-result. Art prices had generally collapsed during the war.
71 Elizabeth Butler, Letter to Wilfrid Meynell, 16 June 1917.
72 Paul Fussell, *The Great War and Modern Memory* (Oxford: Oxford University Press, 2013), pp 132–3.
73 Dick Butler, Letter to Elizabeth Butler, 28 July 1917. Downside Abbey Archive.
74 Dick Butler, Letter to Elizabeth Butler, 15 October 1917. Downside Abbey Archive.
75 Dick Butler, Letter to Elizabeth Butler, 31 July 1917. Downside Abbey Archive.
76 Ibid.
77 Dick Butler, Letter to Elizabeth Butler, 28 July 1917. Downside Abbey Archive.
78 Dick Butler, Letter to Elizabeth Butler, 6 December 1917. Downside Abbey Archive.
79 Dick Butler, Letter to Eileen Gormanston, 20 December 1917. Downside Abbey Archive.
80 Dick Butler, Letter to Elizabeth Butler, 30 April 1916. Downside Abbey Archive.
81 Catherine Wynne, *The Colonial Conan Doyle: British Imperialism, Irish Nationalism and the Gothic* (Westport, CT: Greenwood Press, 2002), pp 112–15.
82 Dick Butler, Letter to Elizabeth Butler, 29 April 1918. Downside Abbey Archive.
83 Dick Butler, Letter to Elizabeth Butler, 10 March 1918. Downside Abbey Archive.
84 Dick Butler, Letter to Eileen Gormanston, 16 December 1918. Downside Abbey Archive.
85 Elizabeth Butler, Letter to Alice Meynell, 17 March 1918.
86 Butler, *Autobiography*, p. 261.
87 Ibid., p. 262.
88 Butler, *Autobiography*, p. 261.
89 'Battle of Vimy Ridge', Canadian War Museum. www.warmuseum.ca/the-battle-of-vimy-ridge.
90 Elizabeth Butler, Letter to Wilfrid Meynell, 24 February 1919.
91 Elizabeth Butler, Letter to Wilfrid Meynell, 25 April 1920.
92 Elizabeth Butler, Letter to Alice Meynell, 6 February 1921.
93 Elizabeth Butler, Letter to Alice Meynell, 10 May 1921.
94 Elizabeth Butler, Letter to Wilfrid Meynell, 19 May 1921.
95 Elizabeth Butler, Letter to Alice Meynell, 30 June 1921.
96 Elizabeth Butler, Letter to Alice Meynell, 26 September 1921.
97 Elizabeth Butler, Letter to Manchester Art Gallery, 4 August 1921.
98 Curator, Manchester Art Gallery, Letter to Elizabeth Butler, 9 August 1921.
99 Elizabeth Butler, Letter to Wilfrid Meynell, 2 August 1921.
100 Elizabeth Butler, Letter to Wilfrid Meynell, 4 January 1922.
101 Elizabeth Butler, Letter to Wilfrid Meynell, 27 January 1922.
102 Elizabeth Butler, Letter to Wilfrid Meynell, 9 April 1922.
103 Elizabeth Butler, Letter to Alice Meynell, 6 June 1922.
104 Elizabeth Butler, Letter to Alice Meynell, 13 August 1922.

105 Alice Meynell, Letter to Elizabeth Butler, 27 September 1922.
106 Elizabeth Butler, Letter to Alice Meynell, 3 October 1922.
107 Elizabeth Butler, Letter to Alice Meynell, 4 October 1922.
108 'Lady Butler's Pictures: Son's Dash to Save Them', *Daily Mail*, 28 October 1922.
109 Ibid.
110 Elizabeth Butler, Letter to Olivia Sowerby, 14 November 1922.
111 Elizabeth Butler, Letter to Wilfrid Meynell, 27 November 1922.
112 Elizabeth Butler, Letter to Wilfrid Meynell, 4 December 1922.
113 Elizabeth Butler, Letter to Wilfrid Meynell, 5 December 1922.
114 Elizabeth Butler Letter to Wilfrid Meynell, 23 December 1922.
115 Elizabeth Butler, Letter to Wilfrid Meynell, 26 January 1923.
116 Elizabeth Butler, Letter to Wilfrid Meynell, 30 January 1923.
117 Elizabeth Butler, Letter to Wilfrid Meynell, 1 June 1923.
118 O'Byrne, 'Lady Butler: The Painter of the "*Roll Call*"', p. 592.
119 Gormanston, *A Little Kept*, pp 60–1.
120 Elizabeth Butler, Letter to Wilfrid Meynell, 17 February 1924. This is the equivalent of around £12,320 in today's currency. Currency Converter: 1270–2017: The National Archives. ttp://www.nationalarchives.gov.uk/currency-converter/#currency-result
121 Elizabeth Butler, Letter to Richard Butler, 1 March 1932.
122 Elizabeth Butler, Letter to Richard Butler, 12 March 1931.
123 Elizabeth Butler, Letter to Wilfrid Meynell, 1 January 1928.
124 Elizabeth (Coos) Kingscote, Letter to Wilfrid Meynell, 1 October 1933.
125 Patrick Butler, Letter to Wilfrid Meynell, 5 October 1933.
126 Elizabeth Butler, *Sketch-Book*, pp 73–4.
127 Colonel M. Browne, Letter to Richard Butler, 15 September 1954. Manchester Art Gallery.
128 Wilfrid Meynell, 'Lady Butler's Autobiography', *The Observer*, 28 January 1923.
129 John Oldcastle [Wilfrid Meynell], 'Our Living Artists', *Magazine of Art*, p. 258.
130 Alice Meynell, 'A Father of Women', *Collected Poems*, pp 118–19.

Bibliography

LETTERS AND JOURNALS

Collections of Letters and Journals

Letters of Elizabeth Butler, Meynell Archive, Greatham, West Sussex.
Letters of William Butler, Meynell Archive, Greatham.
Letters of Eileen Butler (Gormanston), Meynell Archive, Greatham.
Letters of Elizabeth (Coos) Kingscote, Meynell Archive, Greatham.
Letters of Thomas Thompson, Meynell Archive, Greatham.
Letters of Alice Meynell, Meynell Archive, Greatham.
Journals of Christiana Thompson, Meynell Archive, Greatham.
Elizabeth Thompson, Journal fragment, Gormanston Archive, London.
Letter of Christiana Thompson to Fanny Edelmann, Gormanston Archive, London.
Letters of Richard Butler, Downside Abbey, Somerset.
Letters of Patrick Butler, Downside Abbey, Somerset.

Individual Letters

Butler, Elizabeth, Letter to Manchester Art Gallery, 4 August 1921. Manchester Art Gallery.
Browne, Colonel M., Letter to Richard Butler, 15 September 1954. Downside Abbey, Somerset.
Curator, Manchester Art Gallery, Letter to Elizabeth Butler, 9 August 1921.
Leighton, Frederic, Letter to the President and Council of the Royal Academy, 13 May 1874. Royal Academy of Arts Archive, London.

PRINTED AND ELECTRONIC SOURCES

'Academy Banquet', *The Times*, 2 May 1874. *Times Digital Archive*. www.galegroup.com. Accessed 1 July 2013.
'The Academy, the New Gallery and the Guildhall', *Fortnightly Review*, July 1899, pp 101–12.
Adams, Iain, '"Over the Top": Images of the Football Charges of the Great War', *Journal of Sport History*, 43:2 (Summer 2016), 192–211.
'The Antiquary among the Pictures', *The Antiquary* (June 1899), 169–74.
'Art and Artists: The Leicester Galleries', *The Observer*, 30 May 1915. *The Guardian and The Observer Archive*. www.proquest.com. Accessed 10 January 2017.
Arthur, George (ed.), *The Letters of Lord and Lady Wolseley, 1870–1911* (London: Heinemann, 1922).
Asher, Michael, *Khartoum: The Ultimate Imperial Adventure* (London: Penguin, 2005).
Austen, Jane, *Emma,* ed. James Kinsley (Oxford: Oxford World Classics, 2008).
Badeni, June, *The Slender Tree: A Life of Alice Meynell* (Padstow, Tabb House, 1981).

Bainbridge, Beryl, '*The Remnants of an Army* (1879) by Elizabeth Thompson (Lady Butler)' in Judith Collins and Elsbeth Lindner (eds), *Writing on the Wall: Women Writers on Women Artists* (London: Weidenfeld & Nicolson, 1993), pp 1–4.

Baldry, A.L., 'The Royal Academy Exhibition of 1903', *Art Journal* (June 1903), 161–82. *British Periodicals*. www.proquest.com. Accessed 20 June 2016.

Barrett Browning, Elizabeth, *Letters of Mrs Browning*, vol. 2, ed. Frederic G. Kenyon (London: Smith, Elder, 1897).

'The Battle of Vimy Ridge', Canadian War Museum/Musée Canadien de la Guerre. www.warmuseum.ca/the-battle-of-vimy-ridge/

Baumgart, Winfried, *The Crimean War, 1853–1856* (London: Arnold, 1999).

Blackburn, Henry (ed.), *Academy Notes: Facsimiles of Sketches by the Artists* (London: Chatto and Windus, 1879).

— *Academy Notes 1885: Facsimiles of Sketches by the Artists* (London: Chatto & Windus, 1885).

— *The Academy Notes 1895 with Illustrations of the Principal Pictures at Burlington House* (London: Chatto & Windus, 1895).

Blunt, Wilfrid Scawen, *My Diaries: Being a Personal Narrative of Events 1888–1914*, Part 1 [1888–1900] (New York: Alfred Knopf, 1922).

Bodenheimer, Rosemarie, 'Dickens Fascinated', *Victorian Studies*, 48:2 (Winter 2006), 268–76.

Bowen, Claire, 'Lady Butler: The Reinvention of Military History', *La Revue LISA*, 1:1 (2003), 127–37. www.unicaen.fr/mrsh/anglais/lisa. Accessed 20 April 2011.

Bowen, Desmond and Jean Bowen, *Heroic Option: The Irish in the British Army* (Barnsley, Yorkshire: Pen & Sword, 2005).

'Boz in Liverpool', *Preston Guardian*, 2 March 1844. *19th Century British Newspapers*. www.galegroup.com. Accessed 12 May 2013.

Brighton, Terry, *Hell Riders: The Truth about the Charge of the Light Brigade* (London: Penguin, 2004).

Brontë, Anne, *The Tenant of Wildfell Hall*, ed. Herbert Rosengarten (Oxford: Oxford World Classics, 2008).

Butler, Elizabeth, *Autobiography* (Seven Oaks, Kent: Fisher, 1993).

— *From Sketch-Book and Diary* (London: Burns and Oates, 1909).

— *Letters from the Holy Land* (London: Adam and Charles Black, 1903).

Butler, Patrick, *A Galloper at Ypres and Some Subsequent Adventures* (London: T. Fisher Unwin, 1920).

Butler, William, *The Campaign of the Cataracts: Being a Personal Narrative of the Great Nile Expedition of 1884–5* (London: Sampson Low, Marston, Searle & Rivington, 1887).

— *Charles George Gordon* (London: Macmillan, 1889).

— *Far Out: Rovings Retold* (London: Isbister, 1910).

— *The Light of the West* (London: Methuen, 1909).

— *Red Cloud: The Story of a Solitary Sioux* (London: Sampson Low, Marston, 1892).

— *Sir William Butler: An Autobiography* (London: Constable, 1911).

— *The Wild North Land: Being the Story of a Winter Journey, with Dogs, Across Northern America* (London: Sampson Low, Marston, Low, & Searle, 1874).

Buzard, James, *The Beaten Track: European Tourism, Literature, and the Ways to Culture, 1800–1918* (Oxford: Oxford University Press, 1993).

Canziani, Estella, *Round About Three Palace Green* (London: Methuen, 1939).

Cardoso, Denis Rafael, 'Drawing or Design? The development of the National Art Training School' in Christopher Frayling and Clare Catterall (eds), *Design of the Times: One Hundred Years of the Royal College of Art* (Shepton Beauchamp: Richard Dennis/Royal College of Art, 1995), pp 20–4.

Caton Woodville R., *Random Recollections* (London: Eveleigh Nash, 1914).

'C. Dickens, Esq., (Boz) in Liverpool', *Liverpool Mercury*, 1 March 1844. *19th Century British Newspapers*. www.galegroup.com. Accessed 12 May 2013.

Chalmers, F. Graeme, *Women in the Nineteenth-Century Art World: Schools of Art and Design for Women in London and Philadelphia* (Westport, CT: Greenwood, 1998).

'Chat about Books', *Daily Mail*, 21 August 1896. *Daily Mail Historical Archive 1896–2004*. www.galegroup.com. Accessed 6 October 2016.

Cherry, Deborah, *Painting Women: Victorian Women Artists* (London: Routledge, 1993).

Churchill, Winston Spencer, *The River War: An Historical Account of the Reconquest of the Sudan*, vol. 2, ed. Col. F. Rhodes (London: Longmans, Green).
Clarke, Meaghan, *Critical Voices: Women and Art Criticism in Britain, 1880–1905* (Aldershot: Ashgate, 2005).
Courtney, W.L., 'Sir William Butler's Autobiography', *The Telegraph*, 2 March 1911. Meynell Archive [press cutting].
'Current Literature', *Daily News*, 24 September 1872. *British Library Newspapers*. www.galegroup.com. Accessed 17 June 2016.
Dakers, Caroline, *The Holland Park Circle: Artists and Victorian Society* (New Haven: Yale University Press, 1999).
De Bois-Gallais, Frédéric Lepelle, *Memoir of Mademoiselle Rosa Bonheur*, trans. James Parry (New York: Williams, Stevens, Williams, 1857).
'*The Defence of Rorke's Drift*', *The Times*, 18 March 1880. *Times Digital Archive*. www.galegroup.com. Accessed 16 November 2013.
Denny, Margaret, 'Framing the Victorians: Photography, Fashion and Identity' in John Potvin (ed.), *The Places and Spaces of Fashion, 1800–2007* (London: Routledge, 2009), pp 34–51.
Di Bello, Patrizia, 'Elizabeth Thompson and "Patsy" Cornwallis West as *Carte-de-Visite* Celebrities', *History of Photography*, 55:3 (August 2011), 240–9.
Dickens, Charles, *Pictures from Italy*. Ed. Kate Flint (London: Penguin, 1998).
— *The Pilgrim Edition of the Letters of Charles Dickens*, vol. 7. Ed. Graham Storey, Kathleen Tillotson & Angus Easson (Oxford: Clarendon, 1993).
— *The Pilgrim Edition of the Letters of Charles Dickens*, vol. 3. Ed. Madeline House (Oxford: Clarendon Press, 1977).
— *The Pilgrim Edition of the Letters of Charles Dickens*, vol. 4. Ed. Kathleen Tillotson (Oxford: Clarendon Press, 1977).
'The Dudley Gallery', *The Examiner*, 27 January 1872. *British Periodicals Collection II, 1842–44*. www.galegroup.com. Accessed 12 May 2013.
'The Dudley Gallery', *The Examiner*, 8 February 1873. *British Periodicals Collection II, 1842–44*. www.galegroup.com. Accessed 12 May 2013.
'The Dudley Gallery', *The Pall Mall Gazette*, 5 March 1873. *19th Century British Newspapers*. www.galegroup.com. Accessed 22 October 2013.
'The Dudley Gallery', *The Pall Mall Gazette*, 13 February 1872. *19th Century British Newspapers*. www.galegroup.com. Accessed 22 October 2013.
'The Dudley Gallery', *The Times*, 11 November 1872. *Times Digital Archive*. Accessed 1 June 2013.
Du Maurier, George, 'Varnishing Day at the Royal Academy', *Punch*, 19 June 1877. *19th Century UK Periodicals*. www.galegroup.com. Accessed 15 March 2015.
Duberly, Frances Isabella, *Mrs Duberly's War: Journal and Letters from the Crimea, 1854–6*. Ed. and intro. Christine Kelly (Oxford: Oxford University Press, 2007).
E.M.C., 'Letters from the Holy Land', *The Dublin Review*, July 1903. *British Periodicals*. www.proquest.com. Accessed 20 March 2017.
'The Emperor of Russia at Woolwich', *Bradford Observer*, 21 May 1874. *19th Century British Library Newspapers*. www.galegroup.com. Accessed 14 May 2014.
'Essence of Parliament', *Punch*, 8 August 1874. *19th Century UK Periodicals*. www.galegroup.com. Accessed 12 May 2014.
'Exhibitions', *Fun*, 20 April 1881, p. 163. *British Periodicals Collection II*. www.galegroup.com. Accessed 1 January 2016.
'Exhibition of Miss Thompson's Pictures', *Huddersfield Chronicle*, 27 September 1879. *British Library Newspapers*. www.galegroup.com. Accessed 12 April 2013.
'The Exhibition of the Royal Academy', *Birmingham Daily Post*, 30 April 1881. *British Library Newspapers*. www.galegroup.com. Accessed 12 April 2013.
'Exhibition of the Royal Academy', *The Times*, 2 May 1874. *Times Digital Archive*. www.galegroup.com. Accessed 20 October 2014.
'The Exhibition of the Royal Academy (Second Notice)', *The Times*, 12 May 1879. *Times Digital Archive*. Accessed 16 November 2013.

Fenn, W.W., 'Echoes from the Royal Academy', *Belgravia*, June 1874, p. 421. *British Periodicals*. www.galegroup.com. Accessed 10 June 2013.
'Fine Arts', *The Graphic*, 9 May 1874. *19th Century British Library Newspapers*. www.galegroup.com. Accessed 14 May 2014.
'Fine Arts', *Illustrated London News*, 27 June 1874. *The Illustrated London News Historical Archive*, 1842–2003. www.galegroup.com. Accessed 14 March 2015.
Fitzgerald, Edward, *The Letters of Edward Fitzgerald*, vol. 3. Eds. Alfred McKinley Terhure and Annabelle Burdick Terhure (Princeton: Princeton University Press, 2015).
Frayling, Christopher, 'Design at the Royal College of Art: the head, the heart and the hand' in Christopher Frayling and Claire Catterall (eds), *Design of the Times: One Hundred Years of the Royal College of Art* (Shepton Beauchamp: Richard Dennis/Royal College of Art, 1995), pp 8–13.
Freeman, Michael, *The Undercliff, Isle of Wight: A Geographic History* (Newport: Crossprint, 2012).
'From Sketch-Book to Diary', *The Athenaeum*, 15 January 1910, p. 64. British Periodicals. www.proquest.com. Accessed 12 May 2017.
Fussell, Paul, *The Great War and Modern Memory* (Oxford: Oxford University Press, 2013).
'General Butler's Recall', *Daily Mail*, 16 August 1899. *Daily Mail Historical Archive, 1896–2004*. www.galegroup.com. Accessed 19 May 2016.
Gerrish Nunn, Pamela, *Canvassing: Recollections by Six Victorian Women Artists* (London: Camden Press, 1968).
Gillett, Paula, *The Victorian Painter's World* (Gloucester: Alan Sutton, 1990).
Gormanston, Eileen, *A Little Kept* (London: The Catholic Book Club, 1954).
'Gossip of the Clubs', *The Lancaster Gazette*, 24 October 1874. *19th Century British Library Newspapers*. www.galegroup.com. Accessed 14 May 2014.
Greer, Germaine, *The Obstacle Race: The Fortunes of Women Painters and the Work* (New York: Martin Secker & Warburg, 1979).
Gretton, A.L.V., *Vicissitudes of Italy, Since the Congress of Vienna* (London: Routledge, 1859).
Grubb, G., 'Charles Dickens and His Brother Fred', *Dickensian*, 50 (1 January 1954), 123–31. *Periodicals Archive Online*. Accessed 25 September 2013.
Hagarty, Parker, 'Pictures at the Royal Academy', *Western Mail*, 27 May 1895. British Library Newspapers. www.galegroup.com. Accessed 12 May 2016.
'"Halt!" A Reminiscence of Aldershot', *The Graphic*, 18 July 1874. *British Library Newspapers, Part I, 1800–1900*. www.galegroup.com. Accessed 12 January 2013.
Hatton, Joseph, *Club-Land: London and Provincial* (London: J.S. Virtue, 1890).
Hichberger, J.W.M., *Images of the Army: Military in British Art, 1815–1914* (Manchester: Manchester University Press, 1990).
Hourani, Albert, *Europe and the Middle East* (Berkeley and Los Angeles: University of California Press, 1980).
'How the Boer War was Made', *The Star*, 2 March 1911. Meynell Archive [press cutting].
Hutchings, Richard J., *Dickens on an Island* (1970; Freshwater Bay: Hunnyhill Publications, 2012).
'Impressions of the Academy', *Lloyd's Illustrated Newspaper*, 8 May 1887. *British Library Newspapers*. www.galegroup.com. Accessed 20 January 2015.
'Ireland in 1840', *The Manchester Guardian*, 12 April 1937. *19th Century British Library Newspapers*. www.galegroup.com. Accessed 12 November 2013.
Jordan, Anne, *Love Well the Hour: The Life of Lady Colin Campbell* (Leicester: Matador, 2010).
Kaplan, Fred, *Dickens: A Biography* (Baltimore: Johns Hopkins UP, 1988).
Krebs, Paula, *Gender, Race and the Writing of Empire: Public Discourse and the Boer War* (Cambridge: Cambridge University Press, 1999).
Laband, John, *The Transvaal Rebellion: The First Boer War, 1880–1881* (London: Routledge, 2005).
'Ladies Page', *Illustrated London News*, 12 June 1915. *The Illustrated London News Historical Archive*, 1842–2003. www.galegroup.com. Accessed 2 January 2017.
'Lady Butler's Pictures: Son's Dash to Save Them', *Daily Mail*, 28 October 1922. *Daily Mail Historical Archive*. www.galegroup.com. Accessed 18 January 2017.
'Lady Colin Campbell', *Merry England*, 4:20 (December 1884), vi. *British Periodicals Collection II: 1883–1895*. www.galegroup.com. Accessed 20 April 2016.

Lalumia, Matthew. 'Lady Elizabeth Thompson Butler in the 1870s', *Women's Art Journal*, 4:1 (Spring–Summer 1993), 9–14.

—, 'Realism and Anti-Aristocratic Sentiment in Victorian Depictions of the Crimean War', *Victorian Studies*, 48:1 (Autumn 1983), 25–51.

'London and Paris Gossip', *Trewman's Exeter Flying Post Or Plymouth and Cornish Advertiser*, 13 May 1874. *19th Century British Library Newspapers*. wwgalegroup.com. Accessed 30 October 2015.

Loy Smith, George, *A Victorian RSM: From India to the Crimea* (London: Costello, 1987).

Lubin, David M., *Grand Illusions: America Art and the First World War* (Oxford: Oxford University Press, 2016).

Mancoff, Debra N., *Danger! Women Artists at Work* (London: Merrell, 2012).

Markovits, Stefanie, *The Crimean War in the British Imagination* (Cambridge: Cambridge University Press, 2013).

McAllister, Annemarie, '"A Pair of Naked Legs and a Ragged Head Scarf": An Overview of Victorian Discourses on Italy' in Alessandro Vescovi et al. (eds), *The Victorians and Italy: Literature, Travel, Politics and Art* (Milano: Polimetrica, 2009), pp 19–43.

McCourt, Edward, *Remember Butler: The Story of Sir William Butler* (London: Routledge and Kegan Paul, 1967).

Metz, Kathryn, 'Ellen and Rolinda Sharples: Mother and Daughter Painters', *Woman's Art Journal*, 16:1 (Spring–Summer 1995), 3–11.

Meynell, Alice, 'Agostino', *Pall Mall Gazette*, 19 January 1898: 3. *19th Century British Library Newspapers*. www.galegroup.com. Accessed 10 June 2013.

— 'Dickens as a Man of Letters', *Hearts of Controversy* (London: Burns & Oates, 1917), pp 23–52.

— 'Elizabeth Butler', *St Nicholas*, 1 January 1883, pp 12–15. *British Periodicals Online* www.galegroup.com. Accessed 10 May 2013.

— 'A Father of Women', *Collected Poems* (London: Burns and Oates, 1921), pp 118–19.

— 'The Maidservants', *Pall Mall Gazette*, 26 January 1898, p. 3. *19th Century British Newspapers*. www.galegroupcom. Accessed 30 March 2015.

— 'To O –, Of Her Dark Eyes', *Collected Poems* (London: Burns and Oates, 1921), p. 131.

— 'Pictures', *Merry England* 15:85 (May 1890), 70–3. *British Periodicals*. www.proquest.com. Accessed 4 March 2015.

— 'A Question of Propriety', *The Tablet*, 6 June 1885. www.thetablet.co.uk. Accessed: 1 January 2014.

— 'A Remembrance', *The Scots Observer*, 9 August 1890. *19th Century British Newspapers*. www.galegroup.com. Accessed 28 October 2013.

— 'Reviews and Views', *Merry England*, 4:24 (April 1885), 427–8. *British Periodicals Online*. www.galegroup.com. Accessed 20 March 2014.

— 'Reviews and Views', *Merry England*, 13:74 (June 1889), 133–42. *British Periodicals Online*. www.galegroup.com. Accessed 1 November 2016.

— 'Summer in England, 1914', *Collected Poems* (London: Burns, Oates and Washbourne, 1921), p. 123.

Meynell, Viola, *Alice Meynell: A Memoir* (London: Jonathan Cape, 1929).

— *Francis Thompson and Wilfrid Meynell, A Memoir* (London: Hollis & Carter, 1952).

Meynell, Wilfrid. *A Dickens Friendship* (London: privately printed, 1931).

— 'The Life and Work of Lady Butler', *The Art Annual* (London, 1898).

— 'Lady Butler's Autobiography', *The Observer*, 28 January 1923. Proquest Historical Newspapers. www.proquest.com. Accessed 1 May 2017.

— 'Sir William Butler', *The Tablet*, 11 June 1910.www.thetablet.co.uk. Accessed 3 July 2016.

'Miscellaneous', *Hampshire Advertiser and Salisbury Guardian*, 14 August 1847. *19th Century British Library Newspapers, Part II. British Newspapers 1600–1950*. www.galegroup.com. Accessed 24 September 2013.

'Miss Christiana Weller', *Musical Examiner*, 15 June 1844. *British Periodicals Collection II, 1842–44*. www.galegroup.com. Accessed 12 May 2013.

'Miss Christiana Weller's Concert', *The Musical World*, 17 July 1845. *British Periodicals Collection II*. www.proquest.com. Accessed 1 June 2013.

'Miss Christiana Weller's Concert', *The Manchester Times and Gazette*, 24 February 1844. *19th Century British Newspapers*. www.galegroup.com. Accessed 12 May 2013.

'Miss Elizabeth Thompson', *The Graphic*, 8 May 1875. *British Library Newspapers, Part I.* www.galegroup.com. Accessed 5 June 2015.
'Miss Elizabeth Thompson's *Return from Inkerman*', *The Graphic*, 28 April 1877. *British Library Newspapers, Part I.* www.galegroup.com. Accessed 8 September 2015.
'Miss Kate Greenaway', *Illustrated London News*, 16 November 1901. *The Illustrated London News Historical Archive*. www.galegroup.com. Accessed 2 April 2014.
'Miss Thompson's *Balaclava*', *The Sporting Gazette*, 6 May 1876. *19th Century British Newspapers*. www.galegroup.com. Accessed 23 March 2016.
'Miss Thompson's *Quatre Bras*', *Birmingham Daily Post*, 8 May 1875. *British Library Newspapers* www.galegroup.com. Accessed 14 April 2014.
'Miss Thompson's New Picture', *Daily Telegraph*. Rpt. *Nottinghamshire Guardian*, 28 April 1876. *British Library Newspapers*. www.galegroup.com. Accessed 23 March 2016.
'Miss Thompson's New Picture', *The Morning Post*, 22 April 1876. *NewsVault*. www.galegroup.com. Accessed 7 March 2014.
'Miss Thompson's New Picture', *Daily Telegraph*. Reproduced in *Nottinghamshire Guardian*. 28 April 1876. *19th Century British Newspapers*. www.galegroup.com. Accessed 17 April 2014.
Moss Sidney P. and Carolyn J. Moss, 'Frederick Dickens: From Courtship to Courtroom', *Dickensian*, 90 (Summer 1994), 102–12.
Mulock Craik, Dinah, *Olive*, ed. Cora Kaplan (Oxford: Oxford World Classics, 2000).
'Multiple News Items', *The Morning Post*, 28 July 1847. *British Newspapers 1600–1950*. www.galegroup.com. Accessed 24 September 2013.
'Multiple News Items', *The Morning Post*, 28 July 1847. *British Newspapers 1600–1950*. www.galegroup.com. Accessed 24 September 2013.
'New Engravings', *The Times*, 31 May 1882. *Times Digital Archive*. Accessed 4 December 2014.
[Nightingale, Florence], Letter from Florence Nightingale to Mr C. Aldous, 4 June 1879. Florence Nightingale Digitization Project.http://hgar-srv3.bu.edu/web/florence-nightingale/home
Norman, E.R., *Anti-Catholicism in Victorian England* (London: George Allen and Unwin, 1968).
Norman, Edward, *The English Catholic Church in the Nineteenth Century* (Oxford: Clarendon Press, 1984).
Norris, John, *Marching to the Drums: A History of Military Drums and Drummers* (London: History Press, 2012).
O'Byrne, M.K., 'Lady Butler: The Painter of the *Roll Call*', *The Irish Monthly*, 78 (December 1950), 590–2. www.jstor.org
O'Connor, Maura, *The Romance of Italy and the English Imagination* (Basingstoke: Macmillan, 1998).
Oldcastle, John [Wilfrid Meynell], 'Our Living Artists: Elizabeth Butler (née Thompson)', *The Magazine of Art* (January 1879), 257–62. *British Periodicals Collection II*. www.proquest.com. Accessed 1 September 2011.
'Our Royal Academy Guide – Or Guy'D', *Punch*, 9 May 1885. *19th Century UK Periodicals*. www.galegroup.com. Accessed 14 December 2013.
Pakenham, Thomas, *The Boer War* (London: Abacus, 1991).
'Palestine in the Spring', *The Speaker* (April 1903). *British Periodicals*. www.proquest.com. Accessed 20 March 2017.
'Partly, though not Wholly, Responsible', *Daily Mail*, 6 November 1899. *Daily Mail Historical Archive 1896–2004*. www.galegroup.com. Accessed 10 November 2016.
Pemble, John, *The Mediterranean Passion: Victorians and Edwardians in the South* (Oxford: Clarendon Press, 1987).
Perugini, Kate and Walter Dexter (eds), *Mr & Mrs Charles Dickens: His Letters to Her* (London: Constable, 1935).
'Philharmonic Concert', *The Liverpool Mercury*, 31 March 1843. *19th Century British Newspapers*. www.galegroup.com. Accessed 12 May 2013.
Phillimore, Francis [Wilfrid Meynell], 'A Group of Painters', *Merry England* (June 1893), 134–9.
Phillips, Claude, 'Fine Art: The Royal Academy', *The Academy*, 24 May 1890, p. 361. *British Periodicals Collection I*. www.proquest.com. Accessed 17 March 2014.

— 'The Royal Academy', *The Academy, 1869–1902*, 16 May 1885. *British Periodicals Collection I.* www.proquest.com. Accessed 14 March 2014.

Physick, John, 'The Government School of Design: foundation, rebellion, investigation, and the triumph of Henry Cole' in Christopher Frayling and Claire Catterall (eds), *Design of the Times: One Hundred Years of the Royal College of Art* (Shepton Beauchamp: Richard Dennis/Royal College of Art, 1995), pp 14–19.

Picken, Eleanor, 'Recollections of Charles Dickens, His Family and Friends', *Temple Bar*, 82 (1888), 81–506.

— 'Reminiscences of Charles Dickens from a Young Lady's Diary', *English Domestic Magazine*, 10 (1871), 336–44.

Plomer, William (ed.), *Kilvert's Diary, 1870–1879: Selections from the Diary of the Revd Francis Kilvert* (London: Jonathan Cape, 1944).

'The Prince of Wales on Hunting', *Jackson's Oxford Journal*, 9 May 1874. *19th Century British Library Newspapers.* www.galegroup.com. Accessed 8 October 2015.

'Probate, Divorce and Admiralty Division', *The Times*, 21 March 1902. *The Times Digital Archive.* www.galegroup.com

'Prophet and Soldier: General Butler's Autobiography', *The Daily News*, 2 March 1911 Meynell Archive [press cutting].

'The Queen and Miss Thompson's Picture', *The Sheffield and Rotherham Independent*, 15 May 1874. *19th Century British Library Newspapers.* www.galegroup.com. Accessed 14 May 2014.

Rathbone, Charles, *General Lord Wolseley (of Cairo), A Memoir*, 2nd ed. (London: Richard Bentley, 1883).

Robb, George, *British Culture and the First World War* (Basingstoke: Palgrave Macmillan, 2002).

'The Roll Call', Daily News, 19 May 1874. *British Library Newspapers.* wwwgalegroup.com. Accessed 14 May 2014.

'The Roll Call', Birmingham Daily Post, 6 November 1874. *19th Century British Library Newspapers.* www.gale group.com. Accessed 14 May 2014.

'The Roll Call', The Newcastle Courant, 23 October 1874. *19th Century British Library Newspapers.* www.gale group.com. Accessed 14 May 2014.

'The Royal Academy Exhibition. Second Notice', *Illustrated London News*, 9 May 1874. *The Illustrated London News Historical Archive.* www.galegroup.com. Accessed 14 May 2014.

'The Royal Academy Exhibition: Second Notice', *Fun*, 13 May 1885. *British Periodicals Collection II.* www.proquest.com. Accessed 20 March 2014.

'The Royal Academy, Third Notice', *The Athenaeum*, 5 June 1897, pp 750–2. *British Periodicals Collection I.* www.proquest.com. Accessed 19 February 2016.

'The Royal Academy', *Daily News*, 30 April 1881. *British Library Newspapers.* www.galegroup.com. Accessed 12 April 2013.

'The Royal Academy', *Glasgow Herald*, 9 June 1881. *British Library Newspapers.* www.galegroup.com. Accessed 12 April 2013.

'The Royal Academy: Fifth Notice', *The Athenaeum*, 20 June 1885. www.proquest.com. Accessed 20 March 2014.

'The Royal Academy: Fourth Notice', *The Times*, 27 June 1881. *Times Digital Archive.* Accessed 16 November 2013.

'The Royal Academy: Second Notice', *Liverpool Mercury*, 4 May 1897. *British Library Newspapers*, www.galegroup.com. Accessed 20 April 2016.

'The Royal Academy: Second Notice', *The Athenaeum*, 17 May 1890. *British Periodicals Collection I* www.proquest.com. Accessed 15 February 2016.

'The Royal Academy: Third Notice', *Saturday Review*, 17 May 1890. *British Periodicals Collection II: 1855–1938.* www.proquest.com. Accessed 2 February 2016.

'The Royal Academy', *Essex Standard*, 24 May 1879. *British Library Newspapers, Part II, 1800–1900.* www.galegroup.com. Accessed 20 August 2013.

'The Royal Academy', *The Times*, 1 May 1875. *Times Digital Archive.* www.galegroup.com. Accessed 12 January 2013.

'Royal Academy Exhibition', *The Graphic*, 17 May 1879. *British Library Newspapers, Part I, 1800–1900*. www.galegroup.com. Accessed 12 January 2013.
Rudman, Harry W., *Italian Nationalism and English Letters: Figures of the Risorgimento and Victorian Men of Letters* (London: George Allen & Unwin, 1940).
Russell, W.H., *The War: From the Landing at Gallipoli to the Death of Lord Raglan* (London: George Routledge, 1855).
Rutter, Frank, *Theodore Roussel*, intro. G. Reginald Grundy (London: The Connoisseur, 1926).
Ryan, Martin, *William Francis Butler: A Life, 1838–1910* (Dublin: Lilliput Press, 2003).
Sackville-West, Vita, 'Introduction' to *Alice Meynell: Prose and Poetry, Centenary Edition* (London: Jonathan Cape, 1947).
Said, Edward, *Orientalism* (New York: Pantheon, 1978).
Sala, George Augustus, *Twice Round the Clock, or, The Hours of the Day and Night in London* (London: Richard Marsh, 1862).
Schazmann, Paul-Emile, *Charles Dickens in Switzerland*, trans. H.P.B. Betlem (Geneva: Swiss National Tourist Office, 1972).
Scirocco, Alfonso, *Garibaldi: Citizen of the World* (Princeton and Oxford: Princeton University Press, 2007).
'Scotland For Ever', *Liverpool Mercury*, 1 September 1882, *British Periodicals Collection II*. www.proquest.com. Accessed 30 January 2016.
'Sketches of Life and Character in Egypt', *The Graphic*, 9 February 1889. *British Library Newspapers, Part I, 1800–1900*. www.galegroup.com. Accessed 12 February 2016.
'Sir William Butler', *The Speaker*, 6 January 1900, p. 362. *British Periodicals Collection II*. www.proquest.com. Accessed 1 January 2016.
Smiles, Samuel, *Self Help* (London: John Murray, 1908).
Smith, Alison, 'Elizabeth Butler' in Alison Smith (ed.), *Artist and Empire* (London: Tate, 2015), pp 110–11.
Spielmann, Marion, 'Pictures of the Year – I', *The Magazine of Art* (January 1881). *British Periodicals Collection II*. www.proquest.com. Accessed 1 January 2016.
— 'Pictures of the Year – I', *The Magazine of Art* (January 1879). *British Periodicals Collection II*. www.proquest.com. Accessed 1 November 2014.
— 'The Exhibition of the Royal Academy, II', *The Magazine of Art*, January 1897. *British Periodicals*. www.galegrop.com. Accessed 25 April 2017.
Spielmann, M.H. and G.S. Layard, *Kate Greenaway* (London: Adam and Charles Black, 1905).
'A Soldier and a Man', *Evening Standard and St James's Gazette*, 2 March 1911. *British Library Newspapers*. www.galegroup.com. Accessed 1 May 2016.
Soueif, Ahdaf, *The Map of Love* (London: Bloomsbury, 1995).
Stoker, Bram, *Personal Reminiscences of Henry Irving*, vol. 1 (London: William Heinemann, 1906).
'Summary of this Morning's News', *Pall Mall Gazette*, 18 May 1881. *19th Century British Newspapers*. www.galegroup.com. Accessed 22 October 2013.
Sutherland, Kathryn, 'Dickens and Women', *Critical Quarterly*, 25:3 (September 2007), 17–19.
'Theatre Royal', *Freeman's Journal*, 5 December 1842. *19th Century British Newspapers*. www.galegroup.com. Accessed 12 May 2013.
Thompson, Elizabeth, '*The Roll Call*', *The Times*, 12 May 1874. *Times Digital Archive*. Accessed 12 May 2014.
— '*The Roll Call*', *The Times*, 16 May 1874. *Times Digital Archive*. Accessed 12 May 2014.
Tomalin, Claire, *Charles Dickens: A Life* (London: Penguin, 2012).
'The Tour of the Royal Academy', *Punch, or, The London Charivari*, 24 May 1879. *19th Century UK Periodicals*. www,galegroup.com. Accessed 15 March 2015.
'The Tour of the Royal Academy', *Punch, or, The London Charivari*, 24 May 1879, 229. *19th Century UK Periodicals*. www.galegroup.com. Accessed 17 September 2016.
'Two Great Men', Meynell Archive [press cutting]
Usherwood, Paul, 'Elizabeth Thompson: A Case of Tokenism', *Woman's Art Journal*, 11:2 (Autumn 1990–Winter 1991), 14–18.
— 'Elizabeth Thompson Butler: The Consequences of Marriage', *Women's Art Journal*, 9:1 (Spring–Summer 1988), 30–4.

Usherwood, Paul and Jenny Spencer-Smith, *Lady Butler: Battle Artist, 1846–1933* (London: National Army Museum, 1987).
Von Amin, Elizabeth, *The Enchanted April* (London: Vintage, 2015).
Walkley, Giles, *Artists' Houses in London, 1764–1914* (Aldershot: Scolar Press, 1994).
'The Waterloo Centenary – The End – Wellington', Illustrated London News, 12 June 1915. *The Illustrated London News Historical Archive*, 1842–2003. www.galegroup.com. Accessed 10 January 2017.
Wilde, W.R., *Narrative of a Voyage to Madeira, Tenerife, and along the Shores of the Mediterranean*, vol. II (Dublin: William Curry, 1840).
Wilkinson-Latham, Robert, *Uniforms and Weapons of the Crimean War* (London: B.T. Batsford, 1977).
Willis, Martin and Catherine Wynne, 'Introduction' in Martin Willis and Catherine Wynne (eds), *Victorian Literary Mesmerism* (Amsterdam: Rodopi, 2006), pp 1–16.
'Winter Exhibitions – The Dudley Gallery', *The Tablet*, 30 March 1872, www.thetablet.co.uk. Accessed 20 May 2016.
Wolseley, Viscount, *The Story of a Soldier's Life*, vol. 2 (London: Constable, 1903).
'The Woman's Century: How Feminine Influence has Effected the Golden Age', *Daily Mail*, 31 December 1900. *Daily Mail Historical Archive*. www.galegroup.com. Accessed 17 November 2016.
'Women in the Queen's Reign', *Daily Mail Queen Victoria's Diamond Jubilee Extra*, 23 June 1897. *Daily Mail Historical Archive 1896–2004*. www.galegroup.com. Accessed 12 November 2016
Wright, Christopher, *From Victorian to Edwardian: The Ferens Art Gallery Collection of Victorian and Edwardian Art* (Hull: Hull Museums, 2009).
Wynne, Catherine, 'Christiana Weller Thompson's Unpublished Journal (1845–6): Sidelights on Dickens', *Notes and Queries*, 61:4 (2014), 548–53.
— *The Colonial Conan Doyle: British Imperialism, Irish Nationalism and the Gothic* (Westport, CT: Greenwood Press, 2002).
— 'Elizabeth Butler's Artistic and Literary Landscapes: Ireland, Egypt and the Holy Land', *Prose Studies: History, Theory, Criticism* 31:2 (August 2009), 126–40.
— 'From Waterloo to Jellalabad: The Irish and Scots at War in Elizabeth Thompson Butler and W.F. Butler', *Journal of European Studies*, 41 (June 2011), 143–60.
Yeldham, Charlotte, *Women Artists in Nineteenth-Century France and England*, vol. 1 (New York: Garland, 1984).
Zakreski, Patricia, *Representing Female Artistic Labour, 1848–1890: Refining Work for the Middle-Class Woman* (London: Routledge, 2006).

Index